The WREATH
of
WILD OLIVE

The WREATH *of* WILD OLIVE

Play, Liminality, and the Study of Literature

Mihai I. Spariosu

State University
of New York Press

Published by
State University of New York Press

© 1997 State University of New York

For information, address the State University of New York Press,
State University Plaza, Albany, NY 12246

Production by Bernadine Dawes • Marketing by Dana Yulanavich

Library of Congress Cataloging-in-Publication Data

Spariosu, Mihai.
    The wreath of wild olive : play, liminality, and the study of
literature / Mihai I. Spariosu.
        p.   cm.
    Includes bibliographical references and index.
    ISBN 0-7914-3365-X (hardcover : alk. paper). — ISBN 0-7914-3366-8
(pbk. : alk. paper)
    1. European literature—History and criticism. 2. Play
(Philosophy)—History. 3. Literature—Aesthetics. 4. Ethics in
literature. I. Title.
PN521.S63   1997
809'.93384—dc21   96-37257
                                                             CIP

1 2 3 4 5 6 7 8 9 10

For Diana and Ana-María

Contents

Acknowledgments

I wish to express my deep gratitude to several colleagues and friends who have read this work in its various stages and have offered their generous comments: Ronald Bogue, Matei Calinescu, Stanley Corngold, Mikhail Epstein, Dorothy Figueira, Wolfgang Iser, Giuseppe Mazzotta, Virgil Nemoianu, Frederick Turner, Donald Wesling, and William N. West. Particularly helpful have been Cal Clements, who has provided an early version of and commentary on the diagrams in chapter 2; Marcel Cornis-Pope, who has offered a thorough critique of the whole manuscript and persuaded me to revise some of its rhetorical strategies; and Florin Berindeanu, who has assisted me with proofreading and with part of the index. Last but not least, I am very grateful to Carola Sautter, whose accomplished editorial skills, unfailing and uncompromising critical taste, and wonderful personality will be sorely missed at SUNY Press; as well as to Wyatt Benner, my copy editor, for his remarkably astute and sympathetic editorial suggestions; and to Bernadine Dawes, my production editor, for her promptness and good grace in dealing with my various requests.

Introduction

In the preface to his collection of essays, *The Crown of Wild Olive* (1866), John Ruskin elucidates the Hellenic reference in his title: according to ancient legend, the wreath of wild olive was the sole reward that Zeus originally bestowed upon the victors in the Olympic games. Thereby Zeus, says Ruskin, wanted to show mortals that not "in war, not in wealth, not in tyranny, was there any happiness to be found for them—only in kindly peace, fruitful and free."[1] By rewarding the Olympic champions with no more than a wreath of wild olive branches, the God ironically transfigures the competitive values of his worshipers and points, through a paradox, to an incommensurable, alternative world in which all contest becomes cooperation, all war becomes peace. In other words, under the magic hands of Zeus, the barren wild olive turns into a tame and fruitful one—an irenic symbol later on adopted by Christianity as well.

The cultural symbolism of the olive wreath can further be enriched in light of book 5 of *The Odyssey*, where Odysseus, washed away on the shores of Skheria, finds shelter under a wild olive bush inextricably intertwined with a tame one:

> He made his way to a grove above the water
> on open ground, and crept under twin bushes
> grown from the same spot—olive and wild olive—
> a thicket proof against the stinging wind
> or Sun's blaze, fine soever the needling sunlight;
> nor could a downpour wet it through, so dense
> those plants were interwoven.[2]

For me, the intertwined plants, situated "above the water on open ground," represent the liminal space or no-man's land between sea and shore, between wilderness and civilization, where Odysseus builds his temporary hideout, not yet knowing where he is or what to expect, his future fraught with both peril and exciting possibility.

It is this twofold cultural symbolism of ludic liminality and irenic transformation that the title of my book intends to convey. *The Wreath of Wild Olive* thus represents both a continuation of and a departure from my previous work—indeed, it represents the other, incommensurable side of it. In *Literature, Mimesis and Play* (1982), *Dionysus Reborn* (1989) and *God of Many Names* (1991), I have attempted to sketch a broad genealogical outline of the concept of play in Western thought, with special emphasis on the agon between aesthetics and ethics, or between poetry and philosophy, as initiated by Socrates in Plato's *Republic*. I have also sought to provide answers to such questions as: What is the essential relation between art, ethics, and politics in ancient and modern Western communities? What is the nature of the interplay between aesthetic and philosophical-scientific knowledge in Western discursive practices? What is the role of literature within a mentality of power? In the present work, by contrast, I move back and forth between a genealogical and a speculative approach, envisioning the possibility of an alternative human mentality that is not based on power but on another formative principle, such as primordial peace (Emmanuel Levinas's phrase).[3] Can humans in general and Westerners in particular gain access to or build alternative mentalities, or even alternative worlds? What would the ontoepistemology and ethopathology of an irenic world look like? And how can literary discourse specifically contribute to the creation of such a world? These are some of the questions for which I shall suggest at least partial answers in the present volume.

Given the largely speculative nature of my topic, I have organized it not as a linear narrative, but as a series of tentative studies approaching the idea of ludic liminality and irenic worlds in a concentric or metonymic manner, from various historical and thematic perspectives. Part 1 comprises three essays dealing with the primary questions involved in developing a ludic-irenic theory of liminality in modern thought, literature, and culture. Chapter 1, "Nietzsche or Schopenhauer: Can One Construct an Alternative Mentality?" begins with an examination of

Nietzsche's critique of rationalist and Christian values in *The Genealogy of Morals*. It demonstrates that Nietzsche conducts this critique from the standpoint of an archaic or voluntaristic mentality, grounded in the principle of "might makes right," which he offers as a basis for an alternative ethics. Nietzsche also (mis)interprets Schopenhauer's notion of "mystical" knowledge, derived from nondoctrinaire Buddhist and Christian thought, as just another manifestation of the Will to Power in a distorted, "ascetic" guise. My essay suggests, however, that a genuine ethical alternative can be grounded in neither a voluntaristic nor a rationalist mode of thought, feeling, and behavior but, rather, in an irenic mentality that is incommensurable with a mentality of power as a whole. One can furthermore retain Schopenhauer's and Nietzsche's intuition that art, aesthetics, and the imagination are extramoral categories in the sense that they can generate, rather than be generated by, various ethical codes. By the same token, however, they can, due to their liminal nature (largely ignored by both Nietzsche and Schopenhauer) assist in producing irenic worlds, which they may then elect not to destroy, but to nurture and preserve.

Chapter 2, "Liminality, Literary Discourse, and Alternative Worlds," attempts to emancipate the idea of liminality in general and literature as a liminal phenomenon in particular from an agonistic way of thinking that is never seriously questioned in contemporary theory and criticism. Prominent scholars such as Mikhail Bakhtin and Victor Turner have seen liminality in the context of a dynamic between the center and the margin of a given system, with the margin either reinforcing or undermining the center. My essay, by contrast, attempts to develop a ludic-irenic view of liminality as a margin that permanently detaches itself from the center (any center), thus providing a playful opening toward alternative worlds that are incommensurable with ours. From this perspective, literature is best seen not as fictional or marginal, but as a liminal phenomenon that can not only undermine or reinforce a certain state of affairs in the historical world but also act as a threshold or passageway from one historical world to another.

In turn, chapter 3, "Difference, Identity, and Otherness: A Ludic-Irenic Perspective," examines the implications of an agonistic philosophy of difference in Western culture, attempting to reorient it in terms of a ludic-irenic notion of liminality and alternative worlds. After a brief genealogical sketch that traces the Western concept of difference from Greek antiquity to modernity, the essay focuses on the poststructuralist avatars of this concept. Then it considers the possibility of irenic models of difference, including Western kinds, such as those of Bakhtin and Levinas, and Eastern kinds, such as that of Huang Po, a ninth-century Ch'an (Zen) Buddhist. Needless to say, both my genealogical sketch and my alternative models of difference have a purely propaedeutic value, and much work (and fruitful debate) will be required before they can achieve the status of cultural blueprints, let alone cultural realities.

Part 2 includes three analytical studies that view a number of modern literary works and literary traditions from the ludic-irenic perspective developed in part 1. Chapter 4, "Homicide as Play: Dostoevsky, Gide, Aiken," places the ethical issues debated in chapter 1 in the context of certain aestheticist and antiaestheticist trends in modern fiction, showing how through the common literary theme of "murder as play" Fyodor Dostoevsky's *Crime and Punishment*, André Gide's *Lafcadio's Adventures*, and Conrad Aiken's *King Coffin* not only stage but also question Nietzsche's voluntaristic ethics. At the same time, they take up the issue of the relation between literature and religion, demonstrating how literature as ludic-liminal staging can often challenge the divided nature of Christian values and can point to fresh cultural alternatives that do not necessarily reject Christianity (as Nietzsche does) or religion in general, but hark back to a holistic view of the cosmos that both precedes and founds the sacred.

Chapter 5, "Race, Ethnicity and Irenic Mentality: Rebreanu, Eliade, Devi," focuses on several literary treatments of the agonistic notions of cultural difference examined in chapter 3. It shows how two modern East European novels (Liviu Rebreanu's *The Forest of the Hanged* and Mircea Eliade's *Maitreyi*) as well as an Indian one (Maitreyi Devi's *It Does Not Die*) stage the negative existential consequences of conflictive difference—whether sexual, ethnic, racial, or social—and plead for an irenic, integrative kind. These novels go beyond both a rationalist and a poststructuralist dialectic of identity and difference, positing an irenic consciousness of the oneness of all beings that is not unlike Schopenhauer's "mystical" knowledge or Huang Po's nondifferential perception.

Finally, chapter 6, "Allegory, Power, and the Postmodern Game of Interpretation: Nabokov, Lowry, Orwell," concentrates on post–World

War II literary treatments of the ethical and axiological issues examined in part 1 from the specific viewpoint of the changing relationship between author and reader as well as the changing nature of authorship/authority in postmodern fiction. It starts from the premise that the relation between many postmodern authors and their readers is no longer based on a shared code of communication deriving from a traditional hermeneutics centered on allegorical and hierarchical modes of reading, but on an arbitrary and unruly power game of distrust, (dis)simulation and one-upsmanship. Consequently, literary works such as Vladimir Nabokov's *Pale Fire*, Malcolm Lowry's *Under the Volcano* and *Dark as the Grave Wherein my Friend is Laid*, and George Orwell's *1984*, will often take an antiallegorical stand, either by building and then destroying allegorical structures within their own fictional framework, or by postulating a world of simulacra without depth, center, or meaning, where events are governed not by necessity or causation, but by pure chance. These works, therefore, also turn against all (traditional) interpretation, denying either its possibility or its legitimacy. By pointing to the arbitrary and authoritarian nature of interpretation and truth, they equally point to the performative character of these categories, revealing their origin in a preallegorical, archaic mentality of power that had at one time been naked and unashamed. At the same time, however, they imply the need to find viable alternatives to this mentality by proposing a pluralistic concept of allegory as the ludic-liminal discourse of the Other and otherness defined not as hidden truth or agonistic rivalry, but as irenic, responsive understanding.

Behind the analytical section of my book lies the general theoretical assumption (discussed at some length in part 1) that literature can play a central role in an irenic way of thinking precisely because of its essentially ludic nature. Since literary discourse belongs to a playful, liminal mode of being, it is not bound by the logical and analytic methods of philosophical and scientific discourse and, therefore, can also propose alternative worlds based on irenic principles. Furthermore, literature as a form of aesthetic play can both involve and transcend the sociocultural context in which it arises. Unlike other types of discourse, it can adopt an *as if* stance toward the ethical norms of a certain community or culture. Consequently it can produce, in the imagination, new sets of values that can later be adopted by ethical and sociopolitical thought as well. By playfully staging a real or an imaginary world and presenting it from various perspectives, literature contributes to a better understanding of the ethical choices open to a certain community and hence can assume an important role in bringing about historical change.

Part 3 comprises chapter 7,"Criticism as Irenic Play: The Case of the Victorian Sages," and is devoted to an irenic reassessment of the function of cultural criticism at the present time. It examines several essays by Matthew Arnold, John Ruskin, and Oscar Wilde, arguing that, unlike most contemporary criticism that (whether inspired by left-wing or right-wing agendas) is rooted in a mentality of power, the cultural criticism often practiced by these Victorian thinkers is based on a ludic-irenic view of human culture and is designed not to control or divide the community but, rather, to heal it and make it whole. My study attempts thus to revitalize a nineteenth-century form of cultural criticism that, at its best, represented a liberal alternative to the hermeneutics of suspicion instituted by Marx and Nietzsche during the same historical period. This revitalized form of criticism might in the long run transform itself into a genuinely irenic cultural activity; in the short run, it might at the very least counterbalance the excessive weight that its counterpart, the aforementioned hermeneutics of suspicion, has gained in the humanities today.

PART ONE

TOWARD A LUDIC-IRENIC THEORY OF LITERATURE AND CULTURE:
Intellectual Historical Background, Basic Principles

NIETZSCHE OR SCHOPENHAUER
Can One Construct an Alternative Mentality?

In the *Genealogie der Sitten: Ein Angriff* (1887), Nietzsche attacks what he perceives to be the fatal flaw of the modern Western mentality: its ethics of "guilt" and "pity." He carries out this attack from the standpoint of the ethics of the overman, which he proposes in *Thus Spake Zarathustra* (1884) and which, as I have argued elsewhere, can be seen as a return to the archaic or heroic mentality present, for example, in Hellenic and medieval epic.[1] In the *Genealogy of Morals*, however, Nietzsche changes his rhetorical strategy and largely employs the language of the historian and the psychologist rather than that of the prophet. I shall review Nietzsche's principal arguments in the three essays comprising the book and shall assess the relevance of these arguments to contemporary cultural history. I shall finally reassess them in terms of an alternative mode of thought, behavior, and pathos, to which Schopenhauer also refers at the end of his monumental work, *Die Welt als Wille und Vorstellung*, and which is based on neither an archaic nor a modern mentality of power. Indeed, Western philosophy could have taken a completely different turn in the twentieth century if it had chosen to develop Schopenhauer's imaginative insights as thoroughly as Nietzsche's.

The basic questions that Nietzsche wishes to address in the *Genealogy* are: "Under what conditions did man construct the value judgments good and evil?" "Have [these value judgments] thus far benefited or retarded mankind?" "Do they betoken misery, curtailment, degeneracy, or, on the contrary, power, fullness of being, energy, courage in the face of life, and confidence in the future?"[2] In order to answer these questions in a satisfactory manner, he proposes in the first essay, entitled "'Good and Evil,' 'Good and Bad,'" to bring the method of historical hermeneutics into traditional metaphysics, elaborating an *Entwicklungsgeschichte der Begriffe*. He directs this historical method primarily against nineteenth-century German idealist philosophy that claims universal validity for its abstract metaphysical and ethical concepts. For Nietzsche, philology in general and etymology in particular are important instruments of historical interpretation (and here he shows his classical training): they can point to the origin of a philosophical or a moral concept, following its historical metamorphosis from a concrete, physical meaning to an abstract, metaphysical one.

When applied to moral "goodness," the historical method yields the startling insight that, contrary to common belief, this notion does not originate with the beneficiaries of a good deed. On the contrary, "it was the 'good' themselves, that is to say the noble, mighty, highly placed, and high-minded who decreed themselves and their actions to be good, i.e., belonging to the highest rank, in contradistinction to all that was base, low-minded and plebeian" (160). According to Nietzsche, the origin of the opposition between good and bad is to be found in the "pathos of distance" between the ruling elite and the lower, dependent social groups. The lords have the power of bestowing, indeed calling, names, and in this sense one "would almost be justified in seeing the origin of language itself as an expression of the rulers' power." By saying "this *is* that or that," the lords can "seal off each thing and action with a sound and thereby take symbolic possession of it" (160). From the outset, then, Nietzsche links the notions of good and bad to the Will to Power, and thus distances himself not only from Christian, Kantian, and idealist ethics in general but also from the English utilitarians (including the Darwinian evolutionists), who see morality largely as a function of the struggle for survival.

The aristocratic genealogy of good and bad, Nietzsche further argues, can also be supported etymologically. He points out that a close look at the words denoting "good" in several Indo-European languages shows that they invariably had the original meaning of "noble" in a social-hierarchical sense and only afterwards came to mean "nobility of spirit," regardless of social distinctions. In turn, words denoting "bad" can be traced back to terms with which the aristocracy characterized the situation of the commoner and meant "unhappy," "pitiable," "base," and "humble" rather than morally bad or "evil."[3]

Nietzsche distinguishes between the valuation set of good and bad and that of good and evil, contending that these sets have divergent historical sources. The first set belongs to the aristocratic code of conduct, or a "master ethics," while the second is the outcome of a rancorous "slave ethics." For Nietzsche, however, both these ethics have upper-class origins, being different manifestations of the same Will to Power.

They come into being as a result of a "jealous clash" between the warriors and the priests. The values of the warrior caste presuppose "a strong physique, blooming, even exuberant health, together with all the conditions that guarantee its preservation: combat, adventure, the chase, the dance, war games."[4] Whereas aristocratic values arise in and are defined as agonistic play, priestly values are founded upon deadly serious "morality," and Nietzsche points to the historical origin of the conflict between play and (modern) ethics in the conflict between the physically strong and weak: "As we all know, priests are the most evil enemies to have—why should this be so? Because they are the most impotent. It is their impotence which makes their hate so violent and sinister, so cerebral and poisonous. The greatest haters in history—but also the most intelligent haters—have been priests. . . . Human history would be a dull and stupid thing without the intelligence furnished by its impotents" (167). Nietzsche thus relates both ethics and sociology to physiology and biology: a strong or a weak physique largely predetermines the kind of ethical and sociological views that an individual is likely to adopt in his or her community. He even suggests, in a note at the end of the first essay, that a philosophical investigation of morality requires a proper knowledge not only of linguistics and etymology but also of physiology and medicine (188).

In addition to a sociological and a physiological dimension, for Nietzsche the valuation sets of good/ bad and good/ evil have an ethnic and a racial component as well. He singles out the Jews as a historical example of a "priestly people," opposing them to the "aristocratic" Romans. According to Nietzsche, the Jews "dared to invert the aristocratic value equations good/noble/ powerful/ beautiful/happy/favored-of-the-gods and maintain, with the furious hatred of the underprivileged and impotent that 'only the poor, the powerless are good; only the suffering, sick, and ugly truly blessed'" (167). What the noble warrior values as good, the priest values as evil, and vice versa—an "inversion of values" that is responsible for both the decadence of the Western world and the interesting turn its history has taken. Starting from his typological opposition of Roman and Jew, Nietzsche proposes his own version of Western history in terms of a fierce agon between the "two sets of valuations, good/bad and good/evil" (186). The Roman aristocratic idea, which is also the "classical" one, witnesses a "strong and splendid awakening" during the Renaissance, but is buried again owing to "the plebeian rancor of the German and English Reformation, together with its natural corollary, the restoration of the Church" (186). The French Revolution means another triumph of "Israel over the classical ideal," despite Napoléon, who appears as "a last signpost to an *alternative* route," being the "most isolated and anachronistic of men, the embodiment of the noble ideal" (187).

Nietzsche closes the argument of the first essay by assigning himself the historical role of a latter-day harbinger of the aristocratic ideal and its impending reawakening. He insists that by the "dangerous slogan" on the title page of his previous book, *Beyond Good and Evil*, he had hardly meant "beyond good and bad." On the contrary, he had urged a revival of the valuation standard of good and bad, and a return to a "true hierarchy of values," based on aristocratic contest (188).

What is the merit of these cultural historical theses? As far as the history of the Western mentality is concerned, Nietzsche's dichotomy between a "master" and a "slave" ethics provides an important insight, even though it is less a historical account than a highly personal value judgment. A cursory look at the history of the Western world shows that over the centuries our mentality has invariably remained divided between two basic sets of values: an archaic one, which rests on the principle of "might makes right" and is particularly prevalent in traditional communities; and a modern or a "median" one, which prevails mostly in large-scale, democratic societies and which attempts, with various degrees of success, to separate might from right, often enlisting the help of religion to this purpose. These two valuation sets can be traced back to certain social groups, such as a warrior aristocracy, whose viewpoint largely determines cultural values, say, in archaic Greece or early medieval Europe, and various median groups (priests, rich farmers, merchants, craftsmen, artists, and so forth) whose viewpoint gains considerable influence, say, in classical Greece or modern Europe. Thus, what Nietzsche disparagingly calls a "slave ethics" can neutrally be called a median morality, the aim of which is to restrain and moderate the often self-destructive, violent competitiveness of warlike communities.[5]

It is a historical error, however, to identify too closely, as Nietzsche often does, a certain mentality with a specific social group. Although one can retain Nietzsche's insight that both a "master" and a "slave" ethics originate with the rulers, these ethics are far from belonging exclusively to either a warrior or a priestly caste. Historically speaking, Greek archaic communities, for example, seem to have made no distinction between lords and priests, and Hellenic religious beliefs were far from excluding a "master" ethics, as can be seen in Homer and Hesiod.[6] Nietzsche himself acknowledges that a priestly caste can equally share in the mentality of might makes right when he observes that "it at first creates no difficulties (though difficulties may arise later), if the ruling caste is also the priestly caste and elects to characterize itself by a term which reminds us of its priestly function."[7] He also claims, not without some historical accuracy, that religious terms like "pure" and "impure" initially oppose each other as signs of class and only later become ethical notions independent of social hierarchies.

In the absolute monarchies (based on divine right) of the Middle Ages and of later times, moreover, the king was the head of both the state and the church, and the separation of political power from the religious one is a relatively recent development in Western history. The two sets of values that Nietzsche associates with specific social groups can often be shared by aristocrats and commoners alike. Napoléon, Nietzsche's prime example of a noble "Roman," was a commoner who rose through the ranks from noncommissioned officer to emperor; conversely, there are aristocrats who have decisively contributed to the rise of a "slave" ethics, such as Solon and Plato in antiquity, or Leibnitz and Schiller in the Age of Reason. Finally, there are modern priests who adopt a thoroughly warlike, aristocratic mentality (e.g., the papal state throughout the Middle Ages and the Renaissance, the Maltese and Teutonic orders, and so forth).[8]

In sum, although both the "master" and the "slave" ethics originate with the ruling classes, they appear on the historical record from the earliest times and can indifferently be adopted by any individual or social group. The question of a shift from one valuation set to another is not an evolutionary one, nor is it determined by biology, physiology, and temperament, although it may itself determine the specific nature of all three; rather, it is a question of cultural emphasis: whereas the archaic mentality seems to dominate the beginnings of a certain community, settlement, or city (ancient and modern alike—witness, for example, the Anglo-Saxon communities in the Middle Ages or those of the Wild West in nineteenth-century America), it gradually recedes into the background and allows its counterpart to become more visible. The two mentalities thus engage in an incessant contest, with one or the other gaining temporary, inconclusive victories. In this light, Nietzsche and his poststructuralist heirs such as Eugen Fink, Georges Bataille, Gilles Deleuze, and Michel Foucault can themselves be seen as modern proponents of an archaic mentality; in turn, Nietzsche's ethical radicalism can be seen as a reversal of the median values that prevailed in nineteenth-century rationalist thought. It is in this sense (but only in this sense) that one can say that Nietzsche constructs an alternative genealogy of morals, aimed at replacing the predominantly median genealogies of his time.

If identifying the "master" and the "slave" ethics with monolithic social groups is highly questionable, associating them with ethnic, national, or racial entities is downright misleading. For example, Nietzsche's typological opposition of Roman and Hebrew has little historical merit. Rancor or resentment can hardly be the attribute of a whole people or a whole race. According to Nietzsche himself, this resentment can appear within any class or group of individuals, including the aristocracy (compare Nietzsche's argument that the slave ethics originated with the ruling classes, in the conflict between the physically strong and weak). In the third essay of the *Genealogy*, moreover, Nietzsche seems to undermine his own racial typology when he praises the Old Testament as an expression of aristocratic (that is, "Roman") values and attacks only the New Testament as an expression of slavish rancor:

> The Old Testament is another story. I have the highest respect for that book. I find in it great men, a heroic landscape, and one of the rarest things on earth, the naïveté of a strong heart. What is more, I find a *people*. In the New Testament, on the other hand, I find nothing but petty sectarianism, a rococo of the spirit . . . to say nothing of that occasional whiff of bucolic mawkishness which is characteristic of the epoch (and the locale) and which is not so much Jewish as Hellenistic. . . . These little men are fired with the most ridiculous of ambitions: chewing the cud of their private grievances and misfortunes, they try to attract the attention of the Great Demiurge, to force him to *care!*[9]

Here Nietzsche ends up with the proposition that the Jews of the Old Testament are more "Roman" than the Romans and that the late Hellenistic world is more "Jewish" than the Hebrews—an obvious philosophical paradox of dubious historical value.

Furthermore, examples of what Nietzsche calls a "slave" ethics and what I have called a median mentality abound in many ancient texts that predate the New Testament, and this ethics or mentality certainly emerged in the Graeco-Roman world long before the latter's extensive cultural contacts with the Hebraic one. For instance, in Hesiod's *Works and Days*, such terms as μέτριος (moderate), μέσος (in the middle), and καιρός (due measure) describe the life proper to a rich farmer. In the early sixth century B.C., sayings like "Know thyself" (γνῶθι σεαυτόν), "Nothing in excess" (μηδέν ἄγαν), "Measure [μέτρον] is best," "Understand due measure" (καιρός), "Honor moderation" (σωφροσύνη), and "Flee from sensuous pleasure" (ἡδονή)" are attributed to some of the Seven Sages, such as Cleobulus, Chilon, Pittacus, and Solon. During the same century, "Know thyself" and "Nothing in excess" are inscribed over the entrance of Apollo's temple at Delphi, and Apollo's shaman-priests preach due measure and restrain. With the growth of the Hellenic polis, these injunctions become more and more common, for example, in the poetry of Theognis, Alcman, Pindar, Phocylides, Bacchylides and others, as well as in fifth-century Greek tragedy. The origins of these sayings are largely aristocratic and, as such, they are used by statesmen like Pittacus of Mytilene and Solon to support εὐνομία (good rule under aristocratic law), even though they gradually acquire a democratic flavor, being placed in the service of ἰσονομία (equality before the law), for instance in classical Athens. The example of ancient Greece shows again that a median ethics is not necessarily connected with any particular social class, let alone any ethnic or racial group, being used indifferently by any culture based on a mentality of power.

One should also note that although Nietzsche cannot in all fairness be accused of anti-Semitism, his ambivalent evaluation of the role of the Jews in Western culture is unfortunate because this evaluation was taken over without any philosophical qualifications or niceties by Nazi ideology—itself a prime example of social rancor and only superficially related to the "aristocratic" or archaic kind of values advocated by Nietzsche. The self-serving Nazi appropriation of his racial speculations is all the more ironical because, in the *Genealogy* itself, Nietzsche ridicules German anti-Semitism, prophetically pointing out its fatal danger for the German nation: "I am equally out of patience with those newest speculators in idealism called anti-Semites, who parade as Christian-Aryan worthies and endeavor to stir up all the asinine elements of the nation by that cheapest of propaganda tricks, a moral attitude. (The ease with which any wretched imposture succeeds in present-day Germany may be attributed to the progressive stultification of the German mind. The reason for this general spread of inanity may be found in a diet composed entirely of newspapers, politics, beer, and Wagner's music)" (294–95).

Despite some glaring ambiguities in his historical argument, Nietzsche's contribution to the history of Western civilization is nevertheless durable, because he accurately locates the historical origins and the prevailing value-systems of this civilization in a mentality of power. He shows that both archaic and modern ethics stem from this mentality and implies that the exorbitant psychological price of modern civilization may offset the latter's benefits. In fact, Nietzsche appears most persuasive as a diagnostician of the diseased modern psyche, fatally split between might and right, between willful pleasure and guilty self-denial.

In his second essay, entitled "'Guilt,' 'Bad Conscience' and Related Matters," Nietzsche chiefly develops two theses that are directly connected with his view of human history as a relentless agon between aristocratic and priestly values. The first thesis is that human civilization is a result of a violent suppression of the animal instincts and that man had to pay a high price for "reason, seriousness, control over his emotions . . . those grand human prerogatives and cultural showpieces." Behind all good things lies a tremendous amount of "blood and horror" (194). Nietzsche's historical examples in support of this thesis include archaic ludic forms, such as the religious festival, in which the ancient Greeks "could offer their gods no more pleasant condiment than the joys of cruelty" (201). Punishment, too, had its "festive features": witness the Middle Ages, when no royal wedding or public celebration would have been complete without "executions, tortures, or an *auto da fé*" (198). Nietzsche thus points to the archaic link between play, pleasure, and violence, a link that was severed when Hellenic philosophy separated play from immediate power and turned it into a rational instrument. As I have shown elsewhere, this separation has been endorsed and perpetuated by a median mentality throughout the history of Western

rationalism.[10] According to Nietzsche, however, rationalist thought itself is not a renunciation of the Will to Power, but a covert and, in some
cases, even perverted form of it. He will come back to this idea in the
third essay, when attacking modern scholarship and the modern scientific mentality as distorted expressions of the ascetic ideal.

Nietzsche's second thesis, related to the first, is that guilt and bad
conscience are among the highest prices paid by culture for suppressing
man's violent instincts:

> All instincts that are not allowed free play turn inward. This is
> what I call man's interiorization [*Verinnerlichung des Menschen*]; it alone
> provides the soil for the growth of what later is called man's *soul*. Man's
> interior world, originally meager and tenuous, was expanding in ev-
> ery dimension, in proportion as the outward discharge of his feelings
> was curtailed. The formidable bulwarks by means of which the polity
> protected itself against the ancient instincts of freedom . . . caused
> those wild extravagant instincts to turn in upon man.[11]

Nietzsche sees the phenomenon of the "animal soul" turning in upon
itself as one of the "most unexpected throws in the game of dice played
by Heraclitus's great 'child,' be he called Zeus or Chance" (219), that is,
as a highly ambiguous historical development. On the one hand, he considers it a positive step in the (self-)creation of civilized man, even though
this step is neither necessary nor predictable, as his dice metaphor indi-
cates. On the other hand, Nietzsche sees the *Verinnerlichung des Menschen*
as a devastating malady, for it is at the root of both guilt and bad conscience: "Hostility, cruelty, the delight in persecution, raids, excitement,
destruction all turned against their begetter. Lacking external enemies
and resistances, and confined within an oppressive narrowness and regu-
larity, man began rending, persecuting, terrifying himself, like a wild
beast hurling itself against the bars of its cage" (218). Nietzsche further
describes guilt and bad conscience as man's "sickness of himself, brought
on by the violent severance from his animal past . . . by his declaration
of war against the old instincts that had hitherto been the foundation of
his power, his joy, and his awesomeness" (218).

Nietzsche is fully aware of the paradoxical character of his argument
and at the end of his second essay imagines the reader asking him: "Are
you constructing an ideal or destroying one?" His predictable answer is

that he is doing both, for the "raising of an altar" requires the breaking of another (228). Here Nietzsche temporarily abandons his historical-genealogical project and relapses into the prophetic language of Zarathustra, whom he appropriately invokes in the last sentence of the essay. He echoes the closing argument of his first essay by predicting the arrival of the overman, who will restore archaic, warlike values and thus free humanity of pity, guilt, and bad conscience.

Nietzsche's psychological theses constitute the point of departure not only of the twentieth-century psychoanalytical movement but also of some of its contemporary opponents.[12] They offer a plausible explanation of the schizoid character of the Western collective psyche, divided between mind and body, love and hate, contest and cooperation, gentleness and violence, law and transgression, peace and war. But they also offer a holistic, psychosomatic view of individuals inseparable from their physical and social environment. It has by now become clear, I hope, that Nietzsche attempts more than a genealogy of morals in his book. He probes into the nature of Western mentality as a whole, and it is for this reason that he insists on regarding ethics as being inextricably linked not only to axiology but also to physiology, biology, medicine, pathology, psychology, linguistics, and etymology.

A mentality comprises not only a community's ethos (mode of thought and behavior) but also its pathos, i.e., the psychoemotional investment or interest that both underlies and upholds its values, whether material or spiritual. Furthermore, a certain ontoepistemological framework is always the expression of a certain ethopathology, rather than the other way around. As Nietzsche notes, "Our thoughts should grow out of our values with the same necessity as the fruit out of the tree."[13] To "thoughts," Nietzsche would certainly agree to adding "behavior," since for him "ethos" means both. Indeed, in the context of the present study, one should always understand "ethos" as "thought-behavior," because for me, as for Nietzsche or any other holistic thinker, behavior is a mode of thought, and thought is a mode of behavior. As Nietzsche's psychosomatic view further implies, one cannot change one's world without first changing one's mentality (i.e., ethos and pathos), and this is why in subsequent works he will seek to elaborate an alternative ethopathology for his overman, a project in many respects as ambitious as the one Socrates envisioned for his philosopher-king in the *Republic*.

On the other hand, the experience of two devastating world wars, several communist and fascist dictatorships, and the rapid rise of a ruthless multinational technocracy with global hegemonic interests, all within the present century, ought to render us very skeptical of the Nietzschean overman, called upon to heal the diseased Western collective psyche through a return to an archaic ethopathology. Full and lasting changes in this psyche can be achieved neither through social, ethical, and axiological hierarchies based on warlike contest nor through a periodical, violent erasure of all individual differences in Dionysian collective ecstasy. We need to look outside a mentality of power, whether in its archaic or median guise, for such radical changes. One alternative would be to construct an irenic mentality, based on an integrative ethopathology that would in turn ground and support a variety of nonviolent sets of values. But wouldn't this irenic mentality be just another "ascetic ideal," as Nietzsche would undoubtedly charge? This question cannot be answered in a satisfactory manner before examining the third and last essay of the *Genealogy*, in which Nietzsche critically defines and explores such ideals.

"What Do Ascetic Ideals Mean?" is an extended commentary on one of Zarathustra's aphorisms that equally belongs to an aristocratic warrior's mentality: "Wisdom likes men who are reckless, scornful and violent; being a woman, her heart goes out to a soldier" (231). In the end, however, Nietzsche's answer to the question he poses in the title of the essay remains profoundly ambivalent: ascetic ideals may mean different things in the case of different temperaments and they can both further and retard the healthy development of mankind. But, ultimately, they are "indicative of a basic trait in the human will, its fear of the void" (231). In other words, for Nietzsche, ascetic ideals are both products and instruments of a mentality of power and, as such, they can be both good and evil.

Nietzsche concentrates mainly on four personality types that profess embracing ascetic ideals: the artist, the philosopher, the priest, and the scientist or the scholar. He sets the first two in opposition, comparing the specific cases of Wagner and Schopenhauer. One may immediately point out that whenever philosophers embark upon such comparisons, they almost inevitably tend to favor their brethren. Nietzsche is hardly an exception to this rule, and his partiality to the philosopher cannot be put down simply to his personal preference for Schopenhauer rather than Wagner. The charges he brings against artists are age-old: artists are protean, they lack any sense of commitment or loyalty to anyone including themselves, they are political opportunists. Behind Nietzsche's ironic sentences one can hear the condescending voice of Socrates ridiculing Ion: "Artists have never stood sufficiently proudly and independently in (or against) the world for their changes of attitude to be deserving notice. They have ever been in the service of some ethics or philosophy or religion, and all too often they have been tools in the hands of a clique, smooth sycophants either of vested interests or of forces newly come to power. . . . Artists never stand resolutely for themselves; standing alone goes against their deepest instincts" (236). In other words, artists cannot be taken seriously when they claim to pursue *any* ideal, including the ascetic one, and thus cannot be the object of a serious, philosophical discussion.

In turn, the philosopher, as embodied by Schopenhauer, seems at first to get his share of ridicule under Nietzsche's merciless, ironic scrutiny:

> We must take account of the fact that Schopenhauer, who treated sexuality (including woman, that *instrumentum diaboli*) as a personal enemy, absolutely required enemies to keep him in good spirits; . . . that he would have sickened, become a *pessimist* (which he was not, much as he would have liked to be) had he been deprived of his enemies, of Hegel, of woman, of sensuality, of the human will to survival. . . . Just as with the ancient Cynics, his rage was his balm, his recreation, his compensation, his specific against tedium, in short, his happiness. (241)

This time, however, there is a positive valuation behind Nietzsche's ironic tone: for Schopenhauer, just as for the Cynics (and, one might add, for the Sophists, Socrates, Plato, and Nietzsche himself), taking on a worthy opponent is a vital source of both enjoyment and creativity, a particularly productive form of intellectual play. As to the ascetic ideal, Nietzsche tells the reader confidingly, most philosophers exhibit an inveterate prejudice against the senses. This prejudice is no proof, however, of their moral purity, saintliness, or chastity. It is simply that asceticism provides the philosopher with "the condition most favorable to the exercise of his intelligence." Far from denying existence, the philosophers affirm their existence alone, "perhaps even to the point of *hubris: pereat mundus, fiat philosophia, fiat philosophum, fiam!* It is clear: these philosophers are by no means unprejudiced witnesses and judges of the value of the ascetic ideal. They think only of themselves" (243). In the case of the philosopher, then, the ascetic ideal appears as a positive manifestation of the Will to Power, in which a dominant instinct—the instinct to create—subordinates and channels all the other instincts, attaining the conditions most favorable to optimal functioning.

One can certainly argue that there is no reason why this creative instinct should not prevail in the artist as well. Elsewhere, Nietzsche himself relates the ascetic ideal to the artist in the same positive way that he relates it to the philosopher. In *The Will to Power*, for example, he writes: "Artists are *not* men of great passion, whatever they may like to tell us and themselves. And this for two reasons: they lack any sense of shame before themselves . . . and they also lack any sense of shame before great passion. . . . Secondly, however, their vampire, their talent, grudges them as a rule that squandering of force which one calls passion.—If one has a talent, one is also its victim: one lives under the vampirism of one's talent."[14] Therefore, artists, no less than philosophers, are fully able to subordinate all of their instincts, including the sexual one, to the instinct to create, and know how to gather and channel their force into their work, without dissipating it in useless passion. Along the same lines, Nietzsche points out, in another note of *The Will to Power*, that sexual chastity has nothing to do with morality, but with a "will to mastery" that manifests itself particularly in the artistic personality: "A relative chastity, a prudent caution on principle regarding erotic matters, even in thought, can belong to the grand rationale of life even in richly endowed and complete natures. This principle applies especially to artists, it is part of their best wisdom of life." Consequently, the artist, "under the pressure of his task, of his will to mastery," is "actually moderate, often even chaste." His dominant creative instinct "does not permit him to expend himself in any casual way, for the "force that one expends in artistic conception is the same as that expended in the sexual act: there is only one kind of force."[15] If there is "only one kind of force," then it will manifest itself equally in all intellectual and creative endeavors, including philosophical and artistic ones.

In light of Nietzsche's remarks about artistic chastity as focused force in *The Will to Power*, Wagner no less than Schopenhauer can be said to be a prime example of the ascetic ideal as a positive expression of the Will to Power. Yet Nietzsche, like Socrates, ultimately sides with the philosophers in their contest with the artists. To this purpose, he even changes the connotation of the word "artist," just as Socrates did in Plato's *Republic* when he transferred the meaning of σοφός from the poet to the philosopher. As I have shown in *Dionysus Reborn*, for Nietzsche only the philosopher, the soldier, and the statesman are "true artists." Although what is usually called *art* may exhibit traces of a warlike, archaic mentality, Nietzsche sees it only as an intermediary stage in his project of transvaluating all values.

In the *Genealogy of Morals*, the case of the priest as an embodiment of the ascetic ideal is even more ambivalent than that of the artist. Although religious asceticism is equally a manifestation of the Will to Power, it assumes largely a negative form because, through it, the Will turns in upon itself and becomes perverted. According to Nietzsche, the priest is a typical modern hybrid of strength and weakness. On the one hand, the priest ministers to the sufferers, because he is one of them. He "must be sick himself, he must be deeply akin to all the shipwrecked and diseased, if he is to understand them and be understood by them."[16] On the other hand, the priest "must also be strong, master over himself even more than over others, with a will to power that is intact, if he is to be their support, overlord, disciplinarian, tyrant, god" (262). He is a new kind of beast of prey, waging "a war of cunning ('intellect') rather than of brute force" (263).

Consequently, according to Nietzsche, the priest's mission is double-edged. He defends his sick flock against healthy predators by sowing among the latter "pain, inner division, self-contradiction—confident of his rule over all sufferers." But he also defends his flock against themselves, "against all the wickedness and malice smoldering within the herd and whatever other troubles are bred among the sick" (263). The priest, moreover, carries out his double-edged mission through a subtle, sophistic twist: "Every suffering sheep says to himself, 'I suffer; it must be somebody's fault.' But his shepherd, the ascetic priest, says to him, 'You are quite right, my sheep, somebody must be at fault here, but that somebody is yourself. You alone are to blame—you alone are to blame for yourself'" (264). The priest thus wages "a clever, hard, secret battle against anarchy and disintegration, always aware of the piling-up of rancor, that most dangerous of dynamites" (263).

Despite its positive effect of controlling the rancorous herd, however, the priest's reasoning is "not only bold but also abundantly false" (264). In the short term, this kind of remedy has a certain curative virtue, raising a protective barrier between the healthy and the sick. In the long run, however, it cannot result in a physiologically effective cure, because it does not tap the "vital instinct . . . for the rehabilitation of the personality" (265). In other words, it ultimately fails to be effective, because its source is not in the affirmation but in the denial of the Will to Power. It is for this reason that religious asceticism is ultimately more destructive than creative, and Nietzsche ranks its pernicious effect on the health of humanity among the three deadliest, ahead of alcohol and syphilis (280).

Nietzsche also sketches a typology of the modern scholar or scientist, who claims to have rendered his rival, the priest, obsolete through a cultivation of the scientific "counterideal." This counterideal allegedly is "a truly realistic philosophy" that "believes only in itself, has the courage of its convictions, and has managed splendidly thus far to get along without God, transcendence and restrictive virtues" (284). But, to Nietzsche, this is only "noisy propaganda," for the scholar or the scientist is little more than a latter-day avatar of the priest. Barring a few exceptions, "learning today is a hiding place for all manner of maladjustment, lukewarmness, self-depreciation, guilty conscience. Its restless activity thinly veils a lack of ideals, the want of a great love, dissatisfaction with a continence imposed on it from without" (285). Nietzsche contends that scholarship often is an opiate for sufferers who, in a way, are even worse than priests, because they are "unwilling to admit their suffering to themselves," turning into "stupefied and unconscious men, mortally afraid of regaining their consciousness" (286). In that sense, Nietzsche asks, "Haven't we all grown familiar with learning as a drug?" (285). Since the contemporary world still shares, implicitly or explicitly, Nietzsche's mentality of power, perhaps it is superfluous to point out that his observations about the ailing ethopathology of Western academia and the Western scientific community in general are as pertinent today as they were a hundred years ago.

After he analyzes the four personality types that embrace and promote ascetic ideals, Nietzsche implicitly acknowledges that in the end
no one type is higher than the others, because all of them "still believe
in truth" (287). In this regard, all of them should learn what the Christian Crusaders in the East should have learned from "the invincible
Society of Assassins, that order of free spirits *par excellence*, whose lower
ranks observed an obedience stricter than that of any monastic order"
and whose higher ranks reserved for themselves the liberating slogan:
"Nothing is true; everything is permitted" (287). In the absence of such
genuine intellectual and emotional freedom, which would do away with
any kind of ideal, the ascetic ideal remains of utmost importance in the
life of mankind. This is so, Nietzsche concludes, because up to now it
has been the only ideal that has given human life some meaning, and
"any meaning is better than none" (298). Although the ascetic ideal
signifies "a will to nothingness, a revulsion from life, a rebellion against
the principal conditions of living," it nevertheless "is and remains a *will*,"
and man "would sooner have the void for his purpose than be void of
purpose" (298–99). Here Nietzsche reveals the central tautology of any
thought that makes power its grounding principle. For such thought,
power must always constitute its own justification or raison d'être. No
matter how perverted the ascetic ideal may be, it is "justified" because
it remains an expression of the Will. Indeed, it is a strong bulwark against
what power abhors most, the void or nothingness.

The Genealogy of Morals, then, is an "attack" not only on those idealist philosophers who do not recognize that power is at the root of Western mentality but also on "pessimistic" thinkers such as Schopenhauer—
the latter understands the sorry state of human affairs only too well and
attempts to offer, if not a remedy, at least some palliative for it. In fact,
"What Do Ascetic Ideals Mean?" can be read as a direct response to the
last few chapters of *Die Welt als Wille und Vorstellung*, Schopenhauer's
philosophical masterpiece. In this regard, Nietzsche's contrast of
Schopenhauer and Wagner has a hidden subtext as well: an implied comparison between Schopenhauer and Nietzsche himself. Even though
Nietzsche has wrestled himself free of Richard Wagner, the idol of his
youth whom he now largely dismisses as a histrionic, irresponsible court
jester, he still feels the need to distance himself from Schopenhauer, to
show in what ways he departs from his master's thought.

But what is the basic difference between Nietzsche and Schopen-hauer as revealed in the *Genealogy?* It resides precisely in their sym-metrically opposite valuations of the ascetic ideal and its cultural agents. A far-ranging critique of the ascetic ideal is of vital importance to Nietzsche, as he takes seriously Schopenhauer's claim that "no philoso-phy can leave undecided the theme of quietism and asceticism," be-cause "this theme is in substance identical with that of all metaphysics and ethics."[17]

According to Schopenhauer, asceticism and quietism are moral po-sitions (in my terms, ethopathological stances) that humans can assume in regard to the "Will to Live" *(der Wille zum Leben)*, Schopenhauer's philosophical first principle. The Will to Live is immanent in the cos-mos as well as in humans, but humans can adopt two contrary attitudes toward it: affirmation or denial. The affirmation of the Will means in-volvement in the physical world of becoming, violence, and death. All life, at bottom, means striving, suffering, and perishing. The Will to Live is therefore involved in a "delusion," and "injustice, wickedness, cruelty are signs . . . of deep entanglement in that delusion" (610). Con-versely, moral virtues such as justice and philanthropy are signs that "the appearing will is no longer firmly held in [its] delusion, but that disillusionment already occurs" (610). Clinging to life and its pleasures must now "make way for a universal renunciation," which also brings about a denial of the Will. This denial is demanded by human intelli-gence itself, which "can only be reaction to the will; but since all willing is error, the last work of intelligence is to abolish willing, whose aims and ends it has hitherto served" (610). Hence Schopenhauer's positive valuation of the religious teachings of Gautama Buddha and Christ, which seem to him to start from a denial of the Will to Live. For him, the Buddhist and the Christian renunciation of the Will is the highest manifestation of philosophical consciousness in its heroic, if ultimately futile, attempt to transcend itself. In turn, asceticism is a major step toward this renunciation and must therefore be valued positively.

Nevertheless, Schopenhauer contends that asceticism, when defined in a narrow sense as "the giving up of all property, the deliberate search for the unpleasant and repulsive, self-torture, fasting, the hairy garment, mortification of the flesh" (607), is a violent manifestation of the denial of the Will to Live. So Buddhism, for example, rejects this "strict and excessive" form of asceticism, contenting itself with "celibacy, voluntary poverty, humility, and obedience of the monks, with abstinence from animal food, as well as from all worldliness" (607); Buddhism, that is, contents itself with quietism.

Moreover, according to Schopenhauer, certain Oriental thinkers are fully aware of the mentality of power that lies behind asceticism both in a narrow and in a broad sense: "The Vedanta philosophy rightly says that, after the entrance of the true knowledge with complete resignation in its train, and so after the arrival of the new birth, the morality or immorality of the previous conduct becomes a matter of indifference" (107). Here Schopenhauer alludes to his fundamental distinction between philosophical knowledge and "mystical" or "true" knowledge. In his view, philosophical knowledge can concern itself only with the individual and nature, that is, with Will both in its subjective guises (what one may call "ego-will") and its objective guises (what one may call "natural will" or play of physical forces). Because reflection itself is an instrument of the Will, "there is a limit up to which [it] can penetrate, and *so far* illuminate the night of our existence, although the horizon remains dark. This limit is reached by my doctrine in the will-to-live that affirms and denies itself in its own phenomenon. To want to go beyond this is, in my view, like wanting to fly beyond the atmosphere" (591–92).

But, of course, mystical knowledge does just that: it "flies beyond the atmosphere" or beyond the point at which philosophy must inevitably stop. If mystical knowledge begins where philosophical knowledge ends, then it must begin with nothingness. This fact explains, Schopenhauer notes, the negative nature of his philosophy, which ends with the denial of the Will, that is, with nothingness. Yet, he adds, the consolation may be offered that this is a relative rather than an absolute nothingness: "For, if something is no one of all the things that we know, then certainly it is for us in general nothing. Yet it does not follow from this that it is nothing absolutely, namely that it must be nothing from every possible point of view and in every possible sense, but only that we are restricted to a wholly negative knowledge of it; and this may very well lie in the limitation of our point of view. Now it is precisely here that the mystic proceeds positively, and therefore, from this point, nothing is left but mysticism" (612). From the standpoint of the mystic, nothingness can be described positively as a "consciousness of the identity of one's own inner being with that of all things, or with the kernel of the world" (610). This holistic consciousness is the opposite of the consciousness leading to the affirmation of life, of the *principium individuationis* expressed through "the phenomenal world, diversity of all beings, individuality, egoism, hatred, wickedness" (610). The latter consciousness is equally holistic, but it springs from a different root, the Will to Live.

For Schopenhauer, the two kinds of consciousness mark the difference between the mystic and the philosopher. The mystic starts from within, whereas the philosopher starts from without. The mystic begins from his "inner, positive, individual experience, in which he finds himself as the eternal and only being." But since none of this is communicable, he is "unable to convince." On the other hand, the philosopher is able to do so, for he starts from "what is common to all, the objective phenomenon lying before us all, and from the facts of self-consciousness as they are to be found in everyone" (611). These two experiences are incommensurable, and Schopenhauer's philosophy remains necessarily suspended between them, with the paradoxical effect that what it affirms, it negates, and what it negates, it affirms.

One can now readily see how Nietzsche both subscribes to and revises Schopenhauer's philosophy of the Will. One of Nietzsche's lasting contributions to the history of Western thought is to have replaced, in his mature work, Schopenhauer's philosophical principle of the *Wille zum Leben* with that of the *Wille zur Macht*. He thus brings into focus the Will's objective, which is not life for the sake of living, but life for the sake of power. As in the case of the Will to Live, the Will to Power is immanent in the cosmos, and humans can adopt only two attitudes toward it: affirmation or denial. Unlike Schopenhauer, however, Nietzsche advocates the affirmation of the Will to Power at all costs, that is, the affirmation of the world of becoming, multiplicity, and individuality—a world that equally includes violence, suffering, death, and the void. Consequently, for Nietzsche the denial of the Will is a sign of weakness, of physical and cultural decadence rather than one of strength or supreme self-knowledge. Hence his highly ambiguous, mostly negative, valuation of Buddhism and Christianity as a manifestation of a perverted Will to Power. In the context of the present study, then, it becomes clear that the main difference between Nietzsche and Schopenhauer is actually one of pathos, which in turn underlies and supports two symmetrically opposite forms of ethos or thought-behavior.

Yet Schopenhauer's willingness to entertain the possibility of a "mystical" knowledge that is not based on the Will opens a number of ethical and ontoepistemological choices that Nietzsche effectively bars again. In Nietzsche, the world is eternally returning to the same agonistic game of ego-wills and natural forces that, to paraphrase Heidegger, play because they play, causing humans to oscillate perpetually between the extremes of a tragic and a sublime ethopathology.[18] Thus, whereas Nietzsche's justification of the Will to Power is tautological, his attitude (or pathos) toward this Will is both ambivalent and self-contradictory. If power exists only for the sake of power, or if power is its own justification, then there is no good reason why Nietzsche should not joyfully and unequivocally hail the advent of modern ethics as the greatest achievement of the Will. For one can argue that the Will disguises itself under the garb of justice, rationality, and compassion simply to enable a fistful of overmen to dominate the herd with enhanced effectiveness. It is a well-known historical fact (brilliantly dramatized by Orwell in *1984*, as chapter 6, section 3 below will show) that the most efficient rulers are not those who rule in their own name or as unmediated presences, but those who rule as representatives or surrogates, in the name of some abstract idea such as God, the People, Freedom, Universal Equality, and so forth.

As to "man's interiorization" *(Verinnerlichung des Menschen)*, there is no reason why Nietzsche should not welcome it as an entirely positive development, for now power becomes immanent and invisible, operating from within the consciousness of the slave. This interiorization, moreover, may apply only to some "men," not all men (here women, as implied in Zarathustra's aphorism introducing the third essay, presumably have no role to play, being nothing but mirrors of the male Will). Contrary to what Nietzsche often implies in tragical overtones, the consciousness of a master need not be affected at all by that of a slave, for true masters will never waste their energies on pity and guilt; otherwise they will lose their ability to rule and will no longer be what they are. On the other hand, it is not clear at all that one can readily manufacture "overmen" out of "slaves" (in the sense of median humans) any more than one can manufacture cats out of mice. My discussion of *Crime and Punishment* and other novels dealing with "murder as play," in chapter 4 below, will show that the modern ethopathology of power is endemically and chronically split, and that a Nietzschean philosophical program designed wholly to replace a median mentality with its archaic counterpart is bound to fail: as Nietzsche unwittingly proves by his own final breakdown in Turin, it is easier, from the viewpoint of power, to teach a cat to behave like a mouse, than a mouse to behave like a cat.

From the standpoint of what Schopenhauer calls "mystical" knowledge, however, might one not discern some basic element in asceticism that could, after all, be emancipated from a mentality of power and be enlisted in the service of an alternative kind of ethics? In the *Genealogy*, Nietzsche presents asceticism in its Schopenhauerian narrow sense, purely as an instrument of power. As such, his historical evaluation of the priest's position, mode of operation, and impact within a world of power is certainly accurate. When Christianity, for example, enters the world of history, it creates, through the Bible and the Church, a number of power-oriented ideologies and institutions that are partly based on the slave ethics described by Nietzsche. In this particular historical case, he seems justified in saying that the Schopenhauerian denial of the Will is only its roundabout affirmation.

On the other hand, Nietzsche ignores Schopenhauer's distinction between a narrow and a broad kind of asceticism as well as his distinction between asceticism, quietism, and mysticism. A broad kind of asceticism does not go to extremes in the "intentional mortification of one's will" (Schopenhauer's definition of asceticism in general), acting more like a tempered wisdom of the middle way, akin to that of the Seven Sages, the Delphic oracle, and the Stoa of ancient Greece. It acknowledges, moreover, that violence, be it only against oneself, will breed further violence and will therefore defeat the practitioner's self-emancipatory purposes. Thus, while narrow asceticism often leads to a violent resurgence of the Will to Power in a distorted, unhealthy form, the broad kind is mostly a harmless expression of the practitioner's need to move away from the Will as such. In this sense, it is related to quietism, defined by Schopenhauer as "the giving up of all willing," through which the religious practitioner drops out of the power struggle altogether and chooses the largely peaceful, nonviolent values of the *vita*

contemplativa. The contemplative life can in turn lead the religious practitioner to the irenic experience of the harmonious interconnectedness
of all things or to what Schopenhauer calls "mysticism." At this point,
however, the practitioner should be able to leave behind religion itself,
including asceticism and quietism, which he or she will now regard as
mere expressions of a mentality of power, promoted not only by religious beliefs and institutions but also by the so-called *vita activa* as a
whole. It is this "mystical" or irenic experience that Nietzsche, in the
wake of innumerable Western thinkers beginning with Aristotle, char-
acterizes as vacuous or void and that the inhabitants of power-oriented
worlds invariably value negatively as tedious, utopian, and defeatist.

We are now in a position to give at least some preliminary answers
to the question raised at the beginning of our discussion of Nietzsche's
evaluation of the ascetic ideal: Is an irenic mentality based on nonviolent values anything more than a distorted manifestation of such an ideal?
One may observe, first of all, that this kind of mentality, far from sharing the nature and goals of asceticism in Nietzsche's sense, is incommensurable with a mentality of power. This does not mean, of course,
that power cannot partially employ it for its own purposes, as Nietzsche
conclusively demonstrates. In developing an irenic ethopathology, therefore, one must take into consideration both Nietzsche's and Schopenhauer's versions of the philosophy of the Will, in order to understand
how one can best move away from this philosophy altogether. It is at
this point that Nietzsche's substitution of the Will to Power for Schopenhauer's Will to Live becomes extremely important, not only because
power and life can now be thought of as separate but also because one
can imagine a life that is no longer subordinated to power, no longer
defined as "merely a special case of the will to power."[19] So the way is
clear to envision not only one kind but many kinds of life, not only one
world (defined by both Schopenhauer and Nietzsche as a world of suffering and death) but many different kinds, organized on a potentially
infinite number of alternative principles.

Furthermore, perhaps suffering and death, as Schopenhauer and
the Christian tradition in general believe, may indeed serve as passage-
ways from worlds based on a mentality of power to alternative kinds.
They may acquire an irenic pathos especially when they are not sought
out deliberately or made to serve a higher purpose—for example, in

sacrificial rituals, such as Christ's passion, or in self-sacrifice, such as Christian martyrdom—but occur spontaneously as liminal phenomena. Conceivably, even deliberate self-mortification could be a way of gaining access to alternative worlds, even though this way would be a highly paradoxical and ambivalent one. Because of its deliberately violent nature, self-induced suffering could easily lose its liminal quality, thus leading back to, rather than away from, a mentality of power. The present study will return again and again, in subsequent chapters, to the notion of suffering and death as liminal phenomena, as well as to the concept of liminality in general. In the end, however, there is no compelling reason to believe either that asceticism is the only way to attain the "mystical" experience of integrative harmony or that this experience need be mystical at all. Actually, what Schopenhauer calls "mystical" and what I have called "irenic" experience can be seen as truly incommensurable with ascetic ideals and practices, even though it may often seek to find expression through them. From an irenic standpoint, therefore, one needs to revise Schopenhauer's argument that whoever professes either quietism, asceticism, or mysticism is "gradually led to the acceptance of the others, even against his intention."[20] There is a possible, but not necessary, relation between these three practices, and neither asceticism nor quietism will infallibly lead to an irenic ethopathology or away from a mentality of power. Nor is mysticism, as it has generally been thought and practiced in the Western world, entirely emancipated from this mentality: more often than not, "mysticism" is one more label through which power seeks either to appropriate or to dismiss what for it remains essentially an alien and threatening experience.

From a historical or pragmatic standpoint, however, one may still find it difficult to grasp intuitively the existence of an irenic cosmos, when our experience reveals to us precisely the opposite—an inscrutable, violent totality or Being that, in Heideggerian terms, plays with Dasein its dangerous game of life and death, necessity and chance, unveiling and withdrawal. As Schopenhauer notes, the existence of a nonviolent, harmonious world is philosophically (and historically) incommunicable. We have no positive language or pathos to express it, and it exists only in the consciousness of a few mystics, who would be unable to convince us, even if they had the desire to do so. It would seem, then, that no option is left beyond the here and now. Yet this is the kind of circular argument employed by any philosophy of power. We cannot demonstrate the existence of worlds outside those based on a mentality of power, because this mentality is all *we* know. As Schopenhauer shrewdly observes, the nature of the demonstrative activity itself requires that "what is unknown must everywhere be explained from what is better known, not *vice versa*" (643), hence we can never escape the hermeneutic circle of knowledge.

The question remains, however, how to effect the passage from what is better known to what is unknown, from an ethopathology of power to a different kind of mentality. One of the ways of getting around this hermeneutic dilemma is familiar to Western thinkers at least since Xenophanes: it is the hypothetical cognitive game that Hans Vaihinger has called the "philosophy of *as if.*" Although Western thought has often employed this cognitive game to endorse and justify its own mentality, there is no reason why one cannot play it in alternative contexts as well. Thus, we may proceed *as if* something (authentic irenic worlds, for example) were known outside our world of power, even though that something may be incommensurable with our own knowledge. Venturing outside our circle of knowledge would not mean denying the worlds we live in or dismissing them as "delusions" in a Buddhist, Christian, or Schopenhauerian manner. Rather, it would mean gradually moving away from them or turning our back on them, as it were. And we can begin moving away only when our imagination accepts the possibility of worlds outside those with which we are already familiar. Once we entertain rather than exclude this possibility, new worlds and new values will slowly emerge as we muddle along.

Another way of approaching the question of the accessibility of alternative worlds can be found in Schopenhauer's own philosophy of the Will as ethical choice. He claims that his philosophy is "the only one that grants to morality its complete and entire rights; for only if the true nature of man is his own *will*, consequently only if he is, in the strictest sense, his own work, are his deeds actually entirely his and attributable to him. On the other hand, as soon as he has another origin, or is the work of a being different from himself, all his guilt [*Schuld*, also debt, responsibility] falls back on to this origin or originator. For *operari sequitur esse*" (589–90). Although Schopenhauer is certainly not the first to have proclaimed humanity to be the "measure of all things" (Protagoras's phrase), he reemphasizes the fact that humans create and are fully responsible for their world. But if what we do follows from what we are *(operari sequitur esse)*, it is no less true that what we are follows from what we do. Once we change our actions, thoughts, and feelings, we also change our nature or what we are. Nothing can stop us from creating ourselves anew, from producing alternative values and, consequently, new worlds, if we become dissatisfied with our old ones.

From an irenic perspective, humans can also redefine their will, not as a Will to Power nor as a struggle for existence, but as a will to universal love and peaceful harmony. Quietism in this sense would no longer be defined negatively as the giving up of all willing, but positively as an inclination toward an irenic world. Humans would no longer need to practice asceticism and even less mysticism, because mysticism or "that which is hidden" remains hidden only to (or by) a mentality of power. Instead, we would proceed *as if* the inner experience of cosmic integration were no longer "mystical" but open to all humanity. This would in turn bring about sweeping changes in our ethopathology; indeed, it would alter the nature and quality of our perceptual experience as a whole. Chapters 2 and 3 of the present study will deal at length with the notion of incommensurability of various mentalities based on different perceptual experiences, as well as with possible ways of accessing or constructing irenic worlds. Here I can suggest only the general direction that such an irenic project might take.

One of the first tasks would certainly be that of creating a language appropriate for an irenic perceptual experience as well as a history of ethos commensurate with it. As Paul Feyerabend remarks in a different context and to a different purpose, "one must learn to argue with unexplained terms and to use sentences for which no clear rules of usage are as yet available."[21] In this—and here Feyerabend equally employs a game metaphor—we can follow the lead of an infant at play, "who starts using words without yet understanding them, who adds more and more uncomprehended linguistic fragments to his playful activity, discovers the sense-giving principle only *after* he has been active in this way for a long time." Like a playing child, the creator of an alternative world should "be able to talk nonsense until the amount of nonsense created by him and his friends is big enough to give sense to all its parts."[22]

Another task would be to disseminate the values of an irenic mentality throughout the community. In this respect, education or παιδεία
would clearly be a crucial factor, a truth that Plato fully recognized when
he had Socrates elaborate his playful model of an ideal republic. But the
irenic model that I have in mind here is neither ideal nor utopian, for it
does not advocate a particular kind of community or sociopolitical entity. Rather, it advocates a certain mentality or a certain way of responding to the world and to other beings, that is, a form of human responsibility that transcends national, ethnic, social, or political differences. This
does not mean, however, that such a mentality cannot in turn create an
infinite variety of national, ethnic, social, or political realities.

Finally, one can reassess, from the standpoint of an irenic mentality,
the role of various scientific and artistic fields within an irenic world,
starting from the essential relation between aesthetics and ethics, as
Nietzsche (in the wake of Schopenhauer) envisions it. What does
Nietzsche mean when he says that existence can "be justified only in
aesthetic terms" and that "art rather than ethics, constitute[s] the essential metaphysical activity of man"?[23] These statements can again be
best understood in terms of Schopenhauer's philosophy of the Will. Since
humans are creators of both themselves and their world, they are artists
in the broadest sense. According to Schopenhauer (and Nietzsche),
morality itself is a work of fiction (from the Latin *fingere*, to construct,
make, but also to counterfeit) and, in this sense, it is subordinated to
aesthetics, rather than the other way around. Nietzsche, moreover, sees
aesthetics as providing a strong antidote to the poisonous effect of modern ethics based on a slave mentality. For this reason, he considers art to
be more of a counter to the ascetic ideal than science can ever be. According to *The Genealogy of Morals*, for instance, both science and the
ascetic ideal "are one in their overestimation of truth, in their belief that
truth is incommensurate and not susceptible to criticism."[24] Whereas
scientific truth is motivated by guilt and bad conscience, that is, by a
slave morality, in art "the lie becomes consecrated, the will to deception
has good conscience at its back" (290). The artists "lie" deliberately in
the interest of "life."[25] This is why Plato, whom Nietzsche sees as one
of the first promoters of the ascetic ideal, attacks the poets: "Plato vs.
Homer: here we have the whole authentic antagonism; on the one hand
the deliberate transcendentalist and detractor of life [read: detractor of

the Will to Power], on the other, life's instinctive panegyrist. An artist who enlists under the banner of the ascetic ideal corrupts his artistic conscience."[26]

According to Nietzsche, art is the most immediate manifestation of the Will to Power, just as modern ethics is its most indirect manifestation. His highly positive valuation of art and aesthetics does not contradict his low opinion of artists, because, as we have seen, for him the true artists are not the professional ones such as the poet, the painter, the sculptor, and the musician, but the philosopher, the warrior, and the statesman. Moreover, the professional artist is no more than "the condition of the [art]work, the soil from which it grows, perhaps only the manure on that soil" (235). For Nietzsche, art is ultimately a violent form of play, in the sense that the Will to Power can arbitrarily create and destroy physical forms or even entire worlds, just as a child at play can willfully build and demolish sand towers on the beach, or as a sculptor can mold and remold clay figures in his workshop. Art therefore is profoundly amoral, for it can not only create ethical codes but also discard them at will.

But could one imagine art outside a mentality of power and, at the same time, outside a morality of good and evil? One can certainly retain Schopenhauer and Nietzsche's intuition that art, aesthetics, and the imagination are extramoral categories in the sense that they can produce, rather than be produced by, various ethical codes. By the same token, however, they can choose to create nonviolent, peaceful worlds, which they may, in turn, elect not to de(con)struct, but to nurture and preserve.

Then literature as a form of irenic play can equally assume a culturally transcendental dimension, in the sense that it can go beyond its immediate historical context. It can become a playground suitable for the creation and imaginative enactment of human values that are often incommensurable with those embraced by the community out of which the literary work arises and to which it is normally addressed. In other words, literary discourse can offer fresh cultural alternatives precisely because it is a form of play, that is, an *as if* mode of activity and being, in which the world of actuality and that of the imaginary become interwoven and create an intermediary world separate from, yet contingent upon, the other two. By staging a real or imagined state of affairs and presenting it from various perspectives, literature can contribute to a better understanding of the existential choices open to the polis and can play a significant role in proposing modes of historical change. Like other ludic manifestations, therefore, literature is a liminal phenomenon in the most profound sense, and it is this liminal nature that both Nietzsche and Schopenhauer, as well as their twentieth-century heirs, do not sufficiently take into account when they define aesthetics solely in terms of a mentality of power. From an irenic standpoint, both literature and literary criticism cease to be instruments of a differential power struggle between various social, ethnic, racial, and sexual factions. Instead, they become effective means of healing the human community and making it whole. The last four chapters of this study will examine modern works of literature and literary criticism that explicitly or implicitly point to an irenic mentality, staging imaginative ways in which their readers can turn away from a (self-)destructive ethopathology of power.

In conclusion, both Schopenhauer's *World as Will and Representation* and Nietzsche's *Genealogy of Morals* remain fundamental texts for the twentieth century, because they bring to a crisis—understood not only in the negative sense of an impasse but also in the positive sense of a liminal opportunity—the conceptual problems and contradictions that a mentality of power has produced over several millennia of its troubled history. Indeed, they can be seen as a *ne plus ultra* of any thought founded on power. At the same time, they reveal the self-imposed blinkers of such a thought and implicitly (in Nietzsche's case) or explicitly (in Schopenhauer's case) plead for the necessity to go beyond it, even if this would mean "flying beyond the atmosphere" and venturing into the unknown.

LIMINALITY, LITERARY DISCOURSE, AND ALTERNATIVE WORLDS

In the past three decades, contemporary theory has attempted to re-think, among many other issues, the relationship between margin and center in Western culture. One has by now become familiar with Aron Gurwitsch's phenomenological notion of "marginal consciousness," with Michel Foucault's reflections on Georges Bataille's notion of transgres-sion, or with Jacques Derrida's theses on the margins of (rational) dis-course. It is widely accepted, especially in poststructuralist circles, that the center and the margin express a power relation and that they are mutually interdependent, locked in an unstable, easily reversible dia-lectic. The interplay between philosophical and literary discourse in Western culture is one of the prime examples of how margin can con-vert into center and vice versa.[1] Mikhail Bakhtin, in his essays on the dialogic imagination in Rabelais, Dostoevsky, and the Western novel in general, has traced the agonistic relation between literature and poli-tics, showing how novelistic discourse is among the subversive, carni-valesque, centrifugal forces that resist the centripetal, canonical pull in Western culture. Within the field of poetry, Harold Bloom has traced the agon between influential literary figures and schools in terms of an implicitly reversible, Nietzschean dialectic of weak and strong. Current studies on gender and race attempt either to redefine the position of various marginal groups in relation to a cultural center or to do away with this center altogether.[2] Finally, Yuri Lotman's cultural-literary semiotics and Itamar Even-Zohar's polysystem theory expand the Russian formalists' cultural functionalism and Bakhtin's dialogism by envisioning a dynamic series of oppositions between multiple centers and margins that form what Even-Zohar calls a "stratified heterogeneity" characterized by continuous intersystemic struggles, shifts, and read-justments.[3]

All of the theoretical strands mentioned above, as well as many oth-ers, start from the premise of the essential complicity between center(s) and margin(s), assuming the agonistic nature of this systemic or inter-systemic correlation. In the present essay, I shall attempt to show how literary discourse as a marginal cultural phenomenon can also detach itself from the center, transcending its immediate, agonistic context and pointing to values that are outside a mentality of power. In other words, I shall attempt to redefine literary discourse not as marginal, but as liminal—that is, as a threshold or passageway allowing access to alternative worlds that may subsequently become actualized through communal choice and sociocultural practice. The liminal character of literature derives from its ludic nature, for play is the liminal time-space par excellence, as thinkers point out again and again throughout the history of this concept. I shall begin by examining the anthropological notion of liminality as developed by Victor Turner and then I shall look at its various historical antecedents and applications in literary discourse, concentrating especially on the best known "defenses of poesie" from Gorgias to Sidney to Schiller to Shelley as well as on some of the contemporary versions of these defenses. Finally, I shall review some current notions of actual, possible, and fictional worlds and propose an alternative way of considering literary and artistic productions in general as liminal worlds.

1. Liminality as Anthropological Phenomenon

In *From Ritual to Theatre: The Human Seriousness of Play* (1982), one of the last books Victor Turner published before his untimely death, he continues to develop a cultural anthropological theory, the foundations of which he had laid in such important studies as *The Ritual Process: Structure and Anti-Structure* (1969) and *Dramas, Fields, and Metaphors: Symbolic Action in Human Society* (1974). In *From Ritual to Theatre*, Turner explores avenues of linking his theory, based on extended field studies of certain African tribal communities, with a study of the complex, large-scale industrial societies. In "Liminal to Liminoid in Play, Flow, and Ritual," the first and the most important chapter of his book, Turner suggests that the concept of liminality can be a good starting point for a comparative study of large-scale and small-scale societies. He borrows the term from Arnold van Gennep who, in his *Rites de passage* (1908), employs it in order to describe rituals associated with both seasonal changes and individual or communal life changes in small-scale societies.

As Turner points out, van Gennep distinguishes three stages in a rite of passage: separation, transition, and incorporation. In the first stage, the "initiand" or neophyte is isolated from the rest of the community through a rite that separates sacred from secular time and space; during the transition, which van Gennep calls "margin" or "limen" (meaning "threshold" in Latin), the initiand goes through an ambivalent social phase or limbo. During the final stage of incorporation or "reaggrega-tion," the initiand returns to a new and relatively stable position in the society at large. Of particular interest here is the second stage of a rite of passage, the transitional or liminal stage. During this stage, the initiands experience a blurring of all social distinctions or a "leveling" process; they are "stripped of names and clothing, smeared with the common earth, rendered indistinguishable from animals"; they become identi-fied with "such general oppositions as life and death, male and female, food and excrement, simultaneously, since they are at once dying from or dead to their former status and life, and being born and growing into new ones."[4] Turner calls this transitional or liminal stage an "anti-struc-ture" because it inverts or dissolves the normal (and normative) struc-tural order prevalent in the rest of the community.

By temporarily removing the initiands from established social struc-ture, passage rites produce ambiguous social status as well as a tempo-rary release from behavioral norms and cognitive rules. In this respect, the liminal stage may not only include subversive and playful events but also be regarded as the ludic time-space par excellence. Referring to Brian Sutton-Smith's paper entitled "Games of Order and Disorder" (1972), Turner in effect sees liminality as a game of disorder out of which new orders emerge.[5] He defines liminal situations as "seeds of cultural creativity" that generate new models, symbols, and paradigms. These new symbols and paradigms then "feed back into the 'central' economic and politico-legal domains and arenas, supplying them with goals, aspi-rations, incentives, structural models and *raisons d'être*."[6]

One may note that, for Turner, liminality is not only a form of tran-sition but also a potentiality. As he argues in previous studies, it opens the possibility of "standing aside not only from one's own social posi-tion but from all social positions and of formulating a potentially unlim-ited series of alternative social arrangements."[7] By social arrangement or structure Turner understands "jural-political-economic structures, usually institutionalized, which have as important features, hierarchy, official classification, differentiation, stasis." These structures operate in what he calls "the indicative mood" of sociocultural process and should be distinguished from liminal processes, which operate in the subjunctive mood, "the mood of may-be, might-be, as-if, fantasy, hypothesis."[8]

According to Turner, because small-scale societies display relatively stable, cyclical, and repetitive systems, the liminal stage of their rites of passage has a limited creative potential when compared to that of large-scale societies. Tribal liminality, "however exotic in appearance, can never be much more than a subversive flicker. It is put into the service of normativeness as soon as it appears."[9] Turner further argues that in large-scale societies the term "liminality" applies only metaphorically, and it is for this reason that he proposes the concept of "liminoid" to describe certain Western cultural phenomena. While not identical with ritual liminality, liminoid phenomena are, nevertheless, either like it or related to it. According to him, examples of liminoid phenomena include postmodernist theater, film, art, television, rock concerts, opera, miming, clowning, carnivals, festivals, processions, pilgrimages, and even revolutions.

The main differences between the liminal and the liminoid stem from the different social structures of tribal and large-scale communities: "[O]ptation pervades the liminoid phenomenon, obligation the liminal. One is play and choice, an entertainment, the other is a matter of deep seriousness, even dread, it is demanding, compulsory" (43). In tribal ritual even the normally rule-abiding members of the community are expected to be unruly. Tribal liminality concerns the whole community, which operates on Durkheim's principle of "mechanical solidarity," implying a "*homogeneity* of values and behavior, strong social constraint, and loyalty to tradition and kinship" (42). By contrast, the liminoid concerns only certain sections of the population in communities with "organic solidarity," implying ever shifting contractual relations and a heterogeneity of values and behavior. Consequently, in large-scale societies liminoid phenomena are increasingly detached or free from social constraint and increasingly creative. Whereas innovation is introduced very slowly in tribal cultures, in large-scale societies it may be sudden and wide-sweeping, as in the case of violent social revolutions.

Turner's distinction between liminal and liminoid assumes a historical or diachronic dimension as well. In many instances, he argues, liminoid phenomena are direct historical descendants of tribal liminality or secular equivalents of tribal ritual. As cases in point Turner cites secret societies, social clubs, university fraternities and sororities, carnivals, festivals, and charivari, as well as secular drama. He further speaks of a "watershed division" between large-scale societies that "have developed before and after the Industrial Revolution" (30). According to him, the key to understanding this division is to be found in the concepts of work, play, and leisure. Relying on the research of contemporary sociologists of leisure such as Joffre Dumazedier and Sebastian de Grazia, Turner argues that traditional Western societies (as well as tribal communities) operate in terms of a play-work continuum or what he calls a "play-and-work ludergy" (43). With the advent of capitalism and industrial societies, work and play become separated.

Modern industry has equally produced the binary opposition of work and leisure, and in defining leisure Turner adopts Isaiah Berlin's distinction between "freedom from" and "freedom to." On the one hand, leisure can be seen as the individual's freedom from both institutional constraints stipulated by technological-bureaucratic organization and the "forced, chronologically regulated, rhythms of factory and office," giving the worker a chance to "recuperate and enjoy natural, biological rhythms again" (37). On the other hand, leisure involves freedom to both create "new symbolic worlds of entertainment, sports, games, diversions of all kinds" and transcend social structural limitations by playing with ideas (in philosophy), with fantasies and words (in literature), and with social relationships (in friendship, sensitivity training, psychodrama). In this respect, leisure "is potentially capable of releasing creative powers, individual or communal, either to criticize or buttress the dominant social structural values" (37). For Turner, therefore, leisure is one of the most important liminoid developments in modern industrial societies.

Turner's theory of liminality has been and continues to be a very helpful conceptual tool not only in the human sciences but also in literary criticism.[10] It is for this very reason that one may wish to reconsider some of its assumptions and formulations, not in a polemical, but an exploratory spirit, undoubtedly characteristic of Turner himself.[11] For example, one may wish to reexamine his distinction between liminal and liminoid. Turner often wavers between these terms when he tries to define specific cultural phenomena in large-scale societies. At the end of his essay, for instance, he calls "liminal" the activities of churches, religious sects, and movements, as well as the initiation rites of clubs, fraternities, Masonic orders, and other secret societies, even though according to his earlier argument they ought to belong to the liminoid. By the same token, he now reserves the term "liminoid" only for the "leisure genres of art, sport, pastimes, games, etc., practised by and for particular groups, categories, segments and sectors of large-scale industrial societies of all types."[12]

Turner's use of the traditional categories of play and work, or play and seriousness, is also rather ambiguous. Although he correctly points out that the distinction between play and work is of relatively recent historical vintage, he later on employs this distinction in an inappropriate historical context. For example, after saying at the beginning of his argument that the liminal implies a play-work continuum, toward the end of his essay he proceeds nevertheless to distinguish between the liminal and the liminoid in terms of work and play: "The *liminoid* is more like a commodity—indeed, often *is* a commodity, which one selects and pays for—than the *liminal*, which elicits loyalty and is bound up with one's membership or desired membership in some highly corporate group. One *works* at the liminal, one *plays* with the liminoid" (55). What has happened to the "play-work ludergy" or the "serious-play" quality that Turner has earlier attributed to liminal phenomena in both tribal and preindustrial, large-scale cultures? In order to be consistent here, he ought to acknowledge that both the liminal and the liminoid are ludic categories and that the difference between them resides not in their degree of seriousness, but in their degree of freedom.

Turner experiences further difficulties when deploying his categorical distinctions in historical terms. At times it seems as though the liminoid had replaced the liminal in large-scale societies, especially after the Industrial Revolution; at other times it seems as though they still coexisted side by side. In one place, Turner argues that liminoid phenomena are largely products of a capitalist society originating in the early

Renaissance. In another place, he notes that they "perhaps begin to appear on the scene" much earlier, in the city-states and empires of the Graeco-Roman type as well as in the European feudal societies, "but also in the far less 'pluralistic' Japanese, Chinese, and Russian types of feudalism or quasi-feudalism" (55).

Such theoretical ambiguities seem to indicate that liminality might not be the best criterion to employ in working out the fundamental distinctions between large-scale and small-scale communities (that such fundamental distinctions exist, nobody would of course deny, although a consideration of what they are would take us too far afield here). Indeed, liminal phenomena are so widespread in both types of communities that one could even argue that liminality is a universal anthropological element. This universality is acknowledged, for example, in such Buddhist texts as *The Tibetan Book of the Dead*, where liminality appears under the name of *bardo*. According to the commentary of Chögyam Trungpa, Rinpoche, *bardo* signifies "gap"; the word is made up of *bar*, which means "in-between," and *do*, which means "island" or "mark." *Bardo* is thus "a sort of landmark which stands between two things. It is rather like an island in the midst of a lake. The concept of bardo is based on the period between sanity and insanity, or the period between confusion and the confusion just about to be transformed into wisdom; and of course it could be said of the experience which stands between death and birth. The past situation has just occurred and the future situation has not yet manifested itself so there is a gap between the two."[13] The bardo experience, concludes the Rinpoche, is "part of our basic psychological make-up" (1). Likewise, in his *Republic* Plato employs the Pythagorean doctrine of metempsychosis in the myth of Er, referring to a middle station between heaven and earth, where souls meet to choose their next lot. Christian dogma equally acknowledges the concept of liminality when it posits "limbo" (a word that shares its Latin roots with *limen*) as a place between heaven and hell, where certain souls are in an intermediate or transitional state.

One may wish, therefore, to give up the distinction between liminal and liminoid altogether and simply say that in some tribal communities liminality is put to uses different from those in some large-scale communities and that, moreover, these uses may vary from period to period and from community to community. What gives specificity to these functions is the degree of sociocultural flexibility and imaginative freedom that a particular community allows itself at a given time.

One can, however, adopt Turner's notion of liminality in a general sense, applicable to certain cultural phenomena in most if not all human communities: "an interval, however brief, of *margin* or *limen*, when the past is momentarily negated, suspended or abrogated, and the future has not yet begun, an instant of pure potentiality when everything, as it were, trembles in the balance."[14] One can also agree with Turner that liminality is more than a passive, negative condition or the intermediary-mediating phase between two positive conditions (one in the past, the other in the future). Liminality contains both positive and active qualities, especially when the *threshold* "is protracted and becomes a 'tunnel,' when the 'liminal' becomes the 'cunicular'" (41).

Finally, one can partially agree with Turner that meaning in culture "tends to be *generated* at the interfaces between established cultural subsystems, though meanings are then institutionalized and consolidated at centers of such systems. Liminality is a temporal interface whose properties partially invert those of the already consolidated order which constitutes any specific cultural 'cosmos'" (41). Here Turner offers an excellent description of the agonistic interplay between center and margin mentioned at the beginning of this chapter. But one should also point out that even though the margin can oftentimes redefine the center, the liminal as the cunicular may not necessarily always lead back to a center; on the contrary, it may, under certain conditions, lead away from it in a steady and irreversible fashion. It is clear, then, that one needs to distinguish between marginality and liminality, although not necessarily in Turner's terms.[15] In my view, marginality refers to an agonistic relation (between the center and the margins of a structure, system, subsystem, polysystem, or world), whereas liminality refers to a neutral relation (between two or more structures, systems, subsystems, polysystems, worlds, etc.), such as obtains, say, in a no-man's land between two or more state borders. Marginality cannot provide access to or initiate new worlds, whereas liminality can do both. In this sense, a margin can be liminal, but a limen cannot be marginal. In my view, therefore, liminality can both subsume and transcend a dialectic of margin and center.[16]

2. Literary Notions of Liminality: A Brief Historical Overview

One can readily see how Turner's anthropological theory of liminality can apply to literary discourse, although one needs again to reconsider Turner's distinction between liminal and liminoid. On Turner's view, literature generally belongs to the liminoid; in the case of drama, more-over, it can be both a direct descendant from and a functional equivalent of ritual. But Turner also sees literature as liminal, especially in traditional societies, where poetic works can be read as ultimately supporting the dominant social order. This, for instance, is his reading of satire:

> Many artists in many genres, also buttress, reinforce, justify, or other-wise seek to legitimate the prevailing social and cultural mores and political orders. Those that do so, do so in ways that tend more closely than the *critical* productions to parallel tribal myths and rituals—they are "liminal" or "pseudo-" or "post-" "liminal" rather than "liminoid." Satire is a conservative genre because it is *pseudo-liminal*. Satire exposes, attacks, or derides what it considers to be vices, follies, stupidities, or abuses, but its criterion of judgment is usually the normative structural frame of officially promulgated values. Hence satirical works, like those of Swift, Castlereagh, or Evelyn Waugh, often have a ritual of reversal form, indicating that disorder is no permanent substitute for order.[17]

It is by no means clear, however, that satire is always liminal or "pseudo-liminal" in Turner's sense. No literary theorists worth their salt will confine their reading of, say, *Gulliver's Travels* to a monological interpretation, be it conservative, liberal, or radical. In using Gulliver as an unreliable narrator, Swift never spells out the ethical standard underlying his satire; this standard remains implicit and, therefore, open to interpretation throughout the work. A literary text, moreover, is always already "liminoid" in Turner's sense, because it transcends its immediate personal and social context, addressing itself to many subsequent generations of readers from many different cultures. They will in turn bring their own horizons of expectation to this text, which will thus say different things to different people. It is conceivable, therefore, that for some present or future reader, *Gulliver's Travels* will appear as radically challenging the dominant axiological system of the West in the name of some unspecified set of values the reader believes in. (One can also point out, incidentally, that Turner's use of terms such as "pseudo-" or "post-liminal" in this context further confuses his distinction between liminal and liminoid. Are we to assume that genuinely liminoid phenomena are always critical or subversive of their cultural environment? This surely cannot be the case of such modern cultural activities as sports and games, which Turner, at least toward the end of his essay, classifies as "liminoid." Are we to assume, on the other hand, that liminal activities are always conservative? But, then, how can we explain sociocultural changes in traditional societies through a liminal process as Turner seems to do?)

Turner's casual remarks on satire indicate that his distinction between liminal and liminoid breaks down in a literary context as well. It would, therefore, be best to drop the term "liminoid" altogether from our theoretical vocabulary and treat literature as a liminal activity with varying degrees of cultural freedom within different communities during different historical periods. In the history of Western literary theory, the concept of liminality has appeared under at least three, often interrelated, guises. Literature has thus been seen as either supportive or subversive marginality, as mediating neutrality, and as self-transcending plasticity. In all three guises, liminality has often appeared as an instrument of a mentality of power that has posited it as the groundless ground of its own existence.

In the Western world, literary discourse becomes a self-consciously liminal phenomenon during the transition from an oral to a literate culture in ancient Greece, when the central archaic cultural complex known as μουσική breaks down into various disciplines that start competing for cultural authority in the polis. This agonistic process transpires in Plato's *Republic*, where Socrates lays the theoretical foundations for the emergence of philosophy (defined as the master science of Being) as a hegemonic discourse in Western culture. At the same time, Socrates marginalizes poetic discourse as *mimesis* or ludic (dis)simulation of true, philosophical discourse, separating it from all claims of authority-power on both ontoepistemological and ethical grounds.[18]

That poetry as authoritative discourse comes under attack in philosophical quarters even before Socrates delivers it the coup de grace is evident in Gorgias's paradox attempting to defend tragedy as a liminal ground between fiction and truth: "By its stories [μύθοις, myths in the sense of traditional stories, narrative matter] and emotions, tragedy generates a deception in which the deceiver is more just [δικαιότερος] than the non-deceiver, and the deceived is wiser [σοφώτερος] than the non-deceived."[19] This paradox gains even more clarity in the light of two others: the first says that "One must mar [διαφθείρειν] the opponent's seriousness [σπουδήν] with jest, and the opponent's jest [γέλωτα] with seriousness" (DK B 12); the second says that "Being [ἐναι] is unknowable if it fails to appear [ἀφανές], appearance is weak [ἀσθενὲς] if it fails to be [ἐναι]" (DK B 26).

In the last two paradoxes, Gorgias plays with the conceptual and ethical oppositions between play and seriousness, being and seeming, truth and illusion, which he also invokes in DK B 23. In the latter fragment, he obviously defends tragedy against the accusations of falsehood, deception, and irresponsible play that must have been current in his day and that subsequently crop up in the Platonic dialogues as well. Although tragedy employs traditional stories and emotions in order to create an appearance of truth (an illusion or, in ethical terms, a deception), it cannot properly be called a lie because it never claims to be true (i.e., partaking of being) in the first place. For this very reason, however, it is more true or honest than any discourse that claims the opposite. If you are wise, therefore, you can learn more about the apparent nature of truth, or the truthful nature of appearance (that is, about the phenomenal nature of being, or the ontic nature of phenomena) from tragic poetry than from any other discourse. Gorgias in effect employs tragedy to challenge the conceptual and ethical polarities between being and seeming, or truth and deception. At the same time, he locates dramatic poetry in the no-man's land between essence and appearance, or between truth and illusion, thus initiating an important theoretical topos in the history of literary criticism.

In Aristotle's *Poetics*, the liminal nature of poetry is indirectly invoked in the notion of *mimesis*, which for both Plato and Aristotle means not so much "imitation" as "simulation."[20] Poetry is a form of play that simulates other kinds of discourse for pleasurable purposes and, for this reason, cannot be held to the same standards of truth as philosophy and history. If Gorgias situates tragic poetry in the liminal space between being and appearance, Aristotle implicitly situates it in the liminal space between philosophy and history. This becomes clear when he observes, on the one hand, that "the artist may imitate [simulate] things as they ought to be";[21] and, on the other hand, that "poetry is more philosophical and a higher thing [φιλοσοφώτερον και σπουδαιότερον, more abstract and more serious] than history; for poetry tends to express [λέγει, select for expression] the universal, history the particular" (1451b5–7). Here, at first sight, Aristotle seems simply to draw a comparison between poetry and history on philosophical grounds. Insofar as tragic poetry simulates philosophical discourse, which is concerned both with the "universal" and with what could or ought to be (possibility), it is more abstract and more serious than history, which is concerned with the "particular" or with what has been (necessity). Aristotle obviously implies, however, that poetry simulates not only philosophy but also history and, consequently, is an in-between form of discourse that concerns both possibility and necessity; in other words, tragic poetry can in principle mediate between philosophy and history, correcting philosophy's predominant concern with abstraction or with what ought to be, and history's predominant concern with facticity or with what has been. In Aristotle, then, we can indirectly glimpse the traditional idea of literary discourse as mediator between other kinds of discourse.

Of course, through the notion of *mimesis* both Plato and Aristotle attempt to keep poetic discourse subordinated at all times to philosophical discourse, assigning it a marginal (rather than a liminal), supportive role. But subsequent theorists, taking a second look at the Platonic dialogues, also point out that insofar as any literary imitation, let alone simulation, can never be a simple copy, it will always escape or exceed its model(s)—whether they belong to a constituted or surmised reality, or to the art realm itself. Literary simulation may either reverse or undermine the model (as in mime, satire, parody, and the burlesque); but it may also tacitly or openly revise or redefine the model (as in utopian fiction and science fiction, or in what we understand by fantastic or imaginary literature in general). In other words, literature can be seen as either subversive or supportive-corrective marginality. Moreover, its supportive-corrective role can be correlated with its mediating role, and it is this correlation that can often be found in the traditional defenses of poetry from Sidney to Schiller to Shelley.

In his *Defense of Poesie* (1583), Sir Philip Sidney invokes *Poetics* 1451b in support of the view of poetry as a liminal space between philosophy and history. He argues that while the philosopher "giveth the precept" and the historian "the example," the poet does both.[22] The poet can, moreover, be seen as a "moderator" or mediator between the moral philosopher and the historian: "Now whom shall we find . . . to be moderator? Truly, as me seemeth, the poet; and if not a moderator, even the man that ought to carry the title from them both, and much more from all other serving sciences" (419). Later in the same passage, Sidney also suggests that by assuming a mediating role, the poet can disseminate the community's ideals of education better than the moral philosopher and the historian, which for Sidney means better than anybody else:

> For as for the divine [i.e., the theologian], with all reverence it is ever to be expected, not only for having his scope as far beyond any of these [the philosopher and the historian] as eternity exceedeth a moment but even for passing each of these in themselves. And for the lawyer, though *Jus* be the daughter of Justice, and Justice the chief of virtues, yet because he . . . doth not endeavor to make men good, but that their evil hurt not others . . . so he is not in the deepest truth to stand in rank with these who all endeavor to take naughtiness away and plant goodness even in the secretest cabinet of our souls. And these four [philosopher, historian, theologian, and law-giver] are all that any way deal in the consideration of men's manners, which being the supreme knowledge, they that best breed it deserve the best commendation. (419–20)

Like Gorgias, Sidney goes against the vulgar prejudice that dismisses the poet as liar. He contends that the effectiveness of poetic art, unlike that of philosophical or scientific writing, does not depend on a rhetoric of truth and falsehood: "Of all writers under the sun the poet is the least liar and, though he would, as a poet can scarcely be a liar." Unlike the astronomer, the geometrician, the physician, and all the other scientists, the poet can never be a liar because he does not claim to know anything: "[H]e nothing affirms and therefore never lieth" (439). The poet never "maketh any circles about your imagination, to conjure you to believe for true what he writes," nor does he cite undisputed authorities to support his tales. On the contrary, he openly admits the fictional nature of his discourse and "even for his entry calleth the sweet Muses to inspire into him a good invention" (440).

By freeing his discourse from the inflexible demands of truth, however, the poet is paradoxically able to open up and redefine the conventional borders between truth and falsehood. Thus, Sidney in effect sees poetic fictions as breeding grounds for intellectual and moral truths: "And therefore as in history, looking for truth, they may go away full fraught with falsehood, so in poesy, looking but for fiction, they shall use the narration but as an imaginative ground-plot of a profitable invention" (439–40). Sidney also hints at the crucial role that the imagination plays in the generation of sociocultural truths, which, ontologically speaking, are little more than "profitable inventions"—and here he could have invoked no less an authority than Socrates in Plato's *Republic* to support his view.

Sidney's idea of poetry as a liminal ground between truth and falsehood—an idea that had some prominence in Renaissance literary theory in general and in the poetics of Casteveltro, Mazzoni, and Trissino in particular, but was given less importance in neoclassical mimetic doctrines of art—is taken up by the romantics, especially by Schiller and Shelley, who turn against the neoclassical notion of poetic imitation. Schiller attempts to revise this notion in his *Letters on the Aesthetic Education of Man*, where he links poetic discourse to play as the highest manifestation of man's creative faculty.[23] In keeping with the triadic thinking typical of such German idealist thinkers as Kant and Fichte, Schiller sees art-play as a third realm, that of aesthetic phenomena, which mediates between the realm of necessity (matter) and the realm of freedom (spirit). Through the play drive, which in art manifests itself as aesthetic semblance or illusion (*Schein*), art detaches humankind from its sensuous nature and directs it toward its spiritual and moral nature:

> The transition from a passive state of feeling to an active state of thinking and willing cannot, then, take place except *via* a middle state of aesthetic freedom. And although this state can of itself decide nothing as regards either our insights or our convictions, thus leaving both our intellectual and our moral worth as yet entirely problematic, it is nevertheless the necessary pre-condition of our attaining to any insight or conviction at all. In a word, there is no other way of making sensuous man rational except by first making him aesthetic.[24]

Here Schiller, like Sidney, attempts to raise art to the level of a mediator, but always under the supervision of Reason. The play drive itself is a useful fiction or an *as if* concept in Hans Vaihinger's sense, invented by Reason in order to deal with the realm of necessity. In the next paragraph of the same letter, Schiller insists that aesthetic illusion has no cognitive value outside the dialectic of necessity and possibility, nature and morality, intellect and will: "It has been expressly proved [by Kant] that beauty can produce no result, neither for the understanding nor for the will; that it does not meddle in the business of either thinking or deciding; that it merely imparts the power to do both, but has no say whatsoever in the actual use of that power. In the actual use of it all other aid whatsoever is dispensed with; and the pure logical form, namely the concept, must speak directly to the understanding, the pure moral form, namely the law, directly to the will" (letter 23, 161). In one sense, then, by positing art as a third realm mediating between truth and lie, Schiller reinforces Sidney's notion of poetry as a liminal space, even though he does not challenge the neo-Aristotelian subordination of poetry to Reason. In this respect, he also preserves the traditional link between the supportive-corrective and the mediating roles of literature as a ludic-liminal form of discourse.

In "A Defence of Poetry," Shelley echoes Schiller's theory of the aesthetic state when he declares poets to be the "unacknowledged legislators of mankind." Like Schiller, Shelley sees the poetic faculty both as a precondition of and a corrective to the practical pursuits of humanity. For Shelley, however, the Imagination (not Reason) has its immediate source in that unity of Being which becomes fragmented in the modern age. Unlike Schiller, therefore, Shelley does not see poetry as a conscious illusion devised by Reason, but as the highest "expression of the imagination," that is, as a direct manifestation of the unity of Being. Reason is "the principle of analysis, and its action regards the relation of things, simply as relations; considering thoughts not in their integral unity, but as the algebraic representations which conduct to certain general results."[25] By contrast, imagination is "the principle of synthesis, and has for its objects those forms which are common to universal nature and existence itself" (23). Reason reveals the differences, whereas imagination reveals the similarities among things. As an instrument of the imagination, poetry both precedes and guides reason.

In the wake of Sidney, Shelley argues that poetry operates at a higher level than "the ethical science" (as well as the political one), which only "arranges the elements poetry has created, and propounds schemes and proposes examples of civic and domestic life" (33). Poetry, on the other hand, "awakens and enlarges the mind itself by rendering it the receptacle of a thousand unapprehended combinations of thought." It furnishes the imagination with "thoughts of ever new delight, which have the power of attracting and assimilating to their own nature all other thoughts, and which form new intervals and interstices whose void forever craves fresh food" (33).

Shelley's idea of intervals and interstices whose void produces a constant need for renewal and change goes a long way toward defining liminality in terms of self-transcending plasticity, a notion taken up and developed by contemporary thinkers such as Jean-Paul Sartre and Wolfgang Iser. In this regard, Shelley implies that the poets necessarily function as *unacknowledged* legislators and prophets because they can and should operate only at a liminal level: by constantly pointing to such ineffable, imaginative categories as "the eternal, the infinite, and the one," they implicitly set ever-new goals for the spiritual development of humankind. They are social harbingers, not because they predict the form, but because they predict the spirit of events. A poet "not only beholds intensely the present as it is, and discovers those laws according to which present things ought to be ordered, but he beholds the future in the present," and his ideas are both "the germs of the flower and the fruit of latest time" (27). Through its liminal nature, poetry both precedes and anticipates the paradigms of thought that other forms of discourse take up and concretize in a particular historical manner. Poetry is "at once the center and circumference of knowledge; it is that which comprehends all science, and that to which all science must be referred. It is at the same time the root and the blossom of all other systems of thought" (53).

Shelley, then, stands on its head the Socratic doctrine of the good and the beautiful: it is poetry, not philosophy, that is now the carrier of this doctrine and is entrusted with the reformation of humankind. By the same token, however, Shelley remains within Plato's idealist system, whose idea of Being equally pervades his poetic legislative project. It matters little, from an anthropological standpoint, whether reason or the imagination, philosophy or poetry, is entrusted with the carrying out of the Socratic program. No less than Schiller, therefore, Shelley maintains a correlation between the supportive-corrective and the mediating roles of literary liminality.

Whereas in the Neoplatonic tradition poetry as mediator among various kinds of discourse remains under the tutelage of Platonic Being and is nearly always made to serve its interests, in a postmodern age it becomes emancipated from this tutelage but falls under the dominion of Becoming, especially in Nietzsche and the artist-metaphysicians. I have demonstrated in *Dionysus Reborn* how an aesthetic view of the world as ceaseless Becoming, where all that is is a play of simulacra or illusion, gives poetry the task of undermining the world of Being as eternal truth. In the present context, what is relevant is that the internal conflicts within the realm of philosophy have revealed the various functions poetic discourse has been assigned over the centuries and that these functions are historically and culturally determined. What has gradually emerged, in the modern age, is the awareness of a functionalist dialectic of reality and fiction, where certain fictions or imaginative constructs perform as truths according to various cultural needs and interests. In line with this functionalist dialectic, contemporary theorists have further developed the notion of literary liminality by correlating its various elements, such as the ideas of the imagination, self-conscious illusion or fiction, and play.

The idea of imagination in particular has been revolutionized by the contemporary phenomenological and psychoanalytic schools, culminating in Jean-Paul Sartre's notion of the imagination as the groundless ground of human consciousness.[26] In *The Psychology of Imagination* (1972), Sartre notes: "The imaginary appears 'on the foundation of the world,' but reciprocally all apprehension of the real as world implies a hidden surpassing towards the imaginary. All imaginative consciousness uses the world as the negated foundation of the imaginary and reciprocally all consciousness of the world calls and motivates an imaginative consciousness as grasped from the particular *meaning* of the situation."[27] According to Sartre, imagination is a form of nothingness or void that is "*lived*, without even being posited for itself," and is thus able to create all meaning. Because the apprehension of the void or nothingness that is the imagination cannot occur by an immediate unveiling, it develops through the free succession of various acts of consciousness. Consequently the imagination, "far from appearing as an accidental characteristic of consciousness, turns out to be an essential and transcendental condition of consciousness" (218). In this respect, Sartre's view of imagination as a liminal, creative "nothingness" is a phenomenological version of Shelley's notion of poetic imagination as a series of "new intervals and interstices whose void forever craves fresh food" and thus also contributes to the idea of literary liminality as self-transcending plasticity. By constantly confronting past and present human achievements with the all-devouring void of the imagination, literature ceaselessly produces new paradigms of thought and action in a tireless effort to satisfy this void.

In addition to pointing out the liminal nature of the imaginary and the fictive, contemporary literary theorists have further developed the traditional concept of literary liminality as marginality (either supportive-corrective or subversive), mediating neutrality, and self-transcending plasticity. Most notably, Giuseppe Mazzotta, in *Dante, Poet of the Desert* (1979) and *The World at Play in Boccaccio's Decameron* (1986), creatively employs Turner's theory of liminality in discussing the medieval and early Renaissance literary tradition. For example, in his book on the *Divine Comedy*, Mazzotta sees Dante's exile as a liminal condition that the poet shares with literature in general. According to Mazzotta, in the Christian tradition the liminal figures par excellence are Christ and, closer to Dante, St. Francis of Assisi, who is presented in canto 11 of *Paradiso*. By renouncing his wealth and marrying Lady Poverty, St. Francis "moves to the fringes of society, to a symbolic area where the forms of the world lose whatever fixed and stable sense convention has imposed on them."[28] St. Francis thus places himself in a liminal space, between social structure and the divine dispensation. Through the foundation of the mendicant order he institutionalizes "the area of mediation between the world of contingency and history, and the absolute model of Paradise and a Christ-like existence" (111). St. Francis's mendicant community becomes a "scandalous utopia which is disengaged from history and yet has a radical historicity both because it is predicated as the *telos* of history and because it provides the perspective which makes possible a fresh and renewed apprehension of the structures of the world" (112).

According to Mazzotta, Dante's exile, not unlike that of St. Francis, is "far from being a mystical escape into some sort of visionary privacy." On the contrary, it is "the stance affording the detached vantage point from which he can speak to the world and impose his sense of order on it" (112). For Dante, exile is equally "the very condition of the [literary] text, its most profound metaphor" (145). He deliberately oscillates between "the vision of order in the empirical, concrete city of Florence and the 'attender certo' of the glory of Jerusalem." His liminal poetic world "places us in history and against history, in a garden which is a desert where nomads are always on the way" (146).

In his book on Boccaccio, Mazzotta continues to develop his theory of literature as an exilic, liminal space. According to him, in Boccaccio's *The Decameron* literature figures as a "middle-ground between two absences, between utopia and social structures, a provisional retreat from the city in an atemporal space."[29] From this marginal state, literature can reflect "both on itself and on the chaos of the world," and then return to the world "with a vitally renewed apprehension of its structures" (55). Mazzotta implies that in Boccaccio, no less than in Dante, the liminal poetic world can in principle mediate between the divine and the historical worlds: by constantly pointing to the divine ethical standards, literature can perpetually revise and modify the historical ones; in this sense, it also reveals human nature as self-transcending plasticity.

Unlike Dante, however, Boccaccio does not write on the margins of the City of God, and therefore for him (secular) literature falls short of providing the hope that it provides for Dante. According to Mazzotta, Boccaccio expresses this dilemma through "a state of tension between two types of literary mediation, the erotic mediation and the prophetic mediation" (72). In this sense, Boccaccio is already a modern poet: he can regard the mediating nature of literature only in parodic, ironic terms, as a negative potentiality. The "inevitable marginality of the literary act" can accomplish little more than to "efface the fictions—literary and spiritual—of society" (72). In the conclusion of *The Decameron*, Mazzotta argues, Boccaccio "abdicates responsibility for the effect of the book on the audience, tries to disclaim authorship for the tales and finally releases them in a moral vacuum as neutral and autonomous objects to be interpreted by the reader. The marginality is total, which is to say another void; the reader is abstracted from history waiting to reemerge into history; the writer even denies any centrality for himself" (72–73). The radical "uselessness" of literature relegates it to a "perennial marginality." Mazzotta returns, however, to the earlier insight of his Dante book, adding that the profound (ethical) value of literature resides precisely in its uselessness, "with its power to challenge, even as it is fascinated with, the utilitarian, 'real' values that have currency in the social world" (74).

Mazzotta probes into the liminal nature of literature as both a form of exile and a mediator between theology and history. Virgil Nemoianu, concentrating especially on the romantic and the modernist periods, complements Mazzotta's project by examining the nature of the relationship between the central and the marginal, or what he calls "primary" and "secondary" in culture. In *A Theory of the Secondary* (1989), Nemoianu concedes that literary discourse has a secondary cultural importance in relation to philosophy, history, jurisprudence, economics, politics, and so forth, but then he redefines the "secondary" in terms of a functional relation to the "principal." Whereas the positional roles of principal and secondary remain the same, the content of the two terms ceaselessly shifts around in Nemoianu's dynamic view of culture: what appears as principal in a certain age may assume a secondary position in another. Finally, the principal always collapses back into the secondary, which for Nemoianu is an inevitable but positive form of defeat: "Far from relying on erective and harmonizing energies, the secondary finds artistic expression through disorder, relaxation and idleness. Negligence, tolerance, and procrastination are its allies, lack of energy and purpose provide its strength. Literature as the secondary in society and history is a force for defeat, and thus for renewal. Since every progress can be true to its name only at its very inception, the defeat of further advances can only be seen as a beneficent strategy, the condition for a new inceptive progress"[30] For Nemoianu, therefore, literary discourse as marginality has ultimately a supportive, if paradoxical, role in continuously redefining the nature and the meaning of the center (which for him represents not so much an ontological plenitude as an ontological void).

With Wolfgang Iser's *The Fictive and the Imaginary: Charting Literary Anthropology* (1993) the history of the concept of literature as ludic liminality reaches its full expression. Although Iser does not use the term "liminality" as such, he in effect regards literature as a form of liminal play that not only mediates between imagination and actuality but also becomes a primary manifestation of human nature as perpetually self-transcending plasticity.

Iser's view of the ludic comes close to that of Schiller (without the latter's emphasis on rationality), while his view of the imagination expands and modifies those of Shelley and Sartre. Iser posits literary play as a triadic interaction between the imaginary, the fictive, and the real. Literary fictionality is a halfway house located between the real and the imaginary, where the fictive brings together and mediates between what is and what is not yet. As Iser puts it, the "act of fictionalizing" implies "a crossing of boundaries." On the one hand, this act crosses the boundaries of a given social or physical reality and strips it of its rigid determinacy by selecting, recombining, and bracketing some of its constituent elements; on the other hand, it crosses into the world of the imaginary (characterized by endless plasticity), giving it a certain direction or determinacy. So literary discourse "crosses the boundaries both of what it organizes (external reality) and of what it converts into a gestalt (the diffusiveness of the imaginary). It leads the real to the imaginary and the imaginary to the real, and it thus conditions the extent to which a given world is to be transcoded, a nongiven world is to be conceived, and the reshuffled worlds are to be made accessible to the reader's experience."[31] Hence, the fictive in literature becomes a "transitional object," a ludic, borderline phenomenon, "always hovering between the real and the imaginary, linking the two together."[32] In one sense, it can be said to exist because "it houses all the processes of interchange." In another sense, however, the fictive "does not exist as a discrete entity, for it consists of nothing but these transformational processes" (20). Here, then, Iser redefines in phenomenological terms the Kantian and Schillerian notions of the aesthetic as a mediator between imagination and reason.

In Iser's thinking, as well as in my own, one of the most important features of literary play is staging, through which the literary work brackets an extratextual reality, putting it on display, as it were, and thus allowing the audience to distance itself from and conceive possible alternatives to it. Through staging, which is a highly self-conscious act, literature in general becomes an anthropological phenomenon that features "the extraordinary plasticity of human beings" (297). Citing

Cornelius Castoriadis's work on the imagination, Iser observes that fictionality is "the ideal reflection of the creative act." Because the creative act constantly reveals itself as fiction, it perpetually denies itself authenticity. This self-denial, however, is far from being unproductive; on the contrary, it enables the self "to be simultaneously inside and outside itself, making it possible for the self to create itself" (78).

According to Iser,, because humans seem to possess an indeterminate nature, they "can expand into an almost unlimited range of culture-bound patternings. The impossibility of being present to ourselves becomes our possibility to play ourselves out to a fullness that knows no bounds, because no matter how vast the range, none of the possibilities will 'make us tick'" (296). Through the act of staging, therefore, "literature becomes a panorama of what is possible, because it is not hedged in either by the limitations or by the considerations that determine the institutionalized organizations within which human life otherwise takes its course" (296). Furthermore, because literature constantly monitors the ever changing manifestations of human self-fashioning without ever completely coinciding with any of these manifestations, it "makes the interminable staging of ourselves appear as the postponement of the end" (296). Here Iser, like early Heidegger and other existentialist phenomenologists, places human play within the borders of birth and death, with the self constantly attempting to outstrip itself in order to defer the inevitable end. In this respect he equally inscribes himself in the German anthropological tradition of Arnold Gehlen and Helmuth Plessner who stress the creative or constructive side of power, rather than its dark, (self-)destructive side. Hence, Iser can also be seen as the latest and one of the most brilliant representatives of a long line of theorists who consider literary liminality in both its mediating and supportive-corrective roles vis-à-vis a mentality of power.

A view of literary liminality almost diametrically opposed to that of Iser (as well as to those of Mazzotta and Nemoianu) appears in Gustavo Pérez-Firmat's *Literature and Liminality* (1986). In this study, Pérez-Firmat concentrates on the agonistic relation of the periphery to the center within a certain Hispanic literary tradition, seeing this relation not as functional, but as highly dysfunctional. In the wake of Bakhtin, de Man, and Bloom, Pérez-Firmat understands liminality as subversive marginality, a concept that he pushes to its ultimate consequences. Invoking Turner's notion of antistructure, Pérez-Firmat borrows the medical metaphor of cancer from Luis Martín-Santos's influential novel, *Tiempo de silencio* (1962), in order to explain the subversive relationship between the liminal as the marginal and the central order: "The liminal structure behaves like a phase insofar as its peripheral components do not abide in the margins. They occupy the periphery only transitorily, while maintaining the center under constant siege. The impending return does not, however, as in van Gennep's conception, bring about an integrative reunification—any more than a cancer's metastasis brings about a reconciliation of the healthy and the diseased cells. On the contrary, the periphery's convergence poses a deadly threat to the central order. In this respect all my conversions are metastatic, since they aggressively repudiate stasis or immobility."[33] For Pérez-Firmat, liminality is a centrifugal force that ultimately invades and destroys the center, annihilating itself in the process. It thus becomes a symptom of a diseased Will to Power that turns against itself, much like Nietzsche's active forces that become reactive and, hence, self-destructive in the *Genealogy of Morals*.

If Pérez-Firmat's deconstructive view of literary liminality (or, rather, marginality) may seem extreme, it nevertheless obeys the logic of a mentality of power that, as we saw in our discussion of Nietzsche in chapter 1, would annihilate itself rather than change its nature. In *Literature, Mimesis, and Play* (1982), I attempt to present a more balanced view of literary liminality from the standpoint of power, a view not incompatible with those of Iser, Mazzotta, and Nemoianu. There I see literary discourse as a mediating, neutral space where new discursive games of power are being ceaselessly (re)created and old ones, constantly tempered. Literature as fiction becomes the hidden condition of the possibility of all true discourse, guaranteeing the optimal functioning of the discursive mechanism of power throughout the modern history of Western culture. The question now is whether literature as ludic liminality can also give us access to actual and imaginary worlds that are incommensurable with ours. Or, to restate the question in more general terms: Does the concept of ludic liminality belong exclusively to a mentality of power? In order to provide a satisfactory answer to this question, one needs first to examine the current notions of alternative worlds and their underlying theoretical assumptions.

3. *Literature, Liminality, and Alternative Worlds*

The notion of a plurality of worlds has a long history in Western thought from Aristarchus of Samos to Giordano Bruno to Leibnitz. Most recently, this notion has been revived and debated in Anglo-American analytic philosophy by modal logicians such as Alvin Plantinga, Paul Davies, Raymond Bradley, Norman Swartz, and Saul Kripke.[34] In the wake of Leibnitz, they address the issue in terms of a logical and ontological distinction between "actual" and "possible" worlds. Their argument is that the actual world is only one possible world among an infinity of possible nonactual worlds or "pnaws." Pnaws can in turn be divided into those which can become actual because they obey the physical laws of the actual world, and those which can never become actual because they contain purely imaginary elements that disobey such laws. Consequently, although on the face of it analytic thinking appears to postulate a plurality of worlds, in effect it only postulates a plurality of *possible* worlds within one actual (physical) universe. According to this thinking, imaginary or fictional worlds of the literary kind generally belong to the pnaw subdivision that cannot be actualized. The logical division between imaginary and actual worlds is also indirectly supported by speech-act theorists who draw a rigid distinction between actual (or "sincere") and fictional (or "feigned") speech acts. On this view, literary speech acts are a violation of the "sincerity rule" and thereby turn actual speech-acts into mere pretense.[35]

The logical divisions of analytic philosophy have, however, been challenged on functionalist grounds by an array of contemporary constructivist and nonessentialist thinkers. According to these thinkers, the real world is no less "mind-dependent" than the fictional world, and the so-called "physical laws" are no less context-bound and conventional than human laws. Constructivist thought usually posits a plurality of worlds with multiple frames of reference, the boundaries of which are flexible, if not indeterminate. For example, Nelson Goodman states: "Many different world-versions are of independent interest and importance, without any requirement or presumption of reducibility to a single base."[36] According to Goodman, the pluralist needs to go beyond a naive concept of science embraced by "the monopolistic materialist or physicalist who maintains that one system, physics, is preeminent and all-inclusive, such that every other version must eventually be reduced to it or rejected as false or meaningless." The pluralist's willingness to consider world versions other than physics "implies no relaxation of rigor but a recognition that standards different from yet no less exacting than those applied in [traditional] science are appropriate for appraising what is conveyed in perceptual or pictorial or literary versions" (4).

In the wake of Goodman, Floyd Merrell argues that the actual world is "by and large socially formed and interculturally variable" and that all fictions can become "real worlds."[37] The boundaries between real worlds and fictional ones remain necessarily vague: "We can ordinarily distinguish relatively well and at tacit levels between a fiction and what we believe to be the 'real world'. And at the same time we seem to be tacitly aware that there is a boundary between them, but that the boundary is not precise and absolute" (39). Apparently unaware of Turner's theory of liminality, Merrell nevertheless identifies a "fuzziness" between these boundaries, or an "overlapping zone," where "the excluded middle is inoperative, where nothing is exactly identical with itself, and where contradictions are synthesized." It is precisely this fuzzy, overlapping zone or, in my frame of reference, the liminal space, that "enables us to continue being creative" (39).

Whereas Goodman and Merrell develop a nonessentialist, constructivist approach to reality in general, Thomas G. Pavel applies this approach to literary fictions in particular, challenging what he calls the "segregationist view" of speech-act theory: "By taking for granted the existence and stability of linguistic conventions, speech-act theory neglects the dynamism of their establishment and their inherent fluidity."[38] Pavel concludes that the "demarcation between fiction and nonfiction is a variable element and that as an institution fiction cannot be attributed a set of constant properties, an essence" (136). Hence one should operate on the nonsegregationist assumption that social behavior contains two sides: "an adventurous, creative side and a tendency to ossify successful novelties into the conventions of normality" (26). Normal and marginal behavior, moreover, belong to a continuum. Myths and literary fictions "manifest the innovative side of referential processes and are perceived as marginal only in contrast to some culturally determined ossification into normality" (27).

Like Merrell and other thinkers outside the mainstream of the analytic philosophical tradition, Pavel employs Alexis Meinong's theory of "nonexistent" objects to account for the ambiguous ontological status of fictions.[39] Meinong, starting from Brentano's phenomenological claim that all mental states are directed toward something and thus acquire distinguishing features, suggests that what is not is as important as what is. Knowledge pertains not only to "existents," that is, to the empirical objects of science and metaphysics, but also to "nonexistents" (the arts, the imagination, and all inner experiences). In fact, theories about the real world can come about only through the mediation of imaginary worlds (Einstein's theory of relativity is a familiar case in point). Invoking Meinong's theory, Pavel draws a functionalist distinction between fictional landscapes and ontological ones: "At the margins of ontological landscapes, one finds leisure worlds, or worlds for pleasure, which often derive from older discarded [ontological] models. Each culture has its ontological ruins, its historical parks, where the members of the community relax and contemplate their ontological relics. Greek and Roman gods performed this function till late in the history of European culture. Or marginal models may be used as training grounds for various tasks" (141). Paraphrasing Nelson Goodman's phrase, "When Is Art," Pavel suggests that fiction is when "world versions find secondary users" and ultimately defines it "as a peripheral region used for ludic and instructional purposes" (143).

Like Pavel, Doreen Maitre goes against the mainstream of the analytic philosophical tradition when she describes the interaction between actual worlds and fictional worlds as both dynamic and reciprocal. She argues that literature "makes us aware of both the continuities and the discontinuities between the actual and the possible. We come to see that what we take to be actual does not *have* to be so, that what seem like inevitabilities are not so inevitable, that what *is* could be given alternative explanations and could be changed into something different."[40] Finally, by staging nonactual states of affairs, the literary imagination "enables us to consider what alternative states of affairs *could* be the case" (117). One can go farther and say, with Shelley, Sartre, and Iser, that what is not *actively* creates what is, i.e., that literary play ceaselessly mobilizes our imagination to shape and modify our reality.

If a constructivist approach is to be consistent, it must ultimately give up the logical and ontological distinction between actual and possible worlds, or that between fictional and real ones, even though one may wish to preserve these distinctions in a nonessentialist, functional form. For instance, one may divide alternative worlds into actual and imaginary ones, but without placing strict ontological barriers between them. In principle, all worlds become possible or can be actualized as soon as they arise in the imagination, or, to put it differently, actual worlds will always start out as imaginary ones. Why some imaginary worlds eventually become actualized and some do not is hardly an ontological issue; rather, it is a question of communal choice and sociocultural practice. From a strictly ontological viewpoint, on the other hand, one could treat imaginary and actual worlds as being governed by alternative, equally valid ontological principles rather than by a relation of ontological subordination. Merrell, for instance, acknowledges the conventional nature of our real and imaginary worlds: "Given the assumed possibility of fictions becoming 'real worlds,' it must be admitted that any and all 'real worlds' could have been something that at least in part they are not. Hence to be critical of a given aspect of a particular 'real world' as it is ordinarily conceived and perceived is to be aware that the perspective from which the criticism was derived could equally have been in part something other than what it is. To embrace this relativism presents a quandary from which there is no ultimate escape."[41]

One should, however, note that Merrell's quandary has no exit only from the perspective of a mentality of power, which can conceive of itself only in terms of being and nonbeing, negation and affirmation, inclusion or exclusion. That Merrell shares this mentality is evident in his first postulate: "The Initial Cut in the Flux of Experience Results in an Elemental Negation Whereby That which *Is* Is Contrasted with That which It *Is Not*" (1). After acknowledging the logical necessity of relativism for all constructivist forms of thought, Merrell nevertheless adopts the Nietzschean position with which we are by now familiar from the last essay of the *Genealogy of Morals*: the play of power must be reaffirmed at all cost. In the present instance, Merrell uneasily combines the Nietzschean idea of contest with the Darwinian idea of the struggle for survival and the logical-positivist idea of scientific progress: "I submit, nevertheless, that one must provisionally take a stand, that one must present a conjecture and then argue for its validity. Methodological and theoretical pluralism entails competition between ideas, the survival value of these ideas being determined by their ability most effectively to account for the phenomena upon which they focus" (x).

In this passage, Merrell remains ambivalent precisely because he does not wish to give up a power-oriented frame of reference in advancing his version of relativism and pluralism. But one can conceive of a different kind of relativism and/or pluralism in which there are myriads of worlds that incessantly appear, disappear, clash, intersect, intertwine, coexist, or steer clear of each other; some of these worlds can be power-oriented and some of them can be built on principles other than power. As Nelson Goodman points out, worlds are constituted through composition, selection, combination, weighting, ordering, deletion, supplementation, deformation, and so on.[42]. Of particular interest for the present argument is Goodman's notion of weighting or accent: "Some differences among worlds are not so much in entities comprised as in emphasis or accent, and these differences are no less consequential. Just as to stress all syllables is to stress none, so to take all classes as relevant kinds is to take none as such. In one world there may be many kinds serving different purposes; but conflicting purposes may make for irreconcilable accents and contrasting worlds, as may conflicting conceptions of what kinds serve a given purpose" (11).

One may add that it is weighting or accent that creates a particular frame of reference through which all the elements of an emerging or extant world are organized and evaluated and through which one world is recognizably different from another. In this sense, power may be only one weighting principle that creates certain types of worlds among an infinity of others. One may also introduce the notion of subworlds, whose weighting principles derive from but are not identical with the overall weighting principle of an actual or an imaginary world. For example, subworlds can be constituted along historical, geographical, spiritual, psychological, religious, ethnic, political, economic, biological, sexual, physical, cosmological, and aesthetic lines, according to the specific nature of their local weighting principle.

One may also point out that not all of the relationships among alternative worlds (whether actual or imaginary) need be seen as conflictive or competitive, as Goodman and Merrell seem to imply. One may propose four basic types of relationships among alternative worlds and/or their subworlds: compatible, incompatible, commensurable, and incommensurable. Compatible worlds and subworlds have similar weighting principles or kindred, easily interadjustable, frames of reference. Examples may include the communities that belong to the same small-scale or large-scale cultures or subcultures (the tribal communities in the Amazon basin, Polynesia, Africa, and the Arctic, the traditional and modern national states around the globe, and so on); the same socioeconomic system (e.g., slave labor-based, feudal, capitalist, socialist, communist, if one were to employ a Marxist model, although many other compatible socioeconomic models are possible); the same political system (the present and former Communist states of Eastern Europe, Asia, Africa, and Latin America, the current Western democracies, and so on); or the same religious system (Christian, Islamic, Judaic, Hindu, and so forth). One can also regard as compatible the worlds and subworlds constituted on Ptolemaic, or Copernican, or Euclidean, or non-Euclidean, or Newtonian, or Einsteinian weighting principles.

In turn, alternative worlds and their subworlds may appear as incompatible when their weighting principles or reference frames clash or are not easily interadjustable. Examples may include most of the worlds mentioned previously: small-scale cultures in relation to large-scale ones; agrarian communities in relation to industrial ones; tribal and ethnic communities in relation to modern nations or states; Western democracies in relation to East European and other totalitarian states; Ptolemaic worlds in relation to Copernican ones; Darwinian worlds in relation to Creationist ones, and so forth. The traditional division between primitive and civilized cultures equally expresses a relationship of incompatibility, as does my distinction between archaic and median communities in chapter 1. When incompatible worlds or subworlds come into contact, one of them will often either annihilate or incorporate the other, or both will fuse into a new world or subworld. Familiar examples include the fusion of the Greek and the Roman worlds, of the Judaic and the Christian ones, of the West Indian and the Spanish worlds of Latin America, and so on.

Alternative worlds and their subworlds can be said to be commensurable when their weighting principles and reference frames are incompatible, but essentially understandable or translatable in each other's terms. For example, many of the worlds and subworlds mentioned so far can be seen as commensurable in relation to each other. Despite their (self-)perceived incompatibility, they may appear, say, to an observer from another planet, as parts of the same universe or of what Even-Zohar calls, in a different context, a "polysystem" and we may provisionally call a "superworld."[43] Although their local weighting principles can differ considerably, they can be seen as having an overall weighting principle in common. What Western scientists imagine to be our physical universe(s), for instance, suggests precisely this kind of superworld or polysystem. Its overall weighting principle can be described in various ways depending on the criteria involved. From an ontological standpoint, for example, this overall weighting principle may be called "phusis," or "becoming," or "matter"; even more comprehensively, it may be called "energy" or "force."

One can also imagine relations of incommensurability among worlds and/or their subworlds, when their local or overall weighting principles or frames of reference appear as incomprehensible or untranslatable in terms of each other. A good illustration of what I mean by incommensurable relationships is offered by Max Jammer's comparison between Western physics and Jaina "physics" in his book, *Concepts of Force*:

> The Jainas, followers of Jina (Vardhamana), an elder contemporary of Buddha, developed a realistic and relativistic atomistic pluralism *(anekantarada)*, without the slightest allusion to the concept of force, in contrast to Western science in which the idea of force plays . . . a fundamental role. In the Jaina physics, the category of *ajiva* is subdivided into matter *(pudgala)*, space *(akasha)*, motion *(dharma)*, rest *(adharma)*, and time *(kala)*. *Dharma* and *adharma* designate the conditions of movement and of rest respectively. Being formless and passive, they do not generate motion or arrest it, but merely help and favor motion or rest, like water, which is instrumental for the motion of a fish, or like the earth, which supports objects that rest on it.

> Essentially, it is "time" that originates "activity" *(kriya)* and "change" *(parinama)*, and it does so without becoming thereby some kind of a dynamic agent, something equivalent to the concept of force in Western thought.[44]

Here Jaina "physics," based on pluralistic, nondynamic principles appears as incommensurable with Western physics, based on principles of force. Indeed, Max Jammer's comparison between the two kinds of "physics" is no more (as he himself is aware) than a failed attempt to translate the Jaina concept of nature in Western terms, for the very rendition into English of Jaina words such as *anekantarada*, *pudgala*, *akasha*, *dharma*, *kala*, *kriya*, and *parinama* is a (mis)interpretation of their original meaning in terms of a vocabulary of force (matter, space, time, motion, rest, change, activity, etc.). "Physics" itself is hardly the proper word for describing the Jaina view of nature, and by putting it in quotation marks I have merely pointed to the essential incommensurability between the Western and the Jaina worlds.

The traditional Western ontological division between real worlds and fictional ones, moreover, can designate not only a relation of incompatibility but also one of incommensurability, pertaining to two unadjustable reference frames. From a constructivist standpoint, fictional or imaginary worlds can best be seen not as "nonexistent objects" but as entities constituted on alternative ontological principles. In fact, their overall weighting principle can better be described in terms of "being," rather than "becoming." When compared to "real" or physical worlds (whose overall weighting principle is "becoming") they appear as indestructible or immortal; therefore, far from being "nonexistent," they paradoxically belong to an enhanced order of "reality." Other examples of incommensurable worlds are the "natural" worlds in relation to the "supernatural" ones, the mystical ones in relation to the philosophical ones (in the Schopenhauerian sense discussed in chapter 1), the "divine" worlds in relation to the "secular" ones, three-dimensional worlds in relation to two-dimensional or four-dimensional ones, and so on. Euripides' *The Bacchae*, Cervantes' *Don Quijote*, Carroll's *Alice in Wonderland*, Pirandello's *Six Characters in Search of an Author*, and Unamuno's *Mist* are some of the most familiar examples of literary works that thematize relationships of incommensurability between worlds.

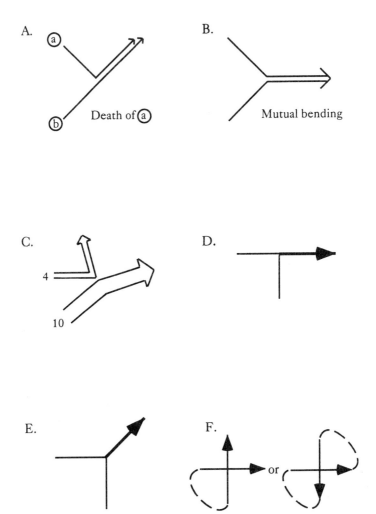

Fig. 1. Modes of Intersection between
Incompatible Worlds

Figures 1, 2, and 3 represent various types of encounters between alternative worlds leading to different outcomes. (Of course, these diagrams hardly claim to present an exhaustive typology of such encounters, a task that would require another book.)[45] Figure 1, Modes of Intersection Between Incompatible Worlds, represents a few types of violent and nonviolent encounters between incompatible, but commensurable, physical realities whose weighting principle is energy or force. *A*, *B* and *C* illustrate violent contacts, in which the qualities of each line become a quantity or applicable force to be directed toward or resisted by the other. In *A*, the clash results in the annihilation of one (or both) of the vectors. *B* results in mutual bending and a loss of original qualities. *C* results in mutual repulsion and also a partial loss of original qualities. In turn, *D*, *E*, and *F* show varying degrees of nonviolent accommodation between incompatible realities. An encounter is perceived as violent when it involves a forceful transgression of physical, psychoemotional, or sociopolitical boundaries that are themselves constructed; and as nonviolent when the boundaries are freely accepted or shift by mutual agreement. In *D*, for example, one line accommodates the other without feeling encroached upon. *E* represents a compromise, with each line adjusting its local weighting principles as it accepts the other. Finally, *F* shows an illusory opposition, in which two lines that perceive themselves as incompatible are in fact aspects of the same vector.

When two incommensurable worlds intersect they do not clash in the same way that incompatible worlds do. Properly speaking no "collision" takes place, and their relationship is necessarily one of *nolo contendere*. Their intersection may be ontologically inconsequential, as in the surrealist movie scenes in which a truck runs through a ghost. Figure 2, Modes of Intersection Between Incommensurable Worlds, represents several ways in which incommensurable physical realities can "miss" each other, even when one (or both) of them is (are) governed by the principle of motion or force. The dotted area in *A* represents a substance that is qualitatively different from the dynamic reality represented by the arrow, which can, for example, be a solid metallic object that passes unimpeded through mist. In *B* a one-dimensional arrow passes through a three-dimensional cube without "cutting" it (as a plane might do). In *C*, two three-dimensional forms are "hinged" together, yet the triangular shape "magically" passes through the cubic

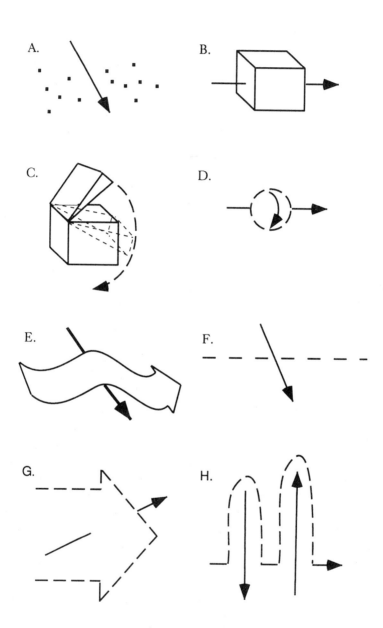

*Fig. 2. Modes of Intersection between
Incommensurable Worlds*

shape; perhaps it swings into a higher dimension. In *D*, a section of the line rotates into a contrary position, a course that normally results in a collision; since the line, however, is no longer present when its contrary rotates, the two lines never cross. In *E*, the two-dimensional arrow actively avoids the one-dimensional one. *F* illustrates a situation in which certain lines exist only cyclically, intermittently, or in phases so that an opportunistic or lucky arrow can slip through the "cracks." *G* represents a shift in scale: the two arrows participate in the same qualitative state, but vary in quantity; their volumes are so disproportionate that they ignore each other's presence. *H* represents a situation of infinite accommodation: one line stretches effortlessly beyond the reach of the other, by either preceding or delaying the moment of contact.

Finally, Figure 3, Intertwining Alternative Worlds, represents "static" rather than "dynamic" situations in which mutually exclusive yet intertwining realities share the same space. In *A*, the face/vase configuration depends on the viewer's negative or positive perception (requiring a logic of either/or). In *B*, the yin/yang figure, like a Zen koan, presents a paradox in which opposites form a single entity (according to a logic of both/and): a certain phenomenon, object, or reality is both present and absent, light and dark, here and there, strong and weak, male and female, etc.

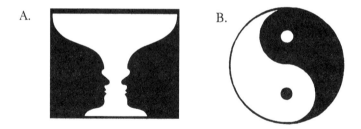

Fig. 3. Intertwining Alternative Worlds

The diagrams above present only a very limited typology of the infinite number of encounters that can take place between alternative worlds. Of primary importance for the present study, however, is the distinction between incommensurable and incompatible realities, and the diagrams have implicitly highlighted essential differences between them. For example, whereas an encounter between two incompatible worlds invariably results in a collision or a shift, an encounter between incommensurable worlds may even go unperceived. When the latter does have a noticeable result, this may simply be the conversion of one weighting principle into the other, rather than a complete annihilation of one of these principles or some kind of accommodation between them, as in the case of clashes between incompatible worlds. Even if the encounter between two incommensurable realities may result in a voluntary, marginal adoption of the other's weighting principle, this would not radically affect either frame of reference. If any "harm" or "violence" does result, it is basically self-inflicted, as a fundamental literary and anthropological document such as *The Bacchae* demonstrates.[46]

A prime example of an incommensurable encounter is that between worlds whose overall weighting principle is power and those whose overall weighting principle is of an irenic nature (it is this particular kind of incommensurable encounter that the present book has focused on). Although most of the alternative worlds that we humans build and classify as "real" are power-oriented, we have also imagined and constructed worlds whose weighting principles and reference frames are irenic. There are many examples of irenic imaginary worlds, but only of a few "real" or actual ones, including certain Oriental and Occidental religious and/ or alternative communities (some of which, however, may upon close inspection turn out to be more liminal than actual—see my discussion of *communitas* below, in this section). It is clear, for instance, that Jaina "physics" is the expression of such an irenic world (in contrast to the power-oriented actual world of Western physics).

One should, moreover, not conceive of the relationship between irenic worlds and power-oriented worlds as one of binary opposition, that is, as one of incompatibility. This would simply mean confusing two radically different reference frames, a confusion that can occur very easily within communities habituated to evaluate everything in terms of power. The New Testament for instance, stages in detail an encounter between an irenic world and a power-oriented one. There is a constant ironic tension between Jesus Christ's ethos and pathos and their (mis)interpretation not only by the powers-that-be but also by his own disciples. Jesus's words and actions are invariably interpreted by the community in terms of a power-based weighting principle, and the radical misreading of their reference frame will culminate in the founding of the Pauline church as a power-oriented institution. The Christian historical or actual worlds have often also chosen to remain within a power-oriented frame of reference, enlisting irenic principles in the service of this frame. In fact, the entire history of Christianity can be read as a series of failed attempts to convert from a world of power to an irenic kind. The New Testament reveals, moreover, that while the irenic or "divine" world emerges intact from the encounter with a power-oriented "human" world, the effects of this encounter on the latter can be devastating, because of the aggressive, totalizing nature of power, which cannot tolerate alterity even at the risk of self-annihilation.

No less than Christ, Gautama Buddha is fully aware of the radical difference between an irenic world and a power-oriented one. For example, the *Mara Suttas* tell of the incommensurable encounter between Mara the Evil One and Gautama, the Exalted One (the Buddha) when the latter meditates on the nature of governance. Gautama asks himself if it were possible to exercise governance "righteously," that is, "without smiting nor letting others slay, without conquering nor causing others to conquer, without sorrowing nor making others sorrow."[47] Whereupon Mara immediately appears to him and says: "Let the Exalted One, lord, exercise governance, let the Blessed One rule without smiting nor letting others slay, without conquering nor letting others to conquer . . . and therewithal ruling righteously" (146). Since Gautama, Mara argues, has already developed the "four stages of potency," which he has repeatedly practiced, applied to perfection, and persevered in, he would even be able to turn the Himalaya into gold if he desired to do so. So why shouldn't he also be able to govern righteously, if that were his wish? But Gautama sees immediately the trap that Mara has set for him: he is considering the question of governance from the perspective of an irenic world, whereas the Evil One wants him to become reenmeshed in the world of power that he has already left behind, where a different reference frame applies (such as turning mountains into gold).

The fact that Gautama meditates on the question of governance while a recluse in a Himalayan leaf-hut also suggests that he is situated in between two worlds, that is, in a liminal space that is part of neither of these worlds and yet can give him access to both. In this respect, it may be helpful to consider a further (nonessentialist) distinction between alternative worlds and liminal ones. Liminal worlds are indeterminate ontological landscapes or gray areas located in between alternative worlds, subworlds, and superworlds. These liminal worlds should therefore not be seen as alternative worlds per se, because they have no firmly established weighting principles while their frames of reference (often borrowed from their immediate neighbors) are ceaselessly being questioned and/or dislocated. But even though they are not themselves alternative worlds, they can nevertheless generate a great number of such worlds by proposing and debating various weighting principles, complete with blueprints of their reference frames. There are numberless examples of actual and imaginary liminal worlds, including religious and nonreligious communes, secular and religious festivals, ceremonies and rituals, public and private games, works of art such as novels, poems, dramas, paintings, sculptures, musical compositions, and so forth. Liminal worlds can also arise through dreams or dreamlike states, travel, pilgrimages, solitary retreat (as in the Buddha's case above) or solitary confinement, voluntary or forced exile, and through the experience of birth, death, and rebirth.

Because of their fluidity, flexibility, and freedom from rigid ontological commitments, liminal worlds are ludic worlds par excellence. The liminal nature of the ludic has indirectly been pointed out, for instance, by Johan Huizinga, who offers this definition of play: "a free activity standing quite consciously outside 'ordinary' life as being 'not serious', but at the same time absorbing the player intensely and utterly. It is an activity connected with no material interest, and no profit can be gained by it. It proceeds within its own proper boundaries of time and space according to fixed rules and in an orderly manner. It promotes the formation of social groupings which tend to surround themselves with secrecy and to stress their difference from the common world by disguise or other means."[48]

One can adopt, in a revised form, several elements from Huizinga's definition of play to describe liminal worlds as well. They stand quite consciously "outside" other worlds, including actual ones, and are "disinterested" in a Kantian sense, allowing themselves complete freedom to adopt any weighting principle or frame of reference they see fit. They have their own proper boundaries of time and space, on the margins of or within an alternative world, subworld, or superworld. Properly speaking, however, they do not have fixed rules and do not proceed in an orderly manner any more than play does; or at least, as in the case of play, rules and order are incidental to their nature. (Here one should make a distinction between play and games, although one could argue that even games only simulate rules and orderly procedure, that is, only pretend to adopt a weighting principle and a reference frame for the sake of play.) Furthermore, as Huizinga implies about play, liminal worlds, like all other worlds, cannot arise outside or independently of specific communities, be it only a community specially assembled for a ludic occasion or a community of one (in which case a larger community always looms in an actual or an imaginary background). On the other hand, just as a community can not only engender but also be engendered by play, it can both initiate and be initiated by a liminal world.

Finally, the idea of community brings us back full circle to Turner's anthropological theory of liminality, where *communitas* as a special type of community plays a crucial role. For Turner, *communitas* is a prototype of human interplay that is obscured by normal social structures but reasserts itself during a liminal event. In a liminal state the initiands engage in spontaneous, immediate, equalitarian interchanges that stand in marked contrast to social hierarchies. Communitas "exists in a kind of 'figure-ground' relationship with social structure. The boundaries of each of these—in so far as they constitute explicit or implicit models for human interaction—are defined by contact or comparison with the other, just as the liminal phase of an initiation rite is defined by the surrounding social statuses (many of which it abrogates, inverts, or invalidates)."[49] According to Turner, communitas does not engage in active opposition to social structure, but merely appears as "an alternative and more 'liberated' way of being socially human." By being detached from a particular human structure while coexisting with it, communitas provides an opportunity to evaluate the historical performance of this structure. It is "a loving union of the structurally damned pronouncing judgment on normative structure and providing alternative models for structure" (51). In its most open form, a liminal event reveals a "model of human society as a homogeneous, unstructured communitas, whose boundaries are ideally coterminous with those of the human species" (47). For this reason communitas no less than liminality is often regarded as dangerous by the powers-that-be who preside over established structure.

Turner argues, however, that communitas can never sustain its immediacy and spontaneity; instead, it develops a protective social structure "in which free relationships between individuals become converted into norm-governed relationships between social personae" (47). Accordingly, Turner distinguishes between three forms of communitas: spontaneous, ideological, and normative. Spontaneous communitas is "a direct, immediate and total confrontation of human identities" and has something "magical" about it—"a feeling of endless power" (47–48). Spontaneous communitas can be experienced in ritual or in mass movements, and the individuals involved in it "become totally absorbed into a single synchronized, fluid event." They relate directly to other individuals as they present themselves in an immediate, natural state, without the "culturally defined encumbrances of . . . role, status, reputation, class, caste, sex or other structural niche" (48).

In turn, ideological communitas is based on the *memory* of the spontaneous one and has a nostalgic relationship to it. It is a "set of theoretical concepts which attempt to describe the interactions of spontaneous communitas" (48). Examples of ideological communitas presumably include various utopian and non-utopian social models from the Platonic republic to the Marxian communist state. Normative communitas on the other hand is, "once more, 'a perduring social system,' a subculture or group which attempts to foster and maintain relationships or spontaneous communitas on a more or less permanent basis" (49). Even though normative communitas has to "denature itself" because spontaneous communitas can never be "legislated for or normalized," it is nevertheless distinguishable from such social entities as clans, tribes, nations, and states that "arise on the foundation of some 'natural' or technical 'necessity,' real or imagined, such as a system of productive relations or a group of putatively biologically connected persons, a family, kindred, or lineage" (49). Examples of normative communitas presumably include religious orders (such as the Franciscans or the Dominicans), religious communities (such as the Puritan settlements in New England, or the Amish settlements in Pennsylvania), hippie communes, kibbutzim, ashrams, and the like.

Turner's notion of communitas can be helpful in understanding the complex relationships between alternative and liminal worlds, but not before it undergoes critical revision. Like his distinction between liminal and liminoid, Turner's typology of communitas turns out to be rather problematic. Both ideological and normative communitas are obviously derived from and subordinated to spontaneous communitas and, consequently, cannot be placed within the same categorical frame as the latter. Not only is ideological communitas also normative but both types already possess a more or less rudimentary social structure and thus differ radically from spontaneous communitas. More simply and logically, therefore, ideological and normative communitas can be seen as types of small communities, to be distinguished from larger types, such as clans, nations, states, confederations, and so forth.

Turner's definition of spontaneous communitas as "a feeling of endless power" sounds very much like Nietzsche's description of the Dionysiac ecstatic community as the intoxication (*Rausch*) of the individual in the presence of "the mystical Oneness"; seized by Dionysiac rapture, the individual forgets himself and becomes at one with other individuals and with the "productive power of the whole universe."[50] Manifestations of spontaneous communitas as understood by Turner can theoretically range from orderly or rambunctious secular and religious festivals to tribal scapegoat rituals to Ku Klux Klan lynchings to Nazi and Communist mass rallies to bloody social revolutions. Moreover, communitas in its "structured," ideological or normative guises is no less of a power-oriented notion. Although Turner points out that these forms of communitas bring upon themselves the persecution of the dominant social structure because of their inclusive, proselytizing tendencies, one should not forget that they can in turn be as repressive and intolerant toward their opponents (or, for that matter, toward their own members) as any prevailing social structure can. In sum, Turner's spontaneous communitas is not so spontaneous after all, but is always already culturally conditioned.

Turner's notion of communitas should ultimately not be separated from his notion of liminality. It becomes obvious from his argument that the ideological and normative kinds of communitas would best be seen as imaginary or actual alternative worlds, while spontaneous communitas would best be seen as a liminal world whose weighting principles and reference frames can shift at will. In this respect, liminal communitas will constantly change its content in relation to the neighboring communities whose weighting principles and reference frames it stages. It would then not remain tied down to a mentality of power but become flexible and open-ended.

Once we emancipate spontaneous communitas from a power-oriented reference frame, we can also envisage it as a liminal world that points to irenic weighting principles and reference frames. Turner's concept of liminality itself could in turn become detached from a mentality of power. Isaiah Berlin's "freedom to" might thus imply venturing not only beyond a dominant system of values with its inversions and subversions but also beyond power-oriented systems in general, toward irenic alternative worlds.

We are now equally in a position to answer the question whether literary works, understood as liminal (rather than fictional) worlds, can also provide access to alternative worlds that are incommensurable with ours. Given their ludic-liminal nature, literary works (as well as works of art in general) are ideally suited, as Wolfgang Iser has shown, to stage any kind of actual or imaginary worlds. Therefore, they can also point to any kinds of ontological alternatives, including irenic ones. In the end, it is up to the community or the communities that receive(s) the artwork to take steps toward embracing and perhaps even actualizing one of these irenic alternatives.

DIFFERENCE, IDENTITY, AND OTHERNESS
A *Ludic-Irenic Perspective*

Looking back at the theoretical scene of American academia in the 1980s, one can say that it was largely dominated, no less than that of the 1970s, by West European thought. Two main schools have had a lasting impact: the French and the German. The French school, known mainly under the name of poststructuralism, included Derridian and de Manian deconstruction, Girardian mimetology, Foucauldian and Deleuzian Nietzscheanism, and Lacanian psychoanalysis. The German school, in turn, offered two brands of hermeneutics: existential-phenomenological (in the Husserlian and Heideggerian tradition), represented especially by Hans-Georg Gadamer and the Konstanz School; and critical-theoretical, represented by the heirs of the Frankfurt School, such as Jürgen Habermas. The American theoretical scene continued, moreover, to be somewhat influenced by East European thought, but not so much by Russian formalism and the Prague Linguistic School as by the dialogic thought of Mikhail Bakhtin (whose major works took almost two decades to be properly translated and received in the United States). Finally, there was a veritable boom of Marxist, feminist, gay, lesbian, and postcolonial critical trends that originated mainly in the 1960s and the 1970s and became entrenched by the end of the 1980s and the beginning of the 1990s.

I should like to suggest that the common intellectual denominator of most of these trends is an agonistic philosophy of difference derived from a mentality of power that has prevailed in the Western world ever since its beginnings in Hellenic culture. In what follows I shall briefly outline the problematic of the Western notion of difference from three closely interrelated standpoints: ontoepistemological, sociopolitical, and psychosexual. I shall then consider a few alternative ways of looking at difference from a nonagonistic, ludic-irenic perspective.

1. Ontoepistemological and sociopolitical models of difference

The concept of difference has a very long history in Western thought and can be traced back to the pre-Socratic notions of the many and the one.[1] These notions arise in the context of physical science, including cosmology and medicine, and stem from the principle of strife (ἔρις) or contest (ἀγών) between various physical forces. The Ionian physicists (φύσικοι) conceive the world in terms of a plurality of warring forces (δύναμεις) that can be either irreconcilable and isonomic (of equal power) or reducible to and subsumable under an ἀρχή or "originating superior force" (such as water, earth, fire, air). As long as the various forces are perceived as part of the same physical cosmos, they may dispute the ἀρχή position and rotate it among themselves. In this sense, their identity depends on an agonistic play of difference and is ceaselessly shifting in relation to their equal or unequal opponents. Heraclitus aptly sums up the archaic notion of difference as strife in one of his oracular statements: "War is the father and king of all, and some he shows as gods, others as men; some he makes slaves, others free."[2] In this view, the difference between the one and the many is only of degree, not of kind, for the gods themselves are many and differ from mortals and from each other only through their degree of power.

The Eleatics and Plato, among others, introduce another phase in the thought of difference when they attempt to arrest its agonistic play and subsume the many under the one. The most effective way of accomplishing this task is to raise the one to the One, that is, to a transcendental level. In this sense, ἀρχή is no longer simply a physical element or force, a *primus inter pares* vying for supremacy with other elements, according to the isonomic principle of government by rotation. On the contrary, it lifts itself above all contest, attaining an unreachable, unassailable position. In Parmenides and Plato, this new, transcendental ἀρχή bears the name of Being, which is eternal and immovable, to be distinguished from Becoming, which is ever-slippery and illusory. In monotheism (the beginnings of which can equally be discerned in the Eleatic and Platonic metaphysics), this ἀρχή bears the name of an invisible yet ubiquitous, almighty God who differs from mortals not only in degree of power but also in (ontological) kind.

If in an archaic mentality all hierarchy or order (including the divine one) is created—and, therefore, can also be destroyed—through the vagaries of war, i.e., by pure chance, in the Eleatic and Platonic views all (transcendental or divine) order is preordained, indestructible, and infinite; that is, it is governed by pure necessity. Whereas in the Ionian physicists difference determines identity, in Plato identity determines difference—not through strife, moreover, but through mimesis. The transcendental One subsumes the many in the form of copies or reflections of itself. These reflections are more or less brilliant or pale, faithful or untrustworthy, according to their relative distance from or proximity to the One. In this respect, the play of the many is denied full power not only in an epistemological but also in an ontological sense (what Nietzsche and his heir, Fink, will call *Seinsmacht*), becoming a mere play of appearances or simulacra. The transcendental One, on the other hand, becomes all-powerful, omnipresent, and omniscient.

Finally, under the impact of Eleatic and Platonic thought, the Ionian pluralistic world will gradually turn into a dualistic world of Being and Becoming, reality and appearance, mind and matter, subject and object. In turn, all that is will eventually be divided into ontological forms of difference such as humans, subhumans (animals, plants, etc.), suprahumans (gods, angels, devils, ghosts, etc.), and extraterrestrials (usually conceived on the model of humans and suprahumans); cultural forms such as race, ethnicity, and gender; and sociopolitical forms such as family, class, tribe, nation, state, ethnic region, commune, federation, kingdom, empire, etc. Geographical space or territory as well as languages or language in general will also function as both a privileged locus and a primary source of antagonistic difference in human cultures.

Needless to say, all the forms of difference I have mentioned so far have often been imagined as hierarchies, as superior and inferior forms of being, and from this brief sketch it has become clear, I hope, how the notions of being and power are inseparable in Hellenic thought and why they will remain inextricably linked throughout the history of Western philosophy, from Neoplatonism to Christian patristics to Cartesian rationalism to German idealism to contemporary poststructuralism.[3] In *Dionysus Reborn*, I have argued that Nietzsche is one of the first modern thinkers who lift the Platonic suspension of the ceaseless play of physical forces by proclaiming the "death of God," that is, by demoting the (transcendental) One to a (physical) one among many. By reversing the Platonic relation between the one and the many, Nietzsche thus returns to the Ionian notion of agon as incessant generator and destroyer of all (cosmic) order or hierarchy. Difference becomes again openly conflictive, and Platonic mimesis is no longer an instrument of containment of the contest among the many, or a primary ordering criterion among them. In Nietzsche Becoming again determines Being, and difference determines identity, rather than the other way around. Nietzsche's far-reaching project of "reversing Platonism" is completed in the twentieth century by such poststructuralist thinkers as Martin Heidegger and Eugen Fink in Germany, and Georges Bataille, Gilles Deleuze, and Jacques Derrida in France. Like Nietzsche, these thinkers go back to the pre-Socratics for their various ontoepistemological notions of difference.

Heidegger, in one respect, can be seen as returning to the Empedoclean moment in the history of the idea of difference, that is, to a dynamic (rather than a stable) correlation between the Eleatic One and the Ionian many. Like Empedocles, he does not entirely give up the Parmenidean notion of Being (conceived by Empedocles as an interplay of Love and Strife, or attraction and repulsion). Heidegger imagines a pluralistic cosmology (similar to the Ionian kind) in which the One does not arrest all conflict but, on the contrary, plays a ceaseless power game (of attraction and repulsion) with the many. For Heidegger, the essential difference is the ontic-ontological one, meaning that Being reveals and conceals itself as both One and the many (now called beings). He rightly insists on distinguishing his dynamic notion of Being from the suspended or static one with which the Platonic ontotheological tradition (including Hegel) operates: "In contrast to Hegel, this is not a traditional problem, already posed, but what has always remained unasked throughout the history of thinking. We speak of it, tentatively and unavoidably, in the language of tradition. We speak of the *difference* between Being [*Sein*] and beings [*das Seiende*]. The step back goes from what is unthought, from the difference as such, into what gives us thought."[4]

Heidegger claims that, although the question of Being is posed at the beginning of Western thought in Anaximander, Heraclitus, and Parmenides, this thought has gradually forgotten the ontic-ontological difference, moving away from Being and increasingly focusing on being(s). It is Heidegger's philosophical world-historical mission, therefore, to refocus thinking on Being. This mission also implies a (re)turn to the origin of thinking in the pre-Socratics, and it is for this reason that Heidegger writes extensively on Being in Hellenic thought.

According to Heidegger, Being ceaselessly draws and withdraws from beings, engaging them in a violent game of revelation and concealment—

what in his later work he will call *das Weltspiel*. As I have demonstrated elsewhere, Heidegger also moves over the course of his career from the notion of Being as Strife *(Urstreit)* to the mystical notion of Being as Love (which he also calls *das Selbe*, the Same, or *das Spiel der Stille*, the play of stillness).[5] He thus seems to enact, in his own thinking, the Empedoclean cosmic dynamics in which Strife and Love wage an eternal contest, ceaselessly advancing and withdrawing with far-reaching consequences for the world of beings (controlled, in turn, by the four ριζώματα, roots, as Empedocles calls the primordial physical forces impelled by Love and Strife to generate various cosmic cycles).

Heidegger's pupil Fink removes the Empedoclean component of Heidegger's thought, and his conception of Being does not oscillate between the vocabulary of power and that of mystical love. Fink's cosmology is an entirely agonistic one, with the world-totality *(Weltall)* as a groundless, meaningless, and impersonal movement of cosmic power, and with human beings *(Dasein)* as both players and toys in a perpetual cosmic game of appearance and disappearance. Difference in this game assumes the form of chance that defies any absolute grounding or necessity and follows the chaotic play of cosmic forces.

Fink also attempts to revise the Platonic relation between the One and the many through his notion of *Erscheinung* (shining forth, spontaneous appearance). He starts from the Platonic ontoepistemology of difference, which rests on two distinctions: between model and copy on the one hand, and between good and bad copies, on the other. Through the notion of *Erscheinung* Fink attempts to erase the Platonic dichotomy between Idea and appearance, or that between model and copy, arguing that in reality the two polarities become a unity. In this sense, Fink conceives Being as a ceaseless play that shines forth or appears not in its totality, but only as a *pars pro toto*, on a limited stage. Thus, he transforms the Platonic metaphorics into a metonymics of totality. In another sense, Fink can be said to preserve the Platonic notion of totality or the One, but in its inverted Nietzschean form: the One is no longer the eternally fixed Idea, but the ever shifting, ever playful Dionysus.

If both Heidegger and Fink maintain the Eleatic notion of a holistic Being, the French poststructuralists problematize this notion; indeed, some of them do away with it altogether, thereby (re)turning to an Ionian pluralistic cosmology. Georges Bataille probably remains the closest to the Heideggerian notion of dynamic totality, because he understands "Being" *(Être)* not in the Platonic, idealist sense of immutable, eternal order, but in the Nietzschean sense of Becoming as a ceaseless play of physical forces. For him Being designates "the movement of free and self-unraveling violence which animates totality and which resolves itself in tears, ecstasy and peals of laughter, revealing their impossibility."[6] Being as cosmic game leads us to silence after exploding in laughter (not unlike Nietzsche's Zarathustra). It defies all project and discourse, assuming the form of an infinite and irreducible game of chance that ultimately escapes even itself. It is this game of chance that produces all difference, which in turn produces identity as an infinite series of heterogeneous singularities.

For Bataille, no less than for Nietzsche and Heidegger, *"Life plays itself: Life risks itself"* (22) in a ceaseless power game. In this respect, Bataille's concept of difference as a cosmic game of chance parallels Fink's and can be traced back to the Nietzschean notion of the agonistic play of a nonrational Will to Power: "In the fight for life against the teleological tendency, against the ordering of means and ends, luck, chance, divinely, ardently, suddenly makes its appearance and comes away victorious in the same manner. Intelligence long ago ceased sensing the universe through reason that reckons. Existence itself recognizes that it is at the disposal of chance when it takes its measure by the starry sky or by death. It recognizes itself in all its own magnificence, created in the image of a universe untouched by the defilement of merit or intention" (21).

Whereas Bataille, like Fink and in the wake of Nietzsche, emphasizes the notion of Being as Becoming under the name of Dionysian mystical experience, contemporary poststructuralists such as Deleuze, Derrida, and de Man return to Ionian physical models of multiplicity as a play of physical forces. They reverse the Platonic relation between the One and the many, interpreting the Platonic notion of difference in terms of *simulacre*. Deleuze and Derrida, for example, argue (against Fink and the German phenomenological tradition) that the crucial distinction in Plato is not between model and copy or Idea and appearance, but rather that between appearances themselves (simulacra), which for Plato can be either good or bad. Reversing Platonism, therefore, consists less in overturning the hierarchy of model and copy, or Idea and image, than in proclaiming the power of the simulacrum. As Deleuze points out, the simulacrum is "a mechanism, a Dionysian machine. It is a question of the false as power, *pseudos* in Nietzsche's sense: the highest power of the false [*la plus haute puissance du faux*]."[7] Thus, for both Deleuze and Derrida the simulacrum is what Nietzsche understands by the Will to Power: a perpetual agonistic play of active forces.

At the same time, however, Deleuze attempts to complete Nietzsche's unfinished project of replacing Being with Becoming by elaborating a philosophy of surfaces or "pure becoming" *(devenir pur)*. Here, again, he starts from Plato, but as modified by the Stoic notion of bodies and "incorporeals." The Stoics, according to Deleuze, redistribute the Platonic cosmic hierarchy of Ideas and matter by postulating (physical) bodies as the only reality or Being, and the realm of simulacra (which Plato banishes to the bottomless depths of the cosmos) as the events-effects of these bodies or "pure becoming." In other words, the Stoics distinguish between "two levels of being: on the one hand, the profound and real being [of the bodies], the force *(la force);* on the other hand, the level of events *(faits)* that play at the surface of being, forming an infinite multiplicity of incorporeal beings."[8] Consequently, for Deleuze the cosmic play of difference also involves two levels: the deep play of forces, combining bodies according to an active-passive principle (a variant of the Nietzschean division of affirmative forces into active and passive); and the "ideal play" *(jeu idéal)* of events-effects, the play of simulacra, affirming chance as a totality of throws or *lancet unique*, which distributes each throw along an unlimited, aleatory line, whose points can in turn be divided into unlimited, coresonant series (not unlike Bataille's series of contending heterogeneous singularities).

Derrida, in turn, is less concerned with the deep play of physical bodies than with the play of pure becoming which he calls *différance* and describes, just like Deleuze, in terms of a linguistic event-effect, or what he calls "writing" *(écriture)*. Although Derrida starts from Heidegger's notion of Being and ontic-ontological difference, he refracts this notion through the Stoic-Deleuzian doctrine of the simulacrum. In this respect, writing as *différance* is also the Nietzschean play of simulacra raised to the highest power.

Like Heidegger, Derrida equates the foundation of Western metaphysics with the concept of being(s) understood as presence (οὐσία). But unlike Heidegger, he focuses on writing as the suppressed Other of a metaphysics of presence, which therefore is also primarily a metaphysics of the spoken word or the *Logos*. In place of this metaphysics, Derrida proposes a "grammatology," based on a concept of language as sign, which he inherits from both Saussure and structuralist linguistics. While preserving the double structure of the sign (signified and signifier), Derrida no longer conceives of reference in terms of a transcendental signified, but precisely in terms of *différance*, a play of differences and oppositions that generates and distributes meaning while it itself remains meaningless. As Derrida points out, "*Différance* is the non-full, non-simple, structural and differentiating origin of differences."[9]

But Derrida's grammatology can also be seen as a Deleuzian philosophy of "pure becoming" where the present as such has no place, being perpetually postponed or "deferred" *(déférer)* as an absent, imaginary origin. Thus, *différance* as a pure play of simulacra has both a spatial and a temporal component. The spatial component concerns the play of differences that Derrida traces back to Nietzsche's play of forces. The temporal component concerns the infinite division of the present into past and future, which transforms Heidegger's ontic-ontological difference into a Deleuzian play of events-effects where the present is always deferred in two directions at once. The spatial and the temporal components of *différance* are inseparable and have to be thought of as one and the same movement: Derrida coins this word in order to convey the meaning of both "differing" and "deferring," an ambivalence that escapes the common French word, *différence*.[10]

Another version of the concept of (agonistic) difference in which a Nietzschean play of simulacra is raised to the highest power can be found in the work of Paul de Man, for whom *différance* is the attribute of literature or fictive discourse in general. For de Man, literary discourse begins with the awareness "that sign and meaning can never coincide." In literature, moreover, "the human self has experienced the void within itself, and the invented fiction, far from filling the void, asserts itself as a pure nothingness, *our* nothingness stated and restated by a subject that is the agent of his own instability."[11] Nothingness here is understood in Nietzschean terms, as a constant void or power vacuum that a mentality of power both fears and hails as the generator of all values. In *The Resistance to Theory* (1986), de Man sees the rhetorical nature of literature as subversive of grammar and logic (unlike Derrida, therefore, de Man considers both *logos* and *gramme* as part of the logocentric ontotheology of Western metaphysics) because its figurality always goes beyond the self-proclaimed rationality of discourse.

What de Man does not mention is that rhetoric is an archaic form of power, older than any grammar, logic, or rational mentality in general. Like poetry, rhetoric traces its history back to and justifies its authority upon orality or an archaic mentality. Isocrates, for instance, praises the power of speech as being able to make people cry or to move stones— hackneyed metaphors that at one time might have been inescapably real. Plato was one of the first rational thinkers to attempt to undermine the archaic (rhythmic, incantatory) power of rhetoric by infusing it with rational self-knowledge and justice. By privileging rhetoric as an antirational instrument, de Man continues the Nietzschean project of reversing Platonism and reinstates rhetoric to its former status as archaic authority. That deconstruction itself can easily turn into a contest for authority even as it claims to subvert all authority has become all too obvious, especially in its less sophisticated versions, currently circulating in the Anglo-American academic world.

The Hellenic idea of difference as either a ceaseless or a suspended strife between the many and the one has produced not only philosophical but also sociopolitical variants throughout the history of Western civilization. Avatars of Greek monistic and pluralistic systems of thought have persistently recurred throughout the history of the Western world, often (but not necessarily) in relation to their counterparts, the various forms of absolute monarchy and dictatorship, on the one hand, and their rivals, the democratic forms of government, on the other. Finally, a third Hellenic differential model that combines monism and pluralism in various manners has been widely employed in the Western tradition. This model, fully developed by Empedocles (and perhaps not unknown to Anaximander and Heraclitus as well), preserves both the strife between physical forces and the unassailable transcendentality of the One, but conceives of the latter as an arbiter or umpire of incontestable authority, rather than as an absolute, eternal ruler. Politically, this model has engendered such diverse governing systems as the modern Austrian-Hungarian empire and the Western parliamentary monarchies.

The notions of identity and totality in Western thought also arise in relation to an agonistic philosophy of difference. Identity can be understood as either that which erases, reconciles, or subordinates all difference, or that which is unique, singular, and irreconcilable, i.e., that which is generated by difference as such. In Parmenides and Hegel, for example, identity is understood as absolute, transcendental mind that is identical with itself, creating and subsuming all difference. In a pluralistic model, on the other hand, identity is conceived as a series of singularities engaged in an ever recurring conflict as in Heraclitus's or Nietzsche's notion of the return of the same or in Bataille's notion of heterogeneity. Bataille, moreover, directly applies the pluralistic model of difference as strife to political structures. For example, in "The Psychological Structure of Fascism" (1933), he sees political entities as configurations of homogeneous and heterogeneous elements, of which the heterogeneous elements are the primordial ones. All order is labile, being founded on violence that breaks out at the slightest imbalance. In this respect, political life as well as existence in general is another name for Nietzsche's Will to Power, "continually drawn in two directions; one leads to the creation of lasting organizations and conquering forces, the other leads, through the intermediary of expenditure of force and increasing excess, to destruction and death."[12]

If in "The Psychological Structure of Fascism," Bataille may still have an ambiguous attitude toward the principle of heterogeneity, in later works he comes to value it in an entirely positive manner under the name of "sovereignty" *(souveraineté)*. For instance, he regards sovereignty in relation to social life as an arbitrary intervention of forces that recognize only their own necessity, imposing the supreme rule of disorder on the precarious order of the homogeneous. It gathers within itself all the antisocial tendencies repressed by homogeneity, such as victimization, luxury, waste, eroticism, gratuity, and uselessness. From this sovereign standpoint, Bataille proposes what he calls an economy of expenditure and loss, in contrast to a capitalist economy of production and profit. Like Nietzsche, he emphasizes the element of uselessness and waste in society, an aristocratic, antibourgeois cultural attitude that favors *otium* over *negotium*, leisure over utility.[13]

Bataille's political model of heterogeneity will be taken up under various forms, serving various ideologies, in French intellectual circles after World War II, from the *Tel-Quel* Maoists' theory of perpetual revolution (which can also be traced back to Trotsky, Gramsci, and the dadaists) to Foucault's and Deleuze's theories of local *régimes* versus global, totalizing ones. The same agonistic model of heterogeneity informs the so-called politics of identity (actually a politics of agonistic difference) of many national, tribal, ethnic, and racial entities throughout the contemporary world.

In turn, the Western mentality of power has operated with at least three distinctive forms of totality, according to the kind of identity each of them embodies. Totality can thus be holistic or all-embracing, reductive, and pluralistic. Holistic totality is best exemplified by the Hellenic notion of εὐνομία (good hierarchical rule) developed among others by Homer, Hesiod, Solon, Socrates, and Plato and resurfacing especially in the neoclassical master narrative of an all-inclusive, hierarchical Great Chain of Being, where everything has and knows its place within a harmoniously organized whole. Politically, this notion of totality finds its (imperfect) counterpart in the Western monarchies of the Enlightenment. In turn, the Parmenidean notion of Being or the Hegelian notion of absolute spirit are common examples of reductive totality, where all that is can ultimately be reduced to the master narrative of an absolute, transcendental entity playing with itself a game of division and reunion. This kind of totality often finds a political expression in the so-called totalitarian states (contemporary right-wing and left-wing dictatorships, for example), in which everything must be reduced to the same common denominator (absolute or centralized power). Finally, the Heraclitian notion of Logos, the Nietzschean notion of the eternal return of the same, and the Heideggerian notion of Being can be seen as versions of a pluralistic totality because they postulate a ceaseless, agonistic play of difference as the groundless ground of all that is. Politically, these models of pluralistic totality have had their counterparts in eunomic, isonomic, and democratic states, the first two being ruled by fiercely contentious aristocratic groups (witness ancient Athens, some of the Italian city-states in the late Middle Ages, etc.), and the last one by somewhat less contentious median social groups (witness the West European democracies, for example).

2. Psychosexual models of difference.

The psychosexual aspect of the Western problematic of difference revolves mainly around the opposition between self and other and can best be discussed in relation to its ontoepistemological and sociopolitical counterparts. The self has traditionally been understood as interiority, subjectivity, and identity, whereas the nonself or the "other" has been understood as exteriority, objectivity, and alterity. In Hellenic thought the concept of identity is related to the Socratic agonistic division of the soul, with its "noble" and "inferior" parts ceaselessly at war: "The soul of a man within him has a better part and a worse part, and the expression self-mastery means the control of the worse by the naturally better part".[14] Identity is, therefore, attained through "self-mastery," the constant disciplining and subordination of the "worse" part (related to the five senses and the world of Becoming) by the "better" part (related to the logos and the world of Being or the Ideas).

According to Socrates, the parts of the soul correspond to the various groups within the Hellenic state. The lower part corresponds to the "mob of motley appetites and pleasures and pains one would find chiefly in children and women and slaves and in the base rabble of those who are free men in name" (4.431b–c). The higher part corresponds to the "simple and moderate appetites which with the aid of reason and right opinion are guided by consideration" and which one "will find in few and those the best born and best educated" (4.431c). Lack of inner discipline means a dissolution of identity into a chaotic play of difference not only inside the individual but also outside him, in the polity at large, leading to στάσις, civil strife, and sedition.

Although the two parts of the soul will in the course of Socrates' argument turn out to be three (if one counts the θυμός, or the "high-spirit" that carries out the commands of reason) so that they can correspond to the three groups of citizens in the ideal republic, the question is ultimately posed in terms of the one and the many, for identity or "unity" arises from the subordination of the many by the one. According to Socrates, the ideal state should assign "one man to one work, in order that each of them fulfilling his own function may be not many men, but one, and so the entire city may come to be not a multiplicity but a unity" (4.423d). Social harmony or unity does not come from a balance of equal forces, but from a "concord of the naturally superior and inferior as to which ought to rule in both the state and the individual" (4.432a). Εὐνομία (good hierarchical rule), therefore, derives from this happy concord between the rulers and the ruled.

The identity or unity of the polis, however, is also created through a contest with the outsiders or the strangers who attempt to penetrate and dominate it. Socrates makes this point when he describes the ideal qualities of the guardian in his model republic, whom he likens to a watchdog: "You surely have observed in well-bred hounds that their natural disposition is to be most gentle to their familiars and those whom they recognize, but the contrary to those whom they do not know. . . . [I]t is not an unnatural requirement that we are looking for in our guardian" (2.375d–e). The noncitizens, and by extension the non-Greeks or the "barbarians," are seen as heterogeneous forces that threaten the identity of the state or the Hellenic people at large and must be kept in check at all times.

What lies behind the politics as well as the psychology of many Western communities is precisely this Socratic double mechanism of disciplining the split individual and civic self through the subordination of certain "inferior," rebellious elements of the body physical and politic by the "superior" force of reason and, in the same movement, of channeling agonistic, "irrational" energies outwardly toward an Other perceived as a common enemy. It becomes equally clear that not only the Western concept of alterity but also the modern notions of relativism and perspectivism are based on the ancient agonistic distinction between friend/ally and enemy. What one cannot engulf, subsume, or override becomes the Other, which one keeps in check by either forming alliances or engaging in war with it. Nietzsche aptly describes the agonistic nature of relativistic perspectivism in one of the notes in *The Will to Power*: "Perspectivism is only a complex form of specificity. My idea is that every specific body strives to become master over all space and to extend its force (its will to power) and to thrust back all that resists its extension. But it continually encounters similar efforts on the part of other bodies and ends by coming to an arrangement ('union') with those of them that are sufficiently related to it: thus they then conspire together for power."[15]

The agonistic view of self and other prevails in Western thought from Socrates' sociopsychological theory of the state, to Hegel's phenomenology of consciousness, to Sartre's existential psychoanalysis, to Lacan's notion of the unconscious as radical alterity, to Foucault's definition of power as interactive contest among social and individual agents. Hegel, for example, derives his notion of self from his Christian theology, which attempts to reconcile the Cartesian split between humanity's two basic components: reflexive subjectivity and "natural" or existential objectivity.

In his early theological writings, Hegel poses this question in terms of a dialectic of the one and the many, or unity and multiplicity: "The multiplicity of life has to be thought of as being divided against itself; one part of this multiplicity (a part which is itself an infinite multiplicity because it is alive) is to be regarded purely as something related, as having its being purely in union; the second part, also an infinite multiplicity, is to be regarded as solely in opposition, as having its being solely through a separation from the first."[16] Thus Hegelian individuality, not unlike the Socratic self, exhibits a split nature, involving both "opposition to infinite variety and . . . inner association with it." According to Hegel, a human being possesses "an individual life in so far as he is distinguished from all the elements and from the infinity of beings outside himself. But he is only an individual life in so far as he is at one with all the elements, with the infinity of lives outside himself. He exists only inasmuch as the totality of life is divided into parts, he himself being one part and all the rest the other part; and again he exists only inasmuch as he is no part at all and inasmuch as nothing is separated from him" (310). This opposition manifests itself in the divided state between dwelling in nature and, concurrently, reflecting on it. Hence, human life is "the union of union and nonunion" (312).

From this standpoint, philosophy is inferior to religion, because it is only "a process of thinking and, as such a process, implies an opposition with nonthinking [processes] as well as the opposition between the thinking mind and the object of thought" (313). Philosophy must reveal "the finiteness in all finite things and require their integration by means of reason." Moreover, it must "recognize the illusions generated by its own infinite and thus . . . place the true infinite outside its confines" (313). For this reason it is not philosophy but religion—specifically the Christian religion of love—that can conceive of, or rather experience, the "true infinite."

Hegel argues that to the extent to which philosophy stresses either the objective or the self-reflective component of human life, it can be either naturalistic, as in Schelling's system, or subjectivistic to the point of solipsism, as in Fichte's thought. The split between subject and object creates conflicting perspectives. Originally, they "seem to be compatible with one another," but the wider apart they grow, "the purer must the Ego be and the further must the object be removed from and above man" (317f.). Furthermore, in Fichte's notion of the absolute Ego, the separation becomes infinite, and it no longer matters which remains fixed, the subject or the object, for in this case the opposition becomes that between the absolutely finite and the absolutely infinite. In Fichte's system, therefore, the opposition between subject and object could never be "overcome in a beautiful union; the union would be frustrated, and opposition would be a hovering of the Ego over all nature, a dependence upon, or rather a relation to, a Being beyond all nature" (318).

According to Hegel, the chronic philosophical imbalance between subject and object is inherent not only in Fichte's notion of absolute Ego but also in the Judaic idea of divinity as completely separated from nature and humanity. For Hegel, the Judaic spirit is embodied in Abraham: "The whole world Abraham regarded as simply his opposite; if he did not take it to be nullity, he looked on it as sustained by the God who was alien to it. Nothing in nature was supposed to have any part of god; everything was simply under God's mastery" (187). By the same token, mastery was "the only possible relationship in which Abraham could stand to the infinite world opposed to him; but he was unable himself to make this mastery actual, and it therefore remained ceded to his Idea" (187). Abraham's spirit was one of "self-maintenance in strict opposition to everything—the product of his thought raised to be the unity dominant over the nature which he regarded as infinite and hostile (for the only relationship possible between hostile entities is mastery of one by the other)."[17]

To Abraham's nomadic impulse toward separation and incapacity to love, Hegel opposes the Christian notion of a loving union between spirit and nature (equally anticipated, Hegel believes, by the Hellenic world). In love, "life has run through the circle of development from an immature to a completely mature unity." When the unity was immature, "there still stood over against it the world and the possibility of a cleavage between itself and the world" (305). As development proceeded, "reflection produced more and more oppositions (unified by satisfied impulses) until it set the whole of man's life in opposition" to objectivity. In the end, love completely destroys objectivity and "thereby annuls and transcends reflection, deprives man's opposite of all foreign character, and discovers life itself without any further defect. In love the separate does still remain, but as something united and no longer as something separate; life [in the subject] senses life [in the object]" (305).

It is clear, however, that Hegel still defines loving union in terms of power: "True union or love proper, exists only between living beings *who are alike in power and thus in one another's eyes living beings from every point of view; in no respect is either dead for the other.* This genuine love excludes all oppositions. It is not the understanding, whose relations always leave the manifold of related terms as a manifold and whose unity is always a unity of opposites [left as opposites]. It is not reason either, because reason sharply opposes its determining power to what is determined. Love neither restricts nor is restricted; it is not finite at all" (304; my emphasis). Although in the last three sentences of this citation Hegel gropes toward a nonagonistic definition of love, he still expresses the relationship between loving individuals in terms of a balance of equal forces. In his later work, moreover, he seems to drop this isonomic notion in favor of the Platonic and Neoplatonic idea of the One (Absolute Mind) subsuming the many.

Starting from these early theological concepts of multiplicity and unity, divisive conflict and unifying love, Hegel will also develop his phenomenology of mind/spirit *(Geist),* including his dialectic of master and slave, self and other, happy and unhappy consciousness. This phenomenology will in turn be taken over by Sartre, but without its theological antecedents. Consequently, Sartre's phenomenology of self and other is based on an irreconcilable conflict, unmitigated by religious love. In *Being and Nothingness*, for example, Sartre imagines "being-for-others" as an entirely agonistic state: "Everything which may be said of me in my relations with the Other applies to him as well. While I attempt to free myself from the hold of the Other, the Other is trying to free himself from mine; while I seek to enslave the Other, the Other seeks to enslave me. We are by no means dealing with unilateral relations with an object-in-itself, but with reciprocal and moving relations. The following descriptions of concrete behavior must therefore be envisaged within the perspective of *conflict*. Conflict is the original meaning of being-for-others."[18]

In the presence of others, being-for-itself experiences itself as an "object-to-be-looked-at." Through his "look" *(regard)*, the Other annihilates my world, by drawing me into his orbit and depriving me of my possibilities. Indeed, the Other appears as the "hidden death of my possibilities" [*la mort cachée de mes possibilités*] (p. 240). I can affirm my freedom only by dissociating myself from the Other, but this is impossible, for the existence of the Other is the only proof of my own existence. I can affirm myself only by transforming the Other into an object. Here one can see that although Sartre's vocabulary is largely Heideggerian (he uses terms such as being-in-itself, being-for-itself, and being-for-others), his phenomenological analyses remain nevertheless largely Hegelian.

The Hegelian background is equally evident in Sartre's self-styled existential psychoanalysis in which the relationship between self and other can be conceived only as a reciprocal, double negation: "The Other must appear to the *cogito* as *not being* me. This negation can be conceived in two ways: either it is a pure, external negation, and it will separate the Other from myself as one substance from another substance—and in this case all apprehension of the Other is by definition impossible; or else it will be an internal negation, which means a synthetic, active connection of the two terms, each one of which constitutes itself by denying that it is the other" (228). Dismissing the "pure, external negation" as logically impossible (ironically, it is precisely this type of negation that will be adopted by poststructuralist thought, including that of Lacan, Bakhtin, and Levinas, which I shall examine shortly), Sartre concentrates on the internal kind. The internal negation is reciprocal and can be described as a double interiority, which "means first that the multiplicity of 'Others' will not be a *collection* but a *totality* (in this sense we admit that Hegel is right) since each Other finds his being in the Other" (228). At the same time, however, as in Hegel, this totality "is such that it is in principle impossible for us to adopt 'the point of view of the whole.'" In other words, one is dealing with "a detotalized totality; for since existence-for-others is a radical refusal of the Other, no totalitarian and unifying synthesis of 'Others' is possible" (228).

For Sartre, the process of differentiation between self and other is a violent one, not least so because it is purely fictitious and arbitrary:

> Consciousness must freely disengage itself from the Other and wrench itself away by choosing itself as a nothingness which is simply Other than the Other and thereby must be reunited in 'itself'. . . . It is necessary that the Other be present to consciousness in every part and even that it penetrate consciousness completely in order that consciousness precisely by *being nothing* may escape that Other who threatens to ensnare it. If consciousness were abruptly to *be* something, the distinction between itself and the Other would disappear at the heart of a total undifferentiation. (259–60)

Because of the violent, arbitrary kind of difference that Sartre's existential psychoanalysis posits between self and other, it is both grounded in and oriented toward entirely negative psychic phenomena: "Fear (the feeling of being in danger before the Other's freedom), pride, or shame (the feeling of being finally what I am but elsewhere, over there for the Other), the recognition of my slavery (the feeling of the alienation of all my possibilities)" (244). For Sartre, love itself loses its Hegelian unifying power and appears as a "conflict" produced by the danger the Other poses for my "freedom" (342–43).

Sartre's existential psychoanalysis is questioned by its poststructuralist counterpart presumably because of its Hegelian roots, of which it can never free itself. For instance, Jacques Lacan, who develops his own notion of psychic void or nothingness notes that existential or pure negativity is equally perceived by "la philosophie contemporaine de l'être et du néant" [the contemporary philosophy of being and nothingness], an obvious allusion to Sartre.[19] According to Lacan, existential psychoanalysis accurately describes the various predicaments of subjectivity: "une liberté qui ne s'affirme jamais si authentique que dans les mures d'une prison, une exigence d'engagement où s'exprime l'impuissance de la pure conscience à surmonter aucune situation, une idéalisation voyeuriste-sadique du rapport sexuel, une personalité que ne se réalise que dans le suicide, une conscience de l'autre qui ne se satisfait que par le meurtre hegelien" [a freedom that is never more authentic than within prison walls, an exigency of engagement that expresses the inability of a pure conscience to surmount any situation, a sadistic-voyeuristic idealization of sexual intercourse, a personality that fulfills itself only through suicide, a consciousness of the other that is appeased only through Hegelian murder] (96). At the same time, however, Lacan argues that the philosophy of being and nothingness misconstrues the roots of the subject's predicaments because it still entertains the illusion of freedom through a conscious choice, of a self based on the Hegelian system of "perception-conscience" as organized by a "reality principle" posited by the rationalist scientific mentality.

Lacan contends, by contrast, that rationalist reality is as fictive as the unconscious Other that constantly creates and destroys it. If in a rationalistic psychology, the Other must always be subordinated and controlled, in poststructuralist psychoanalysis the Other becomes that which can never be dominated, contained, and disciplined. In Hegel, absolute mind (identity) and individual consciousness (alterity) can be reconciled through (happy) universal consciousness, which will eventually achieve the unity of all being(s). For Lacan, on the other hand, individual consciousness remains eternally heterogeneous and the subject, eternally disunited from an unconscious Other. Lacan thus rejects "the dialectic of the consciousness-of-self, as realized from Socrates to Hegel, from the ironic presupposition that all that is rational is real, to its culmination in the scientific view that all that is real is rational" (79). He argues that Freud was the first to "demonstrate that this verifying process authentically attains the subject only by decentering it from the consciousness-of-self, in the axis of which the Hegelian reconstruction of the phenomenology of spirit maintained it" (79–80).

Notwithstanding Lacan's criticism of Hegel and Sartre, he posits the emergence of the subject through a process of differentiation that is as violent and arbitrary as the one imagined by his predecessors. During this process, which Lacan calls the "mirror stage" *(le stade du miroir),* the (infant) self attempts to fashion an individual identity by separating itself from otherness and then seeking to reincorporate this otherness within the new fictional identity. This kind of reincorporation also inevitably involves repression, for whatever the subject cannot integrate, it expels and excludes, just as Socrates has done with the unruly social elements in his ideal republic. But Lacan, in the wake of Freud, points out that this strategy of creating an identity must ultimately fail and that, consequently, the subject becomes conditioned by an Other it can never master.

For Lacan, as for Freud, the real is a perpetual remainder or surplus *(reste)*, not least because it does not exist, or rather, because it exists only as "pure negativity." This Lacanian "radical other"—and here Lacan does depart from both Hegel and Sartre—eludes all assimilation or integration. Indeed, the radical other is that which eternally escapes the scrutiny of reason and is also known as the "unconscious." Moreover, it is the source of aggression and the death principle. As Lacan notes, Freudian psychoanalysis correctly invokes "des instincts de destruction voire de mort, pour expliquer la relation évidente de la libido narcissique à la fonction aliénante du *je*, à l'aggressivité qui s'en dégage dans toute relation à l'autre, fut-ce celle de l'aide la plus samaritaine. . . . Pour une telle oeuvre, le sentiment altruiste est sans promesses pour nous, qui perçons à jour l'aggressivité qui soustend l'action du philantrope, de l'idéaliste, du pédagogue, voire du réformateur" [destructive instincts, that is, the death instinct, to account for the obvious relation of the narcissistic libido to the alienating function of the *I*, to the aggressivity that arises from any relation to the other, be it that of the most Samaritan of aids. . . . In this kind of work, altruistic sentiment holds no promise for us who burst open the aggressivity that underpins the action of the philanthropist, idealist, educator, or reformer] (95–97).[20]

But Lacan does not wish any more than Sartre to go beyond an agonistic view of self and other, whether this Other is conceived as what Sartre calls an internal double negation through which consciousness violently differentiates itself from itself, or as the radical unconscious—what Sartre calls pure, external negation through which "all apprehension of the Other is by definition impossible." From the point of view of the present study, moreover, the Freudian and Lacanian "unconscious" designates the archaic mentality of might makes right mystified as interdicted, impossible, or unspeakable desire (the Nietzschean Will to

Power in its subjective, reactive form) that can only manifest itself indirectly, deviously, or neurotically through its simulacrum-like effects. It
is for this reason that Lacan sees the unconscious as an absence eternally present, a language structured in terms of signifiers and signified,
with the signifiers forever sliding in a ceaseless game of deferred signi-
fication, not unlike the Heideggerian ontological power game of
presencing and withdrawal, or the Derridean game of *différance*.

The same agonistic view of difference is present in those poststructuralist psychologists who proclaim the "death" or "disappearance"
of the subject and attempt to replace the Hegelian and Sartrean dialectic of self and other with a historical materialist view of contending individual and social "agencies."[21] Michel Foucault, for example, develops
(in the wake of Nietzsche) a notion of power as an engagement of active
forces, in which the Other is recognized only insofar as it is an opponent.
For Foucault, as for Nietzsche, power does not exist in a transcendental
form, but only in terms of power relations among (human) "actions" or
"agencies": "[S]omething called Power, with or without a capital letter,
which is assumed to exist universally in a concentrated or diffused form,
does not exist. Power exists only when it is put into action."[22] For
Foucault, moreover, a power relationship "can only be articulated on
the basis of two elements that are each indispensable if it is really to be
a power relationship: that the 'other' (the one over whom power is exercised) be thoroughly recognized and maintained to the very end as a
person who acts; and that, faced with a relationship of power, a whole
field of responses, reactions, results, and possible inventions may open
up" (220).

Seeking to separate his notion of power from both that of arbitrary
violence and that of a social contract, Foucault observes: "In itself the
exercise of power is not violence; nor is it a consent which is, implicitly,
renewable. It is a total structure of actions brought to bear upon possible actions; it incites, it induces, it seduces, it makes easier or more
difficult; in the extreme, it constrains or forbids absolutely; it is nevertheless always a way of acting upon an acting subject or acting subjects
by virtue of their acting or being capable of action. A set of actions upon
other actions" (220). Ultimately, Foucault, just like Nietzsche, sees power
in terms of a contest: "It would be better to speak of an 'agonism'—of a
relationship which is at the same time reciprocal incitation and struggle;

less of a face-to-face confrontation which paralyzes both sides than a permanent provocation" (222).

Power, then, is always a form of action that in some way restricts or limits another action. In this respect, power always depends on a positing of a real or an imaginary "other," i.e., it is mimetic in René Girard's sense. It is clear from Foucault's description that resistance, subversion, and opposition (whether peaceful or passive) are also forms of power rather than alternatives to it and can be neither instruments nor basic elements of an irenic mentality. Thus, even though Foucault starts from Nietzsche rather than from Hegel, his view of self and other leads to practical or *ethical* consequences similar to those deriving from Sartre's and Lacan's views.

Another aspect of the psychosexual problematic of difference is the contemporary notion of gender. Twentieth-century Western philosophers, psychologists, sociologists, and literary critics have amply documented the historical thesis that gender is less of a "biological given" than an evolving, culturally determined construct. What one can further emphasize is that the Western concept of gender is as endemically agonistic as the rest of our fundamental cultural presuppositions. More often than not, generic differences have functioned as instruments of domination or repression of various members of a certain community, including women and so-called sexual deviants. Socrates' attitude toward women, whom, as we have seen, he identifies with the inferior part of the soul (together with slaves, children, and the "base rabble" or the shiftless male citizens), has been shared by ancient and not-so-ancient communities alike. All too often, women have been seen by a patriarchal mentality as the unruly Other that must be overcome, controlled, and strictly regulated, or conversely, as the ineffable, unreachable Other that escapes all rational and imaginative grasp. This patriarchal view has been thoroughly examined and critiqued, especially in our century, and various theoretical alternatives have been suggested, including a new matriarchy based on the privileging of a so-called feminine mentality, supposedly less authoritarian than its masculine counterpart.

In contemporary American academia the main proponents of a new matriarchy are the various "power" schools of criticism, including those advocating feminist, gay, and lesbian power. With a few (but important) exceptions, they operate in terms of a conflictive dialectic of oppressor and victim (or master and slave) that ultimately boils down, just as in the case of other sociopolitical notions of difference, to an agonistic view of self and other. The traditional matriarchal view has recently been challenged within the feminist movement itself by a number of poststructuralist gender theorists, such as Monique Wittig, Luce Irigaray, Barbara Johnson, Jane Flax, Diana Fuss, Diane Elam, and Judith Butler.[23] For example, Butler argues against a feminist politics of identity that all too often becomes a mirror of its patriarchal counterpart: "The political assumption that there must be a universal basis for feminism, one which must be found in an identity assumed to exist cross-culturally, often accompanies the notion that the oppression of women has some singular form discernible in the universal or hegemonic structure of patriarchy or masculine domination. . . . The urgency of feminism to establish a universal status for patriarchy in order to strengthen the appearance of feminism's own claims to be representative has occasionally motivated the shortcut to a categorial or fictive universality of the structure of domination, held to produce women's common subjugated experience."[24]

Butler proposes to replace this totalizing feminist politics of identity with a localized, Foucauldian and Deleuzian version, in which identity is no longer understood as a sublation by the One, but as a series of unique singularities. Consequently, for Butler "the political task is not to refuse representational politics—as if we could. The juridical structures of language and politics constitute the contemporary field of power; hence, there is no position outside this field, but only a critical genealogy of its own legitimating practices. As such, the critical point of departure is *the historical present*, as Marx put it. And the task is to formulate within this constituted frame a critique of the categories of identity that contemporary juridical structures engender, naturalize, and immobilize" (5).

The subtitle of Butler's book—"Feminism and the Subversion of Identity"—already suggests the strategy that she proposes: undermining the rationalist notion of identity through a poststructuralist notion of sexual difference as contending agencies. In the wake of French feminists such as Monique Wittig, Butler sees lesbian feminism as potentially subverting the dichotomy between male and female as well as that between heterosexual and homosexual. All humans should be encouraged to simulate or enact parodically various sexual roles; in this

way, unconventional sexuality becomes a political instrument in opposing not only gender domination but also a "phallogocentric" metaphysics of presence.

Although Butler goes beyond the traditional feminist-lesbian notion
of identity, thus pointing out the interchangeability of sexual roles in a
mentality of power, she does not renounce this mentality, but endorses
subversive tactics (of course, these tactics will always reproduce that
which they claim to destroy). She even criticizes Wittig's ultimate goal
of transcending all power structures, arguing in Foucauldian fashion that
"power can be neither withdrawn nor refused, but only redeployed"
(124). Consequently, for Butler, "the normative focus for gay and lesbian practice ought to be on the subversive and parodic redeployment
of power rather than on the impossible fantasy of its full-scale transcendence" (124). She thus inscribes herself in what has recently been called
"queer theory," a feminist, gay, and lesbian version of the Nietzschean-
Deleuzian postmodern notion of the simulacrum. As Michael Warner
points out, queer theorists are at ease with the idea that "queerness is
necessarily an effect of representation" and that, moreover, sexual fantasy, performance, display, and other representations "are inherently
uncontrollable, queer by nature." According to Warner, this emphasis
on "messy representation" enables "queer theory, like nonacademic
queer activism, to be both antiassimilationist and antiseparatist."[25]

Warner himself, however, reverts to a conventional form of activism
(neo-Marxist social struggle), without entertaining the possibility, any
more than Butler does, of genuine alternatives to a mentality of power.
To bring about significant transformations within the individual and the
community, we should indeed have the intellectual and emotional courage to "fantasize," as Wittig does, about moving away from such a mentality, for most, if not all, genuine change occurs in and through the
imagination. One should also have the courage to fantasize about turning away from any form of "resistance." As we have seen in Foucault's
definition of power, force cannot manifest itself without resistance; it
follows that moving away from a mentality of power means moving away
from both the notion of force and that of resistance. Together, these
notions conspire in creating conflictive difference, including the dichotomy between male and female, heterosexual and homosexual, and
more generally, between self and other. Going beyond both force and

resistance does not mean giving up politics as such, but simply found-ing it on an alternative mode of thought, behavior, and pathos that is incommensurable with a mentality of power.

From a ludic-irenic perspective, one should finally turn away from the traditional dichotomy of victim and victimizer that remains opera-tive not only in much feminist theory but also in its neo-Marxist and postcolonial counterparts, which equally assume that the perspective of the social, ethnic, or racial victim is more humanizing than that of the oppressor. It is not the case, as Monique Wittig and other historical ma-terialists believe, that "once the class 'men' [or exploiters in general] disappears 'women' [or exploitees in general] as a class will disappear as well, for there are no slaves without masters."[26] Wittig's proposition that there are no slaves without masters can once more be turned around in the original Hegelian proposition that there are no masters without slaves. As Hegel has shown, the dialectic of master and slave is all too easily reversible, the mentality of the victimizer going hand in hand with that of the victim.

The example of the various failed communist utopias in Eastern Europe and other parts of the world has clearly revealed that once a dispossessed social group gains the upper hand, it tends to imitate the ethopathology of its former oppressors. The recent demise of interna-tional communism has not led to wiser and kinder human communities but to separatist, nationalistic movements thriving on ethnic conflict in which the former victims become in turn victimizers. Likewise, in con-temporary American culture, a philosophy of conflictive difference (whether Marxian or Nietzschean) has led to bitter social and racial divisions, where special interest groups feud among themselves for po-litical "rights," often ignoring communal responsibilities. Finally, in American academia, many Marxist, postcolonial, feminist, and other his-torical-materialist proponents have revealed their dogmatic tendencies, creating a new orthodoxy popularly known as "political correctness." Some of them have also promptly converted this new orthodoxy into an opportunistic tool of building successful careers for themselves within the traditional academic establishment, thus perpetuating the very power structures they claim to resist.

Although I sympathize with Wittig's proposition of going beyond a mentality of power, I do not believe that any particular social "class" or, for that matter, minority or majority group (one should ultimately give up such dehumanizing political abstractions in favor of genuine human individuality in Oscar Wilde's sense)[27] can occupy a privileged or unique position that would enable them to effect radical transformations in our ethopathology. It seems to me that if such transformations are truly desired, they will eventually occur within each individual as well as through the self-initiated, concerted effort of all the members of a specific community. Meanwhile, one can consider alternative models of difference that might help these transformations along when they are ready to occur.

3. Irenic Models of Difference

Among the many available irenic models of difference, here I should like to discuss two kinds: the ones that are to some extent still embedded in a mentality of power (seeking to change its weighting principle from within) and the ones that turn away from this mentality altogether. Contemporary examples of the first kind include Mikhail Bakhtin's dialogic principle and Emmanuel Levinas's phenomenology of radical alterity. Examples of the second kind include various (nonlogocentric) Buddhist schools of thought in general and Zen Buddhism in particular. Although it will become apparent in the course of this discussion that I favor the second kind over the first (which is simply a question of temperament), all of these models are highly valuable for an irenic mentality, and there is no significant conflict or incompatibility among them. They are different ways of seeking the same difficult ethical objective: what Levinas calls "primordial peace."

At first sight it seems paradoxical to claim that Bakhtin's dialogic principle can be irenic in any sense, given Bakhtin's well-known notions of antagonistic centrifugal and centripetal cultural forces, subversive carnivalesque play, heteroglossia, and so forth. Indeed, Bakhtin, no less than other Marxian or Nietzschean thinkers in general, conceives of cultural and cosmic existence as a struggle between various individual and collective forces. In "Discourse in the Novel," for example, Bakhtin draws a distinction between the centripetal and the centrifugal forces of language that reflect a more general social dynamic remarkably similar to Bataille's non-Hegelian dialectic of heterogeneity and homogeneity:

"Alongside the centripetal forces, the centrifugal forces of language carry on their uninterrupted work; alongside verbal-ideological centralization and unification, the uninterrupted processes of decentralization and disunification go forward."[28] As one of Bakhtin's English translators notes, for Bakhtin (as for Bataille) this "almost Manichean" or "Zoroastrian clash" manifests itself "in culture as well as nature, and in the specificity of individual consciousness; it is at work in the even greater particularity of individual utterances. The most complete and complex reflection of these forces is found in human language, and the best transcription of language so understood is the novel"[29] Indeed, for Bakhtin the novel—and, by extension, fiction in general—is the privileged locus where the agon between centrifugal and centripetal forces is being staged. But what distinguishes Bakhtin from Bataille and other Nietzschean thinkers, is his dialogic notion of otherness, which again shows its clearest manifestation in the novel and which may, in a revised form, go beyond Bakhtin's dynamic of centripetal and centrifugal forces.

For Bakhtin, dialogic alterity begins already within the individual word. A word is "born in a dialogue as a living rejoinder within it; the word is shaped in a dialogic interaction with an alien word that is already in the object. . . . But this does not exhaust the internal dialogism of the word. It encounters an alien word not only in the object itself: every word is directed toward an *answer* and cannot escape the profound influence of the answering word that it anticipates."[30] Starting from the notion of the word as dialogic interplay, Bakhtin develops a seminal distinction between "authoritative discourse" and "internally persuasive discourse." In its authoritative form, the discourse of the other "demands our unconditional allegiance" and, therefore, it is monological rather than dialogical. It "permits no play with the context framing [the word], no play with its borders, no gradual and flexible transitions" (343). In the context of authoritative discourse, the word "enters our verbal consciousness as a compact and indivisible mass; one must either totally affirm it or totally reject it. It is indissolubly fused with its authority—with political power, an institution, a person—and it stands and falls together with that authority" (343).

By contrast, in internally persuasive discourse the word of the other preserves its open and flexible character. Although internally persuasive discourse may at times coincide with authoritative discourse, it is most often at odds with it and, therefore, is dialogical. As opposed to the authoritative kind, internally persuasive discourse consists of the other's word tightly interwoven with one's own. Its creativity consists in the fact that through it someone else's word "awakens new and independent words, [. . .] organizes masses of our words from within, and does not remain in a static and isolated condition. It is not so much interpreted by us as it is further, that is, freely developed, applied to new material, new conditions; it enters into interanimating relationships with new contexts" (345–46).

Bakhtin often tends to describe internally persuasive discourse in agonistic terms as well. He states, for example, that in the context of an internally persuasive discourse language enters "into an intense interaction, a *struggle* with other internally persuasive discourses." According to him, our "ideological development is just such an intense struggle within us for hegemony among various available verbal and ideological points of view, approaches, directions, and values" (346). More generally, however, Bakhtin points out that the semantic structure of an internally persuasive discourse is never "*finite*, it is *open*; in each of the new contexts that dialogize it, this discourse is able to reveal ever newer *ways to mean*" (346). One can therefore retain and develop precisely this idea of dialogic openness, beyond Bakhtin's agonistic terminology that inevitably echoes the fashionable revolutionary jargon of his age.

In fact, Bakhtin himself occasionally attempts to emphasize the open character of the language of the other in a nonagonistic sense. In this regard, his notion of dialogism can ultimately be seen as a failed but important attempt to replace the "Manichean sense of opposition and struggle at the heart of existence" (Holquist's essentialist phrase) with what Bakhtin calls a "creative" or "responsive understanding." This creative or responsive understanding posits the other not in hermeneutical fashion, as translatable or reducible in terms of an identical self, but as "exotopic," that is, situated outside all integration and sublation and, consequently, also outside all struggle. Here, in a sense, one is dealing with the "external negation" judged impossible by Sartre and interpreted negatively by Lacan; Bakhtin, however, tends to interpret it in a non-Lacanian, affirmative manner. For example, in his book on Dostoevsky, Bakhtin notes that Dostoevsky seeks "[n]o fusion with the other but the preservation of his *exotopic* position and of his *excess* of vision and comprehension, that is its correlative."[31] The point for Bakhtin is that Dostoevsky uses this excess not "for objectivation of completion," as Sartre's or Lacan's subject might do, but for "watchful listening" and "active understanding" that "does not reduplicate" but carefully and lovingly preserves the integrity of the other.

It is this active, creative or responsive understanding that Bakhtin calls "dialogical" and attributes, significantly, to literary discourse in contrast to the monological understanding of other types of discourse, including the scientific and the political. Bakhtin ultimately turns away from monologism because it "denies that there exists outside of it another consciousness with the same rights, and capable of responding on an equal footing, another and equal *I (thou)*. For a monologic outlook (in its extreme or pure form) the *other* remains entirely and only an *object* of consciousness, and cannot constitute another consciousness. No response capable of altering everything in the world of my consciousness is expected of this other. The monologue is accomplished and deaf to the other's response; it does not await it and does not grant it any *decisive* force" (107).

The last sentence of the foregoing citation also makes it clear, however, that Bakhtin remains within an agonistic mentality, even as he is trying to find his way out of it. He still thinks of the other, as young Hegel did, in isonomic terms, as a "decisive force" to be respected and reckoned with. His idea of dialogue does not quite transcend the power-oriented, hermeneutical format of question and answer, even as he proclaims the asymmetry between the two.[32] This monological relapse becomes evident in Bakhtin's theory of a "superreceiver." According to him, every dialogue takes place "against the backdrop of the responsive understanding of a present but invisible third entity, hovering above all the participants in the dialogue." Historically, this super-receiver has been variously known as "God, the absolute truth, the fragment, impartial human conscience, the people, the judgment of history, science, etc."[33] Bakhtin argues that the superreceiver should, however, not be regarded as "a mystical or metaphysical entity," despite the fact that some worldviews do accord it such status. Rather, it should be seen as a "constitutive moment of the whole utterance." Thus, the superreceiver "proceeds from the nature of discourse, that always wants to be heard, that always is in search of responsive understanding, and does not stop at *the most proximate* understanding but makes its way further and further away (without limits). For discourse (and, therefore, for man) nothing is more frightening than the *absence of answer*" (111).

From the perspective of a ludic-irenic mentality, one can certainly regard responsive understanding as having an exotopic component, but one needs to revise Bakhtin's theory of the human motivation that lies behind addressing such a component. This theory (according to which mankind's restless search for otherness is motivated by an essential absence or lack inherent in human nature) is reminiscent of Arnold Gehlen's and Helmuth Plessner's anthropologies and comes back full circle to Nietzsche's idea of nothingness as that which is most frightening to the Will to Power. Even though Bakhtin longs for the primordial peace that can manifest itself through dialogue as a form of responsive understanding, he does not quite go beyond a mentality of power, because he shies away from the psychological barrier of nothingness, which is also the psychological barrier of death. In Bakhtin the radical other is not yet completely emancipated from the objectivation or reduplication of the self, hence it must still be sought after and conceptualized by this self, e.g., as superreceiver. It is precisely the complete emancipation of the radical other—understood in a non-Lacanian, irenic sense—from the self that is the project of another East European thinker, the Jewish Lithuanian Emmanuel Levinas.

Whereas Bakhtin's dialogical perspective largely directs itself, as in Sartre and Lacan, from the self toward the other, Levinas's perspective reverses this direction. For example, in one of his major works, *Totalité et infini: Essai sur l'extériorité* (1961), Levinas attempts both a critique of the Western notions of identity and difference and a retrieval (in a Heideggerian sense) of these notions from the standpoint of an irenic mentality. For him, the fundamental question of philosophy is not Being (whether in its Platonic or in its Heideggerian version), but the irreducible and asymmetrical relationship between the same *(le même)* and the other *(l'autre)*. For Levinas the same is synonymous with identity, understood in Hegelian fashion as the reduction of otherness to an all-encompassing totality (thus, the *totalité* in the title of Levinas's book is interchangeable with *le même*). *L'autre*, on the other hand, is understood as radical difference (the *infini* of the book's title) that exceeds identity, but neither in the pre-Socratic nor in the Nietzschean sense of a ceaseless play of physical forces. For Levinas, radical difference is an irreducible, infinite exteriority, which, although it can neither be opposed to nor be sublated by a subjective interiority, nevertheless impinges upon the latter as the visage *(le visage)* and generates an asymmetrical relationship of face-to-face *(le face-à-face)*.

In the inescapable immediacy of the *face-à-face*, the experience of the other is overwhelming and nonrepresentable; although it may arouse violent reactions in the ego, this violence is not immanent but comes from the ego's own totalizing tendencies (or Will to Power). The other is infinitely superior to me, so that I cannot engage it in any kind of mimetic relationship, whether representational or rivalrous: "La vrai essence de l'homme se présente dans son visage où il est infiniment autre qu'une violence à la mienne pareille, à la mienne opposée et hostile et déjà aux prises avec la mienne dans un monde historique où nous participons au même système. Il arrête et paralyse ma violence par son appel qui ne fait pas violence et qui vient de haut. La verité de l'être n'est pas l'*image* de l'être, l'*idée* de sa nature, mais l'être situé dans un champ subjectif qui *déforme* la vision, mais permet précisément ainsi à l'extériorité de se dire, tout entière comandement et autorité: toute entière supériorité" [The true essence of man comes forth in his face, where he is infinitely other than a violence kindred to mine, opposed and hostile to mine, and already caught with it in a historical world where we participate in the same system. He arrests and paralyzes my violence through his appeal that does no violence and comes from high above. The truth of being is not the *image* of being, the *idea* of its nature, but the being situated on a subjective plane that *deforms* vision and, precisely because of that, allows exteriority to express itself, wholly commandment and authority: wholly superiority].[34]

Levinas's notions of *regard* and *visage*, then, are quite different from their Sartrean counterparts. Whereas for Sartre, the "look" (or "gaze") and the "visage" reveal an essentially agonistic and symmetrical relationship between self and other, in which the other is the hidden death of my possibilities, for Levinas they reveal an asymmetrical relationship of infinite superiority, in which the other is the absolute guarantor of my possibilities. In both cases I am dependent on the other, but in the first case I engage the other (mimetically), while in the second case the other engages me (nonmimetically). In Sartre, the other turns out to be an alienated side of my self; in Levinas, the other is radically different (as in the case of Lacan and other poststructuralists), forcing me to search It perpetually. But in Levinas this search is expressly nonagonistic, because the other directs the self toward an originary peace and primordial Goodness. The other is ultimately a divine, an-archic imperative that overwhelms humans with its ethical exigencies, issues irresistible commands such as "thou shalt not kill" and thereby reveals the infinitely irenic, primordial nature of being as exteriority.

According to Levinas, "l'Autre n'est pas la négation du Même comme le voudrait Hegel. Le fait fondamental de la scission ontologique en Même et en Autre est un rapport non allergique du Même avec l'Autre" [the Other is not the negation of the Same as Hegel believed. The fundamental fact of the ontological split between Same and Other is a nonallergic relation of the Same with the Other] (282). The subject constitutes itself as a host *(hôte)* for the other, its relationship with the Other being one of hospitality and service (276). For Levinas, therefore, being can never signify anything else but being for the other *(être pour autrui)* (281). This being for the other, however, is not the manifestation of an essential absence or lack in human nature (as in Bakhtin, Gehlen, Plessner, and others), but, on the contrary, a manifestation of exotopic fullness, to use Bakhtin's phrase. The self or subjectivity is the Other's field of play, within which the Other constantly produces itself.

It is also along these lines, Levinas suggests, that one must emancipate the idea of the infinite from that of totality. The infinite is not a totality reflected or reproduced in the subject. Unlike Hegelian totality, "l'infini se produit dans la relation du Même avec l'Autre" [the infinite produces itself in the relation of the Same with the Other] in the sense that "le particulier et le personnel magnétisent en quelque façon le champ même où cette production de l'infini se joue" [the particular and the personal somehow magnetize the very field within which this production of the infinite plays itself out] (xv). The infinite, then, is not the absolute infinity of the romantics or of the ontotheological tradition in general, but the Heideggerian Being stripped of its agonistic implications. One recalls that in Heidegger Being also takes *Dasein* for its playfield, but its game with *Dasein* is one of presencing and withdrawal and, consequently, is a violent one. It is largely for this reason that Levinas, in his other major work, *Autrement qu'être; ou Au-delà de l'essence* (1974), attempts to go beyond Heidegger's ontological vocabulary, envisioning infinitude as primordial peace and goodness—a nonontological and nontheological retrieval of the Platonic and Cartesian ideas of infinity.

Levinas also attempts to retrieve the traditional notion of the one and the many in irenic terms. For him the One is not a preexisting totality in the Eleatic and the Hegelian sense but, again, an irenic, infinite goodness that produces itself as pluralism: "Le pluralisme de l'être ne se produit pas comme une multiplicité d'une constellation etalée devant un regard possible, car ainsi déjà, elle se totaliserait, se ressoudrait en entité. Le pluralisme s'accomplit dans la bonté allant de moi à l'autre ou l'autre, comme absolument autre, peut seulement se produire sans qu'une prétendue vue latérale sur ce mouvement ait un quelconque droit d'en saisir une verité supérieure à celle qui se produit dans la bonté même" [The pluralism of being does not produce itself as a multiplicity of a constellation displayed before a possible gaze, because as such it would already become totalized or resolved into an entity. Pluralism fulfills itself in goodness proceeding from me to the other, where the other, as absolutely other, can produce itself on condition that no pretended lateral view of this movement have any right to seize a truth superior to the one produced in goodness itself] (282). This pluralism is an inherent unity, but a unity resulting from neither the temporary alliance of various contending forces, as in Nietzsche, nor the totalizing tendencies of a superior force, as in the ontotheological tradition in general. On the contrary, it is a unity derived from primordial peace (282). Since primordial peace, rather than war, is what constitutes the subject (or the many), it comes from both inside the self, as the irresistible aspiration toward goodness, and outside the self, as the ethical judgment of infinite truth (283).

Levinas's notion of radical otherness is very promising for an irenic mentality, but it also reveals the difficulty of developing an irenic philosophical vocabulary within the dominant Western philosophical tradition based on a mentality of power. Levinas wishes to revise this tradition by dislocating it from within. From the perspective of the present study, he attempts to retrieve the Jewish and the Christian ontotheological tradition by changing its weighting principle or frame of reference from primordial power to originary peace. This project, Levinas claims, is already operative in the biblical prophets of both the Old and the New

Testament, who oppose the warlike mentality of the kings by rejecting politics in favor of an ethics based on messianic peace. This peace is not the dialectical opposite of war but antedates war as a primordial relation with the Other: "La conscience morale ne peut supporter le regard railleur du politique que si la certitude de la paix domine l'évidence de la guerre. Une telle certitude ne s'obtient pas par simple jeu d'antithèses. La paix des empires sortis de la guerre repose sur la guerre. Elle ne rend pas aux êtres aliénés leur identité perdue. Il y faut une relation originelle et originale avec l'être" [The moral conscience/consciousness cannot bear the mocking gaze of the political unless the certainty of peace prevails over the evidence of war. Such certainty cannot be obtained by a mere play of antitheses. The peace of empires issued from war rests on war. This kind of peace cannot restore to alienated beings their lost identity. For that one needs an originary and original relation with being] (x). Levinas rightly points out that in the absence of an originary relation between peace and being, Western history has been a ceaseless alternation of war and peace, with peace being simply an instrument of war.

From an eschatological viewpoint, historical peace is a hypocritical lie expressed, for example, in the Roman adage, "If you wish peace, prepare yourself for war," or in the modern politics of nuclear containment. For Levinas, as for the eschatological tradition, peace exceeds history in both directions, which also means that the end of history is the beginning of peace. But, one may ask, what is the most effective way of reaching this originary peace? Should one bring about the end of history from within history, or should one gradually turn away from this history altogether? Both the eschatological tradition and Levinas choose the first path. In this respect, Levinas's project entails a monumental process of retrieval or reinterpretation of Western philosophy from Plato to Descartes to Heidegger in terms of primordial peace. Such a project is undoubtedly crucial for those who cannot envision working outside the Western tradition, although it will probably yield results as ambiguous as those of irenic messianism. It is painfully obvious, for example, that although Christ proclaimed a "new kingdom" on earth long ago, many of the churches built in his name have managed to place this kingdom beyond the reach of the living, thereby not only postponing it indefinitely but also using it in justifying the status quo—a typical example of how a mentality of power will co-opt whatever can serve its purposes.

In turn, Levinas's philosophical vocabulary can be easily retrieved (misinterpreted and co-opted) by a power-oriented mentality. For example, his notion of the infinite Other can easily assume the function of the Platonic One because it is *hors concours*, rendering all contest futile. It also bears a strong resemblance to the Hebrew God of the highest Heights *(le Plus Haut),* imageless and nonrepresentable, yet tormenting his people with his fiercely jealous love. Any attempt at retrieving such figures of power will simply perpetuate the mentality it means to bypass—a fact that Levinas himself is well aware of, for example when he seeks to develop a distinction between the "saying" *(le dire)* and the "said" *(le dit)*.[35] He attempts to translate an incommensurable notion (peace) into traditional philosophical language and therefore partakes of the historical "hypocritical" dualism that he ascribes to that language. His is a dilemma inherent in any hermeneutic project and shared by all of us: if one does not translate one's innovative thought into a familiar language, one will remain incomprehensible, but if one does translate it, one will remain misunderstood.[36]

One can also go outside the Western philosophical tradition and attempt to develop a vocabulary (as well as an ethopathology) that perhaps has less of a chance of being misunderstood, i.e., co-opted by a mentality of power. In this respect, the insights of several Buddhist schools of thought may prove fruitful. It is not so much a question of adopting, say, a Zen Buddhist vocabulary (or ethopathology), as to determine to what extent certain Eastern ways of thinking are addressing ethical and ontoepistemological issues that approximate our own and to what extent they can facilitate reformulating or resolving these issues in our own terms. Of the many relevant Buddhist schools, I have chosen Zen Buddhism not only because I have the most affinities with this school but also because it directly addresses some of the questions that interest us here. For example, the ninth-century Ch'an (Zen) master Huang Po left through his disciples a teaching of the "One Mind" *(hsin)* that is highly relevant in the present context.

Huang Po, like all other Zen masters, identifies the notion of difference in all its aspects (such as the question of one and the many, unity and multiplicity, totality and individuality, self and other, etc.) as the central problem to be dealt with in Zen Buddhist thought-practice. For instance, Huang Po regards what he calls the "differential perception" of the individual ego as the main stumbling block in achieving "Enlightenment" or the Buddha state. Differential perception leads to conceptual dualism, and the first task of the Zen practitioner is to get past this dualism. Huang Po is fully aware that conceptual dualism is endemic to all language, so he dismantles traditional religious terminology in a thoroughly deconstructive fashion. As he instructs his disciples, "You must use that wisdom that comes from non-dualism to destroy your concept-forming, dualistic mentality."[37] But unlike modern Western deconstruction, Huang Po does not merely subvert a logocentric or rationalist philosophical tradition. His teaching, moreover, is neither a philosophical nor even a religious doctrine (in the Western sense), but a psychophysiological practice or "ethics" that goes beyond both Being and Becoming, self and other, and identity and difference, as well as beyond the notion of power itself.

The main verbal symbol that Huang Po uses is the "One Mind" *(hsin)* or the "Absolute" (the Sanskrit *Bhutatathata*), which, however, he also calls "the Great Void" in order to prevent either a substantialist or an eternalist (mis)understanding of the term: "So let your symbolic conception be that of a void, for then the wordless teaching of Zen will make itself apparent to you. Know only that you must decide to eschew all symbolizing whatever, for by this eschewal is 'symbolized' the Great Void in which there is neither unity nor multiplicity—that void which is not really void, that symbol which is no symbol. Then will the Buddhas of all the vast world-systems manifest themselves to you in a flash; you will recognize the hosts of squirming, wriggling sentient beings as no more than shadows. . . . To you, the profoundest doctrines ever heard will seem but dreams and illusions. You will recognize all minds as One and behold all things as one—including those thousands of sacred books and myriads of pious commentaries! All of them are just your One Mind."[38]

One should perhaps caution the Western reader that the Great Void or Nothingness should not be confused with the Hegelian or Sartrian concept of nothingness, nor with that of certain schools of negative theology; these Western concepts ultimately remain within a dualistic mentality because they implicate nothingness or the void in some kind of (synthesizing or nonsynthesizing) dialectic of being and nonbeing or, in the case of some (but not all) schools of negative theology, in a divine

dynamic of light and darkness.[39] Significantly, Huang Po points out—
for the Zen practitioner of his own time—the dangers of distinguishing
between the Absolute as Nirvana and the sentient world as samsara, a
distinction made, for example, by the Hinayana school of Buddhism:

> People become involved in the duality of longing for 'light' and es-
> chewing 'darkness'. In their anxiety to SEEK Enlightenment on the
> one hand and to ESCAPE from the passions on the other, they con-
> ceive of an Enlightened Buddha and unenlightened sentient beings
> as separate entities. . . . Let me assure you again that the Buddha
> dwells not in light, nor sentient beings in darkness, for the Truth al-
> lows no such distinctions. The Buddha is not mighty, nor sentient
> beings feeble, for the Truth allows no such distinctions. The Buddha
> is not Enlightened, nor sentient beings ignorant, for the Truth allows
> no such distinctions. (105–6)

The Hinayana Buddhists, much like some ascetic Christian mystics,
remain trapped in dualism because they seek to renounce their samsaric
life (the realm of illusion) in order to attain Nirvana (the realm of the
Buddha-nature), not realizing that these two realms are just another binary opposition that must be transcended. In this sense, Huang Po effectively preempts Nietzsche's contention that Zen Buddhism is only
another expression of the ascetic ideal (see chapter 1 of the present
study) or a form of nihilism.[40]

Huang Po points out other dualistic fallacies of his time to be avoided
by the Zen Buddhist practitioner: "A student of the Way, by allowing
himself a single samsaric thought, falls among devils. If he permits himself a single thought leading to differential perception he falls into her-
esy. To hold that there is something born and try to eliminate it, that is
to fall among the Sravakas [Hinayanists]. To hold that things are not
born but capable of destruction is to fall among the Pratyekas. Nothing
is born, nothing is destroyed. Away with your dualism, your likes and
dislikes. Every single thing is just the One Mind" (44). The Zen practitioner should equally avoid thinking in terms of being and non-being—
another expression of a dualistic mentality: "If you wish to experience
Enlightenment yourselves, you must not indulge in such [dualistic] conceptions. They are all environmental Dharmas concerning things which

are and things which are not, based on existence and non-existence. If only you will avoid concepts of existence and non-existence in regard to absolutely everything, you will then perceive *THE DHARMA*" (43).

One should also avoid thinking of the One Mind or the Dharma in terms of a more or less refined substance that can be "perceived" or "grasped." According to Huang Po, Gautama Buddha refuted "the notions that Enlightenment will lead to the perception of a universal substance, composed of particles which some hold to be gross and others subtle" (105). From a Western perspective, Gautama Buddha refuted both the materialist and the idealist concepts of energy as they are understood not only in Buddhist but also in Western thought, for example in the so-called New Physics. For Huang Po, the One Mind is not some kind of matter, be it only "mind-stuff" or "energy," because it lacks any internal and external attributes. Nor should the One Mind be seen in idealist fashion as indestructible essence, eternal consciousness, or reconciling-unifying divine totality.

According to Huang Po, the Buddha-nature is both mind and matter, permanence and impermanence, unity and multiplicity, as well as neither. "Emptiness" is what best describes it from a logical standpoint, although it is the nature of logic to attempt to conceptualize and rationalize such descriptions as well. In this regard, Huang Po points out that it is relatively simple to detach oneself from the sentient world or one's physical habits, but very difficult to detach oneself from one's spiritual ideals or mind habits: "Ordinary people look to their surroundings, while followers of the Way look to Mind, but the true Dharma is to forget them both. The former is easy enough, the latter very difficult. Men are afraid to forget their minds, fearing to fall through the Void with nothing to stay their fall. They do not know that the Void is not really void, but the realm of the real Dharma" (41). In turn, the logical mind can describe the Dharma or the Buddha-nature only in a paradoxical way: It is "without beginning, as ancient as the Void, subject neither to birth nor to destruction, neither existing nor not existing, neither impure nor pure, neither clamorous nor silent, neither old nor young, occupying no space, having neither inside nor outside, size nor form, colour nor sound. It cannot be looked for or sought, comprehended by wisdom or knowledge, explained in words, contacted materially or reached by meritorious achievement. All the Buddhas and Bodhisattvas, together with all wriggling things possessed of life, share in this great Nirvanic nature" (41–42).

From the perspective of emptiness, it is pointless not only to privilege the mind over the sentient world or vice versa, but also to affirm or deny their reality, for Dharma as the Great Void can only be experienced, not conceptualized: "Whatever Mind is, so also are phenomena—both are equally real and partake equally of the Dharma-Nature which hangs in the void. He who receives an intuition of this truth has become a Buddha and attained to the Dharma. Let me repeat that Enlightenment cannot be bodily grasped (*attained*, *perceived*, etc.), for the body is formless; nor mentally grasped (etc.), for the mind is formless; nor grasped (etc.), through its essential nature, since that nature is the Original Source of all things. . . . How can you use the Buddha to grasp the Buddha, formlessness to grasp formlessness, mind to grasp mind, void to grasp void, the Way to grasp the Way? In reality, there Is nothing to be grasped (*perceived*, *attained*, *conceived*, etc.)—even not-grasping cannot be grasped" (111).

Huang Po neatly summarizes what he sees as the basic principles of Zen practice in terms of his (non)doctrine of One Mind understood as Void:

> If an ordinary man, when he is about to die, could only see the five elements of consciousness as void; the four physical elements as not constituting an "I"; the real Mind as formless and neither coming nor going; his nature as something neither commencing at his birth nor perishing at his death, but as whole and motionless in its very depths; his Mind and environmental objects as one—if he could really accomplish this, he would receive Enlightenment in a flash. He would no longer be entangled by the Triple World; he would be a World-Transcender. He would be without the faintest tendency towards rebirth. If he should behold the glorious sight of all the Buddhas coming to welcome him, surrounded by every kind of gorgeous manifestation, he would feel no desire to approach them. If he should behold all sorts of horrific forms surrounding him, he would experience no terror. He would just be himself, oblivious of conceptual thought and one with the Absolute. He would have attained the state of unconditioned being. (46)

It becomes clear, then, that for Huang Po, as for other Zen Buddhists, there is no speculative way of attaining the Dharma nor is there any one prescribed practice or "tried and true" path leading to it. It is not that Huang Po does not approve of the six Buddhist *paramitas* or virtues such as charity, righteousness, patience under affliction, industrious application, discipline of mind, and practice of the highest wisdom. These have a crucial place in the life of a community, but they cannot lead to Enlightenment any more than any other purposeful activity: "As to performing the six paramitas and vast number of similar practices, or gaining merits as countless as the sands of the Ganges, since you are fundamentally complete in every respect, you should not try to supplement that perfection with meaningless practices. When there is occasion for them, perform them; and, when the occasion is past, remain quiescent. If you are not absolutely convinced that the Mind is the Buddha, and if you are attached to forms, practices, and meritorious performances, your way of thinking is false and quite incompatible with the Way" (30). Nor can "Enlightenment" be attained through any successive stages or through progressive spiritual growth: "To practise the six paramitas and a myriad similar practices with the intention of becoming a Buddha thereby is to advance by stages, but the Ever-Existent Buddha is not a Buddha of stages. Only awake to the One Mind, and there is nothing whatsoever to be attained. This is the REAL Buddha" (30).

Even though there is no single merit-related path nor any gradual process nor any best method in attaining the Dharma (which does not mean, however, that each practitioner cannot attain it in his or her own way), the Zen practitioner can experience three discontinuous physical-mental states, which Huang Po does not distinguish as such but to which he implicitly refers. During the first state, the Zen practitioner perceives trees, mountains, rivers, clouds, and so forth as distinct from each other; during the second state, s/he perceives them as nondistinct; and during the third, "enlightened" state, as both distinct and nondistinct. The first state is the one most of us are familiar with and wherein we operate on the basis of differential perception, which in turn gives rise to conceptual dualism. This is the normal or "natural" state of the ego, which develops, through conceptualization, an opposition between self and other, unity and multiplicity, female and male, friend and enemy, and so on. In Western terms, this can also be seen as the state of the Will to Power in its subjective guise, as manifested in the onto-theological tradition.

In the second state, the Zen practitioner switches from an ego-related differential perception to a (still ego-related) experience of undifferentiation. In this state, mountains, trees, clouds, and so forth no longer appear as separate but as oneness, even though this oneness is perceived by the ego in negative terms, as nothingness or emptiness. As we have seen, Huang Po describes the second state in some detail, because this is the state that most intellectual Zen practitioners find themselves locked into. As Huang Po remarks (uncannily echoing Nietzsche's observation at the end of the *Genealogy of Morals*) the ego—or in Nietzsche's terms, the subjective Will—feels threatened by the void, that is, by egolessness and cannot let go of conceptual thought, which is its best weapon, even if it now regards it in negative terms. The state of (quasi) egolessness can often be emotionally devastating and approximates, in Western terms, what Nietzsche calls "nihilism" and Paul de Man calls "deconstruction." Confronted with this crisis, the Will can attempt to "joyfully forget itself," as Nietzsche puts it, that is, to objectify itself either by going back and affirming Being as permanence (e.g., in Plato, Kant, and Hegel) or by going even further back and affirming Becoming as impermanence or ceaseless play of forces (e.g., in Nietzsche, Bataille, Deleuze, Foucault, and other so-called poststructuralists). There is, however, no genuine turning back for those who have switched into the second state (the three physical-mental states described by Zen practitioners are discontinuous), so the ego enters a perpetually dissatisfied, split condition that plunges it into an existential vertigo and creates the world of permanent crisis that we find all around as well as inside us.

In the third state, referred to by Huang Po as the One Mind or the Buddha's "enlightened" state, the Zen practitioner experiences the condition of complete egolessness, in which s/he (if indeed in this case we can still meaningfully use grammatical markers of dualistic gender differentiations) no longer operates with dualistic notions such as unity and multiplicity, self and other, totality and individuality, male and female, etc. Now the practitioner perceives trees, mountains, rivers, and so on as both distinct and nondistinct, or in Zen terminology as "suchness" or "thusness." For example, commenting on the Sanskrit term *Tathagata*, Huang Po says: "'Tathagata' means the THUSNESS of all phenomena. Therefore it is written: 'Maitreya is THUS; saints and sages are THUS.' THUSNESS consists in not being subject to becoming or to destruction; THUSNESS consists in not being seen and in not being heard. The crown of the Tathagata's head is a concept of perfection, but it is also no-perfection-to-be-conceived. So do not fall into conceiving of perfection objectively. It follows that the Buddhakaya [the Absolute, the One Mind, or the Buddha-nature] is above all [form-creating] activity; therefore must you beware of discriminating between the myriads of separate forms" (74).

Here, again, Huang Po addresses Zen practitioners who are within the second state and, therefore, has to use dualistic vocabulary to describe what to them (and to us) appears as an *inconceivable* experience. It is perhaps helpful, in this context, to recall the distinction between commensurable and incommensurable worlds or realities employed in the previous chapter. Whereas the first two states can be seen as commensurable albeit incompatible or discontinuous realities, the state of "thusness" or "suchness" as experience of that which is both distinct and nondistinct (as well as neither) appears as incommensurable with the other two. It can be attained neither by conceptual thinking nor by spiritual growth, but only by a mental-physical leap, which in Western terms approximates the experience of conversion. What we call the process of dying itself can be regarded as the prelude to such a leap, and indeed it is not by chance that countless human beings undergo some kind of conversion either on their deathbeds or when confronted with an overwhelming existential crisis.

A Western thinker may wonder about the practical benefits of a "doctrine" that reduces to nothingness all previous doctrines, deconstructing even the concept of deconstruction, and that—most troubling of all—neither exalts virtuous action nor condemns moral iniquity. From a Western standpoint, Zen Buddhism may indeed appear as an amoral and therefore dangerous teaching, doing away even with Levinas's "ethical judgment" of infinite Goodness. But the point is precisely that Zen Buddhism genuinely goes beyond good and evil—not in the Nietzschean sense that there is no absolute truth and therefore everything is permitted (if it can be brought to pass), but in the sense that everything is left up to the practitioner. Realizing that everything is permitted, the practitioner also realizes that nothing is permitted and therefore understands the emptiness of both positions. S/he is now free to fashion a mode of thought, behavior, and pathos in which what is permitted or not permitted becomes irrelevant, i.e., it is no longer a moral issue. It is only within a mentality of power that morality operates in terms of "thou shalt" or "thou shalt not."

By going beyond being and nonbeing, unity and multiplicity, subject and object, self and other, and so on, Zen Buddhist practice effectively transcends the Will to Power and its ontoepistemology, which can operate only through differential perception. Gilles Deleuze, for example, aptly describes "difference as such" *(différence en soi)* as perceived by a mentality of power:

> [I]nstead of something distinguished from something else, imagine something which distinguishes itself—and yet that from which it distinguishes itself does not distinguish itself from it. Lightning, for example, distinguishes itself from the black sky but must also trail it behind, as though it were distinguishing itself from that which does not distinguish itself from it. It is as if the ground rose to the surface, without ceasing to be ground. There is cruelty, even monstrosity, on both sides of this struggle against an elusive adversary, in which the distinguished opposes something which cannot distinguish itself from it but continues to espouse that which divorces it. Difference is this state in which determination takes the form of unilateral distinction. We must therefore say that difference is made, or makes itself, as in the expression 'make the difference'. This difference or determination *as such* is also cruelty.[41]

It is obvious that Deleuze's graphic description of conflictive difference echoes both Hegel's and Sartre's agonistic views, being shared by the whole Western tradition beginning with the biblical book of Genesis (where God, wrenching himself out of the void, separates light from darkness, the waters from the land, and so forth). By contrast, Zen Buddhism shows how difference as cruelty can not only make *(faire)* but also unmake *(défaire)* itself, and in this regard one can say that Zen practice is genuinely *an-archical* since it posits no first principle (ἀρχή), no hierarchy based on order *or* chaos, on either firm or "rising" ground.

Finally, Zen Buddhism reveals the Western concept of nondifferentiation as amorality to be an empty one (or, in Nietzschean terms, a necessary fiction of the Will to Power), in the sense that Zen practice spontaneously develops its own ethics. In other words, it anticipates Levinas's insight that "l'éthique est une optique,"[42] an insight that

Levinas shares with the major thinkers of all ages and traditions, including Buddha, Plato, Christ, and Nietzsche: a certain ontoepistemological
framework is always the expression of a certain ethopathology, rather
than the other way around. The present study obviously shares this insight, for example when it regards politics, in nonpoststructuralist fashion, as an expression of a specific mentality, rather than as an inevitable,
perennial contest between social and cosmic forces. It also starts from
the premise that ultimately all of our perceptions are a question of both
ethos *and* pathos. As I have already pointed out, "ethos" denotes not only
a specific mode of behavior but also a specific mode of thought, the two
being inseparable. Hence, thought can never be mere speculation, but
practice or ethics—it is what the Zen Buddhists mean by (non)thinking
in contrast to the conceptual or dualistic pair of thinking and not-think-
ing. "Pathos," on the other hand, denotes the emotional investment or
interest that permeates any constructed world, shaping its values. For
example, one cannot fail to sense the almost tragic pathos emanating
from Deleuze's foregoing description of agonistic difference. We have
also seen how the notion of emptiness in Nietzsche, Bakhtin, and some
deconstructive thinkers (notably Paul de Man) is invested with tragic
pathos or negative value, and how, by contrast, it is regarded with detachment in Zen Buddhist thought, where it is attributed neutral value.[43]
Power, death, freedom, and ego are other common examples of notions
whose meaning may change radically according to the kind of pathos
invested in them.

Ethos and pathos are also among the determining factors in world
(self-)formation, that is, in establishing ontoepistemological limits, and
it would be very helpful, in the present context, to develop a *peratology*
or a science of limits based on a psychophysiology of perception
(Nietzsche attempted to develop a similar science in *The Will to Power*
but, of course, from the perspective of the Will).[44] Ethos and pathos
equally constitute what is normally understood by psychological barriers,
but without the negative implication of the term—they simply circum-
scribe a certain time-space continuum within which a given community
organizes its physical-mental life.[45] The ethos and pathos of death and
dying in various cultures, for example, can create widely divergent worlds
with widely divergent limits. Michel Foucault—among many others,
including Kierkegaard and Heidegger—aptly describes the Western

ethopathology of death (with its attending negative emotions of horror, anxiety, dread, despair, panic, and so forth) when he relates writing, speech, and language in general to the Western idea of death as (fear of) absence or the void: "Writing so as not to die, as [Maurice] Blanchot said, or perhaps even speaking so as not to die is a task undoubtedly as old as the world. . . . [I]t is quite likely that the approach of death—its sovereign gesture, its prominence within human memory —hollows out in the present and in existence the void toward which and from which we speak."[46]

Significantly, Foucault also links death with what he (as well as Bakhtin and many others) calls "endless striving," i.e., with the Will to Power: "Perhaps there exists in speech an essential affinity between death, endless striving and the self-representation of language. Perhaps the figure of a mirror to infinity erected against the black wall of death is fundamental for any language from the moment it determines to leave a trace of its passage. . . . In this sense, death is undoubtedly the most essential of the accidents of language (its limit and its center): from the day that men began to speak toward death and against it, in order to grasp and imprison it, something was born, a murmuring which repeats, recounts, and redoubles itself endlessly. . . ." (55).

For Foucault, death is a "black wall" as well as both "limit" and "center," meaning both that which cannot be transgressed and that which makes transgression possible. In turn, transgression is nothing but a disguised way (as Foucault himself has shown elsewhere) through which the Will to Power sets ethopathological limits to itself, whereas infinity is nothing but a mirrorlike representation (simulacrum) of the reduplication or repetition of the ego before the impenetrable black wall of death: the Eternal Return of the Same (i.e., of the ego in its objective and subjective guises), indeed. For a mentality of power, death is one of the most important taboos and challenges of the Will, or the (self-constructed) *resistance* most difficult to overcome and therefore the most "productive" and "real." No wonder that our culture is so infatuated with images of violence and death, creating a contradictory mystique of horror, repression, and transgression around them (it is highly relevant that Foucault [pp. 60–66] devotes almost half of his essay to a discussion of Sade and successful eighteenth-century horror fiction).

Although fully aware of the Western ethopathology of death and its limits, Foucault embraces it without much reflection, as one could see from the essentialist and universalist vocabulary of the foregoing citations (e.g., "as old as the world," "human memory," "essential affinity," "fundamental for any language," "from the day men began to speak," and so on). This vocabulary, of course, is part of the tragic-negative pathos of inevitability circumscribing any mentality of power and stands in striking contrast, say, with the Buddhist positive ethopathological vocabulary of death in *The Tibetan Book of the Dead*, in which death is regarded not as a "black wall" or a "center and limit" but as an important (though not the ultimate) threshold, as a liminal gap fraught with peril but also endless opportunity.[47]

We can also have widely different attitudes toward our (self-)constructed worlds, investing them with different kinds of pathos: for example, we can regard them either with various degrees of satisfaction and pride, as the biblical God did at the beginning of the Book of Genesis, or with various degrees of dissatisfaction and malaise. In the latter case, we may either reshuffle them or turn away from them altogether and construct other worlds that are incommensurable with the first ones. In turn, incommensurability can be seen as equally (self-)constructed, to the extent that it depends on what one may call affective-effective perception. In this respect, liminality (which would equally be a proper object of study for peratology) should be understood less as a border or a limit between two already constituted worlds than as a space-time gap, corresponding to an ontoepistemological and ethopathological state of suspension or neutrality, through which a new world gradually emerges or is brought into being. Thus, from the perspective of the present study, the Ch'an/Zen Buddhist *hsin* can also be described as a neutral psychoethical state or disposition conducive to the creation of new worlds. In other words, one could also see Huang Po's Great Void as radical liminality, although a Zen Buddhist's primary project would, of course, be to cease any world-forming activity once s/he experiences the "enlightened" state.

We do not have to believe, however, as Schopenhauer and some Buddhists do, that the sole alternative to "Enlightenment" is falling back into the cycle of reincarnations or into the eternally returning world(s) of power. One can envision many other ontoepistemological alternatives, but always from the perspective of the groundless ground of the Great Void, which would allow us creative access to other worlds. It follows that an irenic world cannot be constituted in relation to another preexistent world (whether or not this relation is one of opposition, reversal, symbiosis, peaceful coexistence, and so forth), but in relation to this originary (non)void or (non)emptiness.

If our project is not "Enlightenment," we can even embrace dualistic, conceptual thinking once again, provided we emancipate it from a mentality of power by constantly confronting it with Huang Po's Great Void. In this respect, the conceptual-imaginative advantage of radical liminality over radical otherness is that the former opens up infinite existential choices for human communities. In Levinas's model, primordial peace is what the face of the Other necessarily impinges upon us with or without a radical (or incommensurable) affective-perceptive conversion on our part. In the modified Zen Buddhist model envisioned here, primordial peace need not derive from any logical, perceptual, existential, or moral imperative, but can simply be one of the paths or reference frames a human community chooses in constructing an alternative perceptual-affective or psychophysical world.[48] From the perspective of a Zen Buddhist or a ludic-irenic mentality in general, emptiness—whether it bears the name of Being, the Other, the Infinite, or God—does not have to be a radical alterity nor a radical sameness. Furthermore, it does not have to be, as in Heidegger, something (or no-thing) that perpetually offers and denies itself. On the contrary, it can be thought *and* experienced as a liminal groundless ground of infinite generosity that perpetually unfolds itself as suchness or thusness.

All of the irenic models presented here, however, imply an ethopathology that would turn away from an agonistic relation between self and other, unity and multiplicity, male and female, and so on, at the same time changing the very meaning of these terms. For any irenic mentality, the other is not an object to be striven for, overcome, or joined in a temporary partnership, but is the originary cosponsor and corespondent of a mutually enriching world. No irenic mentality will experience difference as conflict but, rather, as an openness and an opportunity toward a responsive understanding of other worlds. If, when confronted with an infinity of worlds, an irenic mentality would still choose to imagine a

cosmic whole, it would be only in the sense of a manifold, infinite oneness understood as primordial peace, rather than primordial war. As
Levinas so beautifully puts it:

> L'unité de la pluralité c'est la paix et non pas la cohérance d'éléments
> constituant la pluralité. La paix ne peut donc pas s'identifier avec la
> fin des combats qui cessent faute de combattants, par la défaite des
> uns et la victoire des autres, c'est à dire avec les cimetières ou les
> empires universels futurs. La paix doit être ma paix, dans une rela-
> tion qui part d'un moi et va vers l'Autre, dans le désir et la bonté ou le
> moi, à la fois se mantient et existe sans égoïsme. Elle se conçoit à
> partir d'un moi assuré de la convergence entre la moralité et la realité,
> c'est à dire d'un temps infini qui, à travers la fécondité, est son temps

> [The unity of the plurality is peace and not the coherence of the ele-
> ments constituting the plurality. Peace cannot therefore be identified
> with the end of combats that cease because of lack of combatants,
> with the defeat of some and the victory of others, that is, with cem-
> eteries or future universal empires. Peace should be my peace in a
> relation that proceeds from the I toward the Other, in a desire and
> goodness where the I both maintains itself and exists without selfish-
> ness. This peace arises from an I assured of the convergence between
> morality and reality, that is, of an infinite time, which, through fecun-
> dity, is its time].[49]

PART TWO

LITERARY THEMATICS AND LUDIC-IRENIC HERMENEUTICS

HOMICIDE AS PLAY
Dostoevsky, Gide, Aiken

This chapter initiates my thematical analysis of a number of modern literary works from the ludic-irenic perspective developed in part 1 and focuses on three thematically interrelated novels: Fyodor Dostoevsky's *Crime and Punishment*, André Gide's *Lafcadio's Adventures (Les caves du Vatican)*, and Conrad Aiken's *King Coffin*. Although these works belong to diverse cultural-literary traditions (Russian, French, and American, respectively), all of them reveal the highly ambiguous nature of prevailing Western values, suggesting the need for a thorough reexamination and eventual transvaluation of these values. By choosing homicide as play for their main theme, these novels tap into a rich and complex Western philosophical and literary tradition, which they both question and attempt to modify.

In the modern age, murder becomes a rather common literary theme and is often linked to the larger question of the uneasy relation between ethics and aesthetics in Western thought. In turn, this question has its modern roots in the libertine, romantic, and postromantic traditions of the eighteenth and the nineteenth century (present, for example, in Choderlos de Laclos, the Marquis de Sade, E. T. A. Hoffmann, Pierre-François Lacenaire, Thomas Griffiths Wainewright, Thomas De Quincey, Edgar Allan Poe, Théophile Gautier, Marcel Schwob, Robert Louis Stevenson, Villiers de L'Isle-Adam, Oscar Wilde, and many lesser representatives of the decadent and the art-for-art's-sake movements), but can ultimately be traced back to the ancient quarrel between philosophy and poetry initiated by Socrates in Plato's *Republic*. During the beginning stages of the romantic movement, Kant takes up this quarrel again in his third *Critique* and attempts to resolve it by proposing an aesthetic foundation for his ethics; nevertheless, he eventually subordinates art to morality, which for him becomes the higher purpose of purposeless art.[1]

Thomas De Quincey, in a series of essays entitled *On Murder Considered as One of the Fine Arts*, challenges Kant's subordination of aesthetics to ethics precisely in terms of an ironical transvaluation of homicide as a form of artistic play. In reversing the Kantian relation between ethics and aesthetics, De Quincey becomes a precursor of Nietzsche, who transforms philosophy itself into a fine art, through his notions of the "artist-metaphysician" and the aesthetic transvaluation of all values. But Nietzsche goes even further when he claims, in the second preface (1886) to his *Birth of Tragedy* (1871), that existence itself can be justified only in aesthetic terms and that all process can have only an aesthetic meaning: "A kind of divinity, if you like, God as the supreme artist, amoral, recklessly creating and destroying, realizing himself indifferently in whatever he does or undoes, ridding himself by his acts of the embarrassment of his riches and the strain of his internal contradictions." This god is not Christian, but Hellenic (Dionysus), and by proclaiming his return to the modern world, Nietzsche intends to "resist to the bitter end any moral interpretation of existence whatsoever."[2]

The aestheticist or "decadent" movement at the end of the nineteenth century also rebels against the Kantian notion of art as a higher form of morality and develops the counter concept of "art for art's sake." This concept leads in turn to the realization that art goes back to an older, pre-Platonic version of mimesis, which can no longer be interpreted as a tame imitation of reality, but as an archaic form of play, creating and destroying this reality at will. In *God of Many Names*, I have shown how Hellenic epic and drama stage an archaic world of might makes right, in which the gods themselves are "amoral," playing arbitrarily with men, their delightful toys. In many modern decadent writers, art returns to its origins in archaic play, or in play as an innocent and unashamed manifestation of power. Homicide as a "fine art" becomes naturally a nexus of this whole problematic, because it is the most blatant and radical form of moral transgression: once it is stripped of its ethical and legal (that is, median) accretions, it emerges as a pure and unrepressed form of archaic, violent play. In much decadent fiction, then, homicide as play is presented as a creative act that shatters the normal (middle-class) boundaries of everyday reality and contributes to fashioning a new life, based on Dionysian, tragic principles, where pleasure and suffering commingle indifferently in a joyful, ecstatic affirmation of all that is.

On the other hand, in much antiaestheticist fiction at the end of the nineteenth and the beginning of the twentieth century, homicide as play is often also employed to confront the prevailing values of modern Western culture, but without the violent, transgressive solutions envisioned by its decadent counterpart. Rather, this confrontation is often presented in terms of a perennial literary theme: the gap between art and life, illusion and reality, thought and action, freedom and necessity.[3] In this context, homicide as play turns out to be an illusion (from the Latin word *in-lusio*, literally "in play") engaged in by the protagonists. By the end of these narratives, however, the protagonists often discard their homicidal acts as de-lusion and return to the "real" world of median morality. Should they refuse this return, they are promptly isolated or cast away from their fictional communities. This is the case in much popular fiction, including a host of detective novels in which both the murderer and the detective play a cat-and-mouse game that, far from being subversive, ends up by reestablishing the social and moral status quo.[4]

But in the most interesting of the antiaestheticist narratives dealing with homicide as play, the world of middle-class morality remains by no means unproblematic, and the need for a radical shift in the prevailing mentality is often implied by the end of the work. *Crime and Punishment*, *Lafcadio's Adventures* and *King Coffin* are precisely such antiaestheticist narratives. They stage a direct or indirect dialogue not only with each other but also with Nietzsche and the voluntaristic values that he represents, dramatizing the possibility of turning away from a mentality of power that has repeatedly discredited itself and yet continues to be widely embraced in the Western world.

1. Crime and Punishment: Homicide, Will
to Power, and Christian Mentality

In Dostoevsky's novel, Raskolnikov, a law school drop-out living in squalor in a St. Petersburg slum, decides to kill and rob an old pawnbroker ostensibly in order to finance his studies. He justifies his act in terms of a modern version of the archaic principle of might makes right, taking Napoléon Bonaparte as a role model. In an article he writes for a law review, Raskolnikov makes a distinction between "lower" or "ordinary" people and "higher" or "extraordinary" ones. As he explains it to Porfiry

Petrovich, the examining magistrate, the first group consists of human reproductive material and is by nature obedient, staid, and conservative. The second group, on the other hand, consists of rebels, transgressors, and lawbreakers. Although the members of the second group may be driven by a wide variety of goals, they all desire "the destruction of what exists in the name of better things." If, moreover, it becomes "necessary for one of them, for the fulfillment of his ideas, to march over corpses, or wade through blood, then in my opinion he may in all conscience authorize himself to wade through blood—in proportion, however, to his idea and the degree of its importance."[5] According to Raskolnikov, the function of the ordinary category is to conserve existence by increasing and multiplying, while the function of the extraordinary category is to "move the world and guide it to its goal."[6] Both categories "have an equal right to exist" so that "all men have completely equivalent rights, and *vive la guerre eternelle*—until we have built the New Jerusalem, of course!" (251).

Raskolnikov's theory of higher and lower human types is an age-old cliché from the standpoint of a mentality of power. He uneasily yokes the archaic notion of *la guerre eternelle* to the Christian idea of the New Jerusalem or the new earthly paradise (as described in Revelation 21), implying that humans, even while hoping for a new Christian dispensation, must remain perpetually at war. Raskolnikov thus invokes a traditional correlation that originates in the Middle Ages and the Renaissance and can be found, for example, in Machiavelli and Hobbes, where the archaic principle of the war of all against all, characteristic of the City of Man, is opposed to the eternal peace and love of the City of God. In the context of the novel, Raskolnikov's article elucidates, at least for Porfiry Petrovich, the student's "motive" for killing the old pawnbroker. More importantly, however, it also elucidates, for the reader, Raskolnikov's ethopathology of power which Dostoevsky places at the center of, and questions throughout, his narrative.

In an editorial footnote to *Crime and Punishment* (249), George Gibian suggests that Raskolnikov's views are similar to those expressed by Napoléon III in his book, *Life of Julius Caesar*, which was much debated in the Russian literary press of the period. One may add that Raskolnikov's views are also remarkably similar to those of Nietzsche, who was familiar with Dostoevsky's fiction and referred to it in a number of texts, including several notes collected posthumously in *The Will to Power*. What Nietzsche admires most in this fiction is what he perceives as Dostoevsky's analysis of the Will to Power in its modern, perverted form, which greatly resembles his own analysis in *The Genealogy of Morals*. Indirectly, then, Dostoevsky and Nietzsche engage in an intertextual dialogue that is highly relevant in the present context. Throughout *Crime and Punishment*, Dostoevsky describes Raskolnikov as being emotionally torn between an archaic and a median mentality, an inner conflict which in his case (as in Nietzsche's) assumes the form of a specific contest between voluntaristic and Christian values. It is along these lines that one can best reinterpret the long-standing critical commonplace according to which many of Dostoevsky's characters exhibit a split or schizophrenic personality.

Intellectually, Raskolnikov embraces what Nietzsche calls the Will to Power, which he, like Nietzsche, claims to place in the service of a just future for mankind (one recalls that in *The Will to Power* Nietzsche envisions a new social dispensation of overmen). Raskolnikov's intellectual credo is echoed uncannily in a conversation he overhears, in a café, between an officer and a student, who is clearly his alter ego and who also speculates about killing the old pawnbroker: "For one life taken, thousands saved from corruption and decay! One death, and hundred lives in exchange—why, it's simple arithmetic! What is the life of that stupid, spiteful, consumptive old woman weighed against the common good? No more than the life of a louse or cockroach—less, indeed, because she is very actively harmful" (62–63). Here Raskolnikov's alter ego does not dismiss reason but, on the contrary, enlists it in the service of the Will to Power. Killing is not a question of ethics but of arithmetic, of a neutral and objective science. This rationalist, "scientific" approach to murder can be turned into a gruesome instrument of social engineering and has indeed been adopted, in the twentieth century, by various radical "socialist" ideologies, including Leninism, Stalinism, and Fascism.

Raskolnikov echoes a similar rationalist standpoint later in the novel, for example when he says with unconscious irony: "My life did not die with the old woman! May she rest in peace and—enough, old woman, your time has come! Now comes the reign of reason and light and . . . freedom and power . . . now we shall see! Now we shall measure our strength!" (182). In this context, reason, which a median mentality normally employs as an instrument of mediation between might and right, is directly enlisted in the service of might. Both Raskolnikov and his alter ego show that might can easily justify itself as right in the eyes of a median world, should it choose to do so for opportunistic purposes (of course, from the standpoint of an archaic world, might needs no such subterfuge, since it is by definition its own justification). In order to commit murder, moreover, Raskolnikov puts his reason on "automatic pilot," that is, he allows it to be completely guided by the Will to Power in its naked, archaic (or what Freud and others call "unconscious") form. This is why he appears to act as in a dream during the gory deed and why he can say afterward that it was not "he" (his median, rational self) but the "devil" (402) who killed the "old louse" and her meek and innocent sister, Lizaveta: for a median mentality of the Christian kind, archaic values are at the root of all evil, being relegated to the forbidden domain of Satan.

Once the murders are committed, Raskolnikov returns to his split ego-will and continues to attempt to justify himself in terms of extraordinary versus ordinary people, or, if one adopts a Nietzschean vocabulary, in terms of the strong individual versus the herd. For example, he tells Sonya during their second interview: "And I know now, Sonya, that the man of strong and powerful mind and spirit is their [the herd's] master! The man who dares much is right in their eyes. The man who tramples on the greatest number of things is their law-giver, and whoever is most audacious is most certainly right. So things have always been, and so they will remain" (400).

Raskolnikov dismisses poverty or material need as a motive for his act. Although he plans initially to take the pawnbroker's money, after the murder he stashes it away without ever using it. He instinctively keeps his act "pure," i.e., clear of a bourgeois, utilitarian mentality, thereby puzzling his judges, who consider him to have been temporarily insane. From the predominantly median standpoint of his community, his behavior remains largely inexplicable, but his motivation becomes quite obvious, if one considers it from an archaic perspective. It is power for its own sake that Raskolnikov is after, as he tells Sonya during their first interview: "Freedom and power, but above all, power! Power over all trembling creatures, over the whole ant-heap!... That is a goal!" (317). He further confesses to Sonya that he has killed for the sole reason of performing a power experiment on himself: "I wanted to 'have the courage', and I killed. . . . What I needed to find out then, and find out as soon as possible, was whether I was a louse like everybody else or a man, whether I was capable of stepping over the barriers or not. Dare I stoop and take power or not?" (401–2).

Until the very end of the novel, Raskolnikov does not think he has done anything wrong from the standpoint of an ethics of power. He continues to believe that might is its own justification and, accordingly, that success is the only ethical standard of the Will to Power. So he does not blame himself for breaking the law (or committing a "crime") but failing to live up to the principle of might makes right: "Many benefactors of mankind who did not inherit power but seized it for themselves, should have been punished at their very first steps. But the first steps of those men were successfully carried out, and therefore they were right, while mine failed, which means I had no right to permit myself that step" (521).

Raskolnikov's assumptions are partly shared by other characters in the novel, notably by the examining magistrate. Although Porfiry Petrovich seemingly objects to Raskolnikov's theory, he actually embraces the basic mentality that has generated it. For example, he playfully confesses to Raskolnikov that he loves "the art of war" and that he has missed his vocation: "I ought to have had a military career, really. I might not have become a Napoleon, but I should have become a major, he, he, he!" (328). The examining magistrate admits that he enjoys his job as a detective, because it allows him to play a psychological cat-and-mouse game with his suspects. In fact, throughout the narrative Raskolnikov and Porfiry Petrovich are fully aware that they are playing a game of power with each other, and it is for this reason that when Raskolnikov decides to turn himself in, he goes to another official's office to do so, in order to deprive the examining magistrate of the full satisfaction of his victory.

Despite his cruel cat-and-mouse game with Raskolnikov, Porfiry Petrovich actually sympathizes and partly identifies with the student. He even shows regard for him because Raskolnikov did muster enough courage to act according to his principles, while most people do not. The magistrate's view seems to be not so much that some individuals do not have the right, under special circumstances, to place themselves above the law, but that neither Raskolnikov nor he is such an individual. Judging from his self-deprecating remarks, Porfiry is well aware that his warlike talents could at most have won him a major's commission, but not a generalship or an empire as in Napoléon's case. He thus appears as one of the main representatives of a median mentality in the narrative, and his detective's power game is a form of rational play, confining itself to the median norms accepted by his community. He appropriately taunts Raskolnikov for fancying himself an overman: "Oh, come, who among us in Russia doesn't think himself a Napoleon now?" And Zametov, the police lieutenant, chimes in: "Wasn't it indeed some future Napoleon who last week dispatched our Alena Ivanovna with an axe?" (255). As both Porfiry and Zametov imply, there are also "aesthetic" reasons that preclude certain acts from becoming the mark of an overman, at least in a median community. Raskolnikov himself notes with bitter self-irony: "Napoleon, the pyramids, Waterloo—and a vile, withered old woman, a moneylender, with a red box under her bed—what a mishmash even for somebody like Porfiry Petrovich to digest! . . . How could he, indeed? Aesthetic considerations forbid. 'Does a Napoleon crawl under an old woman's bed?' he will say. Oh what rubbish!" (263).

The magistrate well understands the split nature of Raskolnikov's psyche. As he points out to Raskolnikov, "[Y]ou esteem the human intellect above all things, like all young people," but "abstract reasoning and the play of wit tempt you astray" (327f). Porfiry intimates that no matter how clever and inventive the murderer might be in concealing his crime, he will subconsciously point the finger at himself, because of his feelings of guilt, because he wants to be caught and punished. In solving a murder case, therefore, "the criminal's own [divided] nature comes to the rescue of the poor investigator" (328). Although Raskolnikov can to some extent justify his deed rationally, he fails to justify it emotionally or "aesthetically" (if one uses the latter word not only in Raskolnikov's sense but also in its etymological sense of that which pertains to the senses or feeling). A British chasing metaphor perfectly describes Raskolnikov's situation: he hunts with the hounds and runs with the hare. Raskolnikov remains divided between an archaic and a median mentality, being incapable of choosing between the two. Consequently, throughout the novel he undergoes a severe existential crisis that murder does not resolve but, on the contrary, aggravates.

Raskolnikov's split mentality also greatly impairs his ludic ability, since what appears as mere play to an archaic mind appears as high seriousness to a median one. In a median world, homicide or any other violent act cannot readily be perceived as play, and Raskolnikov fails to overcome his median mentality in this respect as well. He thinks in terms of the typical rationalist dichotomy between play and seriousness or "reality," for example, when he dismisses his murder plan as a mere playful fantasy: "No, of course I'm not serious. So I am just amusing myself with fancies, children's games? Yes, perhaps I am only playing a game" (2). Unlike a Nietzschean overman, Raskolnikov considers homicide a matter of grave moral import rather than an innocent child's game. He is certainly not Nietzsche's "supreme artist, amoral, recklessly creating and destroying, realizing himself indifferently in whatever he does or undoes, ridding himself by his acts of the embarrassment of his riches and the strain of his internal contradictions." Raskolnikov even plays his cat-and-mouse game with Porfiry Petrovich very poorly, becoming incensed at the slightest provocation and being unable to master his bad conscience—thus constantly casting himself in the role of the mouse.

Of course, threatened or sick animals will hardly ever engage in play, and from a Nietzschean viewpoint, Raskolnikov is a very sick animal indeed. Thus, his split ethopathology can equally be seen as the diseased condition of the modern ego-will that Nietzsche calls "decadence" or "nihilism" and with which, according to him, a "Christian" or a "herd" mentality has infected the strong individual in modern society. In his law-review article, for example, Raskolnikov describes violent crime in a typical rationalist fashion as an outward manifestation of a diseased psychophysical state. Dostoevsky presents Raskolnikov himself under great physical and mental stress before he commits murder and as falling ill afterward. Intellectually, the law student believes that "everything is permitted" (263), including murder, and he identifies himself with the aggressor, attempting to play a game of (self-) mastery. Emotionally, however, he constantly identifies himself with the victim, taking the side of "the humble and the oppressed." For instance, at the beginning of the novel, he intervenes on behalf of an inebriated young girl who is in danger of being taken advantage of by a well-dressed gentleman in the street. Upon realizing that his behavior is inconsistent with his overman's principles, Raskolnikov gets angry with himself: "Was it for me to try to help? Have I any right to help? Let them eat one another alive—what is it to me?" (47). He can ill afford to give his money away, yet he helps needy people throughout the novel. He constantly identifies with the sick and the physically handicapped, notably with his first fiancée, whom he describes to his mother and sister with the same bitter self-irony: "I don't really know what attracted me to her; I think it may have been that she was always ill. . . . If she had been lame as well, or hump-backed, I might very likely have loved her even more" (221).

The most significant example of Raskolnikov's ethopathological identification with the victim is his dream of Mikolka's horse. Shortly before committing the murders, he has a nightmare in which, as a little boy, he walks in the street accompanied by his father and witnesses a coachman, Mikolka, savagely beating his horse to death. In the dream Raskolnikov exhibits an extreme emotional reaction toward the slain animal: "The poor little boy was quite beside himself. He pushed his way, shrieking, through the crowd to the mare, put his arms round the dead muzzle dabbled with blood and kissed the poor eyes and the mouth. . . . Then he sprang up and rushed furiously at Mikolka with his fists clenched" (56).

Raskolnikov's dream can obviously be interpreted as his reversion to a Christian mentality (if we define this mentality, in Nietzschean terms, as the ethical standpoint of the victim), which he attempts unsuccessfully to overcome throughout the narrative. Upon awakening, he realizes that his dream was a transparent, subconscious warning against his carrying out the deed, and he spontaneously reverts to prayer: "'Lord!' he prayed, 'show me the way, that I may renounce this accursed . . . fantasy of mine!'" (57) Of equal significance in the dream, however, is Raskolnikov's reaction toward the horse's master: in an unchristianlike manner, he attempts to avenge the victim by doing violence to the aggressor. This is a very common human impulse within a mentality of power and an equally common motivation for social "revolutionary" activity (had Raskolnikov been born a few decades later, one could have easily imagined him in the role of a "commissar of the people" during the October revolution).

Raskolnikov's identification with the victim is a form of mimesis (methexis) and it is against this kind of emotional or pathic mimesis that Raskolnikov constantly struggles. By killing another human being he attempts to sever his emotional ties with, and raise himself above, common humanity. Nietzsche speaks of this kind of antimimetic stance in *The Will to Power*, stipulating that the overman must achieve a "pathos of distance" in relation to the herd by gradually setting himself apart from it through his demeanor and actions. Indeed, Raskolnikov feels that murder has literally set him above everyone else: "In some gulf far below him, almost out of sight beneath his feet, lay all his past, all his old ideas, and problems, and thoughts, and sensations. . . . He felt that he had in that moment cut himself off from everybody and everything, as if with a knife" (109). A while before, at the police station, where he had been summoned in a matter unrelated to the murders, Raskolnikov had experienced the same feeling of having cut himself off from the rest of mankind: "[H]e could never again communicate with these people in a great gush of feeling, as he had just now, or any way whatever. . . . He had never in his life before experienced so strange and desolating feeling, and the most painful thing about it was that it was a feeling, an immediate sensation, and not knowledge or intellectual understanding" (98).

Yet Raskolnikov does not experience his separation from common humanity as a positive emotion or a feeling of exhilaration but as the pain of a terrible loss. The same negative emotion resurfaces when he attempts to comfort his mother by promising to speak to her heart to heart: "[A]gain that same terrible feeling of deadly cold swept through him; again he realized clearly and vividly that he had just uttered a dreadful lie, that not only would it now never be given to him to talk himself out, but that now he could never talk at all, to anybody" (220). Raskolnikov is clearly unable to achieve a Nietzschean "pathos of distance"; he cannot convert to the ethopathology of an overman and continues to identify emotionally with the herd. He himself is quite aware of this problem, for example, when he tells himself: "No, those people are not made like this; the real ruler, to whom everything is permitted, destroys Toulon, butchers in Paris, forgets an army in Egypt, expends half a million men in a Moscow campaign, shakes himself free with a pun in Wilno, and when he is dead they put up statues to him: everything is permitted to him. No! Such people are plainly not made of flesh but bronze!" (263).

Raskolnikov also displays the ambiguous behavior that Nietzsche diagnoses for the modern nihilist. According to Nietzsche, there are two categories of nihilists: the active and the passive. Active nihilists exhibit signs of individual strength, by turning resolutely against current dogmas and existential constraints and by reaching their "maximum of relative strength as a violent force of destruction." By contrast, passive nihilists exhibit signs of weakness insofar as, not believing in the prevailing dogmas, they lack the "strength to posit for [themselves], productively, a goal, a why, a faith."[7] But Raskolnikov's case—no less than Nietzsche's own—reveals that in practice the line between the active and the passive nihilist may be quite blurred. Raskolnikov seems initially to fit the first category as he commits a violent act that transgresses the accepted norms of his community and sets him apart from it. Later on, however, he turns out to belong to the second category because he loses faith in his original goal and acts in a manner completely inconsistent with it.

From a Nietzschean standpoint, Raskolnikov's nihilistic weakness is further aggravated by his partial relapse into the old Christian mentality from which he can never shake himself free. Ironically, Nietzsche himself, despite his anti-Christian philosophical program, apparently reverted to Raskolnikov's passive nihilistic position in real life when, on the brink of insanity, he uncannily reenacted Raskolnikov's nightmare by throwing himself, in the streets of Turin, between a horse and the cruel whip of its master. No less than Nietzsche, Raskolnikov is fully aware of the difficulty of overcoming the split ethopathology of the Will to Power, whose logic dictates that the stronger the ego-will affirms itself, the more violently ill it can become. Hence Raskolnikov's sadomasochistic self-recriminations that only aggravate his diseased condition:

> "Yes, I really am a louse," [R.] went on, clinging to the idea with malicious pleasure, burrowing into it, playing with it for his own amusement, 'if only because, first, I'm arguing now about being one, secondly, I've been importuning all gracious Providence for a whole month, calling on it to witness that it was not for my own selfish desires and purposes that I proposed to act (so I said), but for a noble and worthy end . . . . Finally, I am a louse. . . because, I myself am, perhaps, even worse and viler than the louse I killed, and I knew beforehand that I should tell myself so after I had killed her!"[8]

Human suffering may in turn be seen, in Nietzschean terms, as either a sign of heroic strength or a sign of nihilistic weakness. A Nietzschean overman accepts suffering as an inevitable but fair price to pay for living dangerously, as is the case, say, with the Hellenic or Teutonic tragic hero. According to Nietzsche, humans do not strive for happiness (the measure of which would in turn be the degree of pleasure or pain experienced by the individual). On the contrary, they strive for power, pleasure and pain being simply instruments through which the Will to Power attains its goal: the ceaseless enhancement of the feeling of power for its own sake. Christian suffering, on the other hand, is a form of passive nihilism because it makes itself into a virtue and a necessary goal (martyrdom)—it is only through suffering, patience, and humility, Christians claim, that one can transcend the Will to Power and embrace an all-loving and forgiving Christ. As Porfiry Petrovich observes with regard to the young painter who confesses, ironically, to the murders committed by Raskolnikov: "Do you, Rodion Romanovich, know what some of these [simple] people mean by 'suffering'? It is not suffering for somebody's sake, but simply 'suffering is necessary'—the acceptance of suffering, that means, and if it is at the hands of the authorities, so much the better" (436).

Nietzsche would say, however, that by glorifying suffering, the Christian mentality does not overcome the Will to Power but only reproduces it in a diseased form. Raskolnikov himself has an ambiguous attitude toward suffering. For example, when Razumihin argues that extraordinary men "ought surely not to suffer at all, even for the spilling of blood," Raskolnikov counters: "'Why do you say 'ought'? There is no question either of permitting or forbidding it. Let them suffer if they feel pity for the victims" (254). Here he exhibits an overman's view of suffering as existential accident rather than cosmic or divine necessity. Yet he immediately contradicts himself, as an afterthought: "Suffering and pain are always obligatory on those of wide intellect and profound feeling. Truly great men must, I think, experience great sorrow on the earth" (254). Raskolnikov's ambiguous view of suffering reflects his ambiguous feelings toward Christianity in general. When Porfiry asks him if he believes in God and "in the raising of Lazarus," Raskolnikov emphatically says yes (251). Yet a few pages later, he pointedly tells Svidrigaylov that he does not "believe in a life hereafter" (277). He also scoffs at

Sonya because of her blind faith, but then asks her to read to him the Lazarus story from the New Testament that Porfiry had inquired about.

It would be instructive, from a Nietzschean standpoint, to draw a parallel between Svidrigaylov's and Raskolnikov's types of nihilism. As Svidrigaylov acknowledges (and Raskolnikov heatedly denies) the two men have much in common: they both wish to live outside the norms of their community and are not afraid to transgress them. Both of them are also nihilists in a Nietzschean sense: whereas Raskolnikov can be said to represent the nihilist as revolutionary, Svidrigaylov represents the nihilist as libertine. In this respect, Svidrigaylov's partial seduction of Dunya is very similar to Valmont's seduction of Madame de Tourville in Laclos's *Dangerous Liaisons*. Like Valmont, Svidrigaylov seems to believe in nothing but the world of the senses, which he uses in order to enhance his feeling of power. Like Valmont, moreover, he eventually experiences the possibility of selfless love and, therefore, has the choice of moving beyond a mentality of power. Unlike Valmont, however, Svidrigaylov remains a nihilist to the end, rejecting love as a viable existential alternative.

One may also see Svidrigaylov as a strong nihilist in relation to Raskolnikov, who is mostly a weak one. Whereas Raskolnikov feebly invokes a New Jerusalem that he plans to build after destroying existing social structures, Svidrigaylov believes in no social action whatsoever. While Raskolnikov's morality is divided, which occasionally makes him appear self-righteous and prudish, Svidrigaylov's is quite consistent with what he is. As he himself points out to Dunya during their interview: "I make it a rule to condemn absolutely nobody, since I never do anything myself and don't intend to" (472). He does not embrace traditional Christian values—for example, he delights in subverting the Christian idea of an afterlife of reward or punishment (witness his sardonic depiction of eternity as a small rural bathhouse, black with soot and swarming with spiders [277]). But he does not reject any particular faith just because he himself does not happen to believe in it. Since he is indifferent to good and evil in a Christian sense and acts according to his whim or ludic spirit, Svidrigaylov can spontaneously be cruel, devious, and high-handed, or tender, generous, and merciful (in fact, he helps as many of the dispossessed with whom he comes into contact throughout the narrative as Raskolnikov does, but without the latter's *mauvaise conscience*).

He is indeed the master player that Raskolnikov only dreams of being. His behavior toward Dunya is completely consistent with his overman's mentality. Although Svidrigaylov tries to use Dunya's love for her brother to blackmail her into going abroad with him (all is fair in love and war), he does not take advantage of her when he has the chance. He engages in a dangerous power game with Dunya, but lets her go when she spontaneously gives up this game and appeals to his generosity. He can even experience pity for her. (486)

Svidrigaylov's feelings of "pity" may, of course, also be interpreted as weak nihilism, especially since later on in a dream he expresses anger, just as Raskolnikov did, helping out a young girl: "'Well! Here I am, getting myself involved!' he thought suddenly, with heavy anger. 'How absurd!'" (489). But although Svidrigaylov seems occasionally resentful of the Christian mentality of pity—and Nietzsche argues that such ambiguous emotions are inescapable for any modern Westerner—he does not wallow in this pity, as Marmeladov *père*, for example, does. In this respect, one may wish to draw a distinction between pity and mercy, the first being a median virtue and the second an archaic one. While Raskolnikov, Dunya, Sonya, Marmeladov, and others often show pity, Svidrigaylov mostly shows mercy or generosity.

Even Svidrigaylov's suicide can be seen as a gratuitous game of self-mastery, given his fear of death, to which he freely admits in a conversation with Raskolnikov: "I confess to an unpardonable weakness, but I can't help it: I am afraid of death and don't like to hear it spoken of. Do you know that I am a bit of a mystic?" (452) In this light, Svidrigaylov's theatrical suicide in front of a night watchman to whom he ironically remarks that he is "going to America" can be read as a strong nihilistic act: since he can no longer adhere even to the world of the senses or to his libertinage, he has no reason to live; by killing himself, on the other hand, he can defy or annihilate his own fear of death and plunge himself into the unknown (for the average Russian citizen, "America" was—and still is—the equivalent of the Land of Cocaigne, but for Svidrigaylov it is simply uncharted territory).

Finally, it is not surprising that Svidrigaylov, and not Raskolnikov, shows "mystic" tendencies in the narrative. Because he no longer believes in anything, he is open to everything, including other worlds. For example, it is Svidrigaylov who, in a conversation with Raskolnikov, first interprets illness and death as a liminal time-space fraught with possibility: "Apparitions are so to speak, shreds and fragments of other worlds, the first beginnings of them. There is, of course, no reason why a healthy man should see them, because a healthy man is mainly a being of this earth, and therefore for completeness and order he must live only this earthly life. But as soon as he falls ill, as soon as the normal earthly state of the organism is disturbed, the possibility of another world begins to appear, and as the illness increases, so do the contacts with the other world, so that at the moment of a man's death he enters fully into that world" (277). In this regard, suffering (when not mystified as an end in itself or as Christian or non-Christian martyrdom) can also appear, side by side with illness and death, as a positive liminal state allowing access to alternative worlds.

Although Raskolnikov and Svidrigaylov may be seen as opposite types of nihilists, from the ludic-irenic standpoint of the present study this opposition amounts to very little in (ethopathological) practice. Whether one is a strong or a weak nihilist the outcome is the same: violent (self-)destruction. Even though Svidrigaylov kills himself and Raskolnikov kills two other human beings, their nihilism leads to the same impasse of the ego-will. Raskolnikov is fully aware of this impasse when he tells Sonya: "Did I murder the old woman? I killed myself, not the old creature! There and then I murdered myself at one blow, for ever!" (402). One may, however, wonder, *pace* Nietzsche, if a genuine Christian mode of thought, feeling, and behavior might not offer a way out of this impasse.

Many scholars agree (encomiastically or censoriously) that Dostoevsky was either an orthodox or a mystical Christian who attempted to promote his Christian ideology through his fiction. My assumption here has been, however, that one should consistently distinguish between Dostoevsky's historical and literary persona. Dostoevsky's position toward his fiction seems to be, if anything, one of responsive understanding in the ludic-irenic sense discussed in chapter 3. In a genuine dialogical manner Dostoevsky stages, in his literary works, various ethical models, complete with their existential consequences. *Crime and Punishment* in this respect questions the Christian mentality of his community as well, if by that mentality one understands (as Nietzsche does) the privileging of the perspective of the victim in the guise of the "Crucified." Dostoevsky and Nietzsche can be seen as converging in their diagnosis of the diseased ethopathology that results from the inevitable historical super-imposition of voluntaristic and Christian values. Yet whereas Nietzsche largely advocates a return to an archaic or "innocent" world of power, Dostoevsky's novel seems to point to an incommensurable, irenic mentality that is based on Christ's originary insights (but equally envisaged by many non-Christian sages) and that has yet to actualize itself as a historical world.

In *Crime and Punishment*, the idea of an irenic mentality is hinted at in the epilogue as the existential project on which Raskolnikov and Sonya might work together in the liminal space of Siberia, but this project remains genuinely open-ended. The narrator makes it clear that Raskolnikov still has a long way to go before he can create, together with Sonya, an alternative world for himself and his community. Although we are not told what this world would be like (precisely because its values are incommensurable with the ones embraced by Raskolnikov's fictional society), we are certainly told what it would *not* be like, for example through Raskolnikov's nightmare during his illness in the prison hospital: the feverish prisoner imagines a plague that is caused by microscopic creatures "endowed with intelligence and will," carrying warlike values among all the nations of the world with disastrous consequences for humanity (523–24). Raskolnikov's dream has again liminal qualities insofar as it signals his desire to join those "chosen few, a very few" (523) who are not infected by the plague.

The first step toward the irenic world envisaged by the epilogue, the narrator suggests, is to cease thinking, feeling, and acting in terms of a mentality of power with its dynamic of self and other, master and slave, oppressor and victim. In this sense, it is not only Raskolnikov but also Sonya who has a great deal to learn. We have seen that throughout the narrative, Raskolnikov (like Nietzsche) interprets Christian values from the standpoint of the Will to Power. From this perspective, he is not entirely wrong when he regards Sonya as a religious fanatic, that is, as someone who employs religion in order to enhance her own feeling of power. He sees Sonya's act of becoming a prostitute as the transgressive equivalent of his own homicidal act. He also senses in Sonya the same inability to endure the emotional consequences of her positive nihilistic decisions: "Haven't you done the same [that I, Raskolnikov, have done]? You have stepped over the barrier . . . you were able to do it. You laid hands on yourself, you destroyed a life . . . your own (that makes no difference!). . . . But you cannot endure, and if you remain alone you will go out of your senses, like me. You are like a madwoman even now; so we must go together, by the same path!" (316). Raskolnikov sees Sonya as a fellow sufferer, someone who has had the courage to shatter the barriers of social convention in order to help her family and yet cannot endure living outside these barriers. He instinctively finds in her an ally, which, from the standpoint of the Will to Power, can be interpreted either as a mark of strength (Raskolnikov and Sonya will generously assist each other in converting to a voluntaristic ethopathology) or as a mark of weakness (they need the reassuring comfort and support that the members of the herd seek from each other when they promiscuously huddle together).

Although Raskolnikov obviously attributes some of his own voluntaristic values to Sonya, he correctly senses her Christian identification with the victim. If Raskolnikov can be said to have a Napoléon complex, Sonya has a Christ complex: she seems to seek martyrdom as much as Lizaveta, the pawnbroker's sister and Sonya's friend, who does not even attempt to defend herself against Raskolnikov's ax (a passive mode of behavior that at the time of the murder the murderer interprets as the paralysis of fear, but later on as the meek acceptance of an innocent lamb). The narrator points to Sonya's martyrlike mentality when he observes during Raskolnikov's first interview with her: "An almost insatiable compassion, if one can use the expression, was depicted in every feature of her face" (305). From the perspective of a mentality of power the expression is quite appropriate, since compassion can be as "insatiable" as the ego-will that fuels it. Sonya also urges Raskolnikov to expiate for his crime in a traditional Russian Orthodox manner: "Go at once, this instant, stand at the cross-roads, first bow down and kiss the earth you have desecrated, then bow to the whole world, to the four corners of the earth, and say aloud to all the world: 'I have done murder.' Then God will send you life again. . . . Accept suffering and achieve atonement through it—that is what you must do" (403). Sonya unquestioningly accepts the Christian notion of suffering, interpreted by Nietzsche as a disease of the modern ego-will and by contemporary psychoanalysts as sadomasochism. Raskolnikov does have a point, moreover, when he tells Sonya, "[Y]our greatest sin is that you have abandoned and destroyed yourself in vain. Is that not horrible? Is it not horrible that you live in this filth, which is so loathsome to you, while at the same time you know (you have only to open your eyes) that you are helping nobody by it, and not saving anybody from anything?" (309)

When Raskolnikov finally chooses Sonya's solution of surrendering himself to the authorities, he does so not because he has embraced Sonya's martyrlike perspective. Rather, he has arrived at an emotional juncture where he can accept neither voluntaristic doctrines nor Christian orthodoxy as spontaneously understood by Sonya. Porfiry again intuits very well Raskolnikov's need for "fresh air," i.e., for going beyond the cultural choices his community has to offer him. When Raskolnikov, dismayed by Porfiry's uncanny ability to guess his thoughts, asks him who he really is, the magistrate says: "'Who am I? I am a man who has developed as far as he is capable, that is all. A man, perhaps, of feeling and sympathy, of some knowledge perhaps, but no longer capable of further development. But you—that's another matter: the life God destines you for lies before you (but who knows, perhaps with you, too, it will pass away like a puff of smoke and nothing will come of it)" (441).

Porfiry also realizes that if Raskolnikov were "to pass into a different category of men," he would first need a liminal time-space in which to work out his transformation. A Siberian labor camp could provide just this kind of liminal opportunity: "With your heart you will not pine for comfort! What will it matter if nobody sees you perhaps for a very long time? It is not time that matters, but you yourself. Become a sun, and everybody will see you. The first duty of the sun is to be sun" (441–42). Porfiry Petrovich is equally aware that his suggestion that Raskolnikov confess and then expiate his crime in a labor camp may sound disingenuous coming as it does from an examining magistrate who lacks sufficient incriminating evidence to arrest his main suspect. Raskolnikov can certainly construe it as no more than Porfiry's desire to continue the cat-and-mouse game between them, as the magistrate points out: "And I am willing to bet that you suppose I am trying now to cajole you by flattery. Well, perhaps that is just what I am doing, he, he, he! Perhaps, Rodion Romanovich, you ought not to believe what I say, perhaps you should never believe me completely—I agree that my ways make it undesirable; but I will add only this—I think you ought to be able to judge how far I am a trickster and how far an honest man!" (442). Like all tricksters or royal fools, Porfiry can tell the truth only in jest, and it is indeed up to Raskolnikov to discern what is misleading and what is genuine in the magistrate's game.

But Raskolnikov does see the truth in Porfiry's ludic argument when later on he tells himself that it would be better, after all, to go to Siberia. He thereby does not acknowledge his "guilt" or the necessity for punishment as expiation; he only recognizes his need for a liminal time-space that might restore his ludic ability and thus allow him to move beyond his world, toward an alternative reference frame incommensurable with that world. As the narrator points out in the last paragraph of the novel, however, "that is the beginning of a new story, the story of the gradual renewal of a man, of his gradual regeneration, of his slow progress from one world to another, of how he learned to know a hitherto undreamed-of reality" (527).

4. Homicide as Play in "Lafcadio's Adventures"

In *Crime and Punishment*, the ludic element is constant throughout the narrative, even though it is not foregrounded as such beyond the explicit cat-and-mouse games played by the detective and the killer, or Svidrigaylov's games with Dunya, Raskolnikov, and himself. By contrast, in Gide's *Les caves du Vatican* (best known in English as *Lafcadio's Adventures*), play is at the very core of the novel. Gide's narrative is, by the author's own account, a *sotie* or a parody of a serious Christian morality play. It is also a parody of *Crime and Punishment* or, rather, a parody of the orthodox Christian reading of Dostoevsky's novel. Like Dostoevsky, Gide is fully aware of the conflict between voluntaristic and Christian values in modern Western culture, and many critics seem to believe that, unlike Dostoevsky, he favors the former over the latter, at least in this particular work. But, from the ludic-irenic standpoint of the present study, *Lafcadio's Adventures* exhibits the same kind of responsive understanding that is operative in *Crime and Punishment:* Gide's text stages a conflict between the basic values of a mentality of power, challenging its readers either to accept the full ethopathological consequences of this mentality or to embrace an alternative of ethos and pathos, essentially incommensurable with the old one.

Various characters in the novel, including the narrator, parodically embody various aspects of the axiological reference frame questioned by the text. Thus, Anthime Armand-Dubois is a parody of the modern scientist; Jules de Baraglioul, his brother-in-law, a parody of the conformist writer; and Lafcadio Wluiki de Baraglioul, Julius's half-brother, a parody of the Nietzschean overman. The narrator, in turn, is a parody of the omniscient authorial figure who pretends having complete control over his world and his reader, but who does not know how to solve his hero's Dostoevskian dilemma and leaves his narrative open-ended.

Anthime is partly a comic product of modern science as the Will to Power in its mechanistic and reductive guises (criticized at length by Dostoevsky, Nietzsche, and Heidegger, among others). As the narrator notes ironically, Anthime's "modest pretension, before going on to deal with human beings, was merely to reduce all the animal activities he had under observation, to what he termed 'tropisms'. . . . Organic matter was obviously governed by the same involuntary impulses as those which turn the flower of the heliotrope to face the sun (a fact which is easily to be explained by a few simple laws of physics and thermochemistry)."[9] The narrator implies, however, that Anthime's "modest pretension" is actually false modesty or pride. His project is motivated by the age-old agon between science and religion that, in the wake of the Enlightenment, has often been presented by modern science as a holy crusade of reason against unreason. What is at stake, however, is neither theism nor atheism, but cultural hegemony. If Anthime is successful, then scientific reason can presumably further consolidate its position as supreme cultural authority: "The order of the universe could at last be hailed as reassuringly benign. In all the motions of life, however surprising, a perfect obedience to the agent could be universally recognized."[10]

Here the narrator implies that science no less than religion tends to legitimize a supreme hierarchical principle (whether transcendental or not) to which everything else can be reduced. Through the word "tropism," moreover, the narrator suggests that the allegedly independent and objective world of science is as conformistic and predictable as the mimetic world of high fashion: "Tropism! The word was no sooner

invented than nothing else was to be heard of; an entire category of
psychologists would admit nothing in the world but tropisms. Tropisms!
A sudden flood of light emanated from these syllables!" (7).

Finally, the narrator underlines the similarity between the religious
and the scientific Will to Power when he playfully adopts a religious
perspective, comparing the man of science with a modern Moloch or
bloodthirsty idol, to whom Beppo, the little Italian boy, offers rats, sparrows, mice, and frogs in sacrificial worship: "[W]hile the boy, standing
silent beside the man of science, leaned forward to watch some abomi-
nable experiment, I wish I could certify that the man of science experienced no thrill of pleasure—no false god's vanity—at feeling the child's
astonished look fall, in turn with terror upon the animal, and with admiration upon himself" (7).

The narrator further emphasizes the interchangeability of science
and religion as power instruments, when Anthime converts from atheism to Christianity after the Virgin (whose statue he had desecrated in a
fit of iconoclastic rage) ostensibly cures him of crippling rheumatism
and then back to atheism when the cure proves to be temporary. The
newly converted Anthime, because of his great scientific reputation,
serves as a propaganda tool in the political contest between the liberal
and the conservative press:

> The first enthusiasm of the orthodox press was answered by the
> vituperation of the liberal organs. An important article in the
> *Osservatore*—"A New Victory for the Church"—was met by a diatribe
> in the *Tempo Felice*—"Another Fool." Finally the *Dépêche de Toulouse*
> [a liberal organ] headed Anthime's usual page, which he had sent in
> the day before his cure, with a few gibing introductory remarks. Julius,
> in his brother-in-law's name, wrote a short, dignified letter in reply, to
> inform the *Dépêche* that it need no longer consider "the convert" as
> one of its contributors. The *Zukunft* was beforehand with Anthime
> and politely thanked him for his services, intimating that there would
> be no further use for them. (34)

The narrator clearly implies that in a world of power governed by financial
interest and *Realpolitik* there is no room for atypical behavior such as a
genuine conversion, which is immediately interpreted and assimilated
in partisan terms. A high dignitary in the Masonic lodge, Anthime loses

its financial backing upon his conversion. The Church in turn promises to protect his financial interests, but abandons him as soon as the publicity around his conversion dies down. Anthime's pious wife is at first delighted with his change of heart, but then blames the Church for letting them live in (Christlike) poverty and reproaches her husband for having discontinued his lucrative articles for the atheist press.

Anthime seems initially to accept all "blows with that serenity of countenance which is the mark of a truly devout soul" (34). But this serenity is, ironically, interpreted by Julius, his religious brother-in-law, as a form of inordinate pride: "I was irritated to death by your resignation! And even—since you insist—I must admit, my dear Anthime, that it seemed to me a proof of pride rather than sanctity, and the last time I saw you at Milan that exaggerated resignation of yours struck me really as savouring more of rebellion than of true piety, and was extremely distasteful to me as a Christian. God didn't demand as much of you as all that!" (228). Of course, Anthime is right in observing to the opportunistic Julius: "It's all very easy for you to talk—you, who have never in your life given up anything for Him—you, who profit by everything—true or false. Oh! I've had enough! I want some fresh air!" (231).

Here Anthime invokes disinterestedness as a supreme Christian value, but he also falls short of this ideal when in the end he gives up his martyrlike posture and reverts to atheism: "No! Let me be! I know all that's necessary for my purpose. You can put the rest in a novel. As for me, I shall write to the Grand Master of the Order this very evening, and tomorrow I shall take up my scientific reviewing for the *Dépêche*. Fine fun it'll be!" (231). So Anthime's conversion does turn out not to be genuine after all and, as Julius smugly remarks to himself, it is the return of the scientist's rheumatism that causes him to lose faith again. True to his utilitarian mentality, Anthime has apparently struck a deal in his mind with the Virgin, and since she has not kept her end of the bargain, he sees no reason to keep his.

Whereas Anthime largely embodies the utilitarian scientist, Julius represents the utilitarian artist. Although he belongs by birth to the aristocracy, his values are thoroughly bourgeois. As the narrator ironically observes, the "fundamental distinction of his nature and that kind of moral elegance which was apparent in the slightest of his writings, had always prevented him from giving rein to his desires and from following a path down which his curiosity as a novelist would doubtless have urged him. His blood flowed calmly but not coldly, as many beautiful and aristocratic ladies might have testified" (15). Despite some youthful adventures and "the flattering illusion that nothing human was alien to him, Julius had rarely derogated from the customs of his class and he had very few dealings except with persons of his own milieu" (42).

Julius's literary concerns are equally safe and conventional, and his latest book on the (in)famous career of his own father is written with a view to ensure the author's place in the French Academy—the epitome of the middle-class cultural establishment: "Had not Julius, indeed, retraced in this book the old diplomat's truly representative career? As a companion picture to the turbulent follies of romanticism, had he not glorified the dignified, the ordered, the classic calm of Juste-Agenor's existence in its twofold aspect, political and domestic?" (39). The narrator ironically compares Julius's moral views to those of Descartes—another famous rationalist—implying, however, that this comparison is as much a flattering self-delusion as everything else about Julius: "The moral law which Descartes considered provisional, but to which he submitted in the meantime, until he had established the rules that should regulate his life and conduct hereafter, was the same law—its provisional powers indefinitely protracted—which governed Julius de Baraglioul. But Julius's temperament was not so intractable nor his intellect so commanding as to have given him hitherto much trouble in conforming to the proprieties" (67).

Julius's main failings as an artist include not only a lack of originality and of intellectual and moral probity but also a lack of creative playfulness. For instance, attempting to defend himself against Lafcadio's criticism of his literary endeavors, he waxes pompous and sententious: "'I don't write for the sake of amusement,' he answered nobly. 'The joy that I feel in writing is superior to any that I might find in living. Moreover, the one is not incompatible with the other'" (72). Only after he is temporarily denied a place among the "immortals" of the Academy does he embark upon an antiutilitarian and antiestablishment literary project. But even this project is far from being original, since it has already been anticipated in real life by his half-brother. It is under Lafcadio's influence that Julius turns "immoralist," advocating the doctrine of artistic disinterestedness in the form of a novel revolving around a gratuitous transgressive act such as "perfect murder." He develops the ideas that Lafcadio had suggested to him during their first interview. "You can't imagine," Julius lectures Lafcadio, totally oblivious to the irony of lecturing his own master, "because you aren't in the trade, how an erroneous system of ethics can hamper the free development of one's creative faculties. So nothing is further from my old novels than the one I am planning now. I used to demand logic and consistency from my characters, and in order to make quite sure of getting them, I began by demanding them from myself. It wasn't natural" (196).

Julius's notion of art as a counterbalance to an "erroneous system of ethics" (i.e., median morality) as well as his theory of homicide as play or as a purely gratuitous act is taken not only from Nietzsche but also from the late-nineteenth-century French aestheticist or "decadent" movement. As he explains to Amedée Fleurissoire, his other brother-in-law, "self-advantage is *not* man's guiding principle" and "there *are* such things as disinterested actions" (171). By disinterested actions, Julius does not mean Christian charitable works, as Fleurissoire assumes: "By *disinterested* I mean gratuitous. Also that evil actions—what are commonly called evil—may be just as gratuitous as good ones" (171). When Fleurissoire wonders why one should then commit them at all, Julius replies: "Out of sheer wantonness—or from love of sport." A good Catholic petty bourgeois such as Fleurissoire will always remain bound to a utilitarian view of action, whereas a "contempt of what may serve is no doubt the stamp of a certain aristocracy of nature." Once an individual "has shaken free from orthodoxy, from self-indulgence and from calculation," Julius argues to Fleurissoire's horror, that individual's soul need "keep no accounts at all" (171). In short, as Nietzsche would put it, aristocratic *otium* and not bourgeois *negotium* is the true generator of human values.

As to homicide, Julius contends, a "disinterested" or gratuitous murder can never be traced back to its author—a contention that largely holds true in a predominantly utilitarian society. The (median) legal principle of *is fecit cui prodest* is irrelevant in this case, because the criminal has no material motive, and "the motive of the crime is the handle by which we lay hold of the criminal" (173). Hence, the "criminal" in Julius's projected novel, as he excitedly tells Lafcadio later on, would be an aristocrat who "acts almost entirely in play, and as a matter of course prefers his pleasure to his interest" (197). His crime would have "no motive either of passion or need! His very reason for committing the crime is just to commit it without any reason." In this respect, Julius argues, there is really no good reason "that a man who commits a crime without reason should be considered a criminal [at all]" (198). Ironically, Julius does not know that he is expounding his theory of homicide as play to his own fictional protagonist, as it were, for Lafcadio has already killed Fleurissoire.

When Julius learns of his brother-in-law's death, he immediately drops his aesthetic theories and reverts to his old utilitarian beliefs. He attributes the murder to the Vatican conspiracy and grows angry with Lafcadio for suggesting that there is no motive behind the crime: "'To begin with,' exclaimed Julius furiously, 'there's no such thing as a crime without a motive. He was got rid of because he was in possession of a secret'" (203). The narrator ironically implies that Julius can no more relinquish his utilitarian mentality than Anthime can and that his attempt at genuine (self-)transformation is as short-lived as his brother-in-law's. The narrator drives this point home once more when he has Julius sententiously declare to his wife—upon learning that he will be voted into the French Academy after all—that "not to change" is the highest virtue: "Faithful to you, to my opinions, to my principles! Perseverance is the most indispensable of virtues" (226). And the narrator adds with supreme irony: "The recollection of his recent wild-goose chase had already faded from his mind, as well as every opinion that was other than orthodox, and every intention that was other than proper. Now that he knew the facts, he recovered his balance without an effort. He was filled with admiration for the subtle consistency which his mind had shown in its temporary deviation. It was not he who had changed—it was the pope!" (226).

Even when Lafcadio challenges his orthodox views again by declaring defiantly that he is the true murderer of Fleurissoire, Julius reacts in the most conventional, bourgeois manner: "Lafcadio, I shouldn't like to part from you without a word of advice. It lies entirely with you, I'm convinced, to become an honest man again and to take your place in the world—as far, that is, as your birth permits. . . . The Church is there to help you. Come, my lad, a little courage; go and confess yourself" (236). Of course, Julius's advice is parodically reminiscent of Sonya's in *Crime and Punishment* but, unlike hers, it is obviously not motivated by genuine faith. Julius does not suggest, besides, that the killer go to the authorities, but only that he go to confession, which would have no adverse social consequences for Lafcadio. Julius's advice illustrates the typical utilitarian compromise between one's social and one's religious conscience.

If Julius is the artist as bourgeois, Lafcadio is the Nietzschean aesthete or the artist as aristocrat, and the narrator clearly sympathizes with his predicament in a predominantly middle-class milieu. By birth, temperament, and early education, Lafcadio is outside the accepted norms of his society. The unacknowledged offspring of a secret liaison between a French count and a Romanian demimondaine, Lafcadio spent his childhood moving from country to country and from one paternal figure to another. The figures who influenced him most were several happy-go-lucky noblemen, from whom he acquired his aristocratic tastes and reckless, ludic spirit. As Lafcadio tells Julius, the Italian Baldi was a "juggler, conjurer, mountebank, acrobat . . . forever inventing some new game, some surprise, some absurd joke or other" (77). Bielkowski, the Polish count "who flung himself upon his pleasure with a kind of frenzy" (76), introduced Lafcadio to all kinds of secret, semiforbidden games, including perhaps sexual ones; his English "protector," Lord Gravensdale, took him on "immoralist" trips to the Middle East. By the time Lafcadio entered a select private school in Paris, he was thoroughly "spoiled" at least from the standpoint of a strict, French middle-class system of education. He could never fit into the straitjacket of that system and ran away at the first opportunity. It was at this school that he first met Protos, who would play such an important role in the Vatican swindle and in Lafcadio's life, and the latter was attracted to him precisely because of his rebellious, criminal mind.

The conventional Julius is appalled by Lafcadio's autobiographical account and observes how fortunate it is that his half-brother will inherit a little money, for "with no profession, with no education, condemned to live by expedients . . . you were ready for anything" (82). But Lafcadio counters in true Wildean fashion: "On the contrary, ready for nothing. . . . Nothing hinders me so effectually as want. I have never yet been tempted but by the things that could be of no service to me" (82). Lafcadio's mentality is completely untainted not only by utilitarian but also by traditional Christian values such as identification with the victim, pity, guilt, love of one's neighbor, martyrlike meekness, and so on. Like Svidrigaylov, he can act in a courageous, generous, and merciful manner or, conversely, be cruel, violent, and willful with complete spontaneity. For example, he saves two infants from a Parisian fire and offers their mother the contents of Geneviève's purse, even though he can hardly afford this splendid generosity. At the same time, he scornfully discourages the sycophantic attentions of the crowd that had watched him perform the heroic act. Later on, in Italy, he helps an old Italian woman carry a heavy sack across the mountain, but has impious thoughts about an angelic-looking boy accompanied by a priest.

As Lafcadio himself observes about the beginning of his Italian trip, his actions are hardly motivated by a Christian spirit of fellowship and compassion but, rather, by an irrepressible spirit of adventure and, above all, curiosity. For example, in the scene in which Protos attempts to blackmail Lafcadio, the narrator says: "But if for a moment [Lafcadio] had contemplated flight, curiosity was already getting the upper hand—that passionate curiosity of his against which nothing—not even his personal safety—had ever been able to prevail" (222).

Like Nietzsche's Zarathustra, Lafcadio celebrates life as a ceaseless play of becoming and pure chance: "Nothing ever happens exactly as one thinks it's going to. . . . That's what makes me want to act. . . . One does so little! . . . 'Let all that can be, be!' That's my explanation of the creation. . . . In love with what might be. If I were the Government I should lock myself up" (179). Lafcadio's idea of murdering a complete stranger on a train is part of the same adventurous spirit. Like Raskolnikov, Lafcadio wants to test himself to see if he can rise above common humanity by a violent act of transgression. This could be the crowning act of the self-training program upon which Lafcadio embarks in his adolescence with a view to becoming an overman. In his old diary, surreptitiously read by Julius, Lafcadio had written in Machiavellian fashion: "QUI INCOMINCIA IL LIBRO DE LA NOVA ESIGENZA E DELLA SUPREMA VIRTÚ" (49). He had also recorded the number of *punte* that he had inflicted upon himself as self-punishment whenever failing to follow his program. Ironically but predictably, Julius the moralist had mistaken *punte*—"stiletto pricks" or "marks," for good points—for "a childish and trifling computation of merits and rewards" (49).

Unlike Raskolnikov, however, Lafcadio passes his self-imposed power test with flying colors. He pushes Fleurissoire off the train without much hesitation or moral scruples—only a short while before he had spontaneously offered the stranger a treat and had contemplated helping him with his coat. In considering whether he should kill him or not, Lafcadio completely ignores the ethical implications of the act and only considers the sheer novelty of the experience as well as the challenge it will pose to the authorities: "A crime without a motive," he tells himself, "what a puzzle for the police" (186). Finally, true to his ludic spirit, Lafcadio makes a bet with himself: "If I can count up to twelve, without hurrying, before I see a light in the countryside, the dromedary is saved. Here goes! One, two, three, four (slowly! slowly!), five, six, seven, eight, nine . . . a light!" (187).

After the deed, Lafcadio feels no guilt whatsoever, looking upon it as just another form of adventure: "The crime! This word seemed odd to him, to say the very least; and criminal as applied to himself totally inappropriate. He preferred adventurer—a word as pliable as his beaver and easily twisted to suit his liking" (192). Later on, when Lafcadio finds out who his victim was, instead of fleeing to safety he accepts Julius's distasteful assignment of accompanying Fleurissoire's coffin from Naples to Rome out of the same spirit of *nova esigenza* and *suprema virtú*. In the dining car, his thoughts do not dwell morbidly on the victim but, disdainfully, on his present company. He identifies the train passengers with the Nietzschean herd who, by attempting to minimize chance and individual exposure to danger, transform life into a drab and boring affair: "What mortal dullness exudes from such places as this [the dining car]! . . . Herds of cattle going through life as if it were a monotonous grind, instead of the entertainment which it is—or which it might be" (211).

Although Lafcadio is the Nietzschean overman that Raskolnikov would have liked to be, he is no more successful than his Russian counterpart in asserting his individuality and rising above the herd. The narrator shows that Lafcadio's "perfect crime" is no more perfect than Raskolnikov's. The question is not so much that Protos has to clean up after Lafcadio and remove all the incriminating evidence from the crime scene; or that, as in Raskolnikov's case, little takes place according to

Lafcadio's (or, for that matter, Protos's) plan, with chance playing a great role in the outcome of events. If anything, there is an overdetermination of fate in Lafcadio's crime, which hilariously turns out to be a bourgeois family affair. The narrator deliberately makes himself guilty of loading the dice by introducing too many coincidences into the plot: indeed, in the novel all the roads literally lead to Rome. But this is precisely the narrator's point: he plays with the idea of divine providence, which assumes that nothing happens by chance but according to a divine Will. When stripped of its transcendental, theological guise, this idea can equally apply to any sociocultural context, which effectively predetermines and/or limits an individual's existential options. Lafcadio's attempt at asserting his absolute freedom or individual ego-will through a transgressive act is bound to fail, as Protos points out: "But what astonishes me is that a person as intelligent as you, Cadio, should have thought it possible to quit a society as simply as all that, without stepping at the same moment into another; or that you should have thought it possible for any society to exist without laws" (222).

Protos himself understands that his crooked world—or what he calls the world of the "slim"—is the reverse image of the straight one or the world of the "crusted" (219–20), that there is no God without a Satan and vice versa. The narrator underscores this point when he has Protos acknowledge his cooperation with the police: "Try and take this in, Lafcadio. The police collar people who kick up a row; but in Italy they're glad to come to terms with 'the slim.' 'Come to terms'—yes, I think that's the right expression. I work a bit for the police myself. I've a way with me. I help to keep order. I don't act on my own—I cause others to act" (223). As Protos suggests, the best one can do in a world based on median principles is to work the "system" or the established power structure to one's (material) advantage. Open rebellion, on the other hand, only reinforces this power structure (which, as we have seen in chapter 3, feeds on resistance) and more often than not subverts rather than promotes the individual ego-will. Despite his sophisticated criminal activities, Protos turns out to be a run-of-the-mill confidence man, as utilitarian in his instincts as Julius. Ironically, however, he fails to follow his own power strategies, thereby becoming a victim rather than a master manipulator of the system. From a utilitarian standpoint, Protos makes the mistake of acting spontaneously rather than in his own interest: in a fit of rage, he strangles Carola Venitequa, thus openly seeking (archaic) revenge for what he perceives as betrayal on his mistress's part.

The narrator also demonstrates how ineptly naive a philosophical program of returning to an archaic or heroic mentality can be in a predominantly median world. Lafcadio's "gratuitous" act, belonging to an aristocratic mentality, is immediately interpreted and assimilated in the median terms of *cui prodest* and Lafcadio's pure assertion of the individual ego-will becomes "tainted" by the utilitarian values around him. A median world of power can obviously co-opt not only Christian values—essentially incommensurable with it—but also archaic values that are, in principle, incompatible with it. In this regard, Lafcadio fails not because, like Raskolnikov, he cannot overcome his own split ethopathology, but because he cannot use that of others to his advantage (a technique that, as we shall see in chapter 6, the overmen of Orwell's *1984* have mastered to perfection).

In one sense, *Les caves du Vatican* goes beyond *Crime and Punishment* by demonstrating that the divided ethopathology of median humanity can be overcome by the affirmation of the power of the false (simulacrum) advocated by Nietzsche and the twentieth-century French poststructuralists. Unlike the relatively stable fictional world of *Crime and Punishment*, where the ontological status of truth is not a central issue (as it is, say, in *The Possessed*), the world of *Les caves du Vatican* belongs to a Nietzschean or a postmodern centerless universe where the play of simulacra reigns supreme. Even the obtuse Fleurissoire realizes he lives in such a world when, having embarked upon his pope-saving crusade, he is faced with various interpretations of the same events and cannot decide which of these interpretations are true: "Here we have at once the consequence and the proof of that initial vice—the collapse of the Holy See; everything comes tottering down with that. Whom can one trust if not the Pope? And once the cornerstone on which the Church was built gives way, nothing else deserves to be true" (162). Later on in the narrative, Anthime makes a similar comment to Julius, be it only in blasphemous jest, when the latter tells him about the false pope: "And who knows but what Fleurissoire, when he gets to Heaven, won't find after all that his Almighty isn't the *real* God either?" (230). Of course, Julius, the arch-"crusted" (the staunchest defender of orthodox median values in the novel) rejects the idea as preposterous: "Come, come, my dear

Anthime, you're rambling! As if there *could* be two! As if there could be another!" (231).

Since Lafcadio, however, does not wish to affirm the power of the simulacra (as Protos does, up to his fatal faux pas), he runs out of existential options. For example, when Geneviève, a parodic composite of Dunya and Sonya from *Crime and Punishment*, urges her stepuncle and lover to deliver himself into the arms of the Church ("Lafcadio, the Church is there to prescribe your penance and to help you back to peace through repentance" [240]), the narrator comments ironically: "Geneviève is right; most certainly the best thing Lafcadio can do now is to be conveniently submissive; he will realize this sooner or later and that every other issue is closed to him" (240).

Before spending the night with Geneviève, Lafcadio also contemplates surrendering himself to the authorities, not out of remorse but out of a gallant sense of pride. The narrator, however, is not satisfied with this "Dostoevskian" solution and closes the novel with another ironic statement: "What, is [Lafcadio] going to renounce life? Does he still for the sake of Geneviève's esteem (and already he esteems her a little less now that she loves him a little more), does he still think of giving himself up?" (242). The novel ends on this ambiguous note, because the narrator himself has run out of options and has no other recourse but to fall back on the voluntaristic values that have already failed Lafcadio, thus pointing to the perpetual return of the same that is endemic to any mentality of power. He has taken Lafcadio as far as he could go in terms of the ethical choices available in his culture, and his hero's quest has ended in ambiguity and confusion.

But the reader can go farther than the narrator, choosing to see Lafcadio's state of ambiguity as a liminal one, fraught with alternative existential possibilities. The narrator himself nudges the reader in this direction through the various liminal elements that he introduces in his narrative. For example, he ends his story at dawn—a common literary symbol of temporal liminality: "We will leave our two lovers at cockcrow, at the hour when color, warmth, and light begin at last to triumph over night" (241). One may note that, similarly, the narrator of *Crime and Punishment* has Raskolnikov experience the beginning of his spiritual regeneration in spring—a liminal season par excellence.

Gide's narrator also makes Lafcadio into a liminal figure by giving him the social status of a bastard. (Here one can discern another close parallel with *Crime and Punishment*: as Raskolnikov's name suggests in Russian, he can be associated with a particular group of disgruntled Russian intellectuals of mixed social origins. In this respect, Raskolnikov has an ambiguous place vis-à-vis the established scheme of things and may well feel like a social outcast.) Whereas the bastard is usually regarded as a social, juridical, and psychological monster who can never overcome his or her split identity, Protos points, on the contrary, to the great advantage that can be derived from this ambiguous status: "[B]etween ourselves, what an advantage for the bastard! Just think! a being whose very existence is owing to an erratic impulse—to a crook in the straight line!" (218). Lafcadio's ambiguous social status may be advantageous not only in the sense that, as Protos implies, it gives him access to both the straight and the crooked worlds, but also because it opens up a third path for him: that of renouncing both of these worlds and gaining access to an alternative reality incommensurable with the previous one, where there are neither bastards nor firstborns, neither "slims" nor "crusted"—in a word, where there are no binary oppositions of any sort. Of course, the narrator leaves it up to the reader to imagine what this reality might look like, and in this regard, at least, *Lafcadio's Adventures* is as open-ended as *Crime and Punishment*.

3. Conrad Aiken's "King Coffin" and the Concept of Perfect Murder

Aiken's short novel was reportedly inspired by the famous Leopold-Loeb case that shook Chicago in the twenties. According to Clarence Darrow and Benjamin Bacharach, the criminal defense attorneys in the case, "the civilized world had been startled out of its routine complacency on May 31, 1924, by the amazing confession of these two youths of nineteen and eighteen respectively, of the kidnapping and murder of a young neighbor and acquaintance of Richard Loeb, fourteen-year-old Bobby Franks, purely for the thrill and adventure. The wealth of the three families, their prominence in the community of Chicago, the bizarre and apparently motiveless homicide, and the instantaneous newspaper notoriety which was given the crime from every conceivable angle, aroused public interest throughout the entire civilized world in the fate to be meted out to the young murderers."[11]

The Leopold-Loeb case inspired several works of fiction, including Patrick Hamilton's play, *Rope's End* (on which Alfred Hitchcock based his motion picture *Rope* in 1948) and Meyer Levin's *Compulsion*, but Aiken's novel is perhaps the most intriguing because it places its subject in a long novelistic tradition to which *Crime and Punishment* and *Lafcadio's Adventures* equally belong. Although Aiken borrows certain superficial features from the Chicago case, he goes well beyond his alleged historical source, concentrating on the idea of a crime without a motive, which he develops, like Gide, in terms of the aestheticist notion of homicide as a fine art.

The plot of *King Coffin* is fairly straightforward, although it does contain a final twist. Jasper Ammen, a young man of independent means, has associated himself with a group of anarchists operating in Boston, but becomes disillusioned with their petty goals and decides to follow a path of his own. A great admirer of Nietzsche, whose death mask is one of the few adornments of his "chaste and epicene" room, he considers himself an overman and proposes to live beyond the morals of the herd. To this purpose, not unlike Raskolnikov and Lafcadio, Ammen considers committing "pure murder," for him an act beyond good and evil. After contemplating the possibility of killing one of his friends, he discards the idea because it lacks purity of motive. Instead, he randomly chooses a complete stranger for his target. The stranger's name, appropriately enough, turns out to be Jones.

Ammen studies the habits of Jones for several weeks, managing at the same time to keep his friends interested in his secret life. He learns about their reactions by stealthily reading the diary of his neighbor, the law student Toppan. Also, Jasper makes an alliance of sorts with Gerta (a young woman who is in love with him), sharing with her as much of his project as he considers safe to disclose. He encourages her, moreover, to get sexually (but not emotionally) involved with Sandbach, a Jewish anarchist, so that his own relationship with her will remain "pure." To Toppan he presents his plan of murdering a complete stranger as a purely theoretical problem to be made into the subject of a novel entitled *King Coffin*. Gerta becomes more and more concerned about his odd behav-

ior, while Toppan grows more and more suspicious. Finally an anony-
mous letter is sent, presumably at Gerta's instigation, to Ammen's father, informing him of his son's criminal intentions. Another complica-
tion arises from the fact that Jones's wife has a stillborn child. Ammen
secretly attends the funeral, and instead of killing Jones he tries to kill
himself by turning on the gas in his apartment, but not before sending a
letter to Gerta in the hope that she will arrive in time to save him.

Most American critics have seen Aiken's novel as no more than a
psychological casebook. For example, Vincent McHugh describes the
work as the "crisis-chart of a paranoid psychosis, complete with narcissism, megalomania, sexual symbols and a psychopathic inheritance."[12]
Far from being a psychological case study of aberration, *King Coffin* focuses on the ethopathology of an all too common world of power. In this
respect, Aiken takes up the literary problematic of the "perfect crime"
where Dostoevsky and Gide leave it off. By linking this problematic to
an essentially narcissistic and solipsistic notion of the self only tangen-
tially touched upon by his predecessors, Aiken carries it to its logical
conclusion. In order to commit a perfect crime, the protagonist chooses
a perfect stranger for his victim. In the end, however, this stranger turns
out to be himself. Furthermore, Ammen never commits murder, but
only *plays* at it (so he can hardly be accused of being a psychopathic
killer), and the ending of the novel remains deliberately ambiguous, a
fact that thus far no literary critic has carefully considered.

One may begin by drawing a distinction between what Julius de
Baraglioul understands by "perfect crime" (a notion that belongs to the
tradition of the detective novel) and what Ammen calls "pure murder"
(a notion that belongs to the tradition of aestheticist fiction). As both
Julius de Baraglioul and Lafcadio suggest, a "perfect crime" is a legalis-
tic concept, implying a deed that cannot be detected because it cannot
be traced back to an apparent motive. A "perfect crime" is both a challenge to and a triumph of rationality or logic; it is a mathematical problem. "Pure murder," on the other hand, is ultimately more of an aesthetic and ethical question than a logical one. As Ammen tells himself
while looking for a suitable victim, "the terribleness of the deed must
be kept pure: the problem had become a problem in art-form."[13]

On one level, the two concepts are diametrically opposed, on another
they overlap. Whereas both concepts defy modern ethical standards, a

perfect crime suspends the question of ethics altogether, whereas pure murder is explicitly directed against it (meaning that it proposes to replace a commonly accepted ethical code with another one, incompatible with it). As Jasper Ammen points out to Toppan: "To injure or destroy is natural, it's life itself: to deny that is to deny life. Well, you know it's right, and I know it's right, but society won't agree with us, will it? . . . Consequently what ought to be a public action, and done openly has to be private or secret: unless you make up your mind to go the whole hog and *do* it openly and take the social consequences. That's the way it ought to be, to be perfect, it ought to take place in *sunlight*" (326–27). A perfect crime is perfect only as long as it remains undetected, whereas pure murder remains imperfect *unless* it is committed in broad daylight as Ammen, Lafcadio, and the surrealists argue.[14]

Most importantly, the two concepts point to two incompatible value systems, archaic and median, that were equally present in *Crime and Punishment* and *Lafcadio's Adventures*. Through pure murder, Ammen attempts to reaffirm the archaic principle of might makes right, whereas a perfect crime largely belongs to a median mentality that separates might from right. But since Ammen, not unlike Raskolnikov or Lafcadio, lives in a predominantly median world, he is fully aware that pure murder must also be a perfect crime, and indeed the two notions overlap in several respects. They overlap, for instance, because of their "purity." Thinking of his insane brother, Kay, Ammen rejects the possibility of his own madness by arguing that "purity is not insanity. An action could have the purity of a work of art—it could be as abstract and absolute as a problem in algebra" (319). In other words, the two concepts overlap because they are both ludic in nature: a perfect crime involves a game of hide-and-seek between the perpetrator and the detective, while pure murder involves a cat-and-mouse game between the aggressor and the unsuspecting victim.

Ammen is well aware of the pleasurable, playful quality involved in choosing his victim at random, tracking it down—what he calls "detection for the *sake* of detection" (326)—and eventually annihilating it. Telling Gerta about King Coffin—the name of a physician he had seen on a sign somewhere in Boston or St. Louis—Ammen exclaims: "I'd *like* to play King Coffin. . . . It seemed to me a very good, and very sinister name for a doctor—it sounds a little supernatural. It might not be a *man* at all, but a sort of death-principle" (320). Ammen repeatedly uses the cat-and-mouse analogy in order to describe his playing King Coffin: "As he stood still by the corner, observing first one face and then another, one hand jingling pennies in his pocket, the other holding his unlighted pipe, it occurred to him that a cat must feel something like this: a cat alone in a cellar, sitting perhaps on the top of a flour barrel, and watching the naive and unconscious antics of mice" (310).

The other common analogy Ammen uses for his game is that of the puppeteer pulling the strings of his puppets at will. Once he chooses Jones as the intended victim, he resists the impulse of calling up Gerta to say, "I've found a man, a stranger, and I have him on the end of an invisible cord, a cord three miles long, and with this cord I shall slowly but surely kill him, I shall dangle him there like a puppet, like Punch or Judy, until I want him" (343). Ammen equally thinks of Gerta and his other friends as puppets to be manipulated for his own ends: "They, as much as Jones, were his own creation, they were falling into their grooves, they no longer had any freedom of will. To all intents, they had become [his] puppets" (363).

Ammen sees his game as pure because it has no material object, it is simply a game of enhancing his feeling of power for its own sake. (Compare Raskolnikov's and Lafcadio's similar ideas of purity, which also derive from their aversion toward a herd mentality and bourgeois utilitarianism.) Looking over Boston at sunset, the protagonist feels that the surrounding world is "all Jasper Ammen, a singular magnification or distillation of his own essence, it was himself gone abroad for the greater exercise of his subtlety and power. The tower was his strength, the trees were his strength, the evolving and changing of light were merely, as it were, the play of his thought over an earth everywhere his own" (300). Killing for the sake of killing is part of this feeling of power, which seeks to expand beyond all boundaries, beyond good and evil. In this sense, pure murder can equally succeed as a perfect crime, because its object is transcendental and therefore impossible to trace back to any material motive.

For Ammen, purity also means lack of emotional involvement beyond the sheer pleasure of the hunt, and here he comes closer to Lafcadio than to Raskolnikov. As he reasons with himself, the victim must be a stranger, "someone to whom one could be completely indifferent. He must be neither attractive nor unattractive, not to be loved or pitied, nor hated or feared, some one whose strangeness and anonymity (in the sense that one knew nothing about him and *felt* nothing) was pure. The face must be quite ordinary, just a face, the bearing and gait must be neither offensive nor enviable, the clothes of a sort of universal characterlessness. In short it must be simply 'a man'" (332).

But as Ammen finds out soon enough, Everyman does not exist except in the realm of thought, and therefore he cannot kill Jones outside this realm and still preserve the "purity" of the deed. In the practical realm no deed is "pure," as Lafcadio also discovers after killing his own brother-in-law in the mistaken belief that he was a complete stranger. Ammen gets emotionally involved in Jones's petty existence, just as he had gotten emotionally involved at the meeting with his fellow anarchists, an emotional involvement that he again visualizes through the ludic image of the puppeteer:

> The affair of the meeting [with Sandbach and the other anarchists] had been certainly only a partial success, it was in some measure because he had gone there with his plans unformulated, with nothing but his anger and contempt, and therefore it had got beyond his control: or at any rate, his control had not been quite perfect. This remained tethered to him, as by threads or eyebeams, as if himself, the puppeteer, had become subtly and dangerously entangled in the threads of his own puppets, could not quite escape from them, found their voices still at his ears, like gnats. (314)

Ammen's very motive of committing murder is impure, because it is "polluted" by his rage for purity itself. His object is to separate himself from the crowd by which he feels "contaminated." For instance, he explains angrily to Gerta why he does not want a sexual relationship with her: "I won't be contaminated any longer, by you or anyone else. That's something the exceptional man must learn sooner or later, and I've learned it. Nietzsche speaks of it in *Beyond Good and Evil*. The exceptional man is subject to one great temptation—a sort of desperateness—a sudden weak-kneed longing for the society of the commonplace and orderly, the good little parasites. He thinks he gets a kind of healing from it. It's a flight from himself, from his loneliness. The same with sex" (317).

Here Ammen echoes Raskolnikov's desire to separate himself from the ordinary crowd and achieve a Nietzschean pathos of distance. By killing one of the "good little parasites" (compare Raskolnikov's view of the pawnbroker as an "old louse" or "cockroach"), Ammen hopes to raise himself above the herd: "He was going to *do* something, he must *do* something, there must be the final action by which he would have set the seal on his complete freedom. To escape the company of rats, to express the profundity of his contempt—to *kill* a rat—!" (309). But Ammen does not realize (as Raskolnikov does) that one's need to separate oneself from the crowd is precisely what makes one part of the crowd. A cat does not need to separate itself from the rats to become a cat. A cat is a cat before it kills a rat, not because it kills one.

Ammen's feelings of hate for the crowd, therefore, clearly contradict his idea of purity. Of course, he defines "hate" in a Nietzschean manner, as a dispassionate means of achieving distance from the herd, but he quite obviously fails to live up to this definition, for example, when he associates hate with the impure, physical aspects of humanity. The idea of murder occurs to him "precisely at the moment when the mere physical nearness of a stranger's human body was beginning to oppress and stifle him, making itself felt as an unwarrantable and disgusting intrusion. The feeling of hatred, intolerable hatred, had come like a flash and had revealed to him as never before the rightness of the *deed* . . . the mere presence of the human body had shown him not only what he wanted but exactly why he wanted it" (310).

Moreover, if purity means retreat into the "kingdom of thought," how can one achieve it through a "deed," that is, by moving in the opposite direction? Ammen attempts to solve this dilemma theoretically by expanding his self over the entire world so that the outside object becomes part of the subject. In practice, however, Ammen preserves a distinction between self and world, thought and action: "Between his world and the world outside, a peculiar division had now arrived, and if time still existed importantly for himself, it had no longer any important existence elsewhere: in his own kingdom, the kingdom of thought, he could move as rapidly as he liked, stay as long as he liked, the outside world would meanwhile stand still, and he could rejoin it whenever he wished, and exactly at the point at which he had left it" (310).

Ammen's assumption that the outside world will stand still until he chooses to rejoin it reveals the nature of his problem: despite his idea of a cosmic expansion of the self, he never questions the dualistic notion of subject and object that controls his way of thinking. In order to unite himself with the world-object, he has to act. But by acting he becomes part of the world-object (rather than the object part of himself) and therefore instead of gaining his freedom, he loses it. Ammen knows with half his mind that he is omnipotent only in the "kingdom of thought," that is, as long as his idea remains pure by not becoming fact. (This knowledge, incidentally, distinguishes him from the clinical paranoid and makes possible the final dramatic reversal in the narrative.) For instance, Ammen has the feeling that his idea of pure murder has been "deranged" when he first sets eyes on Jones and instantly chooses him as a victim: "This was no Joseph Kazis [a name Ammen had picked at random from the telephone directory], no abstraction, nothing so remote as a name in South Boston, and in that sense it was already possible to feel an acute disappointment, a definite derangement of the basic idea" (335). By the end of the narrative Ammen recognizes, not unlike Raskolnikov and Lafcadio, that "vision is one thing, action or speech another" (402).

The same derangement of the idea of purity in the face of outside reality is present in Ammen's relationship with Gerta. In order to gain complete freedom, he wants to disentangle himself emotionally from her. In keeping with his subjective view of the expansion of the self (and ironically anticipating his suicide attempt) he reasons, commenting on a Zarathustrian maxim: "Take care lest a parasite ascend with you! But the parasite was actually, in such a case, simply oneself . . . the cause of one's hatred was not without but within; it was not therefore a question of getting rid of Sandbach or Gerta, not at all, but of getting rid of one's *need*" (305). But Ammen miscalculates again his—and Gerta's—capacity for purity or living in the absolute. He loves Gerta, though he rejects this love in order to build a new, "pure" relationship with her, in which he would allow her to share his feeling of power. In this he follows again a Nietzschean precept: "The happiness of man is: I will. The happiness of woman is: he wills." But when Gerta takes him at his word and gets sexually involved with Sandbach, Ammen is visibly hurt and feels betrayed.

The dialectic of subject and object reaches its crisis in the narrative when, like Oedipus, Ammen discovers that the stranger is himself. This is the logical outcome of his subjectivism, the ironical clarification of another Zarathustrian maxim: "But remember, if thou gazest into the abyss, the abyss will also gaze into thee." Early on, Ammen sees Jones as the obscenity of the world and himself as the "destructive positive" or Nietzsche's strong nihilist. By the end, Jones as the obscenity of the world has become part of himself or his double—a sort of Mr. Hyde or picture of Dorian Gray—which effectively undermines his strong nihilism, converting it into a weak kind. It is in this sense that Jones, the victim, now threatens to kill his aggressor. Ammen's contemplated suicide is thus consistent with his notion of pure murder, becoming ironically the "conscious end of the conscious world." Suicide is the only possible actualization of pure murder in a median world, because it presupposes a closed circle in which the murderer becomes his own victim. But also, from a nihilist subjectivist standpoint, to commit suicide means, as in Svidrigaylov's case, to annihilate the whole world, negating its fundamental principle, the Schopenhauerian Will to Live.

The duality of subject and object is also closely connected with the problematic of mimesis-imitation that one can trace throughout *King Coffin*. There are two anthropological notions of mimesis in the narrative, operating in terms of a dialectic of subject and object, or aggressor and victim. There is a good kind of mimesis (love), in which the subject identifies or becomes at one *with* the object, and a bad kind (hate), in which the subject attempts to *identify* the object and distance himself from it in order to control, or even annihilate, it. As we have seen, Ammen practices mostly the bad kind, and this becomes again obvious in his attitude toward Jones: "The stranger had been identified—hadn't he—as Jones, and as such could thus be destroyed: the *strangeness* in Jones had been recognized, with its terror and its pure desirability; it had been observed carefully and inimically as the thing-that-wants-to-be killed; it could be killed. There is no compromise with the object, no placid or reasoned acceptance of it. It is seen, understood, and destroyed" (403).

Once Ammen is motivated by hate, he no longer plays, he imitates, just as Raskolnikov does. Of course, he attempts, as we have seen, to employ the Nietzschean overman's technique of avoiding mimetic conflict by ceaselessly increasing the distance between himself and others. But instead of keeping aloof from his fellow humans, he actually goes to great lengths to spurn them, constantly engaging in a bad mimetic relationship with them. When he finally identifies with Jones, he does so in terms of hate, rather than love. (It is true, he experiences something like "love" for Jones when he tries to protect their "special" relationship of aggressor and victim against the "others"—Gerta, Sandbach, and Toppan—who try to stop him. But this illusory love goes away when he no longer feels threatened.) Ammen does not escape the dynamic of aggressor and victim, eventually seeing himself as a victim, or as Jones's double. Now it is he himself—the strange creature who has failed to rise above the ethics of pity and become an overman—that must be destroyed. Appropriately, when Ammen looks at himself in the mirror, his face momentarily becomes that of Jones or the stranger. This face "was as surprising and as mean, as vital and objectionable, as definitely something to be suspected and distrusted and perhaps destroyed, as some queer marine creature which one might find on overturning a wet rock by the sea. . . . It might have to be killed" (404).

Ammen, however, takes only halfhearted steps toward killing himself. Instead he chooses to turn his suicide into a game. He now appears to rely on the chance that Gerta will receive his letter in time to come and rescue him. In this sense, one could argue that the situation is reversed again and that Ammen's recognition of his strangeness has become a false one. Having discovered the advantages of being a victim, he refuses to give up his game of power and attempts to manipulate Gerta through her need to help him.

But Aiken, by leaving his novel open-ended, also allows for a completely different interpretation of Ammen's final action. Through giving himself up to chance and putting his own existence on the line, Ammen is at last beginning to turn away from his mentality of hate. Throughout the novel, Aiken presents Ammen as literally moving between two incommensurable worlds, or two radically different modes of thinking, feeling, and acting, represented by two symbolic figures: Nietzsche and Buddha. His "chaste and epicene" room contains not only the bust of Nietzsche but also that of Buddha, which is repeatedly referred to at key junctures in the narrative.

The bronze Buddha is mentioned for the first time at the beginning of the novel when Ammen looks at himself in the mirror, admiring his own face: "Yes, it was a noble face, and fine, as Gerta had said—the conscious end of the conscious world. The room was grey and pictureless, there was no ornament save a small bronze Buddha on a scarlet shelf. This he could see behind him in the mirror as he began passing the comb backward through the dark luxury of his hair" (306). Indeed, throughout the narrative the Buddha statue is never confronted by Ammen directly but always through a mirror or an ambivalent play of shadow and light. But of crucial importance here is the phrase "the conscious end of the conscious world." On the one hand, this phrase can be read paranoically as Ammen's megalomaniac belief that with his ego-will the conscious world has reached its "end" in the teleological sense of entelechy or full development. On the other hand, it can be read ironically and prophetically (in view of Ammen's suicide attempt by the end of the narrative) as a loose citation from Schopenhauer's *The World as Will and Representation*, referring to the ego-will's conscious self-denial.

In a sense, then, the presence of the statues of Nietzsche and Buddha in Ammen's room implies Schopenhauer's presence as well. One recalls that Schopenhauer, unlike Nietzsche, assigns a positive value to the religious teachings of Buddha and Christ, because they start from a denial of the ego-will. For him, the Buddhist and the Christian renunciation of the Will is the highest manifestation of philosophical consciousness in its heroic, if ultimately futile, attempt to transcend itself—what Ammen ironically calls "the conscious end of the conscious world." One can therefore argue that, in *King Coffin*, Aiken indirectly stages a dialogue between Nietzsche and Schopenhauer. As we have seen in chapter 1, it is Nietzsche himself who initiates this dialogue in *The Genealogy of Morals*, and Nietzsche obviously remains Ammen's model during much of the narrative. When the Buddha statue reappears in the text a little later, the reader learns that for Ammen it had meant "a brief experiment with the hardening doctrine of yoga, the deep breathings, the concentration on the thought of drowning, the concept of the individual" (307). One is thus allowed to infer that this brief phase in Ammen's spiritual development was replaced by the Nietzschean doctrine of the Will to Power, just as Nietzsche had succeeded Schopenhauer in the history of Western thought. Consequently, the implied question that the novel sets out to answer is whether this historical turn constitutes a form of ethical progress or regress, and it is precisely the protagonist's reversed journey from the Nietzschean affirmation of the Will to its Schopenhauerian denial that Aiken traces throughout his narrative.

At the beginning of the novel, we find Ammen adopting a definite Nietzschean stand. If the world is "a kind of phantasm," he argues, then "how could there be rights or wrongs or obligations? Or injuries or thefts?" (305). If all is as "scattered and meaningless as that, as intangible, or almost intangible, then the only course was to extend oneself violently outward, to thrust everywhere, to occupy the world entirely with one's own length" (306). What Ammen describes here is Nietzsche's Will to Power that must fill the void or nothingness at all costs. Yet, by the end of the novel, Ammen comes to see this Will as a bitter delusion. In a Schopenhauerian manner he renounces his desire to dominate and control, giving himself over to the play of chance and the void. This development is underscored in the narrative not only by the frequent recurrence of the Buddha image, which always hovers at the back of Ammen's consciousness, but also by the protagonist's distaste for violent action, which ought to signal to all but the most obtuse critic that Ammen is no psychopathic serial killer. For example, early on in the narrative, he proves incapable of hurting even a cat: "He [Ammen] remembered first his impulse to drop the cat out of the window, and the curious repugnance which had seemed to rise as if from his hands; then the relief with which he had driven the cat out into the corridor" (329).

King Coffin charts the development of Ammen's consciousness from violently experiencing the fear of nothingness as hate to accepting this nothingness at least conditionally as a first step toward an alternative ethos and pathos. If at the beginning of the narrative Ammen declares that "the essential thing in life is hate" (327), he ends up implying, in his last letter to Gerta, that the essential thing in life may be love. Once he realizes that Jones's stillborn child is in fact a symbol of his own aborted project of pure murder, he is confronted with himself as a stranger, and then as nothingness. In other words, he experiences a Schopenhauerian dissolution of the self. But nothingness in turn becomes a positive, liminal state, or one that allows access to a new mode of being and a new kind of self (what Schopenhauer describes as the irenic "consciousness of the identity of one's own inner being with that of all things"). This transformation is suggested in the novel by Ammen's experiment with the air currents in his apartment a few hours before turning the gas on.

Looking for another way of manipulating Gerta, Ammen believes he can employ the flow of air into and out of his apartment to create the appearance of a bona fide suicide attempt. The steady currents in his living room and bedroom are quite suitable for his purpose. To his disappointment, however, the draft in the kitchen (where his gas source is located) proves unsatisfactory: "But the kitchenette, presumably because its window was shut, or simply because it was out of the path of the main currents, was a disappointment: the movement of the [cigarette] smoke [exhaled by Ammen], whether at floor or ceiling, was scarcely perceptible, sluggish, equivocal. In fact it would go exactly where propelled" (402). Because the gas will flow only slowly out of the kitchen, where Ammen would have to sit if his suicide attempt were to be credible, the case is altered: instead of being completely in control, Ammen would now *have* to gamble with his own life.

It is at this moment that Ammen realizes the liminal nature of his newly discovered playground: "It was like the backwater of a river: it was stagnant; and looking at it he became abruptly aware of the profound nocturnal silence. It was that moment between night and morning when the traffic is stillest, the brief interval between the end of the night life and the beginning of the day—the hour when life is at its ebb" (402). Once he decides to carry out his plan, Ammen has relinquished control, staking his own being in the game. Will Gerta arrive in time to save him? The novel ends on this equivocal note, suggesting that Aiken is fully aware that his protagonist would have to sojourn in a no-man's land, between life and death, before he could reemerge out of this experience with a transformed, ludic-irenic self.

Of course, we shall never know whether Gerta will rescue Ammen or whether he will finally accept her love in an unconditional manner, just as we shall never know what paths Raskolnikov and Sonya, or Lafcadio and Geneviève, will ultimately choose. But the point is precisely that the open-ended, liminal worlds of Dostoevsky, Gide, and Aiken have made it possible for us momentarily to glimpse the reality of such incommensurable paths, thereby offering us imaginative alternatives that we are free to pursue on our own.

CHAPTER 5

RACE, ETHNICITY, AND IRENIC MENTALITY
Rebreanu, Eliade, Devi

As I have suggested in chapter 3, the idea of agon or contest lies at the foundation of the Western philosophy of difference, to which the socio-cultural concepts of ethnicity and race equally belong. There are count-less twentieth-century literary treatments of these concepts, but here I should like to concentrate on two early Romanian examples and a re-lated Indian one: Liviu Rebreanu's *The Forest of the Hanged* (1922), Mircea Eliade's *Maitreyi* (1933), and Maitreyi Devi's *It Does Not Die* (1976), writ-ten in response to Eliade's novel. I have chosen these works mainly because they provide imaginative answers to the questions of national-ism, ethnocentrism, and racism that have resurfaced with great urgency in the posttotalitarian East European communities (although these an-swers are equally relevant in the case of many contemporary Western communities, including North American ones). I shall suggest that Rebreanu, Eliade, and Devi, in taking up such controversial issues as ethnicity and race, show the negative existential consequences of con-flictive, violent difference and plead for an irenic, cooperative kind. All of them seek to go beyond a dialectic of identity and difference to an irenic consciousness of the oneness of all human beings. And all of them imply that the path to this consciousness lies in the liminal experience of exile understood as *atopia* or as a no-man's land that, although unde-finable, is an inexhaustible imaginative source of fresh meanings and values.

1. "The Forest of the Hanged": Nationalism,
Ethnicity, and Liminal Experience

Liviu Rebreanu, the author of *The Forest of the Hanged*, was the foremost Romanian novelist of the interwar period. He was born in 1885 in Transylvania, as the son of a poor rural schoolteacher. In 1906, he gradu-ated from the Budapest Military Academy and, after a short career in the Austro-Hungarian army, he left his native Transylvania for Bucharest.

169

Once in Romania, Rebreanu essentially lived the life of an exile, both because of his Transylvanian origin and because of his literary aspirations. He earned his living as a journalist and as a literary secretary for several theaters. During World War I, Rebreanu was arrested and detained by the Germans in occupied Bucharest for being a self-exiled Austro-Hungarian subject. He managed to escape to Jassy, but was in turn suspected of espionage by the Romanian authorities. When Soviet troops occupied Romania just before the end of World War II, Rebreanu chose to commit suicide rather than live under Communist rule.

Padurea Spînzuratilor (1922; translated as *The Forest of the Hanged*, 1930) occupies a special place in Rebreanu's fiction on several counts. It is a fictionalized account of his brother Emil's desertion from, and subsequent execution at the hands of, the Austrian imperial army. It is also Rebreanu's attempt to understand his own exile, in a world torn between material and spiritual aspirations, between history and myth. On the surface, the novel centers around the moral dilemma of Apostol Bologa, a young Romanian officer of artillery, who seems to waver between a strong sense of duty toward the Austro-Hungarian Empire and an equally strong sense of his ethnic responsibilities. He becomes a half-hearted deserter, and when he is caught and sentenced to death, he eagerly accepts his "martyrdom." In my view, however, Rebreanu is only secondarily interested in presenting a rather common East European psychological case study. Rather, in tracing Bologa's spiritual progress, Rebreanu goes beyond narrow regionalist issues and shows that the cultivation of an individual's inner being within a liminal time-space can lead to an irenic mentality that transcends all violent conflict, including social, national, and ethnic difference. He thereby substitutes the irenic principles of nonviolence and unconditional love for both nationalistic ideal and ethnic myth.

The beginning of *The Forest of the Hanged* presents Apostol Bologa as a zealous participant in the trial and execution of a Czech officer, Svoboda, who attempted to desert to the enemy in protest of the hanging of his father back home. When Otto Klapka, a newly arrived captain of artillery, shows pity for his kinsman Svoboda and readily admits his civilian's distaste for war, Bologa counters by affirming warlike values, which he equates with "real life": "'I'm also a reserve officer,' interrupted [Bologa] with pride. 'The war snatched me from the midst of my studies at the University, where I had almost lost touch with real life, but it did not take me long to wake up, and now I realize that war is the real generator of energy.'"[1] Echoing Nietzsche, Bologa explicitly embraces the notion that warlike contest is the true generator of cultural values. This notion belongs to an aristocratic code of ethics that the imperial army seeks to instill into its officers, a code which Bologa accepts unreservedly. But the radiant, ecstatic look of Svoboda, who welcomes his death as a long-awaited deliverance, creates doubt and anger in Bologa's heart, an initial liminal sign of his spiritual awakening:

> At first this look disconcerted and angered Bologa, but presently he felt distinctly the flame from the condemned man's eyes shoot into his heart like a painful reproach. He tried to look away, but the eyes, which looked so contemptuously at death and were beautified by so great a love, fascinated him. And tensely he waited for the prisoner to open his mouth and utter one of those terrible cries of deliverance which the early Christian martyrs were wont to utter at the point of death, when the vision of Christ was vouchsafed to them. (21–22)

The blazing light in the prisoner's eyes strikes a long-forgotten chord in the Romanian officer's heart. Back in his quarters, Bologa attempts to soothe his troubled conscience and starts reminiscing about his childhood in a small Transylvanian village. His earliest recollections are of his mother's inspiring in him the love of "a kind, gentle, and forgiving Deity, who, in exchange for daily prayers, granted men pleasures on earth and everlasting happiness in Heaven" (30). At the age of six, Apostol had a mystical experience. While he was in church, praying for a divine sign, the sky parted suddenly and "there appeared a curtain of white clouds in the midst of which shone the face of God like a golden light, dazzling awe-inspiring and withal as full of tenderness as the face of a loving mother. And then from the midst of this divine radiance there emerged a living eye, infinitely kindly and magnanimous, which seemed to pierce all deep and hidden places" (33). The young boy's vision lasted only a moment, but it was "so unutterably sweet" that his heart "stopped beating and his eyes filled with a strange, ecstatic light. He was so filled with happiness that he would have been glad to die there and then in the presence of the divine miracle" (33–34). The "strange, ecstatic light" of Bologa's childhood vision is similar to the one he has seen emanating from Svoboda's eyes and will haunt him to the end of the narrative. For the reader, the light also points to the arduous liminal journey that Apostol must undertake, from his original vision in church to his final acceptance of death on the gibbet.

Continuing his reminiscences, Apostol realizes that the gentle influence his mother exercised on him in early childhood was soon pushed into the background when his father came back from prison where he had served a two-year sentence for nationalist activities. Apostol's father sought to infuse the boy with both a "modern," scientific spirit and nationalistic sentiments. He was quite unaware of the fact that his well-meant injunctions contained a potentially tragic double bind: "Always do your duty like a man, and never forget that you are a Rumanian!" (36). From his father, then, Apostol has inherited a strong sense of civic duty that in time will become inevitably divided between his country and his ethnic group.

Throughout the novel, however, Rebreanu shows that an individual's "duty" ought to be first toward his fellow humans and only secondarily toward his nation or ethnic community. This duty can be based neither on the idea of violent revolt against oppressors, as the communists and the anarchists preached all over Europe at the time, nor on the idea of an enlightened, multinational empire of the Napoleonic or Austro-Hungarian type. The novel stages these two ideological positions as alternatives that Bologa will ultimately reject. In a heated discussion among the officers at which Apostol is present, Lieutenant Gross preaches the gospel of anarchic violence as a means toward creating a new international community, whereas Lieutenant Varga invokes a no less false gospel of an imperial, multinational community. Varga, for example, says:

> "Wait! Allow me! Our anarchist would have an International, wouldn't you, comrade? Very well, behold the International!", he added with pride, raising his voice and indicating those present with a sweep of his arm. "Behold! You are a Jew, the captain is Czech, the doctor over there is German, Cervenco is Ruthenian, Bologa is Rumanian, I am a Hungarian. . . . And I'm sure that in the big room over there or in the lobby we would find Poles, Serbs, and Italians, in fine all nationalities. . . . And all fight shoulder to shoulder for a common ideal against a common foe! That's the true International, comrades!" (56)

But Apostol seems to sympathize with a third position, presented by the Ruthenian Cervenco, whom the rest of the officers consider a sort of madman, because he goes into battle armed with a reed wand and singing hymns, claiming that he would rather "chop off his hands than shoot at his fellow-creatures" (52). As an alternative to Gross's anarchistic and Varga's imperialistic internationalism, Cervenco proclaims the Christian gospel of universal love, which he believes, not unlike Sonya Marmeladova and other Russian Orthodox souls in *Crime and Punishment*, to be attainable only through suffering: "We need to suffer much, tremendously. . . . Only amidst suffering can love grow and thrive, that great, real, and victorious love. . . . Love, dear fellows, love!" (57). Yet the novel will eventually suggest that this Christian idea of redemption through suffering is not part of Christ's originary message of universal love, but a subsequent (mis)interpretation of it by a mentality of power that finds it expedient to adopt the standpoint of the victim for its own purposes. Apostol will therefore also need to turn away from Christian "martyrdom," if he is to attain an alternative irenic world based on love.

When Bologa's unit is sent to the Romanian front, he decides to desert to the enemy, but his plan is temporarily thwarted by his being wounded in action. His convalescence is a prime example of a liminal experience in the narrative: through it, Apostol comes to understand the inauthentic nature of his life up to this point. He also comes to realize the real reason for his ambivalent behavior toward his fiancée, Marta. It was in order to win the admiration of this flirtatious and rather superficial Romanian middle-class woman, infatuated with men in uniform, that Apostol had signed up for the army in the first place. While on convalescence leave in his hometown, however, Apostol had broken up his engagement, ostensibly because Marta came to see him accompanied by a Hungarian officer and addressed him in Hungarian. But the truth is that during his convalescence at the Romanian front he had fallen in love with a young Hungarian peasant, Ilona, who had taken care of him. When Bologa returns from his leave and sees Ilona again, it finally dawns on him that genuine love is more important than either social position or nationalistic involvement:

> He had not been indignant because Marta had come accompanied by a strange man, but because she had come with a Hungarian

and had spoken Hungarian. So it was not because he was jealous that he had given her up, but because he loved the other one [Ilona]. If this were so, his indignation against the Hungarian and the Hungarian language had been a farce. What was more, the farce had begun before that—it had begun when he had not regretted in the least that his illness had for the second time prevented him from going over to the Rumanians." (192)

Yet, at this point Apostol is still unprepared to accept the essential unity between physical and spiritual love and continues to deceive himself by reasoning that "it is in vain to seek [spiritual] food in the world of the senses. Only the heart can find it, either in some secret place of its own or else in some new world beyond the reach of mortal eyes and ears" (193). He will eventually realize that his love for Ilona, his love for mankind and, ultimately, his love for God cannot be separated: universal love is unconditional, going beyond friend and enemy, as well as beyond family, ethnicity, and nationality. As Apostol comes to acknowledge, in the past "he had divided the whole world into two halves, one of love and one of hatred" (204). Consequently, he had never known love, but only hatred in various guises: "He had thought that all those who were of his own race were dear to him, but as soon as he had discovered that his hatred found no echo in their hearts, his love was scattered like dust by the breath of the wind. True love never died in the soul of man, but accompanied it right through the portals of death into eternity. But love could not take root in a heart tainted with hatred, and in his own heart hatred had ever dwelt, like a rusty nail embedded in living flesh" (204–5).

Bologa's earlier chance encounter with a Romanian prisoner now helps him understand that his father's ideal of national reintegration is nothing but the mirror image of Austro-Hungarian chauvinism. The Romanian officer bitterly complains about his harsh treatment at the hands of the Austro-Hungarian army, but when Bologa attempts to fraternize with him, the prisoner shows a heart equally "tainted with hatred": "'If you were a real Romanian you would not shoot your brothers', answered the young officer quickly, with such contempt that his whole face was changed by it. 'Your place, sir, would be on the other side, not here'" (155–56). Apostol will eventually understand that the essential question is not how to choose the "right" side in a war of hatred but, rather, how to turn away from a mentality that condones any kind of war. During his visit home, Bologa feels estranged not only from his Romanian fiancée but also from his mother. Like any liminal experience, this visit proves both troubling and enlightening as it helps him shed all the romantic illusions of his youth. His family and friends, however, misunderstand his motives for breaking off his engagement, choosing to see in him the mirror image of his nationalistic father. This false nationalistic image will pursue him all the way to the gibbet, for both his judges and his Romanian priest see him either as a traitor or as a hero, according to their own *parti pris.*

Back on the Romanian front, Bologa attempts to forget the war, immersing himself in his love for the Hungarian peasant girl. He becomes engaged to Ilona, despite the considerable differences in social, cultural, and ethnical background between them, and despite the obvious disapproval of his peers. Apostol is attracted to the girl because of her unquestioned, selfless devotion and loyalty, her freshness, gentleness, simplicity, and humanity. Ilona and her father, as well as other Romanian and Hungarian peasants in the novel, are not exactly idealized, but they seem to fulfill the exemplary function that Tolstoy's and Dostoevsky's honest peasants do: they are unassuming models of humanity and decency in a world dominated by inauthentic values. Additionally, they offer an irenic model of ethnic coexistence in a multicultural region such as Transylvania, perpetually troubled by ethnic conflict.

During a conversation with Constantin Boteanu—a Romanian Orthodox priest with whom Apostol went to school and whom he providentially meets again at the Romanian front—Bologa suddenly realizes that his deep and genuine feelings for Ilona do not go against his mystical notion of love, even though they are far from being spiritual; rather, they are both a first step toward and a necessary condition for this love. When Apostol asks Boteanu if the latter loves his wife as much as he loves God, the priest answers solemnly: "Yes, much—as much as I love God! Love is one and indivisible, exactly like faith. My heart embraces in the same love both God and the companion of my life and the mother of my children! By means of true love the coalescent souls approach nearer to the throne of the Almighty" (249). The priest's answer makes the light "which flamed in Apostol's eyes . . . so bright that Popa

Constantin could hardly restrain his wonder" and it strengthens Bologa's resolve to marry Ilona against the prejudices of his class.

Yet, the realities of an outside world at war intrude again upon the inner universe of the young officer. Although he has discarded his intention to desert as a useless and irrelevant action, Apostol is now forced into it: he is called upon by his commanding officer, General Karg, to sit on a court-martial and is, therefore, faced with the prospect of sending more innocent people to the gallows. As Apostol later on tells his embarrassed and uncomprehending prosecutor, "Sometimes it is more terrible to judge others than to be judged oneself!" (313).

But this time Bologa has no intention of joining the Romanian "holy war"; rather, he aimlessly wanders along the front line until he runs into a border patrol. Bologa's aimless wandering in the no-man's land between the two warring sides is fraught with obvious liminal symbolism. By going over to the Romanians he would simply trade one horn of his dilemma for the other. Hence, he would like to remain indefinitely on the border between his two worlds, no longer able to accept either of them. When he is finally forced into a decision, he chooses death rather than fighting against his fellow human beings on either side of the fence. He also leaves his pistol behind, avoiding the temptation of suicide: like Svoboda, he is determined to go through with his Christlike ordeal.

On one level, then, Bologa's spiritual journey is also the Christian way of the cross, and the novel abounds in Christian symbolism, including the protagonist's first name (*apostol* is the Romanian word for "apostle"). The descriptive contrast between light and darkness that recurs at the end of each chapter is an obvious part of this symbolism. The episode of Apostol's destruction of the enemy searchlight is another case in point. For weeks, a Russian searchlight playfully flashes out of the darkness onto the Austrian positions without any apparent reason. It soon comes to be perceived as a challenge, and the artillery officers vie among themselves to put it out. When Apostol finally destroys it, he is far from experiencing the satisfaction he had anticipated: "Why did he not rejoice as he had rejoiced when the idea had come to him to destroy the search-light? Instead of an answer the white light which he had strangled just now flashed up in his soul, shining like a distant beacon. And the radiance resembled now Svoboda's countenance under the halter, now the vision which he had had as a child in the church before the altar" (93-94). Cervenco sums up the symbolical nature of Apostol's action, when he says: "I am sorry that you have destroyed the search-light, I don't know why. . . . You've killed the light, Bologa!" (94). But Apostol realizes that what he has killed is his own past, beset by doubts and fears, for now the light has moved from outside into his inner being:

> "The light is here!" answered Bologa triumphantly, beating his breast with his hand.
> "Yes, yes, you are right! The light is there, and the suffering, too! The whole world is there!" added Cervenco with a glint in his eyes.
> Apostol went on through the twisting trenches, his back bent, his eyes shining, his soul full of confidence, reconciled and contented as if he had been purified in a bath of virtue. (94–95)

The inner being that, as Cervenco puts it, contains "the whole world" should not be understood simply as a religious or mystical notion (though Bologa tends to think of it in those terms) and even less as a solipsistic escape from reality. Rather, it is the means by which inside and outside melt into a harmonious whole, and human consciousness constructs a cosmic and communal interconnectedness based on love rather than conflict. From the standpoint of an agonistic mentality and its violent politics, this incommensurable consciousness appears, of course, as quietistic, impractical, and naively idealistic. Hence the total incomprehension of Bologa's actions on the part of the jurors and the prosecutor, and even on the part of his Romanian priest, all of whom judge him in practical or political terms.

Another essential image, intimately related to that of light and darkness, is the forest, which significantly appears in the novel's title as well. This forest is undoubtedly Dante's *selva oscura*, a Christian metonymy for the world of suffering and death. But, like Dante's forest, it can be a place of learning or, liminally speaking, a place of transition from darkness to light. At the beginning of the book, Klapka alludes to a "forest of the hanged," which he saw in another section of the front and in which many Czech nationalists were hanged for attempted desertion from the imperial army. Forced to witness the execution of some of his fellow deserters, whom he failed to join at the last moment, Klapka describes his terrifying experience from the standpoint of the unenlightened sufferer, the man who remains immersed in the world of fear, violence, and death, even though he has a momentary glimpse into an alternative world of peace, joy, and light:

> There were no gibbets, but on each tree men were hanging, strung up on the branches. All were bareheaded, and from the neck of each man dangled a label bearing the words "A TRAITOR TO HIS COUNTRY," inscribed in three languages. My heart froze within me, but still I did not dare to tremble. . . . I closed my eyes, thinking with stupid amazement: "This is the Forest of the Hanged". . . . Then all three were hanged simultaneously on the same tree, an old beech with hollow trunk. When the noose was put around their necks I looked at their eyes. They were shining brightly, like stars which announce the coming of the sun, with so much nobility and hope that their faces seemed bathed in a radiance of glory. Then I felt proud of being the kinsman of the radiant three and I longed thirstily for death! But only for a moment, a single moment! Then I became aware of the struggling bodies. I heard the creaking of the branches and my heart trembled silently, timorously thievishly, so that no one near me should hear it. . . . I rejoiced that I was alive, that I had escaped from The Forest of the Hanged. (69–70)

Yet The Forest of the Hanged has followed Klapka everywhere, on the Italian, Russian, and Romanian fronts, and has by now become part of his inner being. In turn, Bologa encounters a similar forest on the Romanian front but, unlike Klapka, he resolves to meet its challenge. He realizes that the desire of escaping The Forest of the Hanged is a short-lived illusion and that he has to confront his fear of death, on which his whole life has been based, before he can gain access to an alternative world. The question now arises if, for Rebreanu, this alternative world can be reached only through suffering and sacrificial death, or through other paths as well.

The Forest of the Hanged can of course be understood simply as a religious symbol and Bologa's martyrdom, as a mystical passage to a future existence bathed in divine light. Indeed, much of the novel is apparently concerned with Apostol's spiritual ordeal due to his loss of faith in God, under the influence of his father's secular and scientific mentality. Bologa's professor of philosophy at the University of Budapest regards him precisely in those terms. To Apostol's mentor it seems that the "young man was typical of a generation which, losing faith in God strives to find something outside the human soul, a scientific God, free from mystery, an absolute truth beyond which there should be nothing and which should contain and explain all things" (39). In this light, Bologa will ultimately regain his early childhood's faith in God and will come full circle to the traditional values represented by his mother.

One could, therefore, see Rebreanu's novel in the same manner in which many critics have seen *Crime and Punishment*—as an attempt to understand a typical East European culture that wavers between transcendental, religious values and secular, materialist modernization. As George Schöpflin points out in a different context, such cultures have a strong agrarian orientation and are dominated by traditional values that resist modernization. The agrarian or peasant mentality (to some extent represented in the novel by the honest peasants of Hungarian and Romanian origin, whom both Bologa and his creator view with obvious sympathy) was historically "strongly influenced and reinforced by religious concepts, particularly that of 'salvation.' Its perception of change was heavily conditioned by its understanding of change in the religious context—its dominant experience of a world outside the village commune—viz. Christian salvation. This lent peasant politics a certain flavor of messianic expectations."[2]

Apostol does come from a small Transylvanian village where peasant politics would undoubtedly acquire a messianic and nationalist flavor, as we can see, for example, from the attitudes of such priests as Father Boteanu, who attempts to console the prisoner before his execution: "In the midst of life's temptations you remained your father's son, Apostol! You did not forget his teachings, but carried them ever in your fiery blood. . . . The storms of life sway the human soul, but they cannot irradicate from it imperishable roots! Pleasing in the sight of the Lord God is he who willingly sacrifices himself for the race of his fathers and for their faith for ever and ever!" (344). As I have already pointed out, however, it would be rather limiting to attribute the priest's Christian nationalistic creed to Rebreanu and give his novel a strictly political or ideological interpretation. According to this interpretation, Bologa's spiritual path would be a circuitous one, genetically and socioculturally determined first by his father's bourgeois, progressive, secular mentality and then by his mother's Christian, agrarian, backward one. The closed world of the novel would then be a faithful replica of the world in which the author lived and wrote, offering no viable alternative.

But, as we have seen, a more imaginative reading is open to us, if we keep in mind that Rebreanu was a perpetual exile and was therefore able to look at his world both with a certain emotional detachment and with the kind of irenic responsive understanding that I have described in chapters 3 and 4. It is therefore not impossible that through the figure of Apostol Bologa, Rebreanu—not unlike Dostoevsky—wished to go beyond both modern, secular values and Christian, traditional ones. Like *Crime and Punishment,* his novel points to an irenic alternative world, the location of which is not necessarily transcendental, but here and now. A life free of conflict, fear, and violence, Rebreanu's text implies, is easily accessible to all human beings—if only one can face The Forest of the Hanged within oneself. The way to attain this life, Rebreanu's novel further suggests, is through the development of inner being, understood not as solipsistic egocentricity but as cosmic interconnectedness based on irenic love—an incommensurable alternative to an ethnic and nationalist ideal that ceaselessly reproduces the same inequities and violent oppressions it attempts to eradicate.

2. "Maitreyi": Orientalism, Racial Difference, and Literary Perspectivism

Rebreanu's exilic perspective, opening the path toward an irenic consciousness, lies behind some of Mircea Eliade's major fiction as well. Eliade is widely known in the West as a historian of religions and as an Orientalist, while his considerable literary output has only recently started receiving significant critical attention. In Romania, on the other hand, his reputation rests mainly on his fiction, and it was only after the fall of Ceausescu's Communist regime in December 1989 that Eliade's scholarly work began to be published and, consequently, commented upon by Romanian scholars.[3]

As Eliade's fiction becomes accessible in the Anglo-American world and his scholarly work in Romania, both communities of readers will realize that his scholarly and literary pursuits are not mutually exclusive but, on the contrary, compatible and complementary. In this Eliade follows a long cultural tradition in Europe and, specifically, in Romania. In the preface to the English edition of his journal, *No Souvenirs*, he notes: "Born in Romania near the turn of the century, I belong to a cultural tradition that does not accept the idea of any incompatibility between scientific investigation and artistic, especially literary, activity." He then goes on to discuss the relevance of his fiction to his scholarly work: "For me, a historian of religions and an Orientalist, the writing of fiction became a fascinating experience in method. Indeed, in the same way as the writer of fiction, the historian of religions is confronted with different structures of sacred and mythical space, different qualities of time, and more specifically by a considerable number of strange, unfamiliar, and enigmatic worlds of meaning."[4] In his preface to *The Forbidden Forest*, Eliade elaborates on the idea of literary fiction as a cognitive instrument: "Just as a new axiom reveals a previously unknown structure of the real (that is, it *founds* a new world), so also any creation of the literary imagination reveals a new Universe of meanings and values. . . . And literature constitutes an instrument of knowledge because the literary imagination reveals unknown dimensions or aspects of the human condition."[5]

It would, therefore, be useful to look at Eliade's scholarly work through his fiction and disclose the similar imaginative patterns underlying his creative and conceptual universe. Indeed, *Maitreyi* (1933) is one of the best illustrations of the subtle relation between Eliade's scientific and literary work. Out of his Indian notebooks of 1928–32 emerged several "Indian" novels, including *Maitreyi*, as well as his first scholarly studies. Eliade himself acknowledges in his preface to *No Souvenirs* that "[f]or years my Indian notebooks and folders supplied not only the materials for two volumes consecrated to India, but they were also used in the preparation of many articles and essays and even some of my literary works."[6]

Maitreyi, moreover, presents an interesting problem in the ontological status of literature because its heroine, Maitreyi Devi—an eminent Bengali woman of letters in her own right—looks back, in *It Does Not Die*, over a span of forty-two years, to the same events that are referred to in Eliade's book and challenges their interpretation by Eliade's narrator and (according to her) alter ego. On the surface, *Maitreyi* is a thinly disguised "autobiographical" narrative referring to Eliade's forbidden liaison with Maitreyi Devi, the sixteen-year-old daughter of his guru, the philosopher Surendranath Das Gupta. But Eliade's autobiographical material is transfigured into a work of art having little to do with the historical events that took place in Calcutta in 1930, just as Devi's narrative is an equally imaginative reconstruction of those events. In fact, both novels offer an excellent example of intertextuality and can best be read in terms of each other: as we shall see, what connects both authors is a kind of responsive understanding that leads, as in Rebreanu, to an awareness of the intimate connection of exilic experience to the irenic unfolding of inner being. Through this awareness, they also question the positivistic notion of reality itself, which favors pure facticity. They imply that reality can comprise many nonfactual elements, including the *as if*, imaginary worlds projected by their novels. For them, literary discourse does not imitate or represent, but often responds to, or even produces, reality; hence, for them, its essential nature is not fictional, but liminal.

But *Maitreyi* is intertextual in another sense as well, for it abounds in topoi that have become familiar from Eliade's scholarly work: escapes from profane into sacred time, hierophanies or revelations of the sacred in everyday experience, nostalgia for origins and for presence, *deus otiosus*, *coincidentia oppositorum*, and the like. Yet, this does not turn *Maitreyi* into a neoromantic extravaganza, as some Romanian critics would have it.[7] Nor should one look at it, as American postcolonial criticism has recently done, as a thinly disguised expression of the author's Eurocentric and racist prejudices.[8] On the contrary, the novel can best be read in terms of a self-critical presentation of its themes. All of its neoromantic topoi are undermined by the literary form in which they are cast, that is, by a separation between the authorial and the fictional perspectives. If Rebreanu tackles the question of national and ethnic difference from an exilic perspective, Eliade raises the issue of racial difference by presenting an imaginary world in which two star-crossed lovers from different continents come together only in order to be separated by their racial and cultural preconceptions. But whereas Rebreanu chooses an omniscient narrative viewpoint and thereby risks having Bologa's perspective confused with that of the implied author, Eliade attempts self-consciously to distance himself from his imaginary world by employing an unreliable narrator, thus producing a form of literary perspectivism.

The term "perspectivism" was apparently introduced in Anglo-American literary criticism by Leo Spitzer in connection with *Don Quijote* and has since then been associated with modernist and postmodern novelistic techniques, but its historical roots can actually be traced back to Plato's *Republic*, in Socrates' distinction between *mimesis* and *diegesis*. According to Socrates, in the diegetic mode the narrative voice coincides with that of the author, while in the mimetic mode the author assumes or simulates the voices and viewpoints of others. Of course, Socrates condemns *mimesis* precisely because it separates authorship from authority and thus generates cognitive and ethical relativism. Ironically, Socrates as a character in the *Republic* implicitly condemns his own creator's dialogic method, through which Plato stages an agon of personalities, ideas, and ethical standpoints. But, in the spirit of Plato's own dialogic imagination, one can, unlike Socrates, grant a positive value to *mimesis* as staging, under the guise of literary perspectivism. From a dialogic viewpoint, perspectivism is a form of responsive understanding. As such, it becomes a valuable narrative technique, emancipating the text from its author-authority and partially handing it over to the reader.

In *Maitreyi*, Eliade employs precisely this perspectivist technique, thus inviting the reader to view his imaginary world from various ethical standpoints. This novelistic perspectivism is achieved specifically through the use of a "diary within a diary," which attempts to reinforce the confessional form of the narrative but ends up creating the opposite effect: it exposes its illusory character. By the end of his narrative, Allan, the narrator, manages not so much to reveal as to conceal the meaning of his confession. As in André Gide's *The Immoralist* or Ford Madox Ford's *The Good Soldier*, the narrator is unreliable and the reader learns the novelistic truth not from him but *through* him.

At the beginning of his narrative, Allan starts a new notebook in which he plans to tell the story of his love for Maitreyi, the sixteen-year-old daughter of his boss and benefactor, the engineer Narendra Sen. For this purpose, he goes back to his old journal, kept during his Calcutta days, in which he had presumably recorded the day-by-day events that had led to his involvement with Maitreyi, their secret marriage, his banishment from Sen's house, his retreat to the Himalayas, his return to Calcutta, and his final departure from India. From the outset his old diary proves useless, however, because it failed to record events that, at the time of their occurrence, seemed insignificant, but that now, at the time of their narration, appear of primary importance to the story. Indeed, the old diary failed to record the very beginning of Allan's involvement with Maitreyi, which makes it impossible for the narrator to begin his own story:

> I have hesitated for so long in front of this notebook because I haven't been able to find the precise date when I met Maitreyi. In my notes of that year I found nothing. Her name appears much later, after I had left the hospital and moved into Narendra Sen's house in Bhawanipore. But that was in 1929, and I had met Maitreyi at least ten months before. And if I somehow suffer in beginning this story, it is precisely because I do not know how to evoke her image of those days and cannot relive my wonder, the uncertainty and the confusion of the first encounters.[9]

Because Allan cannot find a beginning of his story in "recorded history" (his old diary), he invents this beginning, and his new notebook becomes not only a commentary on his old one but also an exercise in imagination. He vainly seeks meaning in his old journal and consequently sets out to create his own meaning. From now on, he will frequently insert into his narrative excerpts from his old diary, which he will attack as falsifying "reality," that is, the reality of his story.

But this imaginative reality in turn is a falsification, because it is controlled by certain Orientalist racial beliefs operative in the Western world. Allan's Indian "experience" does not help him to discard these beliefs but, on the contrary, to reinforce and consolidate them. His love for Maitreyi is determined by two diametrically opposed attitudes that stem from the same Western cultural myth: the "primitivism" of certain Oriental civilizations. The first attitude that Allan assumes in his old diary and exposes in his new one is that of a "white father": he feels superior toward the childlike Oriental who is helpless, irrational, and irresponsible, and therefore needs guidance and protection. Before getting involved with Maitreyi, Allan behaves Kipling-fashion, conscious of his "civilizing mission" in India. For instance, when he is transferred to Assam with the help of Sen, he writes:

> A different India . . . was revealing itself to me then, among tribes, among people hitherto known only to ethnologists. . . . I wanted to

give life to these places . . . their people so cruel and so innocent. I wanted to discover their aesthetics and their ethics, and I would collect stories, take pictures, sketch genealogies. The deeper I penetrated into the wilderness, the more there grew in me an unknown dignity and unsuspected pride. I was good and righteous in the jungle, more correct and self-possessed than in the city. (16)

At first Maitreyi repels Allan because of her "Indian" features. He finds her rather unattractive, "with her eyes too big and too black, with meaty, protruding lips, with her strong breasts of a Bengali maiden, grown too full, like an over-ripe fruit." He likes the color of her skin, of an "uncommon brownness, as though of clay and wax," but, predictably, he idealizes this feature, rationalizing his attraction in mythological terms. For example, he tries to describe to Harold, his snobbish Anglo-Indian friend, "Maitreyi's naked arm and the uncanniness of that dark yellow, so confusing, so unwomanlike, as if it belonged to a goddess or to an icon rather than to an Indian" (3–4).

Throughout the beginnings of Allan's involvement with Maitreyi, racial difference controls the dialectic of attraction and repulsion in Allan's consciousness. For instance, he detects a certain kind of racial envy in Maitreyi's remarks about his white skin: "She pronounced the word 'white' with a certain envy and melancholy, with her eyes unconsciously glued to my arm, as it leaned against the table, half-naked in my work-shirt. I was both surprised and enchanted guessing her envy" (27). Allan also relishes Maitreyi's protestations that she is less "black" than Chabu, her younger sister, although he himself cannot "perceive any difference between them" (27).

But Allan's feeling of racial superiority goes beyond the color of their skin. He reads all kinds of anthropological signs into the games of Maitreyi and Chabu. When Chabu mentions her beloved tree to which she offers her own food, Allan notes: "I was happy and would repeat to myself: pantheism, pantheism. I thought what rare documents I had in front of me" (32). He sees Maitreyi as a primitive human being and this flatters his white male's ego: "I did not understand her. She seemed to me like a child, a primitive. I was attracted by her words, by her incoherent thinking, by her naïveté—and for a long time, later on, I would flatter myself thinking that I was a whole man beside this barbarian" (30).

The few comic scenes in the book rely on a racial type of comedy of errors, i.e., on misunderstandings that result from bringing together members of different cultures for the first time. A good example is the scene in which Allan brings Lucien, a French journalist, into Sen's house to enlighten his friend about the life of upper-class women in Indian society. What follows is familiar to the English reader from E. M. Forster's *A Passage to India*: "These three women, finding themselves before us, huddled together with the same panic-stricken eyes, and the engineer tried in vain to encourage them, to make them talk. . . . Some tea was spilt by mistake on the tray and on Lucien's trousers, and everybody hastened to his aid, the engineer lost his temper and started severely scolding his family in Bengali, while Lucien kept apologizing in French without succeeding in making himself understood" (10).

After Allan falls in love with Maitreyi, he assumes the opposite Western attitude toward the Orient. Now he becomes anxious to convert to Hinduism and to embrace what he believes are Oriental values. It is from the standpoint of this "conversion" that he ridicules his white-father postures from the old diary. When Harold, his Eurasian friend, comes to visit him at Sen's and tries to "save him from the engineer's clutches," Allan vehemently attacks his Eurasian prejudices, without being aware that he equally shares them but in reverse: "It would be my greatest happiness to be received into their world. . . . A live world, with live people who suffer without complaining, who still abide by an ethic code, and whose women are saints, not whores like ours. . . . They are a dead world, our white continents" (93).

If in the past Allan had a condescending view of Indian society, now he idealizes it, placing it within his own Western moral utopia. He has the typical attitude of a traveler who reads his ideological biases into a foreign culture. Maitreyi becomes for him a "passage to India" but also, by the logic of the *coincidentia oppositorum*, an unreachable, inscrutable, and arbitrary Asian goddess. To him she is still a "primitive," but now Allan gives this term a positive value, contrasting it to all that is pretense and superficiality in the West: "I would listen to her as one listens to a fairy tale, but at the same time I felt her moving away from me. How complicated her soul! I understood once again that only we, the civilized, are simple, naive, and transparent; that these people whom I loved so much that I wanted to become one of them hide a history and a mythology impossible to penetrate, that they are rich and deep, complicated and incomprehensible" (83). In turn, Narendra Sen is rather suspicious of Allan's sudden conversion and does not encourage him to change his religion. According to Maitreyi, he has his own plans, based on no less illusory cultural myths: he would like to adopt Allan as his own son and, after his retirement, live with his family in Allan's country where "whites are good and hospitable, not like the British" (92).

That Allan's new attitude toward Maitreyi and her culture is really the old one in an antithetical guise becomes quite clear when, during his fits of jealousy, Allan no longer idealizes Maitreyi's "primitivism" but, on the contrary, reverts to his racial distrust. For example, he believes Maitreyi capable of giving herself to the first stranger and writes: "I could not understand Maitreyi, I could not place her in a definite frame of predictable reactions, and it seemed to me that, being so primitive and innocent, she could give herself to anyone, without pausing to consider the enormity of her act, without any sense of responsibility" (108).

The progress that Allan persuades himself to have made from the old journal to the new one turns out to be a circular movement. For instance, his retreat to the mountains and his encounter with Jenia reveal that the ordeal of his separation from Maitreyi has taught him nothing and that he manages to emerge with all his Western prejudices intact. After Sen turns him out of the house and forbids him to contact his daughter, Allan decides to become a sannyasi or a sadhu (one who has renounced the world). But his retreat to the Himalayas, fraught with liminal promise, actually turns out to be a romantic pose, an abortive initiation rite. When he encounters Jenia, a white South African musician who has fled the Western world and has come to India "in search of the absolute," Allan despises and pities her Orientalist illusions, without fully recognizing in her his own image: "In Jenia's head there was a muddle of inconsistent ideas, side by side with sentimental disappointments and female superstitions (the cult of the 'overman,' of the 'lone wolf,' the isolation, the adventure, the renunciation). I was almost terrified listening to her, for since I had isolated myself I had come to follow a thought to its end, to consider an idea in all its implications and, in spite of myself, I was pained at the hybrid and incongruous substance of the mind of this young woman in search of the absolute" (149).

Despite Allan's claim that he had come a long way since his retreat, his description of Jenia's confused thinking is an accurate picture of his own confusion. His *mauvaise foi* reveals itself when, for instance, he tries to rationalize his seduction of Jenia in terms of a "test": he presumably wants to find out if his love for Maitreyi and his prolonged abstinence have dulled his senses or, worse yet, have destroyed his "will to live" (note that he rationalizes his actions in the same pseudo-Nietzschean terms that he finds objectionable with Jenia). He pities Jenia's will to self-deception when she demands to be made love to as if she were Maitreyi, without questioning his own pitiful, all too human motives in performing his "experiment."

By criticizing his old journal, Allan attempts to create the illusion of having transcended not only his racial prejudices but also his fictionalization of experience, which he always processes through the books he reads. For instance, he derides the sections in his old diary where he describes the intensifying passion between Maitreyi and himself in Vaishnava mystical terms: "(Note: In my diary of those days I was influenced by certain Vaishnava readings and I used the term 'mystical' very often. In fact my comment on this event, which I found in a stray notebook is pervaded throughout by 'mystical experience.' I was ridiculous)" (68). But this fictionalization permeates his new diary as well and is based on the same cultural assumptions that motivated his behavior toward Maitreyi and Jenia.

Of course, Allan rationalizes his will to fiction in terms of art as a reconstruction or reordering of historical events according to an imaginative pattern that is more real than reality. On rereading his notes recording his stay in the mountains, Allan is struck by their inability to convey his devastating grief and rejects them as irrelevant. He writes again parenthetically apropos of his old diary: "(How incapable we are to render, at the time of their occurrence, the substance of an overwhelming joy or grief. I have come to believe that only memory, only distance can give them life. The diary is dry and irrelevant)" (135). Allan implies that this sort of recollection in tranquility, whereby events are recreated and reordered according to an ideal pattern, is emancipated from history. But a second look at his narrative will reveal that his exotic love story set in India is very much historically determined by the narrator's cultural beliefs. In fact, this narrative is little more than the reenactment of a most common Christian myth: the story of the Fall of Man.

Allan presents his story in such a way that we begin to see him repeating the events connected with the Fall: the sojourn in Eden (Sen's house), the temptation and fall through sex (his involvement with Maitreyi), the banishment from the garden of innocence (his forced departure from Sen's house), and the eternal misery and desolation that follows this banishment (his ordeal in the Himalayas and final departure from India). In this context, Narendra Sen becomes God the Father (Allan believes that the engineer wants him to marry his daughter, when he actually wants him to become his son and therefore Maitreyi's brother), Maitreyi becomes Eve or eternal temptation, whereas Allan himself becomes Adam, who misuses God's trust and forfeits eternal bliss through sexual transgression (incest). So, Allan's cultural preconceptions are manifest not only at the surface or immediate level of his narrative, but also at its deep or symbolic level.

But why does Allan fictionalize events in terms of these familiar myths? A partial answer may be found in his attempt to give his story the dignity of tragedy, by implying that his separation from Maitreyi is demanded by the implacable logic of the myth itself. But Allan's appeal to the myth also serves to conceal his rather discreditable role in the denouement of his love affair. It is never very clear why Allan and Maitreyi cannot get married except for the arbitrary, godlike will of Narendra Sen. If, as the narrator claims, he and the girl did exchange hymeneal garlands (the rite of Gandharvavivaha), together with other pledges, such as a wedding ring (laboriously described by the narrator), then, according to Indian custom, Allan could have successfully pressed his claim to Maitreyi's hand. We are never told, moreover, what became of Allan's plans to embrace Hinduism.

The ending of the novel is a far cry from tragedy; in fact it turns into lurid bourgeois melodrama, when Allan reverts once again to his Orientalist fantasies in order to explain why he has given up any attempt to rejoin Maitreyi. Now in Singapore, he runs into an Indian friend who informs him that Maitreyi has caused a scandal by giving herself to one of the servants. Allan remembers that Maitreyi had once suggested a desperate solution: if she were dishonored, then her father would turn her out of the house and she would be free to leave for Europe with her beloved. At first Allan is flattered by this "barbarian" sacrifice to their love. But then he remembers a letter from one of Maitreyi's admirers, which, for some obscure reason, the girl had given to him on her birthday and which Allan had opened only a few days before. From its contents he infers that Maitreyi had not been exactly "faithful" to him. Allan's jealousy assumes again a racial form: the girl is a primitive, unpredictable, and cruel sex goddess who is beyond the Western moral code. The narrative ends on an ambiguous note. Torn between his reawakened love for Maitreyi and his cultural prejudices the narrator is thrown into a deep emotional confusion: "I feel that she did it for me. . . . And what if my love deceives me? Why should I believe? How do I know? I would like to look into Maitreyi's eyes" (158).

From the reader's standpoint, however, it is clear that the barrier between the two lovers is placed there not by an irate father or god, but by the narrator himself, who builds it out of his Orientalist fantasies and confused notions of racial difference. The narrator remains blind to the liminal possibilities inherent in his ambiguous state of crisis and is thus unable to transcend his egocentric, agonistic mentality. His self-induced, paranoid fears ("And what if my love deceives me?" and "Why should I believe?") indicate that his ego-will is far from being ready to melt itself into the ecstatic play of irenic love.

3. "It Does Not Die": Love, Liminality, and Inner Being

Not unexpectedly, Maitreyi Devi's version of this love story challenges both the factual accuracy and the psychological truth of Allan's melodrama. There is no secret marriage in *It Does Not Die*, nor is there any self-dishonoring sexual act, no matter how honorable its motives. Amrita, the narratrix, accuses Mircea Euclid—Devi's fictional character based on young Eliade—of having given her up too easily and of having exaggerated the cruelty and willfulness of her father, though she also judges the latter severely. Amrita makes fun of Euclid's credulity and humorlessness. She constantly teases him about her guru, the famous poet Tagore, of whom Euclid is absurdly jealous. She laughs at his pedantry, at his habit of reading anthropological signs into her childish games.

She accurately senses the immature, adolescent nature of Allan-Euclid's narrative and does not hide her own ambivalent response to it: "This book really has no quality to revive memory, on the other hand it hurts. It wears a mask of truth—it is the work of a delirious mind."[10] Because of Euclid's preconceived notions, Amrita writes, he "failed to understand me. He never grasped my thoughts. I too, of course, gave him little chance. I never opened my mind to him—there was no time. Exactly for that reason, in his book he puts in my mouth absurd confessions. It seems his unsatiated desire made him indulge in a strange fantasy" (227).

In writing her version of the story, however, Amrita wishes less to set the record straight than to understand both Euclid and herself: "It requires colossal daring to try to navigate the inexhaustible, mysterious ocean of the human mind. So I do not judge him. I try only to understand" (227). Amrita acknowledges her deep emotional involvement, so deep that even after a lapse of forty-two years this youthful episode comes back to haunt her. In contrast to Allan, she is no unreliable narrator, and her narrative is a courageous, if painful attempt to explore the nature and meaning of her love both within and outside an ethopathology of power.

If *Maitreyi* revolves around certain Orientalist myths, *It Does Not Die* predictably reveals certain preconceptions and simplistic generalizations about the West. For instance, Euclid often appears as a rational, cold-blooded scholar, who spends his life (and passion) buried in books—his Greek name is an obvious reference to the ancient geometer-philosopher, who in this context replaces Descartes as a symbol of Western rationality. At the end of her narrative Amrita must, both literally and symbolically, negotiate huge piles of books scattered all over Euclid's office in order to reach him. She also accuses him of "unfaithfulness," calls him a "European hunter," and charges that Westerners cannot understand pure (platonic?) love, that for them "the fulfillment of love must be in bed." If anything, a comparison between *Maitreyi* and *It Does Not Die* reveals an identity of human response, manifested through the very wealth of economic, sociopolitical, and ideological differences.

On one level, this identity of human response comes from the fact that the different worlds to which Euclid and Amrita belong basically share the same mentality of power and, therefore, are far from being incompatible. If *It Does Not Die* stopped here, it would largely remain the sociopolitical document that contemporary postcolonial criticism deems it to be. But Devi goes even further than Eliade in spelling out what is wrong with their two worlds and how these worlds can renew themselves. In this sense, *It Does not Die* is not so much a response as it is a sequel to *Maitreyi*, placing it in the proper spiritual perspective. Devi's novel, despite its subtitle, "A Romance and a Reminiscence," is less about what has been (the historical events that concerned her and Eliade in Calcutta, in 1929–30) than it is about what could be if the two lovers— as well as all lovers—would shed their sociocultural and racial prejudices and approach each other from the perspective of an irenic communitas, as two human beings. Devi constructs her narrative around the Hindu myth of the immortality of the soul (the title of her book is an allusion to the sloka of the *Gita* that describes the soul as immortal). But she also shows how this Hindu myth can become reality by temporarily removing it from its specific cultural context and rejuvenating it through the liminal imaginative state that generated it in the first place, along with all other human myths.

At the outset of the novel, Amrita establishes the central point of view of her story. This point of view is decidedly not that of a powerless native female victimized by a colonialist white male, but that of a human being who transports herself to a neutral, liminal time-space that can best be described as a void or nothingness, where she is neither female nor male, neither victim nor aggressor, neither ego-will nor fluid nonentity. Amrita herself first experiences such a liminal state at the age of fourteen, which she describes through the same *via negativa* that I have employed here for lack of better terms: "I actually felt the evening turn into morning at one and the same moment. Time lost its dimensions for a while. I wrote a poem that day: 'Allow me to float away, where my dream goes;' then I described that place. 'It is a place of nothingness, there everything ends, no hope, no speech, no voice, no sound, no traveller shuffles on an empty path, no birth, no death, no time, no night, no day and no morning breaks in that void'" (36).

Here Amrita presents a poetic version of what Buddhists call the liminal state of bardo, rich with endless possibilities and, for that very reason, confusing and terrifying.[11] From within this poetic bardo she can travel to any time and place in history, including her Bhowanipur paternal home of forty-two years ago. And this is precisely where she goes at the beginning of the narrative, on her fifty-eighth birthday. In a sense, this fateful day marks a liminal rebirth for Amrita. While speaking to Sergiu Sebastian, Euclid's young disciple who informs her about his guru's (in)famous novel, she is suddenly transported back to the past: "A weird sensation tingled in the soles of my feet. I was sitting on a low divan, my feet pressed firmly on the floor; but suddenly I was lifted up. I soared, I remained hanging in a void without support. My feet were no more on the ground, the room had no roof. Yes, I know I was staring at Sergiu, he was smiling a little, so was I, and a strong sensation ran through my body. I was turned into a drop of quicksilver, unable to remain steady. I was transported to the verandah of our Bhowanipur house" (15).

It is from this liminal standpoint that Amrita ultimately evaluates not only her father's, Euclid's, and her own past behavior, but also the intercultural and interracial context that led to her separation from the young man she loved. One should also note that because Amrita experiences two different historical times simultaneously, she employs the present and the past tense indifferently throughout her account, so that the reader has initially some difficulty in determining her central viewpoint. To understand Amrita's narrative properly, therefore, the reader needs to be constantly aware of her fluid transitions, back and forth, from her youthful, agonistic perspective—not all that different from Allan-Euclid's—to her mature, liminal one.

Examining her ambivalent relationship with her father (from an agonistic perspective), Amrita reveals the Hindu paternalistic mentality that had controlled it. For example, she observes: "The master of the house is the bread-earner, so he also had absolute right to dismiss all other views and lead every member of the family according to his own views. Maybe this is a necessary and useful custom to maintain discipline in a large joint-family, but it invariably turns the ruler into an arrogant and selfish person. He considers himself to be a god ruling that particular household" (105). Amrita is also aware that this paternalistic fiction created by a Hindu mentality of power, which is very similar to the traditional Western one, becomes essentially untenable when tested against a fluid, reversible dialectic of weak and strong, so she adds ironically: "But actually [the master of the house] is no god; he is just a human being full of weaknesses and bound down by the pleasures and sorrows of life like any other insignificant member of the family" (105).

Not unlike Nietzsche, Amrita detects in her father's love of scholarship a disguised and distorted Will to Power. For her Indian philosopher-father, as for many of his Western counterparts, scholarship is a game of one-upsmanship. As Amrita points out, her father "is well-known for his erudition and feared by many because of it. His scholarship is aggressive; he can easily reduce a person in argument to shambles; he is very fond of his game" (22). Although her father exhibits an open-minded, "modern" attitude in encouraging his talented young daughter to study, he does so only for the purpose of showing her off to his peers-competitors. He has the same attitude toward his students, whom he "loves for his own sake, not theirs" (22). He is "immensely happy" with his disciple Euclid because of his "unquenchable thirst for knowledge" (44). As Amrita notes ironically, "In [F]ather's museum, we two [she and Euclid] were good exhibits" (44). Her father's arduous pursuit of knowledge prevents him from understanding and caring about anyone around him: "Ever eager for that supreme knowledge, [F]ather cared little for the people who endure their petty sorrow-cum-happiness in this world of Karma. The message that man is greater than all else was never acceptable to him" (135). His books are both objects of worship and instruments of power. For example, when her father, upon discovering her romance with Mircea, tears out the dedications from the books that the young scholar had given her but does not dispose of the volumes themselves, Amrita writes: "In any other house the books would have been destroyed. But that cannot be in our house. We also have a Genghis Khan. Only he does not burn books. He can burn human beings but not books. The book is his God" (129).

Amrita has no illusions about the nature of her father's love for her: "My father is full of me, yet I know if I dare go against him the littlest bit he won't hesitate to crush me ruthlessly. My likes and dislikes are immaterial. I have to be happy at his command" (22). Although Amrita denies Allan-Euclid's secondhand report that she was cruelly beaten and physically tortured by her father in the wake of the separation between the two lovers, she acknowledges having undergone a much worse kind of torture at his hands, that of the mind: "Father is like an Emperor who could order anyone crushed under the feet of an elephant or behead anyone, as he thought best. Of course he won't be able to decree physical punishment—but what about the mind? He holds unchallenged sway over our minds. If by any chance he comes to know of what is going on, he will do the same thing that the Great Mogul Emperor Akbar did— not in body but in mind—he will roll a boulder down on this Anarkali [a sixteen-year-old slave girl whom Akbar buried alive] of love" (106).

Whereas Amrita sees her father as representing mostly the aggressive side of the scholarly Will to Power, she sees Euclid as largely representing the ascetic or self-aggressive side of it. She acknowledges that as a young girl she was attracted to this kind of power. For example, Amrita always defers to Euclid when they wage their lovers' battles of will: "After all, [Mircea] is superior to me not only in age but in learning and also in strength of mind. I felt defeated and crushed—but I was happy. I was happy that he had grown taller than me by manifesting his power of self-mortification" (104). Amrita also admires Euclid's retreat to the Himalayas in order to become a sannyasi, flattering herself that he has gone there because of her. She is very impressed by a Himalayan guide's description of the ascetic habits of a hermit, whom she immediately associates with Euclid: "I am always humbled before the power of self-mortification" (142).

Much later, however, Amrita realizes that Euclid's aim in becoming a sannyasi was to increase his power and prestige through self-mortification, not unlike many an ascetic Christian monk. Speculating on the reason why Euclid chose to betray his love for her and remain her father's disciple, she compares him to the mythical hero, Kacha: having been sent by the gods to the priest Sukra to learn from him the secret of reviving the dead, Kacha falls in love with the priest's daughter, but abandons her as soon as he accomplishes his mission, claiming that his work is more important than love. When Amrita learns that Euclid has published eminent scholarly works about Indian philosophy, she muses: "Isn't he really a Kacha once again? A careerist like Kacha himself. I realised then why he did not write to me. It was more necessary to write the book on Yoga. It was necessary to become a specialist in Indian philosophy. 'Greed of fame and erudition,' I told myself" (199).

In the end, Amrita comes to realize that Euclid and her father are actually quite similar despite their different ages and cultural backgrounds. Her judgment of Euclid echoes her guru's judgment of her father: "[P]erfidious man, you have purchased learning at the cost of truth. You may have become a pundit but you are not wise. You are like a wooden ladle that, though it remains soaked in honey, does not taste it" (201). Speaking of her father, Amrita's guru, Tagore had remarked: "Your father came to see me with your husband. I did not find much to talk to him. Only pundits can be so ruthless" (166).

Amrita is also aware that the paternalistic mentality against which she rebels is equally shared by the men and the women in her family, including herself. For example, it is Amrita's mother who creates and maintains the image of the father as a household god. In this regard, Amrita comments: "We never thought that our father could have any fault. For us he was flawless, as pure as a god. Mother was at the root of building this image. . . . She thought children should never even in mind criticize their father. After all, the age-old maxim said, 'Father is heaven, father represents virtue, father is our greatest penance. The gods are pleased if father is pleased'" (105). At the same time, Amrita's mother treats her husband like an irresponsible "child" who must be pampered and indulged despite his naughty behavior, revealing that in Hindu traditional society, as in many other such societies all over the world, paternalism goes hand in hand with the cult of the mother. When Amrita asks her to intercede with her husband on behalf of Mircea and herself, her mother responds with the kind of guilt-inflicting, emotional blackmail employed by authoritarian parents everywhere: "What can I do, Ru? He says if I insist, he will die. Do you want to kill your father? You don't love your father. Is that boy dearer to you than us?" (123).

Although Amrita's mother does sympathize with her daughter, rejecting her husband's suggestion that she malign Euclid and turn Amrita against him for "therapeutic" purposes, she is nevertheless partly responsible for her husband's tyrannical behavior and ultimate betrayal of his family, because of her general tendency to condone hypocrisy and lies in order to preserve social appearances. When Amrita's father starts an affair with a younger female student who will eventually push him into abandoning his family, her mother tries to cover up for him even after he leaves the house and withdraws financial support from them. Amrita does not see her mother as a helpless victim, however, but mostly as someone who will stick to social convention out of fear of the unknown and will even condone an act of injustice rather than cause "unpleasantness."

Amrita equally realizes that her family is part of a dynamic network of social relations that is constantly shifting as India's middle and upper classes attempt to become "Westernized" under the impact of (and against) British colonial power. Not unlike the East European world staged in Rebreanu's novel, Amrita's India is a traditional agrarian culture in the throes of modernization. Although her family considers itself "modern"—e.g., its women are not in purdah, being able to mix freely with foreign male visitors—it preserves many of its traditional Hindu customs and will never go against the caste system. So Amrita writes that Euclid was naive in thinking that her father would ever agree to their marriage, because of his strong Hindu family ties, including a host of traditional relatives in the countryside: "Even if [F]ather is himself willing, he will never be able to give me away in marriage to a foreigner. All these relatives who are really nobody to us, who do not understand half of what we say, are invincible" (91). An argument to this effect between Amrita and Mircea reveals both her father's ambivalent character and the ambivalent nature of modern India as a whole:

> "Mircea, I tell you my father will never agree. Never, never."
> "But, why not? Because my complexion is white? Because I am Christian?"
> "I do not know exactly why, but certainly because you are a foreigner."
> "Do you want to say that the professor is in favour of the caste system? Is there any difference between a Hindu, a Muslim, a Christian, or a Buddhist to a Philosopher?"
> "Of course there is." (83)

Amrita points out that there is a whole chain of prejudices operating in modern India, not only on the part of the traditional social groups but also on the part of the British rulers and their "emancipated" Indian allies. For example, Amrita acknowledges that Euclid was the first to introduce her to the Anglo-Indians, a social group with whom she had never had much contact before and who had their own prejudices, as Euclid describes in his book. Like Allan, Amrita notes that the Anglo-Indians "think of themselves as pure descendants of the British and so much above the Bengalis! They hate Mahatma Gandhi whom they mention as 'Gandy'; and though they themselves are uneducated and narrow-minded, they consider us [Hindus] uncivilized" (87). But then she adds, speaking from her mature, liminal perspective: "But, let's be truthful, don't we also hate them? We call them 'crossbreeds.' Is that a decent word? But I know that we hate each other only because we don't know each other" (88).

There is also conflict and misunderstanding between the traditional Hindus and the Brahmos (a unitarian sect that sought to purge Hindu society of all forms of idolatry, but had its own elitist prejudices). Amrita's description of the magnificent Shankar performance (to which Allan alludes in his narrative as well) is permeated by exquisite social irony directed not only at the Brahmos but also at her own group: "Our pedigree was questionable, since we were 'backward' Hindus. So they [the Brahmos] did not usually recognise us. But that day quite a few from this group of the specially superior elite discarded their superciliousness and, during the interval, came, stood under our box, in batches, and began conversation. Father's attitude was no less overbearing. He was after all accompanied by an exquisitely beautiful wife, a moderately pretty (the views of Mircea notwithstanding) poetess-daughter, and a foreign disciple in Indian dress, and added to all that was the box. Altogether it was an immense affair that reduced the pride of the Brahmos to rubble" (110).

Amrita's look at the Hindu marriage practices is no less ironical. In the wake of Euclid's departure and her father's sexual errancy, Amrita agrees to contract a traditional marriage in order to get away from her parents. Her only condition is to marry outside her caste as an emancipatory gesture, but here again she encounters insurmountable prejudices both within and outside her family. One Bengali suitor is unacceptable to her mother, because of his excessively dark skin: "[W]e Bengalis," Amrita notes, "are no less prejudiced against dark skin than Europeans" (158). She wonders whether she will ever get married at this rate, since fair skin, judging from her parents' treatment of Mircea, seems equally unacceptable to them (159). As it turns out, however, the girl herself is unacceptable to the suitor because she is not tall enough: "He is only five feet four or so, he wants a girl to be at least five feet seven [Amrita is only five feet two]. For if a short boy is married to a short girl, what would happen to the future of the race?" (159). When the Bengali doctor turns down the match, Amrita comments: "I could not blame him of course: just as I want to improve the moral side of the nation, he is trying to improve the biological. Both of us at least have one thing in common: we are patriotic!" (159).

Amrita underscores the irrationality underlying most of these prejudices, largely held by eminently rational people, and then she adds: "But reason does not play a great part either in family life or in politics. The British say, 'Rule, Britannia, Rule the waves, Britons never will be slaves'—but look at what they have done to others and then that is also their pride—'The sun never sets on the British Empire.' Logic is seldom used" (158). Nor was it the right thing (by any standards—traditional or modern) for Amrita's father to turn Mircea out of the house the way he did, and she comments sarcastically: "According to our [Hindu] custom in the month of Bhadra even an animal is not turned out of a home, let alone a human being; but we were a modern family and paid no heed to such superstitions" (148). Her final comment on the bigoted culture that separated her from the young man she loved is no less severe: "Afterwards, whenever I remembered that evening, I thought of the fear that remained interwoven with the experience of a tender love. Was it a crime for a sixteen-year-old girl and a twenty-three-year-old boy to be in love? Where else would God's greatest gift descend on the earth, how else would love be born? What a threatening and frowning society we lived in!" (118).

At this point Amrita completely rejects her own culture, just as Allan rejected his. Her emotional involvement with Euclid can be read as a sign of obvious rebellion, initially directed against her father and then against her society at large. In this respect, Amrita writes from her youthful, agonistic perspective: "[Mircea] does not know how much even our family is bound by these irrational rules. And [F]ather, who is so learned, who knows so much, does not know that happiness never depends on a person's caste or clan name? And me? I don't care about these things. Never, never will I enter into the prison house of prejudice. Even if I am not married to him I will prove with my family that I don't care for these silly customs. I don't care for anything in Hindu society. I don't even like idolatry or icon worship the way Hindus do it" (89).

In the same rebellious voice of the past, Amrita goes on to say: "I am a prisoner. Who will free me? . . . Do not become a Hindu, Mircea. Hinduism will take you nowhere. Look at me, what have I gained by remaining a Hindu? It will not give you strength; it will take it away"

(93). Out of a frustrated rebellious spirit, the young Amrita would like to join the nationalist struggle of liberation from the British, but she feels helpless as a woman, because even this struggle is largely the prerogative of Indian men. Yet her feeling of helplessness makes her realize, in turn, that while nationalist struggle may free the country from foreign rule, it will certainly not free it from its own prejudices: "I know they want to rid the country of the British. I don't know exactly what the British are doing to us—but can they tell me who will free us—can human beings?" (131).

From her mature, liminal perspective, on the other hand, Amrita fully acknowledges that her rebellious attitude could only lead to prejudice in reverse, as well as to more suffering for herself and others. Ironically, it is the Hindu traditional marriage she eventually contracts that helps her transcend her agonistic frame of mind. She follows her husband to the Himalayan forests near Darjeeling, far away from Calcutta, where she relearns how to live with herself and others. Amrita's liminal Himalayan experience, unlike Allan's, is both genuine and productive of new values. As she points out, "When I went to make my home on a tiny hill perched on an arm of the mighty Himalayas I came with a sense of emptiness in me, but when I left the place after twenty-two years, that emptiness was gone. I came back with a full life—full of affection, love and friendship" (196). As in Rebreanu's novel, simple country people (in this case the Ghurkas) prove to possess genuine human values worth embracing; what they primarily teach Amrita is how to be less self-involved and how to care for and serve others.

Amrita's husband, who is an enlightened Hindu, becomes as important an ethical model for her as the Ghurkas with whom he works: "He has no prejudice. He also is against all caste taboos. He is critical of our social customs and rational in his attitude" (172). By "rational" here Amrita means a state of mind akin to responsive understanding: unlike her father (or Euclid, for that matter), her husband cares much more for the well-being of others than for an intransigent adherence to some ideological or religious doctrine. He has a truly irenic disposition that Amrita would like to share, but that she cannot yet fully embrace, especially where the British are concerned: "They [the British women on the Darjeeling tea plantation] kill their time over tennis, bridge, drinking, dancing, and intermittent flirtation with each other's husbands. They care for nothing else. Their menfolk are ignorant and drunkards. Maybe in their inner self they are as human as we are but I have not the eye to see it, nor sensitivity enough to feel it" (178).

Amrita's husband, by contrast, has arrived at the kind of irenic understanding that allows him to feel, think, and act in a nonagonistic, selfless manner. For example, although he is a strict vegetarian, he does not hesitate taking meat at the house of an ignorant and insensitive English woman, in order to spare her feelings as a hostess. So Amrita comments: "I was surprised to hear that the first day he took meat it was beef [cows are, of course, sacred to the Hindus]. . . . But for him it was a simple act of following reason—he was not rebellious—not like me—I am consciously and purposely eager to break all these foolish customs, especially caste. But he is just acknowledging truth simply and naturally" (172). Learning about Euclid's book, Amrita's husband attempts to place himself in Mircea's exilic predicament. When Amrita snaps, "Don't talk of him. . . . A betrayer—he was served right," her husband replies: "How can you have peace if you think like that? You were in your home, with your parents, and that poor young boy, in a foreign country, was turned out in an hour's notice. . . . Really, your father cannot be forgiven" (220).

As one can readily see from the preceding citations, Amrita makes no secret of the fact that she cannot yet fully operate within an irenic mentality despite her liminal perspective. She continues to experience ambivalence about the orthodox Hindus and the British, as well as about her father, whom she nevertheless attempts now to understand from his own point of view, rather than from that of his family: "But to-day I felt, maybe Rama [the woman for whom Amrita's father left his family] was also just a tool. It is someone else's game we are playing. We are marionettes in his hands. Maybe what appeared as loss from the outside was actually [F]ather's gain from another aspect. Sadhu Bijoykrishna Goswami had told father that he would have a fall. Father had the seed of it in him from birth. It was his immense 'ego', and we have all of us tried to preserve that ego. We regretted that [F]ather could not be President of our country. Did he not deserve it, we said. It was only for her that he lost everything, power and prestige, and died in dignity while living in the ignominy of her 'protection'" (226).

Despite her liminal perspective, Amrita continues to have ambivalent feelings toward Mircea as well. She is still very angry with what she perceives to have been his double betrayal (having given her up and having written an ignominious book about it): "Unbearable is the flame of anger burning within me. I resolve that I must avenge myself. I will not, even though many years have passed, accept the injustice done to me" (214). But even as she experiences these agonistic feelings, "a metamorphosis is going on" inside her, making her wonder: "Why are you so angry? Maybe he has written but his letters have not reached you, or maybe your letters have not reached him" (214). She also hears a "third mind" deep within herself, where "no arguments, no logic can ever reach," saying to her: "Can everything be explained only by events and facts; can truth be realised by arguments? Listen to the message that emanates from the soul, listen in silence. Not through the ears, nor by the intellect, but by the heart you will hear the echo of truth. He has not deceived you" (203).

As Amrita listens to this third mind, she realizes that her anger is directed not only at Mircea but also at herself. She realizes that as a young girl she fully shared the cultural prejudices against which she wanted to rebel, that she was no less instrumental than Mircea in letting her world control their fate. Commenting on the agonistic mentality she had for so long been immersed in, she writes: "In the few days that we live—how we make others suffer! We can cause a little happiness, instead we inflict unending suffering" (211). Far from casting herself in the role of a victim, she fully accepts her share of responsibility in the tragic affair: "Actually I could have done much. This was my country. I had many friends and some of them were illustrious men. Was there no one to support me? Why did I not seek help? Just because I had a pre-conceived notion that in these matters the man should take the lead and not the woman. It would be a shameless act on the part of woman to take the initiative. This was a kind of prejudice and also vanity. I was a foolish, vain and worthless girl. I should have realised that as a foreigner his position was vulnerable" (242).

Amrita's anger, then, is far from being all negative; on the contrary, it burns away the negative feelings lodged in her first and second minds, clearing the way, as it were, for her third mind or the bottomless depth of her inner being: "On sleepless nights, the fire of anger burns within me but it burns my pride, prejudice, and all that I thought valuable so long. A taper of fear is coming up from within and is burning everything in its course. I am melting like a candle, and its light is spreading all over. Drop by drop the hard straight candle is slipping like a liquid, melting my vanity, my sense of prestige. Everything is falling in that fire. My ego built through the prejudice of the ages was unbending like that candle" (217).

In turn, what the third mind reveals above all, when listened to attentively, is the harmonious interconnectedness of all beings. Through her liminal perspective, Amrita will eventually be able to experience her true self as the fulfillment of suchness (in the Zen Buddhist sense discussed in chapter 3). While still enmeshed in her agonistic mentality, she can experience this true self only as the negative emotions of fear, anguish, and insatiable desire. In her divided, agonistic state, Amrita observes, "I was not seeking anyone but myself—that part of me which could not express itself used to wring my heart with an unnamed anguish, whereas the other part of me was happily engaged in its circle of daily life" (187). Although on one level Amrita feels fulfilled in both her personal and public life, she still experiences an indefinable emptiness or lack: "Most of the people I know seem to be happy with their lot, why can't I be? I have everything that one can seek or expect. Why this interminable emptiness—as if I could not perform what I was to perform, as if I could not speak what I wanted to speak, as if I could not get what I was aspiring for. This unspecified desire remains ever elusive and unsatiated" (186). Amrita has chosen to ignore the call of this desire most of her life, but in her middle age it has surged with renewed intensity, her painful memory of Mircea serving as a catalyst: "Since some months before I remembered Mircea again—quite a few months before Sergiu came—I used to feel a mysterious yearning in me, of which I have written. I cannot describe the acuteness of that feeling. I continuously hummed those lines—'I am restless, I aspire for far-away things—I forget, I always forget that I have no wings'" (245).

The desire to which Amrita refers here is not the insatiable, agonistic desire of the Schopenhauerian ego-will (as experienced by Allan-Euclid, for example); on the contrary, it is akin to Levinas's notion of the infinite as desire irresistibly melting down the self-centered will to individuation. This desire, understood as the irresistible pull of infinitude or as the love of the Other as incommensurable alterity, plunges

Amrita into the measureless time-space of her inner being, where the ego-will dissolves into an ecstatic play of suchness: "The infinite has picked me up from the world below. Holding me in its lap, it is danc-ing—its loosened hair has covered my eyes, face and whole body. The front and the back have blended; east and west, far and near are the same. My prison is broken. I am emancipated from shame, fear, and all social ties. Only love, unconquered by time, burns like a pole star on the corner of that limitless expanse" (246).

Amrita's liminal perspective eventually allows her to experience love as selflessness or as the infinite calling of the Other. Through it she gains access, like Apostol Bologa, to an alternative irenic world that is incommensurable with the worlds in which she has lived in the past. Now everything that has gone on before appears as misperception, self-delusion, and lack of authenticity and will be removed for good: "It is the fire of love that destroyed everything else and began to emanate light. The light entered into the depth of my being, in every corner of my heart, and all the blind alleys began to brighten up. All my preten-sions, all my self-deceptions are evaporating, eroding; I am starting to see the full image of truth" (217).

Like Bologa, Amrita discerns two kinds of love corresponding to these two incommensurable worlds: agonistic and irenic. As both Apostol and Amrita come to realize, from the standpoint of an irenic world ago-nistic love looks more like hate—hate of self and hate of the other. It is mostly this agonistic, destructive form of love that Amrita and Euclid experience in their youth, as Allan's version of the story amply testifies. Likewise, speaking of Rama's selfish love for Amrita's father, Amrita notes: "Only I have fully realised that there are two different kinds of love which look very similar from the outside, though they are really opposed—one kind can lift a person so high that from there all small-ness and selfishness disappear—it fills one's world with light and fra-grance and makes dear all that was unpleasant before—by its light the usual things appear extraordinary, and dearer—this love does not make you greedy or provoke you to persecute your rival. But there is another kind of love: its appearance is the same, but it deftly puts a noose around the other's neck—or chains one down" (155).

Once Amrita experiences irenic love, her agonistic perception of Mircea loses its emotional hold on her and can no longer affect the way in which she relates to him, in other words, her ethopathology undergoes a process of radical transformation: "I sharpen all these criticisms like little poisoned arrows and throw them at him, but strangely, they vanish no sooner than they leave the bow-string, and do not reach the target. My angry thoughts are like little round pebbles on the waves of my heart. I can't use them to hit him; from moment to moment they slip from my hand, roll off, move away and get lost" (227). This irenic perception also transforms Amrita's conventional sense of space, time, and reality: "Gradually I am being lifted up into another dimension. It is another existence from where the good and bad, the truth and untruth, the fact and the fantasy of this world appear meaningless. The shell of this outer world begins to peel off from me—mind says, praise or blame, all are the same—there are things truer than these" (217). Amrita's notion of death is also completely altered, since an irenic mentality does not perceive death in terms of fear or temporal and spatial barriers: "Love is deathless. My soul, held by him in that Bhowanipur house, still remains so fixed. The infinite is flowing through the finite—the limitless is held in the limits of my body—I am far and I am also near, I am here and also not here" (218).

Amrita is aware that her experience of irenic love is incommensurable and that, as such, it cannot be properly understood or felt by someone operating within an agonistic world. For this reason, she conveys her experience in poetic, liminal terms that may still be within the purview of a mentality of power, but can also point beyond it: "I don't know whether God exists, but I now know the nature of our inner being. All my doubts are vanishing like a moving mirage. This experience cannot be transmitted to others just as light cannot be shown to a blind man. It is an experience that is beyond argument, beyond intellect, which cannot be learnt in books and scriptures. I now realise this timeless, indestructible love will never get crushed by worldly affairs—it will flow from moment to moment and carry me away from the profane state, like the river that grows in speed as it approaches the confluence of the sea" (232).

Someone who thinks in agonistic terms such as a rationalist philosopher or scientist will at best classify Amrita's irenic experience as "mystical" or "supernatural," belonging to the realm of the divine rather than to that of ordinary reality. A rationalist observer would probably argue that although she rejects Hinduism, she seems to return to the religion of her ancestors by invoking the Hindu myth of the immortal soul. Amrita, however, emphasizes not only in the preceding citation but throughout her narrative that she is not religious, that she is neither an atheist nor an agnostic, religion being for her only another expression of a mentality of power. If she invokes the Hindu myth of immortal love, she emancipates it from its concrete religious or nationalist context, just as Rebreanu, in *The Forest of the Hanged*, emancipates its Christian counterpart from an East European context, viewing it from the liminal standpoint of an irenic human communitas, beyond any specific culture. In this regard, Devi's narrative, like that of Rebreanu, follows what one may call a non-Aristotelian apocalyptic pattern.

In a traditional apocalyptic narrative (of the kind Aristotle describes in his *Poetics* in relation to the tragic plot), the ending is always the beginning revealed and recognized—hence the attribute of "apocalyptic."[12] Historical events form a logical, causal chain and lead inexorably to an ending that has already been anticipated in the beginning, for example through a prophecy, vision, or dream. By contrast, in a non-Aristotelian apocalyptic narrative, the final revelation is not related to the historical events preceding it, even though it may have been heralded by an initial vision or dream; on the contrary, it rejects these events as irrelevant. This kind of narrative lacks a plot per se and consists of a succession of disconnected historical events, having no rational meaning, that is, not being related to a whole. Its ending is calculated precisely to reveal this lack of rational meaning, hinting instead at an alternative reality, which is situated outside constituted history and which either assumes a familiar mythical form or remains indefinite. Well-known examples of such non-Aristotelian apocalyptic narratives include Brontë's *Wuthering Heights*, Dostoevsky's *Crime and Punishment*, Forster's *A Passage to India*, Bulgakov's *The Master and Margarita*, and Pasternak's *Doctor Zhivago*, as well as Eliade's mature novel, *The Forbidden Forest*.

When, in Devi's narrative, Amrita sees Euclid again after an interval of over forty years, although their reunion in Chicago is disappointing at the historical level, she circumvents past and present events in favor of a mythical revelation of the future. The ending of *It Does Not Die* is worth citing at length:

Mircea raised his face. His eyes were glazed. Oh no, my worst fears are true—his eyes have turned into stone. He will never see me again. What shall I do?. . . Fear changed me—I am no more Amrita. I turned into just a mortal and I thought like him—forty years, forty years! It is too late indeed.

. . . I walked toward the door crossing the little hillocks of books, when I heard Mircea's voice from the back, "Amrita, wait a little. Why are you breaking down, where you were so brave for so many years. I promise you I shall come to you, and there on the shore of the Ganga, I will show you my real self."

I am not a pessimist. Inside my broken heart a tiny bird of hope was in its death throes but no sooner Mircea's words reached me, than the little bird revived and turned into a phoenix. . . . That huge bird flapped its great wings and then, picking me up, it rose higher and higher as the roof of Mircea's study opened like Pandora's box, and the walls disappeared—all the stony books turned into ripples—I heard the gurgle of flowing water.

That great bird, built with the illusion of hope, whispered to me, as we moved towards an unknown continent, crossing Lake Michigan, "Do not be disheartened, Amrita, you will put light in his eyes."

"When?" I asked eagerly.

"When you meet him in the Milky Way—that day is not very far now," it replied.[13]

There is in this ending a skillful interplay between the novel's historical and mythical themes, with a gradual, subtle substitution of the former by the latter (even the comparison of a university office with Pandora's box has its merits in and out of this context). Amrita suggests that despite temporary setbacks, her and Euclid's inner beings are united in eternal love, and will meet again in a different order of existence, away from samsara, or the world of karmic distraction and suffering.

The same rejection of history as constituted by a mentality of power in favor of a mythical revelation takes place at the end of Eliade's *The Forbidden Forest*. Stefan Viziru, the novel's protagonist, lives through a series of disconnected events (the rise of fascism in Romania, World War II, the postwar period, the exile in France, and so on) without being able to make any sense of them. But at the end of the book he experiences a revelation that also coincides with his physical death in a car accident. He had actually visualized his death scene twelve years before to the day, during a walk with his lifelong beloved, Ileana, in a forest outside Bucharest. At that time, however, he had felt that there was a missing link in the scene: a car that was supposed, for some obscure reason, to pick them up. This car will predictably be, in the completed scene, the agent of their "death-hierophany." Now, years later, Stefan encounters Ileana again, in a forest in France. (Note Eliade's symbolic use of the forest: here, as in Rebreanu's novel, the forest stands for Dante's *selva oscura*, the confusing world of suffering and death, which, nevertheless, can also be "enchanted," i.e., liminal, providing passage to another world.) Their reunion, like that of Amrita and Mircea, is at first unsuccessful because Ileana is in love with someone else. But at the moment of the car accident they both recognize in a flash the long-forgotten scene in the Romanian forest and come together again, in eternity. This death-hierophany, or the revelation of the eternal through the repetition of a certain moment, renders all the other events in the book meaningless and irrelevant. As in *It Does Not Die*, we have a subtle manipulation of two opposed concepts of temporality, the mythical and the historical, or what Eliade calls "sacred" and "profane" time, with the latter being replaced by the former.

In a sense, then, both *It Does Not Die* and *The Forbidden Forest* are fitting sequels to *Maitreyi*, Eliade's youthful work. In *Maitreyi*, Allan is caught in his Orientalist, racial fantasies that belong to a violent philosophy of difference. As such, they fail to yield any meaning because they only serve to separate him from his true inner being, barring his access to the irenic consciousness of the oneness of all beings. Once this consciousness is regained, as Amrita and Stefan Viziru find out, all agonistic differences fall away and the path opens itself toward a nonviolent kind of world, based on acceptance and love, rather than rejection and conflict. As we have seen, this is also the understanding that Rebreanu's protagonist, Apostol Bologa, reaches at the end of *The Forest of the Hanged*, once he emancipates himself from his nationalist and ethnic prejudices.

One can finally argue that the exilic perspective, implicit in Rebreanu and explicit in Eliade and Devi, allows ever new textual meanings to take effect with their readers. From the standpoint of a no-man's land, even our authors' distinctions between sacred and profane time or between history and myth turn out to be merely provisional props. For whatever the human imagination brings forth can become reality, even though only certain existential paths (or modes of thought, feeling, and behavior) are at any given moment accessible to certain individuals and communities, depending on their imaginative choices. In this way, myth will incessantly create history and history will incessantly create myth, until they both melt into what the Hindus call *lila*, or the ecstatic play of the world, in order to be born anew.

ALLEGORY, POWER, AND THE POSTMODERN GAME OF INTERPRETATION
Nabokov, Lowry, Orwell

In the previous two chapters, I have focused on several literary texts that most critics would describe as "modernist" (although Gide's *Caves du Vatican* might prove an embarrassing exception here) and have shown how these texts constantly question the dominant values of their culture, pointing to imaginative alternatives that would radically transform it. In the present chapter, I shall focus on literary works that can be described as "postmodern" (although most critics would still view them as "modernist") and shall examine the various ways in which they deal with kindred axiological and ethical issues. These works are Vladimir Nabokov's *Pale Fire*, Malcolm Lowry's *Under the Volcano* and *Dark as the Grave Wherein My Friend is Laid*, and George Orwell's *1984*.

Considerations of space preclude me from discussing the countless definitions of modernism and postmodernism that have been proposed in the past few decades, so I shall content myself with simply clarifying my own rather restricted use of these terms.[1] For me, "modernism" and "postmodernism" are contemporary labels for a very old cultural phenomenon: the relentless, but inconclusive, agon between archaic and median values that has been central to Western civilization at least since the Hellenic classical period. Thus, what has been labeled as cultural "modernism" often supports median values, even though it presents these values in an ironical, parodic, or problematic fashion. "Postmodernism," on the other hand, often appears as a renewed attempt to affirm archaic values in Western culture. In this respect, Nietzsche is the first "postmodernist" who attempts to undermine the cultural authority of Western median values, including the hegemony of reason and middle-class morality. In the wake of Nietzsche, postmodernism shifts its emphasis from the world of eternal Being, necessity, continuity, and essence, to the world of perpetual Becoming, chance, chaos, and play of simulacra. It perceives traditional hermeneutics as an archenemy, particularly in the guise of allegory—one of the most powerful tools of this hermeneutics.

Webster's Seventh New Collegiate Dictionary defines "allegory" as
(1) "a story in which people, things, and happenings have another meaning, as in a fable or parable: allegories are used for teaching and explaining; (2) the presenting of ideas by means of such stories; symbolical
narration or description." A brief genealogical examination of the term
would show, however, that its meanings go well beyond these narrow,
didactic-literary boundaries. "Allegory" comes from the Greek ἀλληγορία,
which mainly denotes the "description of one thing under the image of
another," but came, originally, from ἄλλος, other, and ἀγορεύειν, to speak
in the ἀγορά, the assembly or marketplace. In ancient Greece, allegory
was clearly related to the birth of the science of interpretation or hermeneutics (which was in turn based upon the archaic science of divination), arising in the wake of the invention of writing and the advent of
the text. In the text, as opposed to speech, the speaker was no longer
there to clarify or stand by his meaning. The written words became
ambiguous, pointing to an authority or a "signified" outside the text.
The notions of truth and falsehood also gained a new usage in connection with the presence or absence of the speaking authority.[2] In archaic
Greece, the word ἀλήθεια meant "unhiddenness" or "unveiledness," or
"that which arises unhindered to presence," but later on came to mean
its opposite: "mediated presence" or "that which one arrives at through
a process of interpretation."

Allegory, then, came into being as the discourse of the absent authority or the Other, for which it substituted. At first it was specifically
used by Homer's apologists to preserve his cultural authority in the Greek
polis: Homer had come under the attack of certain philosophers and
theologians for telling "lies" or "myths" about the gods, so the allegorists
claimed that his true meaning was hidden and had to be revealed or
disclosed; in other words, that it had to be interpreted.[3] Gradually, allegory also came to be employed by religious or mystical sects (from the
Greek word μυστικός, hidden), secret brotherhoods, and so forth, which
encoded their meaning in order to make it inaccessible to outsiders. In
antiquity, therefore, allegory was originally an exegetic instrument that
eventually also turned into a rhetorical or literary figure.

In the Middle Ages and the Renaissance allegory preserved both its
hermeneutical and rhetorical functions, being employed in reading the
Bible and then secular or literary texts, as one can see, for example, in

Dante's famous letter to Can Grande della Scala, in which he explains the various allegorical levels of the *Divine Comedy*. In English literature, Spenser's *Fairie Queene* is the most familiar example of Renaissance allegorical poetry, and allegory as a rhetorical figure and an interpretive device remained in common use until the end of the neoclassical period. With the advent of romanticism, allegory lost its cultural prestige and was replaced by symbol, a related term that was now turned into allegory's symmetrical opposite.[4] The devaluation of allegory was the direct consequence of the loss of the traditional sense of community and social convention, on which both allegory and hermeneutics depend, and the establishment of such romantic notions as individuality, originality, creative freedom, and genius.

Allegory regained some of its prestige in the twentieth century, when a number of artists turned again to the traditional values of antiquity and classicism, even though now these values could often be expressed only in an ironic or parodic mode (e.g., in the works of T. S. Eliot, James Joyce, and Thomas Mann). Allegory also regained its hermeneutical function in connection with the rise of semiotics, for which all literature and, by extension, all language is "allegorical," being an infinite network of deferments, displacements, and substitutions that point to and stand in for an absent, perhaps imaginary, referent or origin.[5]

This brief genealogical sketch implies that allegorical discourse may, as a rule, appear under two interrelated circumstances: when the wealth of experience is felt to be so overwhelming that it can only be dealt with on several levels or a multiplicity of dimensions and will consequently require what one might call a *pluralistic* use of allegory; and when what is felt as truth is, for some reason, concealed, forbidden, inaccessible, or elusive. In the first case, allegory, especially in its ludic-liminal or literary form (emancipated from both a preestablished and a hidden or mystical idea of truth) could also become the open-ended, irenic discourse of the Other and otherness, as implied in chapter 3, section 3, above. In the second case, allegory, because of its double structure of openness and closure that necessarily implies ambivalence, can also be put to what one might call a *totalitarian* use, especially in political discourse. In the latter case, the science of interpretation or hermeneutics, which no less than literature is the allegorical discourse par excellence, ultimately becomes "doublespeak" to borrow Orwell's phrase from *1984*. In a totalitarian political context, therefore, allegory returns to its original, etymological meaning of the discourse of the concealed Other, or that which is not or cannot be spoken of in the agora, or out in the open.

My assumption in this chapter is that postmodern literature attempts to deal with a world in which all discourse has become allegorical, in other words, with a world that is self-conscious about its aesthetic foundations. Hence, postmodern literary texts will often take an antiallegorical stand, either by building and then destroying allegorical structures within their own fictional framework or by postulating a world of simulacra without depth, center, or meaning, where events are governed not by necessity or causation, but by pure chance. At the same time, these texts often turn against interpretation, denying either its possibility or its legitimacy.[6] By pointing to the arbitrary and authoritarian nature of interpretation and truth, postmodern literature also points to the functional character of these categories, revealing their origin in a preallegorical, archaic mentality of power that had at one time been naked and unashamed. Finally and most importantly, some postmodern literary texts, no less than their modernist counterparts or, for that matter, many outstanding literary works from any historical period, imply the need to find viable alternatives to this mentality, which keeps returning in ever more reified and violent historical forms, even though it has already run its logical and imaginative course many times over. These postmodern texts implicitly propose a pluralistic concept of allegory as the ludic-liminal discourse of the Other and otherness viewed not as hidden truth or agonistic rivalry but as irenic, responsive understanding. In what follows I shall explore these theses in connection with *Pale Fire, Under the Volcano, Dark as the Grave Wherein My Friend is Laid*, and *1984*—literary works that stage, but also go beyond, what I consider postmodern issues.

1. "Pale Fire" and the Agonistic Game of Wor(l)ds

At the most obvious level, Nabokov's book is a highly sophisticated and hilarious parody of a respectable, age-old hermeneutical practice, the scholarly commentary on a literary text. The unreliable editor-narrator presents himself as an eccentric, if not insane, exiled king-scholar who edits and annotates a long poem entitled "Pale Fire." This poem is the unfinished labor of an American academic poet who has inadvertently fallen victim to an alleged murder plot designed to eliminate none other than his royal admirer and would-be editor. In the college town of New Wye, Appalachia, Charles Xavier Kinbote, the exiled king, had befriended John Shade, his famous neighbor, hoping that the latter would transpose into verse the story of his reign over and escape from Zembla—a fabulous Northern land, not to be confused with Nova Zembla (an English corruption of Novaya Zemlya), mentioned in one of Alexander Pope's poems, as the commentator himself learnedly points out.

If Kinbote had had his way, Shade would have written a traditional allegorical romance—say, a contemporary version of the *Fairie Queene.* The poet would have dressed the king's adventures and misadventures in an allegorical garb, thus immortalizing him after the fashion of the bards of yore without betraying his disguise. In this traditional sense, Shade would have lived up to both his and his poem's name, being a mere shadow or pale fire of a resplendent royal figure: one recalls that the secondary role of the bard, whose authority derives not from the Muse or from his inner faculties but from the ruler whom he immortalizes, is discussed as early as Plato's *Republic,* where Socrates presents the poet as a pale copy or a mere shadow of Being-Power, twice removed from the king (βασιλεύς).[7] Shakespeare's image of the moon stealing its pale fire from the sun in *Timon of Athens,* mistranslated and misquoted by Kinbote, can obviously serve as an emblem of this power relationship as well.

But John Shade is a thoroughly modern poet who reverses the hierarchical relationship between king and bard, exalting the latter's personality. He chooses to present autobiographical events that lie much closer to his heart than the Zemblan monarch's fate, including the tragic suicide of his sensitive but unattractive teenage daughter in the wake of a fruitless blind date, as well as his own intimations of mortality and immortality. Faced with bitter disappointment in the aftermath of Shade's murder, Kinbote decides to publish the latter's poem anyway, at the same time telling his own story in the critical footnotes. Thereby he does precisely what he says in a note that he has no desire of doing: "twist and batter an unambiguous *apparatus criticus* into the monstrous semblance of a novel."[8]

But Kinbote also does much more: he restores the relation between poet and ruler to its original asymmetry, converting the romantic idea of artist as king (or "legislator of mankind") back to the even older idea of king as artist. He reveals, moreover, that the relationship between artist and critic or scholar is only a mirror of the power relationship between artist and king. Kinbote's territorial and invasive attitude toward Shade's poem does not differ essentially from that of many less whimsical, but equally self-aggrandizing scholars toward their object of study-worship. His foreword to the poem makes up in honesty for what it lacks in subtlety: "Let me state that without my notes Shade's text has no human reality at all since the human reality of such a poem as his (being too skittish and reticent for an autobiographical work), with the omission of many pithy lines carelessly rejected by him, has to depend entirely on the reality of its author and his surroundings, attachments and so forth, a reality that only my notes can provide. To this statement my dear poet would probably not have subscribed, but for better or worse, it is the commentator who has the last word."[9]

Kinbote does not hide his regret that he has to tell his autobiographical tale indirectly through Shade's poem and encourages the reader to see the latter, and not his critical commentary, as a secondary hermeneutical or *allegorical* tool: "To this poem we must now turn. My Foreword has been, I trust, not too skimpy. Other notes, arranged in a running commentary, will certainly satisfy the most voracious reader. Although those notes, in conformity with custom, come after the poem, the reader is advised to consult them first and then study the poem with their help, rereading them of course as he goes through its text, and perhaps, after having done with the poem, consulting them a third time so as to complete the picture" (25). Kinbote's editorial "labor of love" turns out to be self-serving even in a lucrative or pecuniary sense when he suggests that in order to "eliminate the bother of back-and-forth leafings" the reader might wish to purchase "two copies of the same work which can then be placed in adjacent position on a comfortable table" (25).

Through his metafictional parody, Nabokov exposes not only the nature of art and scholarship as Will to Power but also the violent and arbitrary nature of any interpretive act. Although apparently unconnected to the poem's subject matter, Kinbote's commentary creates an intricate "web of sense" around it. He sets up an elaborate framework of correspondences between the poem and his own life, which then becomes fatefully intertwined with that of the poet. The poem, which may be described as a modern version of an Augustan meditation on the human condition in the manner of Pope's *Essay on Man*, gains a fresh perspective in the light of Shade's death at the hands of his own "blind date," Gradus, the regicide manqué. What starts out as sheer chance turns out to be, in Kinbote's self-serving interpretation, an intricate pattern woven by divine providence. Hence the poem, regardless of the original intention of its author, *can* be read as a poetic allegory of Kinbote's life, with Shade's life subordinated to it.

On the other hand, Kinbote's willful editorial project only plays into the poem's original allegory of human existence as a whole, from the perspective of which Shade's and Kinbote's lives are interchangeable. The allegorical nature of all human endeavor is expressed in Shade's sibylline line, *"Man's life as a commentary to abstruse | Unfinished poem"* (67), which Kinbote aptly paraphrases as "human life is but a series of footnotes to a vast obscure unfinished masterpiece" (272). Kinbote's gloss on Shade's aphorism is a delightfully involuted, unconscious self-parody, but it is also the modern aestheticist credo, for one is reminded here of Mallarmé's paradox, "Tout au monde existe pour aboutir à un beau livre," or Nietzsche's aphorism in *The Birth of Tragedy*: "Only as an aesthetic product can the world be justified to all eternity—although our consciousness of our own significance does scarcely exceed the consciousness a painted soldier might have of the battle in which he takes part."[10] If existence is, at bottom, a series of obscure, unrelated events governed by chance, as Shade implies in the wake of Nietzsche and Mallarmé, the act of interpretation is an act of the Will through which humans create a "web of sense" or a world of illusion to interpose between themselves and the abyss. By the same token, the concept of divine providence is nothing but the objective guise of this self-fashioning Will, projected into a transcendental principle.

Kinbote, for one, is fully aware of the subjective, emotional necessity of positing a divine providence as transcendental creative Will. For example, when Shade remarks that "Life is a great surprise" and so "I do not see why death should not be an even greater one," Kinbote replies: "Now I have caught you John: once we deny a Higher Intelligence that plans and administers our individual hereafters we are bound to accept

the unspeakably dreadful notion of Chance reaching into eternity."[11]
Kinbote cannot endure "the idea of one's soul plunging into limitless
and chaotic afterlife with no Providence to direct her" (226). Finally,
however, it is the Will's fear of the void or nothingness that impels
Kinbote to posit the existence of God, be it only through the *via negativa*.
Although he does not know what God is, he thinks he knows what He is
not: "He is not despair, He is not terror, He is not the earth in one's
rattling throat, not the black hum in one's ears fading to nothing in nothing" (227). In this sense, Kinbote is an excellent example of the psychopathology of power that I have discussed in previous chapters. As he
reveals in his genealogical account of the Zemblan monarchy and
throughout his commentary, he is a twisted product of aristocratic haugh-
tiness, religious guilt, and matriarchal authority, further complicated by
conflicting vegetarian, nonviolent, artistic, and homosexual impulses.
Fear, guilt, despair, and a sense of inverted, sadomasochistic pleasure
prevail over his ludic-irenic self, and his alleged aspirations toward a
nonviolent God, selfless Love, the Good, and the Beautiful remain hopelessly entangled in his narcissistic obsessions. One wonders, then,
whether Kinbote is truly mad or only a typical artistic manifestation of
the perverted modern psyche, as described in *The Genealogy of Morals*.

But mad or not, Kinbote reveals a great deal of artistic method when
he muses about the interplay of chance and necessity that allegedly
leads to the selection of the inept Gradus as the would-be assassin of
the king. He also makes the "fatidic moment" of this selection coincide
with the date on which Shade started writing his poem (151). In the
same note, Kinbote as much as admits that he has manipulated divine
providence for artistic purposes: "I have staggered the notes referring
to [Gradus] in such a fashion that the first (see note to line 17 where
some of his other activities are adumbrated) is the vaguest while those
that follow become gradually clear as gradual Gradus approaches in space
and time" (152).

Kinbote unwittingly refers again to his own method of composition
when he criticizes Shade's synchronous arrangement of the themes in
the poem: "[T]he whole thing [the juxtaposition of the television series
in Shade's parlor and the tragic consequences of the blind date] strikes
me as too labored and long, especially since the synchronization device
has been already worked to death by Flaubert and Joyce" (156). Kinbote

also works this device to death, that is, the death of Shade. In the end, however, Kinbote does no more through his commentary than what Shade wants to do through his poem: create order out of chaos. For example, when Shade finds out that his quest for eternal life has been built on a misprint (mountain-fountain), he writes:

> Life Everlasting—based on a misprint!
> I mused as I drove homeward: take the hint,
> And stop investigating my abyss?
> But all at once it dawned on me that *this*
> Was the real point, the contrapuntal theme;
> Just this: not text, but texture; not the dream
> But topsy-turvical coincidence,
> Not flimsy nonsense, but a web of sense.
> Yes! It sufficed that I in life could find
> Some kind of link-and-bobolink, some kind
> Of correlated pattern in the game,
> Plexed artistry, and something of the same
> Pleasure in it that they who played it found.
>
> (63)

Ironically, Shade seems to adopt Kinbote's notion of a transcendental Will that fabricates sense out of the void, although his reference is not to one deity, but to many. Furthermore, Shade presents the demiurgic activities of these higher beings in ludic terms:

> It did not matter who they were. No sound
> No further light came from this involute
> Abode, but there they were, aloof and mute,
> Playing a game of worlds, promoting pawns
> To ivory unicorns and ebon fauns;
> Kindling a long life here, extinguishing
> A short one there; killing a Balkan king;
> Causing a chunk of ice formed on a high-
> Flying airplane to plummet from the sky
> And strike a farmer dead; hiding my keys,
> Glasses or pipe. Coordinating these
> Events and objects with remote events
> And vanished objects. Making ornaments
> Of accidents and possibilities
>
> (63)

Shade describes these superior powers as divine players who play a "game of worlds," and the image of the world as a divine game is as old as the hills, being present in all ancient cultures, from Mesopotamia to India to China to Greece. It is also present in the Age of Reason, whose temper Shade attempts to emulate, in Leibniz's famous dictum, *Cum deus calculat, fit mundus*, which Heidegger translates appropriately as "Während Gott spielt, wird Welt." [12]

Of course, Shade's game is a poetic one and therefore can be said to be primarily a game of words, rather than worlds. On the other hand, these words *can* conjure up a plurality of worlds, if not in actuality, at least in the imagination. But, in turn, poetic worlds are as indifferent to the ontological distinction between the real and the imaginary as Nietzsche's painted soldier is to the distinction between a real and a canvas battle. From an aestheticist viewpoint, therefore, one can properly speak only of a game of wor(l)ds, in which the allegorical fades continually into the literal and vice versa. Shade adopts this aestheticist (and postmodern) viewpoint when he writes:

> I feel I understand
> Existence, or at least a minute part
> Of my existence, only through my art,
> In terms of combinational delight;
> And if my private universe scans right,
> So does the verse of galaxies divine
> Which I suspect is an iambic line. [13]

In turn, Kinbote plays a parallel game of wor(l)ds through his commentary. Although he humorlessly informs the reader that he "abhors such games" (189)—his pompous gravity and professed lack of a ludic sense might again lead to the impression that he is insane—Kinbote clearly imitates the poet in weaving "some kind of correlated pattern" on the analogy of divine play and in deliberately erasing the ontological distinction between the real and the imaginary. For example, he informs us, in the whimsical manner of Tristram Shandy, that we "shall accompany Gradus in constant thought, as he makes his way from distant dim Zembla to green Appalachia, through the entire length of the poem, following the road of its rhythm, riding past in a rhyme, skidding around the corner of a run-on, breathing with the caesura, swinging down to the foot of the page from line to line as from branch to branch, hiding between two words (see note to line 596), reappearing on the horizon of a new canto, steadily marching nearer in iambic motion, crossing streets, moving up with his valise on the escalator of the pentameter, stepping off, boarding a new train of thought, entering the hall of a hotel, putting out the bedlight, while Shade blots out a word, and falling asleep as the poet lays down his pen for the night" (78).

Kinbote also cites Franklin Lane (a sage of Cedarn, Utana—a Western town where Kinbote has allegedly taken refuge from Shade's widow and other greedy would-be editors of "Pale Fire"), who regards Aristotle as another godlike thinker who has forced chaos into order: "What a satisfaction to see him [Aristotle] take, like reins from between his fingers, the long ribbon of man's life and trace it through the mystifying maze of all the wonderful adventure. . . . The crooked made straight. The Daedalian plan simplified by a look from above—smeared out as it were by the splotch of some master thumb that made the whole involuted, boggling thing one beautiful straight line" (261). The merging of Aristotle with Theseus in the image of the Daedalian labyrinth catapults the reader even farther back into regressive time, placing Kinbote's and Shade's game of wor(l)ds within yet another Chinese box or, to change the metaphor, within an infinite house of mirrors. It also points to the agonistic nature of our games of creation, which often conceal either a violent contest or a scapegoat ritual behind them—an image reaffirmed by the "master thumb" that crushes everything into "one beautiful straight line." William Carroll aptly draws attention to the violent nature of Nabokov's games of wor(l)ds when he paraphrases Shakespeare in describing the relation between the author and his characters: "As flies to wanton boys are we to our authors, they kill us for their plots."[14]

Chess, one of the most ancient and beloved royal games, can be seen as the central metaphor around which Nabokov builds his narrative, as Shade's description of the divine players as "promoting pawns / to ivory unicorns and ebon fawns" suggests. And chess is the agonistic "game of worlds" par excellence, with two symmetrical kingdoms pitted against each other and fighting to the virtual death through immobilization of the other's king. This game, moreover, depends on the players' cunning intelligence in using to their advantage not only their opponents' tactical mistakes but also the ever shifting configuration of necessity and chance on the checkered board. So Kinbote sets up his imaginary Zemblan world as a game of chess between the royalist party and that of the Shadows, with himself as the king and Gradus as the enemy's fool (the bishop is called a fool in several European languages). Moreover, he is playing simultaneous chess games not only within his Zemblan world but also outside it, pitting the world of his commentary, where he is again undisputed king, against the world of the poem, in which Shade is king.

Of course, Kinbote is unable to keep the two games separate, collapsing them into each other; hence again the reader's perception that he might be insane. Kinbote insists that he has played a main role in Shade's death—"a tragedy in which I had been not a 'chance witness' but the protagonist, and the main, if only potential, victim."[15] He also implies that he has won this particular game (which allows him to have the last word as the poet's commentator) through the chess stratagem of castling: he removes himself from and places Shade in the line of Gradus's fire; in other words, he sacrifices or scapegoats his own bishop or fool. His stratagem has even tricked some critics into believing, with Kinbote's gardener and Shade's wife, that Kinbote attempted to protect the poet rather than hide behind him.

But Kinbote is too proud of his game not to give it away. Describing his and Shade's hasty retreat from the murderer's gun, he has at first the poet pulling him by the hand while they are running back toward the bushes—which means that at this point Kinbote is still in the line of fire, between the poet and Gradus. As Shade is hobbling along, Kinbote manages to outstrip him, even though the poet tries desperately to cling on to him. Of course, Kinbote presents this struggle for survival at each other's expense as a nobly cooperative, indeed Olympic, relay race: "I felt—I still feel—John's hand fumbling at mine, seeking my fingertips, finding them, only to abandon them at once as if passing to me, in a sublime relay race, the baton of life" (294). But Shade is now clearly behind him, taking one of Gradus's bullets in his place, for Kinbote comments: "His presence *behind me* abruptly failing me caused me to lose my balance, and, simultaneously, to complete the farce of fate, my gardener's spade dealt gunman Jack from behind the hedge a tremendous blow on the pate. . . ." (294; my emphasis).

The preceding scene also dramatizes the agonistic relationship between Nabokov as implied author and his reader-critic, with whom he plays an equally clever chess game. Nabokov lays all kinds of traps and dead ends for his "adversary," thereby obstructing rather than facilitating the traditional (allegorical) game of ferreting out the "real" meaning of the text. These traps and dead ends are too many to list here,[16] but they largely depend on the critic's rationalist belief in an interpretive master plan that accounts for everything and leaves nothing to chance in the literary text, as well as on the equally rationalist assumption that one can separate the real from the imaginary in a work of art or, specifically in this case, that one can ascertain the "real" identity of Shade, Kinbote, and Gradus.

The interpretive master plan is mentioned by Shade at the end of his poem, coinciding with the eighteenth-century rationalist view of the universe:

> I'm reasonably sure that we survive
> And that my darling somewhere is alive,
> As I am reasonably sure that I
> Shall wake at six tomorrow, on July
> The twenty-second, nineteen fifty-nine,
> And that the day will probably be fine;
> So this alarm clock let me set myself,
> Yawn, and put back Shade's "Poems" on their shelf.
>
> (54)

But Shade's deistic, "clockwork" view of the universe as a predictable mechanical game is ironically belied by his own blind date with death (Shade does not wake up the following morning; indeed, he will never wake up again in this world). The blind, irrational, and unpredictable game of chance ultimately prevails both in Shade's poem, left unfinished, and in Kinbote's commentary, which remains equally inconclusive. (Nabokov only pokes more fun at the critics when he declares in an interview that Kinbote, "after putting the last touches to his edition of the poem," must surely have committed suicide on the anniversary of Swift's death and the completion of Pushkin's *Lyceum*, adding that he himself shares, with Pushkin, a fascination with "fatidic dates.")[17]

Pale Fire, then, implies that the game of interpretation is merely a game of semblance, illusion, or simulacrum. As Kinbote points out, Zembla is not a corruption of the Russian *zemlya*, but of "Semblerland, a land of reflections, of 'resemblers'."[18] If Zembla refers, moreover, not only to Pope's Nova Zembla but also to Swift's hellish Land of Criticism, then critical interpretation can equally be seen as an arbitrary play of identity and difference. When an Oxford visitor challenges John Shade to deny, if he can, the "astounding similarity of features" between King Charles and Kinbote, the old poet counters: "I have seen the king in newsreels, and there is no resemblance. Resemblances are shadows of differences. Different people see different similarities and similar differences" (265). Shade implies that interpretation is nothing but willful bias, so much so that everything can be made to resemble, or to differ from, everything else. In this respect, Kinbote can be made to resemble not only the Zemblan king, but also Gradus, the would-be regicide. As Kinbote himself acknowledges, his last name in Zemblan means a "king's destroyer," and he longs to "explain that a king who sinks his identity in the mirror of exile is in a sense just that" (267). So, not only Kinbote and Shade but also Kinbote and Gradus can appear as mirror reflections of each other, as interchangeable doubles. In the end, the arbitrary juxtaposition of Shade's poem and Kinbote's commentary proliferates the intricate web of mirroring reflections to the point that any allegorical framework or system of interpretation gets hopelessly lost. What remains is the Nietzschean play of simulacra, the eternal game of creation and destruction that the world plays with itself, without telos or meaning, for the sheer sake of the game.

By the same token, the identities of all the protagonists in *Pale Fire* are fluid, doubtful, and undecidable. Critics have argued at length as to the "true" identity of Nabokov's narrator: Is Kinbote really the deposed Zemblan king or is he only the mad Professor Botkin—Professor Pnin's colleague in the Russian department? (Pnin is of course another character, perhaps an alter ego, in Nabokov's fiction.) Or is Kinbote really the nom de plume of John Shade, who has written both the poem and the commentary? Or, conversely, is John Shade a mere figment of Kinbote's imagination? And, finally, is Zemblan Gradus really only Jack Grey—the murderous escapee from an Appalachian lunatic asylum, bent on seeking revenge against Judge Goldsworth (Kinbote's landlord and Shade's neighbor), who put him away in the first place?[19]

Nabokov has his critics on a wild-goose chase, providing deliberately ambiguous answers to these questions and leaving behind him an obfuscating cloud of false resemblances, clues, and subterfuges. He has his readers move around in circles, all of which are inscribed within a larger, hermeneutic circle—a vicious one to boot. Nabokov dramatizes this vicious circle by the cross references to the Zemblan crown jewels in Kinbote's index: under *Crown Jewels* we find "See Hiding Place";[20] under *Hiding Place*, there is a cross-reference to *Potaynik*, the Russian word for "hiding place" (307); under *Potaynik*, we are sent to *Tainik*, a Russian synonym for "hiding place" (312); and the entry *Tainik* finally leads us back to *Crown Jewels* (314). Nabokov's irony is all the more exquisite because the vicious hermeneutic circle manifests itself precisely through the crown jewels—the supreme regal insignia, or a metonymy of absolute power. As the "democratic" government of Zembla realizes only too well, those who can find them will take full possession of the king's authority, just as the critics who can uncover Nabokov's secret meaning will presumably achieve full mastery over his text.

The question has often been asked if Nabokov has not pushed too far his critical game of hide-and-seek, or more generally, if the "serious" or ethical dimension of *Pale Fire* has not been impoverished by its author's excessive ludic spirit. Again, the answer to this question depends on the critic's ideological and aesthetic allegiances, including a favorable or unfavorable bias toward the "play-element in culture" (as Huizinga puts it). A reader sympathetic to modernism would ultimately decry Nabokov's anarchic and indiscriminate destruction of all traditional hermeneutic values; a poststructuralist reader would, on the contrary, hail it as a necessary, preliminary deconstructive move, before joyfully affirming perpetual Becoming and the agonistic play of simulacra. Neither of these critics, however, would readily entertain the possibility of *Pale Fire* as a ludic-liminal text, pointing to an irenic alternative world.

Yet the idea of such a world is not entirely absent from the novel. Although it remains inaccessible to Kinbote, who seems to confine himself to an eternal inferno, it is nevertheless implicit in his ambivalent feelings toward Disa, surfacing especially in his dreams. According to

Kinbote's own account, the plot of these dreams "was a constant refutation of his not loving her" (210). Kinbote's "dream-love" for his wife "exceeded in emotional tone, in spiritual passion and depth, anything he has experienced in his surface existence," being like "an endless wringing of hands, like a blundering of the soul through an infinite maze of hopelessness and remorse" (210). His oneiric love for Disa has the same radiant, ecstatic quality that he saw, as an adolescent, reflected on the face of a young monk in the Onhava Royal Palace and, later on in New Wye, on the face of John Shade while at work in his study. At first "guilty disgust" had contorted the Zemblan priest's thin lips, but then "all at once his look changed to one of rapture and reverence," for, Kinbote notes, "there is no bound to the measure of grace which man may be able to receive" (88).

Since the name of Disa derives from splitting the Zemblan word *paradisa* (paradise) in two, the allegorical nature of Charles's unfulfilled love for her is quite transparent, being both reinforced and undermined throughout his commentary (e.g., Villa Paradisa, where the exiled queen lives, is located on the French Riviera, described by Kinbote as an earthly paradise for the rich). The Dantesque allegory of the exiled soul in search of salvation through spiritual love (embodied by Beatrice) appears in *Pale Fire* ironically, as the subliminal, impossible aspirations of an exiled king, burning in a political, ethical, and spiritual hell of his own making. In turn, Kinbote's homosexuality appears as a symptom of his barren narcissism, his paranoid fear of alterity (whether in its feminine or any other guise), his inability to understand and love the Other unconditionally, thus pointing to the essentially narcissistic nature of a mentality of power as a whole.

In *Pale Fire*, the ludic-irenic idea of the Other and otherness as responsive understanding is also implicit in the improper, asymmetrical relationship between artwork and interpreter, at the level of both poem and commentator (Shade and Kinbote) and implied author and reader (Nabokov and his critics). One has seen how Nabokov uses the vicious hermeneutic circle to his advantage, setting (allegorical) traps for the symbol-happy critic. From an agonistic standpoint, the best a reader can achieve is a draw—in chess terms, a Solus Rex situation, meaning a king who has lost his kingdom. (One should not forget that *Solus Rex* was both the title that Kinbote had suggested to Shade for his poem and the title of an early, "unfinished" Nabokov novel.)[21] But Nabokov also implies that the agonistic game between critic and text may differ radically from chess, insofar as it can result in nothing *but* a draw. Otherwise, the winners will always be the losers: at the very moment when the critics think they have caught their quarry and have locked it up in the iron cage of a foolproof interpretation, the artwork has already given them the slip.

Nabokov tantalizingly dramatizes this aesthetic paradox by having Kinbote sum up the plot of his "monstrous" novel as a stage play or "an old-fashioned melodrama with three principals: a lunatic who intends to kill an imaginary king, another lunatic who imagines himself to be that king, and a distinguished old poet who stumbles by chance into the line of fire, and perishes in the clash between the two figments."[22] Nabokov thus collapses the imaginary and the real in his text through the traditional *theatrum mundi* topos, proclaiming with Shakespeare that humans are only "such stuff as dreams are made of" and that, ironically, only lunatics and poets are fully aware of, and act in accordance with, this truth. Nabokov also collapses Kinbote's persona as a narrator-editor into his own persona as implied author when he has his character declare that he will never commit suicide: "God will help me, I trust, to rid myself of any desire to follow the example of two other characters in this work. I shall continue to exist. I may assume other disguises, other forms, but I shall try to exist. I may turn up yet, on another campus, as an old, happy, healthy, heterosexual Russian, a writer in exile, sans fame, sans future, sans audience, sans anything but his art" (301).

One should point out, however, that here Nabokov does not lose his own identity, but simply dramatizes the fact that he is all and none of his characters. In this regard, the Nabokovian collapse of various fictional identities does not lead (as in Lowry's work, which I shall examine shortly) to a repetitive-compulsive pattern of (self-)violence, but to an affirmation of the endless freedom of the creative individual, who can try out a multiplicity of roles and thus invent ever fresh games of wor(l)ds without getting entangled in any of them.

By the same token, it is Kinbote and not Nabokov that draws the readers into the fatal hermeneutic circle of his allegorical life-book, when he compares death with "a bigger, more respectable, more competent Gradus" who, although he is "still rather far away," is nevertheless "buying a ticket, is boarding a bus, a ship, a plane, has landed, is walking toward a million photographers, and presently he will ring at my door" (301). Through the grim, implacable Gradus who will sooner or later call at all of our doors, Kinbote imparts an aesthetically satisfying sense of an ending to his narrative. But he also allows the implied author to posit a moral imperative that concerns every reader—a memento mori that both puts Kinbote's world into perspective and opens up new axiological and ethical possibilities. For, just like the implied author and unlike Kinbote, the reader can always break, at least imaginatively, the vicious circle of life and death that a mentality of power will invariably perceive and evaluate as both tragic and sublime. From an irenic-ludic perspective, then, Nabokov's ideal readers will not attempt to master the text or enter into a competitive relation with it. On the contrary, they will approach it in a spirit of responsive understanding, opening themselves to it and allowing themselves to experience, through it, that liminal time-space which can produce alternative realities and new historical worlds.

2. Playing at Tragedy: Malcolm Lowry and the Modernist Symbol-Making Machine

Not unlike *Pale Fire*, Lowry's *Under the Volcano* can be seen as a self-consuming allegorical narrative, thrown out of joint by the protagonist, who this time is not a mad, exiled king, but an alcoholic, guilt-ridden British ex-consul—an impaired, pathetic figure of authority nonetheless. Like Kinbote, moreover, the Consul rejects the woman he loves and chooses to live in a hell of his own making. Although he does not attempt, like Kinbote, to twist another's artistic creation into a paean of his own life, he does, no less than Nabokov's protagonist, transform his own life into a work of fiction. Here, as in *Pale Fire*, the characters are to their author what flies are to wanton boys, but, unlike Nabokov, Lowry will improperly collapse his identity into that of his protagonists and will eventually get entangled in his own game of wor(l)ds.

Under the Volcano, even more obviously than *Pale Fire*, stages both a scapegoat ritual and a substitution of victims. The difference is that whereas Kinbote scapegoats Shade, the Consul turns the scapegoat mechanism upon himself, internalizing it. In his well-known essay, "*Coriolanus*—Or the Delights of Faction," Kenneth Burke shows how the events and the personae in Shakespeare's play, including the protagonist, are constructed in such a way that they not only conspire to bring about Coriolanus's victimization but also make this victimization acceptable and even aesthetically pleasurable.[23] The same thing can be said about *Under the Volcano*—there are several key references in the book to *Coriolanus* and to other Elizabethan plays—but with a crucial difference: in *Coriolanus*, as in many Greek and Elizabethan tragedies, the victim or the scapegoat does not deliberately promote his own sacrifice, whereas in Lowry's novel he brings about his own victimization. In this respect, the tragic pattern in *Under the Volcano* is Christian rather than Hellenic, if one (mis)interprets the Passion as a tragedy in which Christ promotes his own crucifixion, dying "for us"—a (mis)interpretation that, as I have argued in previous chapters, is typical of a mentality of power and is often endorsed by Christian dogma as well. The Consul is not only the protagonist but also, in more than one sense, the "maker" of his own tragedy. His psychopathology can be seen, much like that of Kinbote, as exhibiting diseased, modern features.

The Consul suffers, no less than Sonya Marmeladova, from what may be called a "Christ complex": he causes himself to be betrayed by Yvonne, Hugh, and Laruelle, as he himself points out. In chapter 3, while lying on Calle Nicaragua, he addresses an imaginary Hugh, attempting to alleviate his half-brother's feelings of guilt about his past love affair with Yvonne: "Yet does this help, what I am trying to tell you, that I realize to what degree I brought all this upon my self? Help, that I am admitting moreover that to have cast Yvonne upon you in that fashion was a feckless action, almost, I was going to say a clownish one, inviting in return the inevitable bladder on the brain, the mouthful and heartful of sawdust."[24] The Consul is also fully aware of the role he played in Laruelle's affair with Yvonne. In chapter 7 he muses about his magnetic influence upon his childhood friend: "Why had Jacques come to Quauhnahuac in the first place? Was it not much as though he, the

Consul, from afar, had willed it, for obscure purposes of his own? . . .
Was it not almost as though the Consul had tricked him into dishonor
and misery, willed, even, his betrayal of him?"[25]

In turn, both Hugh and Laruelle play Judas to the Consul's Christ.
In chapter 4, for instance, Hugh identifies with Judas, whom he imagines
hungover, riding out of Jerusalem, on the morning after the betrayal:
"How joyous all this could be, riding out of Jerusalem—and forgetting
for an instant, so that it really was joyous—how splendid it all might be
had I only not betrayed that man last night, even though I knew perfectly well I was going to, how good indeed, if only it had not happened
though, if only it were not so absolutely necessary to go out and hang
oneself" (111). In chapter 1, Laruelle, on his part, interprets the Consul's
act of lending him the volume of Elizabethan plays that has never been
returned and has now turned up again, as a subtle reminder of his,
Laruelle's, betrayal. At the time, the Consul and Yvonne had already
been separated and the former had given him the volume with a "dia-
bolical look," which, in retrospect, seems to have said: "I know, Jacques,
you may never return the book, but suppose I lend it to you precisely
for that reason, that some day you may be sorry you did not. Oh, I shall
forgive you then, but will you be able to forgive yourself? Not merely
for not having returned it, but because the book will by then have become an emblem of what even now it is impossible to return" (27).
Yvonne's postcard to the Consul, which the latter slips under Laruelle's
pillow, in chapter 7, is an even stronger (if less subtle) reminder of
Jacques's affair with his friend's wife. Both Laruelle and Hugh associate
their betrayal of the Consul with that of humanity in general, while the
Consul, supposedly like Christ, takes upon his shoulders not only their
guilt but the burden of all mankind.

In addition to playing at Christ, the Consul sees himself as Adam,
Faust, William Blackstone, and the black magician of the Cabala. From
his letter of chapter 1, we learn that he was at one time writing a book
on the Cabala that he has never finished. In chapter 4, Yvonne and Hugh
refer to this unfinished project:

> "Geoffrey said something this morning about going on with his book—
> for the life of me I don't know whether he's still writing one or not,
> he's never done any work on it since I have known him, and he's

never let me see scarcely any of it, still, he keeps all those reference books with him—I thought —"
"Yes", Hugh said, "how much does he really know about all this alchemy and Cabbala business? How much does it mean to him?" (118)

The thought suggests itself that the Consul has stopped writing his book and has started playing at it instead. Laruelle's observation, in chapter 1, that "during the last period of his life the Consul had lost almost all capacity for telling the truth and his life had become a quixotic oral fiction" (33) is relevant in this context. If one accepts the premise that, like Don Quijote, the Consul is enacting his own unfinished book, then the cabalistic themes in *Under the Volcano* assume an important function: they are a convenient framework within which he may act out his tragedy. The Consul fictionalizes his entire life through the Cabala; he casts himself in the role of a white magician who, through abuse of his powers, has turned into a black one, and then proceeds to construe in this light all the events that will subsequently lead to his death.[26] The cabalistic correspondences provide the Consul with a unifying poetic principle that, much like Shade-Kinbote's involuted "web of sense," ties together the threads of his plot. An elaborate system of correspondences such as the Cabala satisfies not only man's mystical but also his aesthetic impulse, as Lowry himself pointed out in his letter to Jonathan Cape, his future editor.[27] It has, moreover, the advantage of being able to accommodate within itself all the other fictional material with which the Consul builds his tragedy: Adam's fall, the damnation of Faust, and the Passion itself.

Although the Consul may play at several tragic heroes, his plot is always the same. His game, which is far more dangerous than any of Don Quijote's chivalric or pastoral extravaganzas, is that of self-victimage. In fact, the final chapter of the book could be read as the scenario of a scapegoat ritual. Like Christ (or Antigone), the Consul brings about his own victimization by pointing to himself as scapegoat. The insults that the sinárquistas fling at him reveal his ambivalent nature of φαρμακός-φάρμακον.[28] They call him in turn a "spider" (spy), "bolshevisten", "juden" (jew), "wrider" (writer/artist), "borrachón" (drunkard), and a "pelado."

The Spanish word *pelado* is particularly revealing here because of the antithetical sense that the Consul attributes to it. In chapter 8, Hugh muses about this word, mentioned by his brother in connection with the drunken Spaniard who will rob the dying Indian and will eventually turn out to be in league with the fascist police: "Hugh understood this word finally to be pretty ambiguous. A Spaniard, say, could interpret it as an Indian, the Indian he despised, used, made drunk. The Indian, however, may mean Spaniard by it. Either might mean by it anyone who made a show of himself. It was perhaps one of those words that had actually been distilled out of conquest, suggesting, as it did, on the one hand thief, on the other exploiter. Interchangeable ever were the terms of abuse with which the aggressor discredits those about to be ravaged!"[29] Like the Greek word φαρμακός, which, through its etymological association with φάρμακον (denoting both "medicine" and "poison") reveals the essential ambivalence of the scapegoat as both evil spirit and savior of the community, the word *pelado* reveals the interchangeability between aggressor and victim within a mentality of power. As the Consul lies dying, he recalls the word again:

> Presently the word "pelado" began to fill his whole consciousness. That had been Hugh's [in fact his own] word for the thief: now someone had flung the insult at him. And it was as if, for a moment, he had become the pelado, the thief—yes, the pilferer of meaningless, muddled ideas out of which his rejection of life had grown, who had worn his two or three little bowler hats, his disguises, over these abstractions: now the realest of them all was close. But someone had called him "compañero" too, which was better, much better. (374)

The Consul sees himself not only as the *pelado* but also as the dying Indian from chapter 8, whose last word, significantly, had also been "compañero." And finally, he identifies not only with the "beggars and the accursed" but also with their (and his) victimizers, who turn out to be his own doubles. Sanabria, or the Chief of Gardens, "might have been an image of himself, when lean, bronzed, serious, beardless, and at the crossroads of his career, he had assumed the Vice Consulship in Granada" (359). Before he becomes completely engulfed by violence the Consul experiences, in his delirium, the proliferation of doubles characteristic of the last stages of the sacrificial game (one is reminded here of Pentheus, in Euripides' *Bacchae*, who sees doubles under the influence of Dionysus before he is torn apart by the maenads led by his mother): "He was surrounded in delirium by these phantoms of himself, the policemen, Fructuoso Sanabria, that other man who looked as a poet, the luminous skeletons, even the rabbit in the corner and the ash and sputum on the filthy floor—did not each correspond, in a way he couldn't understand yet obscurely recognized, to some faction of his being?" (361–62).

Significantly, the Consul associates his fall into the barranca with the plunge of mankind into the all-consuming blaze of universal war: "[T]he world itself was bursting, bursting into black spouts of villages catapulted into space, with himself falling through it all, through the inconceivable pandemonium of a million tanks, through the blazing of ten million bodies, falling, into a forest, falling—" (375). Thus, the Consul's self-sacrificial game points to the "meaningless, muddled ideas out of which his rejection of life had grown" (374) and warns mankind of the danger of generalized delirium and violence inherent in any mentality of power. Not unlike *Crime and Punishment*, then, *Under the Volcano* offers one of the most penetrating and devastating descriptions of a schizophrenic psychopathology (further magnified by the intoxicating effect of alcohol), in which the Will to Power must affirm itself even in the distorted, masochistic form of self-victimization and at the price of colossal, needless suffering. In one of his lucid moments, the Consul is fully aware of the sheer perversity of his game, which he carries on solely for the purpose of enhancing his own feeling of power: "You fool, you stupid fool," the Consul tells himself. "You've been insulated from the responsibility of genuine suffering. . . . Even the suffering you do endure is largely unnecessary. Actually spurious. It lacks the very basis you require of it for its tragic nature. You deceive yourself" (219).

If the Consul enacts his book, he leaves the task of writing it to someone else. In his letter to Jonathan Cape, Lowry suggests that his novel can be read, beginning with chapter 2, as Laruelle's film script. After he points out the multiple function of the Ferris wheel at the end of chapter 1 (and at the beginning of the "tragedy"), he adds: "[O]r superficially [the wheel] can be seen simply in an obvious movie sense as the wheel of time whirling backwards until we have reached the year before and chapter 2 and in this sense, if we like, we can look at the rest of the book through Laruelle's eyes, as if it were his creation."[30] Indeed, the novel reads in many places like a detailed film script, and this feeling is enhanced by the centers of consciousness (Yvonne, Hugh, the Consul, and Laruelle himself) through which the narrative moves along and which select, like a camera, only those bits and pieces of external, or, more often, externalized, psychological reality that are relevant to the plot.[31]

Laruelle can be seen, apart from his role as Judas, as a sort of Evangelist, an eyewitness to the Passion, whose mission is to record the event for posterity. In more than one sense, the Consul writes his "tragedy" through him. On the Day of the Dead, Laruelle seems possessed by the spirit of the Consul, whom he sees everywhere. He has not only the Consul's English manner and way of dressing (if we make allowance for the socks) but also his habit of moving through a "forest of symbols." As we have seen, the Consul himself points to Laruelle, in chapter 7, as his double-mediator (209–10). In chapter 1, the film producer and director is even tempted to start reenacting the Consul's "tragedy," or at least its first step, by ordering tequila. However, he overcomes this temptation and burns the Consul's compelling cabalistic letter, and thus he can start writing the story. But Laruelle, if he is indeed the "author," has designed the reading process itself in such a way that it invites eternal return. At the end of the narrative the reader is compelled to go back to the first chapter, which starts "making sense" only after having read the rest of the book, and thus s/he is caught in the reading process again.[32]

By providing an epilogue, "Laruelle" presumably seeks not only to break off this infernal hermeneutic circle, but also to separate himself from the Consul. In this regard, Lowry himself becomes twice removed from his fictional alter ego. Hence, it is rather ironical that critics should generally have seen the Consul as a glorified, neoromantic version of his creator, and the symbolical frameworks of the narrative as belonging to Lowry, rather than to his fictional doubles. Although many scholars have criticized *Under the Volcano* for being overpacked with allegory and symbolism and although its first readers have compared it (unfavorably) with the work of James Joyce and T. S. Eliot, it is clear that Lowry puts his allegorical framework to uses that are significantly different from those of Eliot or Joyce. Even as he devises a complicated symbol-making machine in *Under the Volcano*, Lowry, unlike his modernist predecessors and very much like Nabokov, frustrates the symbol-happy critic by handing it over to his characters. In other words, in Lowry's literary universe the traditional allegorical systems become "self-consuming artifacts," in the manner of Nabokov's world of *Pale Fire* or García Marquez's world of Macondo in *One Hundred Years of Solitude*. So, it is the Consul (as well as Laruelle), and not Lowry, who is a poor master of his craft, not unlike Goethe's apprentice-sorcerer, unable to control this formidable *moulin-à-symbole* gone mad. Just before his death, at the height of his delirium, the Consul literally sputters out the dismantled pieces of his "tragedy," which has, for him, lost all sense and coherence: "The Consul didn't know what he was saying: 'Only the poor, only through God, only the people you wipe your feet on, the poor in spirit, old men carrying their fathers and philosophers weeping in the dust, America perhaps, Don Quijote —' he was still brandishing the sword . . . . 'if you'd only stop interfering, stop walking in your sleep, stop sleeping with my wife, only the beggars and the accursed'" (372).

The Consul unconsciously, yet appropriately, mixes together the rhetoric of the victim with the behavior of the aggressor (he brandishes a sword), implicitly revealing the essential complicity between the two antagonistic positions. In this respect, the Consul's "tragedy" can have meaning only outside the fictional frame of the story; hence the epilogue, which functions as a sort of reality principle in contrast with the Consul's highly fictionalized, delirious world:

> ¿LE GUSTA ESTE JARDIN
> QUE ES SUYO?
> EVITE QUE SUS HIJOS LO DESTRUYAN!

(Do you enjoy this garden which is yours? Don't let your children destroy it!)

The garden here may again be read allegorically as the Garden of Eden or as a symbol of human constructive effort. But, assuming that Laruelle is the author of this epilogue, its message remains highly inconclusive, if not ironical: he is about to leave the desolate, dilapidated garden—the scene of the Consul's tragedy—for an even more troubled paradise, Europe of 1939, poised on the brink of World War II. And as Laruelle himself observes in chapter 1, no matter what the outcome of this war would be, "one's own battle would go on"; in other words, war would not solve, but only aggravate, the axiological and ethical impasse of the modern individual.

Lowry implies, moreover, that allegory in the sense of a story "used for teaching and explaining" can mystify as much as illuminate. If there is any lesson to be drawn from the Consul's tragedy, it is precisely that one should follow Nabokov's advice and stay away from traditional allegorical interpretations; for it is obvious that the Consul, much like Nietzsche, (mis)interprets the Passion as a scapegoat ritual that allows the Will to Power to continue operating even through a shift in ethical perspective from the strong to the weak. *Under the Volcano* thus shows how the myth of redemption through suffering present in the Hellenic tragic world is perpetuated, in a modified form, by the Christian tradition as well, and implicitly warns of the dire consequences of this perpetuation.

One may add, however, that Lowry himself will eventually succumb to the vicious hermeneutic circle that he warns against through the fate of his protagonist. In this regard, he differs radically from Nabokov, who, as we have seen, never gets entangled in his own "tragedies." In order to understand Lowry's place in postmodern fiction one must look beyond *Under the Volcano*, to what was to have been his all-encompassing book, appropriately entitled *The Voyage that Never Ends*, which could only end with its author's death.[33] *Dark as the Grave Wherein my Friend is Laid*, one of the novels belonging to that impossible project, will thus cast further light on the relationship between author and work in a postmodern age. In many ways, the problematic relationship between Lowry and his fiction is an exemplary case for those postmodern artists who, unlike Nabokov, relive both the romantic and the aestheticist tradition of the late-nineteenth and early-twentieth centuries, in which one turns one's own life into a self-consuming art work (examples of this tradition range from Byron's *Don Juan* to Pushkin's *Queen of Spades* to Lermontov's *Hero of Our Time* to De Quincey's *Confessions of an English Opium-Eater* to Sacher-Masoch's *Venus im Pelz* to Wilde's *The Picture of Dorian Gray*). Here, again, both the allegorical structure of traditional hermeneutics and the scapegoat mechanism are key elements in understanding this problematic relationship.

Like *Under the Volcano*, *Dark as the Grave Wherein my Friend is Laid* is a variation on the Pygmalion theme of the artist's entanglement in his own creation.[34] If, in the former work, the author-protagonist dies and leaves behind a double to write his "tragedy," in the latter the process is reversed: a fictional double is sacrificed in the author's place. The writer-protagonist makes his own tragedy as he goes along, but will at the last moment find a scapegoat surrogate to replace him.

Sigbjørn Wilderness, the author of an unpublished novel, *The Valley of the Shadow of Death* (one of Lowry's alternate titles for *Under the Volcano*), and his wife Primrose set out on a trip to Mexico in search of Fernando Martínez, Sigbjørn's Oaxacan friend and a model for Dr. Vigíl and Juan Cerillo, two characters in his book. In a letter to Frank Taylor, Lowry refers to Pirandello's *Six Characters in Search of an Author* in connection with *Dark as the Grave*, saying that he has reversed the play's theme: the characters are no longer in search of an author, but the author is in search of his characters.[35] Figuratively this would be a cliché, but Lowry's meaning here is quite literal: Sigbjørn and Primrose set out in search of the imaginative world of *The Valley of the Shadow of Death*, i.e., in search of Sigbjørn's past Mexican experience in its transfigured, fictionalized form.

The reasons for their trip are ambivalent. Ostensibly they undertake it for Primrose's sake: she wants to identify with her husband's past experiences, but in their harmless, fictional guise. Primrose delights in playing at *The Valley of the Shadow of Death*, and, to a certain extent, so does Sigbjørn, although for him this kind of game is dangerous, as he himself is fully aware: "He was using his wife's necessity and the fact that she had never visited a foreign country as an excuse for indulging his own necessity—for what was it but death? . . . Why had he used Fernando Martínez of all people, as a kind of excuse for going to Mexico? What did his friend, his character Dr. Vigíl, mean to him but a nostalgia for delirium? Or oblivion. And his meeting with him another excuse, even such as the Consul liked to find, for 'celebration'?"[36]

Sigbjørn's nostalgia for delirium turns out to be another game for him, the game of "making tragedies," as his friend Fernando used to say. Like his character the Consul, Sigbjørn is aware that he is acting in a play for which he is both author and protagonist. Much like Shade-Kinbote, he employs the *theatrum mundi* metaphor throughout his book, because to him the world itself looks like a rejected play, or a rejected novel—to be exact, his novel. If Sigbjørn borrows his image of "world as play" from Shakespeare, Calderón, and Pirandello, he adopts his metaphor of the "world as novel" from Unamuno and Ortega y Gasset. In a letter to Albert Erskine, Lowry writes that "Sigbjørn is Ortega's fellow, making his life as he goes along, and trying to find his vocation."[37] In *Toward a Philosophy of History* Ortega says: "Human life transcends the reality of nature. It is not given to man as its fall is given to a stone or the stock of its organic acts—eating, flying, nesting—to an animal. He makes it himself, beginning by inventing it. Have we heard right? Is human life in its most human dimension a work of fiction? Is man a sort of novelist of himself who conceives the fanciful figure of a personage with its unreal occupations and then for the sake of converting it into reality, does all the things he does—and becomes an engineer?"[38]

But Sigbjørn employs Ortega's metaphor for his own purposes. He reads it in a literal sense and starts enacting his own book, which no less than the Consul's is a tragedy. As Sigbjørn attempts, however, to enact his tragedy while still writing about it, he will soon run into compositional problems: the sense of doom is weakened instead of being enhanced as he goes along, since there is no external agent to precipitate his fall; besides he cannot die and at the same time record his death. He solves these problems by introducing doubles into his plot. First he dissociates himself from what he calls his "daemon," a cross between God and his own creative genius. This enables him both to write and to be written; hence his feeling of being both within his book, as the protagonist caught up "in the great chain of the infernal machine of his life," and outside it, as "a God who has just lifted the lid of a box of toys, the burros, the flowers, the tortillas, the little pigs, the Indian women, the dancers in fringes of scarlet . . . and Cuernavaca, the town of his novel."[39]

But Sigbjørn creates his tragedy as he goes along in yet another sense: his daemon is also Mallarmé's *démon d'analogie*, which possesses him as much as it possesses Kinbote. He sees in every event of his life a correspondence with the past and a foreshadowing of the future. One such coincidence is renting Laruelle's tower in Cuernavaca, which intensifies his feeling of living within his book. The correspondences, as numerous here as in *Under the Volcano* (and in *Pale Fire*), serve to build a circular or oracular structure present in most tragedies—for instance, many classical and neoclassical tragedies begin with an oracle or a prophetic dream that will come true at the end of the play despite the protagonist's efforts to circumvent it. Sigbjørn sees their trip to Mexico as a spiritual analogue of their Canadian home burning down: he finds himself back in the place from which he has started, in a spiritual wasteland.

This principle of the perpetual recurrence of the same is suggested in the novel through the obvious image of a circle. When their plane lands in Los Angeles, Sigbjørn sees this event as symbolic: Primrose and he had first met in that city and now, at least geographically, they are back where they had started from. This is the closing of a circle, which at first he is inclined to see positively as ecdysis. But the reptilian metaphor conjures up the image of the snake biting its tail (the Ouroboros) and immediately assumes a sinister connotation in Sigbjørn's mind: he feels himself caught "in the suction of the future." He realizes with horror that if one circle has closed (that of Los Angeles-Vancouver-Los Angeles), he is now caught in the greater circle of Oaxaca-Vancouver-Oaxaca and for him, as for the Consul, Oaxaca means death. The Ouroboros, a symbol of the Great Chain of Being, has for Sigbjørn the same sinister implication of doom that it has for Macbeth, who struggles in vain to avoid what he construes as an inexorable chain of events leading to his destruction:

> We have scotched the snake, not killed it
> She'll close and be herself whilst our poor malice
> Remains in danger of her former tooth.[40]

But unlike Macbeth, who defies his fate, Sigbjørn is a "lighthouse" that only too eagerly "invites the storm."

The same snake imagery recurs at a crucial moment in the novel, when after long circuitous wanderings, Primrose and Sigbjørn finally reach Oaxaca. They start looking for the Banco Ejidal where Fernando, by now inexorably associated with Sigbjørn's fate, may still be working. But all they find, by yet another coincidence, is the ominous public sign that had so much terrified the Consul in *Under the Volcano*: "¿Le gusta este jardín que es suyo? Evite que sus hijos lo destruyan!" Upon noticing the sign (at one time commonly displayed in Mexican public parks), Sigbjørn "was staggered," feeling as if he were "wrestling with an invisible enemy" or as if he "were being by some strange magnetism, sucked from a distance into the maw of a lampalagua, that serpent which in fact resembled Mexican Immigration that while extremely sluggish in its motions, it yet captures its victims by following them into their burrows."[41]

The tragic circular pattern has also a psychological sense in *Dark as the Grave*: Sigbjørn's voyage, like most Lowry voyages, is a voyage of the self. One of Sigbjørn's motives for going to Mexico is to find a subject for his novel, which would compensate for *In Ballast to the White Sea*, lost in the fire. But in this case he travels again, like Oedipus, in a circle: he sets out in search of a subject for his book only to discover that he himself is this subject. Sigbjørn is well aware that his problems do not lie in Mexico: the only ghost that needs to be exorcised is himself, his self-destructive impulses, but he is not at all sure he wants to be exorcised. This exorcism will nevertheless take place and the tragedy will eventually be consummated.

But what tragedy does Sigbjørn enact in *Dark as the Grave*? Since he is playing at his own book, *The Valley of the Shadow of Death*, the tragedy will again be that of the Passion, (mis)interpreted as self-victimage and scapegoat ritual. Sigbjørn himself suggests this, when he hesitates to go down the elevator in the lobby of the hotel Cornada, where the scene of his parting with Ruth, his first wife, had taken place years before: "No wonder he did not want to go down in the lift! It was like a station of the cross, in the unfinished Oberammergau of his life, shadowy understudy even in that, it was much as if he'd left his cross here while he went off and got drunk on Pilsener one night and then had done something else, and forgotten the part he was playing: and now he'd had to come back here to pick up again and finish whatever it was he had begun. Or was it he had left his cross in Oaxaca, c/o Fernando Martínez, to be left till called for?" (77).

In *The Valley of the Shadow of Death*, Sigbjørn has appeased his daemon by the Consul's death. But since he is now playing at the Consul's tragedy, the daemon has to be appeased again. By killing the Consul, Sigbjørn had broken the circle: he had separated himself from his fictional double. In *Dark as the Grave*, however, he becomes again his own character—his identity collapses into that of his fictional double, and if he is to survive (his halfhearted attempt at suicide is hardly a convincing solution even to himself), another separation is needed. This time his friend

Fernando will perform the function of the scapegoat. Sigbjørn's transference of his death wish onto him is made easier by yet another providential coincidence. Fernando had died precisely in the manner of the Consul: he had been shot years before in a bar, after drinking a bottle of mescal, perhaps at the very moment that Sigbjørn was writing the last sentence of *The Valley of the Shadow of Death*. He thus also becomes, as it were, the Consul of *Dark as the Grave*, replacing Sigbjørn as victim of his own tragedy. The daemon is, for the moment, appeased. The book can now be written, indeed it has already written itself, not unlike, Sigbjørn suggests, Parsifal's garden, which had bloomed in his absence. If Mexico has previously appeared to him as a wasteland, now it becomes a garden in bloom: "It was all so different from eight years ago, and also the look of the animals, which were not shabby or starved looking but had strong well-fed looks and shining coats that came from proper feeding and care, and the fields themselves were rich. Oaxaca had become the granary of nearly all Mexico and the Valley of Etla had become the granary of Oaxaca" (255).

Sigbjørn attributes the miraculous change to the Banco Ejidal, that is, to Fernando, its employee, who has mediated between him and the land of death. He establishes a subtle correspondence between his book and Mexico, which also becomes Parsifal's garden. The Consul's ritualistic murder at the end of *The Valley of the Shadow of Death* corresponds to Fernando's death and therefore is mystically responsible for the fertility of the land. Sigbjørn's tragedy has after all turned out to be a divine comedy, a fitting conclusion to the Passion. This happy ending is achieved only when Sigbjørn separates himself from his novel by sacrificing his double.

Yet Sigbjørn realizes that playing at tragedy as scapegoat ritual is a highly dangerous game. In the Consul's case it has resulted in loss of creative power and in self-destruction, and Sigbjørn himself narrowly escapes the same fate. Neither the Consul nor Sigbjørn can function in the immediate world, which simply becomes an allegorical projection of their respective books. As in *Don Quijote*, play or literature spills into life, and fiction interposes itself between its creator and lived experience. Sigbjørn suggests this, for instance, when he complains that he cannot enjoy anything except in retrospect, in a fictionalized form; he cannot make real friends because he always thinks of other people as characters. As in *Pale Fire*, moreover, the solipsistic fictionalization of experience results in the ultimate impoverishment not only of this experience (which loses its quality of otherness) but also of the writer's imagination, although Sigbjørn, unlike Kinbote, never loses his sense of humor or capacity for self-parody: "There were of course people in the bus, but he did not notice them; they sat there like blocks of inchoate, illegible notes. Phrases and paragraphs bumped by; and the unwritten octet of the blue sky.... Sigbjørn watched the lost prose sliding past the window" (197–98). Here one can also see that the allegorization of experience is interchangeable with the literalization of fiction—a paradoxical effect brilliantly described by Oscar Wilde in *The Picture of Dorian Gray*, where Dorian's portrait becomes interchangeable with his soul, so that when he attempts to stab the painting, he stabs himself.

Finally, since the act of literary creation in the modern age often symbolically repeats the violence of an archaic scapegoat ritual, Sigbjørn is aware of the sacrificial nature of art within a world of power. Prying into the "mysteries" of Monte Albán, for example, Sigbjørn descends into a dark tomb and listens to the guide's explanations, with his dead friend, Fernando, in mind:

> "One of the strangest finds at Monte Albán was relief sculptures of human beings, all of whom have some bodily deformity. Some show the heads too flat, while others show them extraordinarily elongated. In some the extremities, usually the feet, are twisted, others are bent, and so forth." Who were the authors of these writings, and why did they prefer to show cripples in their sculptured stones? Was it their intent to ridicule certain enemies? Or should we see in these sculptures a representation of the sick who came to a temple in which there was a god who performed miraculous cures? Could Monte Albán be a kind of Lourdes? Was there not some identity with modern art—yes, and modern writing—in this? Was art at bottom a form of propitiation? (226–27)

Sigbjørn realizes that within his world the relation between the artist and his creation is equally agonistic. The novelist becomes an author-authority that must constitute itself in the play of difference between reality and fiction, with the creative act being a negative affirmation: the novelist shapes his world by separating himself from it, by rejecting it as fiction. Delirium or madness is precisely the moment of undifferentiation, when the authorial self loses its identity at the same time that it acquires all identities. The Consul experiences this moment, as we have seen, in the last chapter of *Under the Volcano*, and this is what Sigbjørn calls his nostalgia for delirium, which also tempts Laruelle, under the guise of tequila, in chapter 1. And this moment requires a reestablishing of difference, an act of "propitiation," as Sigbjørn suggests. In this respect, Lowry's immediate predecessor is less Pirandello or Ortega y Gasset than Unamuno.

At the end of Unamuno's *Niebla*, for example, the protagonist Augusto pays a visit to the author, complaining about his fate and threatening suicide. When Don Miguel (Unamuno as implied author) tells his character that he cannot die because he is only a figment of the author's imagination, Augusto turns the tables on his creator: "Could it possibly be, my dear Don Miguel . . . that it is you and not I who are a creature out of fiction, the person who actually does not exist, who is neither living nor dead? Could it not be that you are a mere pretext for bringing my story to the world?"[42] Don Miguel becomes enraged and insecure at Augusto's suggestion and finally manifests his authority as creator by decreeing that Augusto must indeed die. Augusto makes good on his threat to commit suicide in order to assert his independence from Don Miguel: even though now he appears to follow his creator's decree, at least he chooses his own manner of death. Unamuno, therefore, equally stresses the negative, agonistic nature of the relation between an artist and his creation, particularly when the work is treated as a form of otherness (i.e., an allegory) that threatens the artist's identity as author-authority and therefore must be purged or scapegoated.

In a certain sense, then, the proper functioning of literary discourse within a world of power often depends on its allegorical or double structure, which manifests itself as an agonistic interplay between reality and fiction (thus, accounting for the novelist's tireless insistence, at least since Cervantes, that art and life must remain separate both within and outside their work). Once this allegorical structure is removed, the author-character distinction collapses as well, and the creator may often become entangled in his own creation. Hence the danger incurred by Don Miguel when he kills Augusto, or by Sigbjørn when he destroys the Consul and, with him, the allegorical framework of *The Valley of the Shadow of Death*.

It also becomes obvious, from a ludic-irenic perspective, that a literary work can effectively transcend a mentality of power only when it functions as liminal rather than fictional discourse, i.e., when it places itself in a no-man's land, outside an agonistic dialectic of truth and fiction or reality and appearance. Of course, Lowry's work remains open to an irenic liminal perspective, but Lowry as author-authority unfortunately closed himself off from this perspective in his own life. Like Sigbjørn, he was fully aware that through his symbolic game of scapegoating he reaffirmed a mentality of power that could easily erupt into literal violence, yet he chose to follow its appalling logic to the end. Like Sigbjørn Wilderness, Lowry created several doubles, through which he separated himself from his fiction and "propitiated" delirium and violence. But in the end his identity collapsed into that of his fictional doubles, and he became what Sigbjørn was afraid he had become: a character in his own book. He stopped writing, and like Byron, his *Don Juan* unfinished, he started enacting his own fictions. Dr. Hippolyte's warning to Sigbjørn seems prophetic of Lowry's fate:

> But remember what I told you, Sigbjørn. In Voodoo, there is a great lesson. There is great discipline. The dancers do not leave the blazing circle. If you like to call it neuroses that they get rid of, then that is what they do. And even if the priest becomes possessed, the ceremony goes on. A bell is rung when it has reached a certain point beyond which it may become dangerous. You have to be your own priest and ring your own bell. Yes, I will tell you. You are possessed too. You are possessed by Sigbjørn Wilderness. (151–52)

In *Dark as the Grave*, Sigbjørn found himself caught up in the great circle of Oaxaca-Vancouver-Oaxaca and broke away. In "Through the Panama" he will find himself caught in the even greater circle of England-Canada-England, but this circle will eventually prove fatal both to him and to Lowry, his creator.

3. George Orwell and the Will to Power as Utopia/Dystopia

In *Pale Fire*, the Will to Power appears mostly as aesthetic play, the violence of which is essentially turned into farce. In *Under the Volcano* and

Dark as the Grave Wherein My Friend Is Laid, this Will assumes both an aesthetic and a solipsistic, existential guise through the kind of self-scapegoating that belongs to a median ethopathology. By contrast, in Orwell's *1984* the Will to Power unambiguously reverts to its violent, archaic ludic form. One does not usually think of Orwell's novel as being a playful book, perhaps because the original, archaic link between power, violence, and play becomes obscured within a predominantly median mentality such as ours. As I have shown in *God of Many Names*, play did have a central role within an archaic mentality (such as that of early Hellenic civilization), being the primary way in which power presented itself. With the advent of a median mentality, play became separated from power, which began to present itself as reason, knowledge, morality, and truth. Consequently, play lost its centrality in culture, being tamed and repressed alongside all the other archaic values. A return to these values—and my assumption has been that "postmodernism" is precisely such a return—also presupposes a revaluation of play by reestablishing its connection to power.

As we have seen in chapter 1, the modern thinker who initiates the return to an archaic mentality is Nietzsche and, in this sense, his thought is crucial in understanding the postmodern age. In Nietzsche play again becomes the exuberant, violent impulse, beyond good and evil, that tirelessly engenders and destroys innumerable worlds; in other words, play becomes the most authentic mode of expression of the Will to Power. Nietzsche, therefore, is also one of the initiators of the "aesthetic" turn in modern thought, whereby art and play again become fundamental ways of conceptualizing experience. Orwell's *1984* can, then, also be understood as an imaginary construction of a world based on a naked, unashamed, and playful Will to Power, evaluated from symmetrically opposite perspectives: from a Nietzschean perspective this naked and unashamed Will is valued positively, as political utopia (the ideal product of a "master race" that Orwell calls "oligarchical collectivism"), whereas from a median perspective it is seen negatively, as political dystopia. A comparison between Nietzsche and Orwell would yield some useful insights not only into the latter's work but also into the governing assumptions of what I call "postmodernism" in general. Here I can only touch upon some of the main points that such a comparison would entail, concentrating on what interests me most in the present context: the notion of interpretation and its corollary, the notion of allegory.

In *1984*, Orwell has his main character, Winston Smith, an ordinary intellectual with traditional, middle-class values, move in a Nietzschean world of overmen who have organized themselves according to the principles of oligarchical collectivism, reminiscent of a Leninist-Stalinist brand of communism. Smith engages in a game of passive and then active resistance against the authorities, a game in which he has as much chance of winning as a mouse has against a cat. Once in the hands of the thought police, O'Brien, his torturer-teacher, plays with him an elaborate power game that results in Smith's understanding and full emotional acceptance of the archaic principle of might makes right. He not only renounces any thought of resistance against Big Brother but also comes to love him, embracing what he perceives to be the latter's unbeatable strength.

In the eternally bright cells of the thought police, Smith's rational, commonsensical view of reality receives blow after blow from O'Brien's sophisticated, perspectivist view of the world as a manifestation of the Will to Power. O'Brien is the "philosophical man of power" or "artist-tyrant" described by Nietzsche in *The Will to Power*:

> [T]he possibility has been established for the production of international racial unions whose task will be to rear a master race, the future "masters of the earth";—a new tremendous aristocracy, based on the severest self legislation, in which the will of philosophical men of power and artist-tyrants will be made to endure for millennia—a higher kind of men, who, thanks to their superiority in will, knowledge, riches, and influence, employ democratic Europe as their most pliant and supple instrument for getting hold of the destinies of the earth, so as to work as artists upon "man" himself.[43]

Like Nietzsche's artist-tyrant, O'Brien works upon Smith the way a sculptor works upon clay or stone, molding him according to his own will or, rather, the collective will of the Party. In order to achieve his purpose, O'Brien sets out to prove to his victim that there is no reality outside the reality of power, which, as in Nietzsche, consists of nothing but a feeling of power. In order to achieve this feeling of power one has to merge one's individuality with the collective (un)consciousness, the equivalent of the Nietzschean ecstatic Dionysian experience (hence the two-minute hate periods in *1984*, during which the individual merges into and identifies with the collective frenzy typical of an archaic scapegoat ritual). Only this collective feeling of power creates "reality," the rest is an illusion.

O'Brien's philosophical position, as he explains it to Smith, is not a form of solipsism, but a form of perspectivism. The collective mind of the Party is the active, subjective part of the Will to Power that is called upon to give shape to its passive-resistant or objective part. In this sense, "reality" has no content or meaning outside the one that the collective Will imposes on it. As O'Brien puts it: "Only the disciplined mind can see reality, Winston. You believe that reality is something objective, external, existing in its own right. You also believe that the nature of reality is self-evident. When you delude yourself into thinking that you see something, you assume that everyone else sees the same thing as you. But I tell you, Winston, that reality is not external. Reality exists in the human mind, and nowhere else. Not in the individual mind, which can make mistakes, and in any case soon perishes: only in the mind of the Party, which is collective and immortal. Whatever the Party holds to be truth *is* truth. It is impossible to see reality except by looking through the eyes of the Party."[44]

According to O'Brien, then, reality is a matter of interpretation. But for him, as for Nietzsche, interpretation is no longer the process of cognition through which the agent discovers the world as it is already constituted; on the contrary, it is the process through which he creates the world as he goes along. In this respect, O'Brien is an antipositivist, and Nietzsche's criticism of the positivist assumption of the existence of "facts" independent of interpretation is also O'Brien's criticism of Smith's commonsensical notion of reality. In *The Will to Power*, for example, Nietzsche writes: "Against positivism which halts at phenomena—'there are only facts'—I would say: No, facts are precisely what there is not, only interpretations."[45] To positivism, Nietzsche opposes his notion of perspectivism based on an ever active Will to Power. According to him, the world "has no meaning behind it, but countless meanings— 'Perspectivism.' It is our needs that interpret the world; our drives and their For and Against. Every drive is a kind of lust to rule; each one has its perspective that it would like to compel all the other drives to accept as a norm" (note 267). In other words, it is the Will to Power (which O'Brien calls the disciplined collective mind of the Party) that "interprets." The Will constantly "defines limits, determines degrees, variations of power. Mere variations of power could not feel themselves to be such: there must be present something that wants to grow and interprets the value of whatever else wants to grow. Equal *in that*—In fact interpretation is itself a means of becoming master of something" (note 342).

    Like Nietzsche's, O'Brien's perspectivism can thus be understood as a multiplicity of interpretations where truth and fiction, taken in their traditional epistemological and ethical sense, are relative and interchangeable. But this perspectivism, which the Party calls "doublethink," is far from leading to political pluralism or tolerance of the other's viewpoint; nor does it lead to axiological relativism; on the contrary, its context is strictly agonistic and hierarchical. Nietzsche is helpful again in understanding O'Brien's brand of perspectivism as Will to Power. As one recalls from chapter 3 of the present study, Nietzsche argues that perspectivism is "only a complex form of specificity. My idea is that every specific body strives to become master over all space and to extend its force (its will to power) and to thrust back all that resists its extension. But it continually encounters similar efforts on the part of other bodies and ends by coming to an arrangement ('union') with those of them that are sufficiently related to it: thus they conspire together for power" (339). Translated into political terms, Nietzschean perspectivism becomes not only the fundamental principle of oligarchic collectivism as expounded by Goldstein-O'Brien but also the principle of agonistic (rather than peaceful) coexistence among the three superpowers of *1984:* Oceania, Eurasia, and Eastasia. Since these superpowers cannot destroy each other, they continuously form and break alliances with each other, thus conspiring together for power.

    Just like Nietzsche, O'Brien does not regard truth and fiction as purely epistemological or ethical categories. In this he reverts again to an archaic mentality, where truth and fiction or lie have a *performative* value and may be used indifferently as long as they further the goals of power. O'Brien would fully endorse Nietzsche's argument that, epistemologically speaking, truth is not something to be found or discovered in the nature of things, but rather "something that must be created and that gives a name to a process." It is a *"processus in infinitum,* an active determining—not a becoming-conscious of something that is in itself firm and determined." Truth, then, is also an agonistic notion, indeed it is a "word for the will to power," and its criterion "resides in the enhancement of the feeling of power" (note 290). For instance, in the revolutionary manifesto that elucidates the aims and methods of oligarchical collectivism and that is attributed to Goldstein but is written by O'Brien, among others, O'Brien echoes Nietzsche when he describes the fluid and dynamic relation between truth and fiction inherent in the Party's notion of doublethink. Doublethink is a political, totalitarian version of not only Nietzsche's concept of perspectivism but also his concept of joyful forgetfulness:

> *Doublethink* lies at the very heart of Ingsoc, since the essential act of the Party is to use conscious deception while retaining the firmness of purpose that goes with complete honesty. To tell deliberate lies while genuinely believing in them, to forget any fact that has become inconvenient, and then, when it becomes necessary again, to draw it back from oblivion for just so long as it is needed . . . all this is indispensably necessary. Even in using the word *doublethink* it is necessary to exercise *doublethink.* For by using the word one admits that one is tampering with reality; by a fresh act of *doublethink* one erases this knowledge; and so on indefinitely, with the lie always one leap ahead of the truth.[46]

O'Brien also informs Smith that a proper philosophical comprehension of the nature and objectives of the Will to Power is only the preliminary and the easiest step toward his rebirth or "reintegration" in the cells of the Ministry of Love as a worshiper of oligarchical collectivism. According to O'Brien, there are three stages in this process of reintegration: learning, understanding, and acceptance (215). Whereas the first two stages involve intellectual or thought processes, the third stage involves psychoemotional transformations and is the hardest to achieve. Evaluating Smith's "progress" after interminable sessions of physical and mental torture, O'Brien observes: "You are improving. Intellectually there is very little wrong with you. It is only emotionally that you have failed to make progress" (232).

O'Brien is fully aware that to convert Smith's mentality back to an archaic one, the Party must change not only his mode of thought and behavior but also his feelings or pathos. Rather than simply obeying Big Brother, Smith must accept and love him as the highest embodiment of the Will to Power. In Newspeak terms, "doublethink" cannot be successful without "bellyfeel." Smith's pathic transformation is the most difficult to effect because of the median accretions that are built into his psychophysiological constitution and that function as "tacit knowledge" or an unconscious set of assumptions and beliefs, resisting any conscious logic and determining both his perceptions and his emotional responses. Such tacit knowledge includes his perceptions of right and wrong, likes and dislikes, love and hate, and so on. As Smith reasons halfway through his "reeducation" process, he has surrendered his mind to the Party, but he can still "keep the inner heart inviolate." With his mind he now "knew he was in the wrong," but with his heart he "preferred to be in the wrong" (231). Likewise, in an earlier conversation with Julia, Smith reassures her and himself by arguing that, under torture, the Party can make them say anything, but cannot make them believe it: "Confession is not betrayal. What you say or do doesn't matter; only feelings matter. If they could make me stop loving you—that would be the real betrayal" (137). Smith's "inner heart" or tacit knowledge lends integrity or dignity to his ego or image of himself as a distinct and stable individual.

It is Smith's self-image founded on his median ethopathology that O'Brien has to destroy before he can remold him in Big Brother's collectivist image. O'Brien performs this destruction in two stages: first, he destroys Smith's physical self-image when after prolonged torture he has Smith contemplate himself in a mirror (223–25); secondly, he confronts him, in Room 101, with his worst phobia (rats) so that Smith believes that he has "to interpose another human being, the *body* of another human being, between himself and the rats" (235) and screams frantically: "Do it to Julia! Not me! Julia . . . Not me!" (236). By abjuring his feelings for Julia, Smith has fully abjured his old self-image and is now ready, in O'Brien's eyes, to transfer not only his intellectual but also his emotional allegiance to Big Brother.

One may wonder, with Smith, why those who rebel against oligarchical collectivism need to be "reeducated" in such a ghastly manner, since they will be put to death anyway and cannot constitute a real danger to the all-powerful Party. This question cannot be answered, however, without first understanding the motives and the objectives of the Will to Power in its oligarchical collective guise. O'Brien offers a Nietzschean insight into these motives and objectives when he says: "The Party seeks power entirely for its own sake. We are not interested in the good of others; we are interested solely in power. Not wealth or luxury or long life or happiness: only power, pure power" (217). O'Brien notes that the oligarchies of the past, including the German Nazis and the Russian Communists, have failed because "they never had the courage to recognize their own motives," pretending or perhaps even believing that "they had seized power unwillingly and for a limited time, and that just round the corner there lay a paradise where human beings would be free and equal" (217). By contrast, oligarchical collectivism is fully aware that "no one ever seizes power with the intention of relinquishing it." For O'Brien and the Party, therefore, power is never a means, but always an end: "One does not establish a dictatorship in order to safeguard a revolution; one makes the revolution in order to establish the dictatorship. The object of persecution is persecution. The object of torture is torture. The object of power is power" (217).

If the object of power is power itself, then it can be attained only by tirelessly exercising it. And power cannot be exercised unless it encounters resistance. O'Brien implicitly acknowledges this fact when he tells Smith: "We do not destroy the heretic because he resists us; so long as he resists us we never destroy him" (210). Heretics like Smith are no less indispensable to a mentality of power than authority figures like O'Brien. If they do not exist, they must be invented, as O'Brien openly acknowledges both when he coauthors the revolutionary manifesto attributed to Goldstein and when he says to Smith: "Goldstein and his heresies will live for ever. Every day, at every moment, they will be defeated, discredited, ridiculed, spat upon—and yet will always survive" (221). Hence, the Party revives the archaic scapegoat ritual, which, however, it stages in a conscious and deliberate manner so that it will never lose its effectiveness again.

The Party will forever reenact the Dionysian dramatic cycle of creation and destruction, and all human beings will not only accept it but will ecstatically identify with and participate in it, much as they used to participate in the archaic mysteries of Dionysus. O'Brien openly acknowledges the artistic-dramatic nature of the Party's power game, because its stagelike quality does not make it any less real: "This drama that I have played out with you during seven years will be played out over and over again generation after generation, always in subtler forms. Always we shall have the heretic here at our mercy, screaming with pain, broken up, contemptible—and in the end utterly penitent, saved from himself, crawling to our feet of his own accord. That is the world that we are preparing, Winston. A world of victory after victory, triumph after triumph after triumph: an endless pressing, pressing, pressing upon the nerve of power" (221).

Power for its own sake involves not only a perpetual staging of the scapegoat ritual but also the incessant, deliberate cultivation of a negative ethopathology. As Goldstein-O'Brien points out in his pamphlet, in addition to the political and the economic conditions, one must provide "the emotional basis for a hierarchical society" (158). Positive emotions such as love, trust, joy, and physical well-being become strictly subordinated to their negative counterparts such as fear, hate, distrust, envy, humiliation, and physical and emotional discomfort, which in turn create the kind of paranoid, oppressive psychological climate that a mentality of power finds most congenial to operate in. The ordinary member of the Party "is expected to be competent, industrious, and even intelligent within narrow limits, but it is also necessary that he should be a credulous and ignorant fanatic whose prevailing moods are fear, hatred, adulation, and orgiastic triumph. In other words it is necessary that he should have the mentality appropriate to a state of war" (158). As O'Brien cynically remarks to his victim later on, pain or suffering is the main instrument of this mentality, hence the necessity of developing ever more effective forms of mental and physical torture (as well as self-torture) so that power can be constantly reaffirmed and reassured:

> Power is in inflicting pain and humiliation. Power is in tearing human minds to pieces and putting them together again in new shapes of your own choosing. . . . It is the exact opposite of the stupid hedonistic Utopias that the old reformers imagined. A world of fear and treachery and torment, a world of trampling and being trampled upon, a world which will grow not less but *more* merciless as it refines itself. Progress in our world will be progress toward more pain. . . . All competing pleasures will be destroyed. But always—do not forget this, Winston—always there will be the intoxication of power, constantly

increasing and constantly growing subtler. Always, at every moment, there will be the thrill of victory, the sensation of trampling on an enemy who is helpless. If you want a picture of the future, imagine a boot stamping on a human face—forever. (220)

Smith himself believes that power as suffering is the true standard of existence when he notices that he "seemed to have lost the power of intellectual effort, now that the stimulus of pain had been removed" and when he defines well-being negatively as the absence of pain (227).

Now one can also see why allegory is impossible, as well as unnecessary, in O'Brien's world of unashamed power, where reality is openly manufactured rather than discovered: in the context of such a world, the image of "a boot stamping on a human face" is not allegorical but metonymical. Allegory, as we have seen, depends on a notion of reality or truth that is hidden and needs to be brought out in the open; in other words, it depends on a dichotomy of presence and absence characteristic of a median mentality. But once the Will to Power manifests itself openly or as eternal Becoming, it no longer needs allegory or any metaphysical language behind which to hide itself. Consequently, O'Brien's world is antiallegorical: unmediated power ceaselessly destroys allegorical systems, and representations in general, as being ambiguous, superfluous, and inimical to its goals. Smith's fatal mistake, according to O'Brien, is that he still relies on traditional hermeneutics to uncover the "real" meaning behind the Party's statements and slogans, instead of taking them at face value.

Smith's dream of meeting O'Brien in "the place where there is no darkness" is a good example of the constant destruction of allegory as a hermeneutical principle throughout the narrative. Smith interprets this phrase to mean "the imagined future, which one would never see, but which by foreknowledge, one could mystically share in" (87). However, after Smith is arrested and O'Brien proves to be not an ally but an enemy, the "place where there is no darkness" turns out to be, very literally, the cells of the thought police that are kept brightly lit day and night.

The mutability of the past is another antiallegorical principle of archaic power that only recognizes a continuous present (or what Nietzsche calls "the eternal return of the same"). Allegory, like truth, depends not only on a dichotomy of presence and absence but also on a dichotomy of Being and Becoming. Unmediated power dispenses with the notion of

Being and conceives of itself as an eternal play of simulacra. The mutability of the past implies endless Becoming as well as eternal return and joyful forgetfulness. Goldstein-O'Brien thus writes in his revolutionary pamphlet:

> The mutability of the past is the central tenet of Ingsoc. Past events, it is argued, have no objective existence, but survive only in written records and in human memories. The past is whatever the records and the memories agree upon. And since the Party is in full control of all the records and in equally full control of the minds of its members, it follows that the past is whatever the Party chooses to make it. It also follows that though the past is alterable, it never has been altered in any specific instance. For when it has been recreated in whatever shape is needed at the moment, then this new version is the past, and no different past can ever have existed. This holds good even when, as often happens, the same event has to be altered out of recognition several times in the course of the year. At all times, the Party is in possession of absolute truth, and clearly the absolute can never have been different from what it is now. (176)

Doublethink is, again, ineffective unless it is accompanied by the right kind of bellyfeel. The Party, therefore, favors the development of an archaic type of memory that automatically processes all past events selectively, as eternal returns of the present. In this sense, Goldstein-O'Brien writes: "It will be seen that the control of the past depends above all on the training of memory. To make sure that all written records agree with the orthodoxy of the moment is merely a mechanical act. But it is also necessary to *remember* that the events happened in the desired manner. And if it is necessary to rearrange one's memories or to tamper with written records, then it is necessary to *forget* that one has done so. . . . In Oldspeak it is called quite frankly 'reality control'" (176).

The Party also wishes to return to an archaic language that is purely transparent and univocal, i.e., completely free of allegory. Although Newspeak necessarily starts from an allegorical structure required by doublethink, its ultimate goal is to do away with all ambivalence and ambiguity, that is, with allegory itself. For instance, the ministries of Love, Truth, Peace, and Plenty may appear at first as allegorical terms, since in Oldspeak (standard English) they mean exactly their opposites. As Goldstein-O'Brien notes, the "Ministry of Peace concerned itself with war, the Ministry of Truth with lies, the Ministry of Love with torture and the Ministry of Plenty with starvation" (178). But, again, following the model of a mythical mode of thought (the vestiges of which resurface in dreams, as Freud among many others has pointed out), the Party replaces the median or rationalist logic of either/or by the atavistic logic of both/and, which operates neither on the principle of binary oppositions nor on the principle of *tertium non datur*. As Goldstein-O'Brien puts it, "These contradictions are not accidental, nor do they result from deliberate hypocrisy: they are deliberate exercises in *doublethink*. For it is only by reconciling contradictions that power can be retained indefinitely" (178).

The play of simulacra is precisely this reconciliation of logical contradictions or erasure of differences in which essence and appearance, model and copy are accorded the same ontoepistemological value. By the end of the novel, it becomes obvious that the titles of the ministries are scrupulously literal, at least from the perspective of the inner Party, which is the only perspective that matters. The Ministry of Love, the seat of the thought police, sees to it that Big Brother is loved by everyone; the Ministry of Peace, the seat of the army, guarantees peace for Oceania by waging war on the other superpowers; the Ministry of Truth, the seat of the official propaganda machine, sees to it that the inner Party's lies become truth; and the Ministry of Plenty, the seat of the economy, sees to it that the inner Party prospers through the starvation of the rest of the population. The noncontradictory nature of these titles (from the univocal perspective of oligarchical collectivism) is appropriately expressed by their Newspeak equivalents: Minitruth, Miniluv, Minipax, and Miniplenty. Here, again, the irony—and one should not forget that irony, like literature, is the allegorical discourse par excellence—can be perceived only by those raised in the ambivalent mode of thought of a median mentality or, as Newspeak would have it, by "Oldthinkers" who "unbellyfeel Ingsoc"; retranslated into Oldspeak or standard English, this would of course mean, by those "whose ideas were formed before the revolution" and, consequently, "cannot have a full emotional understanding of the principles of English socialism" (251).

Newspeak, then, is language stripped of all its metaphorical accretions, all its ambiguities, and all its allegorical possibilities. As Symes, an ardent supporter and creator of Newspeak, says about The Eleventh Edition of the Newspeak Dictionary, the "definitive edition": "You think, I dare say, that our chief job is inventing new words. But not a bit of it! We're destroying words—scores of them, hundreds of them, every day. We're cutting the language down to the bone. The Eleventh Edition won't contain a single word that will become obsolete before the year 2050" (48). The destruction of Oldspeak would mean, in the first instance, the destruction of the literature of the past (together with its unacceptable allegorical ambivalence): "By 2050—earlier, probably— all real knowledge of Oldspeak will have disappeared. The whole literature of the past will have been destroyed. Chaucer, Shakespeare, Milton, Byron—they'll exist only in Newspeak versions, not merely changed into something different, but actually changed into something contradictory of what they used to be. Even the literature of the Party will change. Even the slogans will change. How could you have a slogan like 'freedom is slavery' when the concept of freedom has been abolished? The whole climate of thought will be different. In fact there will be no thought, as we understand it now. Orthodoxy means not thinking—not needing to think. Orthodoxy is unconsciousness" (50). Here, again, orthodoxy as "unconsciousness" means a de facto return to an archaic mentality, in which thinking does not denote (self-)reflecting but doing or performing (scholars have often noticed the "literal" character of Homeric language, for instance), and Symes's argument can be construed as ironical only from Smith's or the reader's median standpoint.

Critics have often interpreted *1984* as Orwell's warning against totalitarian political systems of the Nazi or the Communist type. But, as O'Brien himself points out, oligarchical collectivism far surpasses Nazi and Communist mentality. My argument has been, therefore, that the model of this oligarchical collectivism is neither Fascism nor Stalinism, but Nietzsche's race of the "masters of the earth." Just like O'Brien, Nietzsche would have dismissed the Nazis and the Communists as representatives of a "herd mentality," promoting petty bourgeois ideals, being motivated by ressentiment and shying away from the aristocratic principle of might makes right. The point that I made about pathic distance in connection to Raskolnikov and Jasper Ammen in chapter 4 applies in the present context as well. Distance is what equally distin-

guishes the O'Brien "masterly" type from a Nazi or a Communist dicta-
tor. One remembers that, according to Nietzsche in *The Will to Power*,
proper distance precludes any danger of the master getting caught up in
a mimetic relationship with the slave: "Absurd and contemptible form
of idealism that would *not* have mediocrity *mediocre* and, instead of feeling a sense of triumph at a state of exceptionalness, becomes *indignant*
over cowardice, falsity, pettiness, and wretchedness. *One should not desire these things to be different!* and should make the gulf *wider!* . . . *Chief
viewpoint:* establish *distances*, but *create no antitheses.* Dissolve the *intermediate forms* and reduce their influence: chief means of preserving distances."[47] In this sense, one should speed up, rather than retard the
process of homogenization in democratic societies, so that the true masters can emerge rapidly and decisively: "The homogenizing of European man is the great process that cannot be obstructed: one should
even hasten it. The necessity to create a gulf, distance, order of rank, is
given *eo ipso*—not the necessity to retard this process" (note 898).

As Goldstein-O'Brien demonstrates in his revolutionary pamphlet,
the inner Party is fully aware of Nietzsche's principle of distance, for it
allows the proles to do whatever they please and concentrates its "re-
educational" efforts only on the members of the outer Party. In other
words, the inner Party knows that in order to achieve distance it must
act in two directions, by both homogenizing the proles and eliminating
the "intermediate" or median elements represented by the outer Party.
The inner Party also takes fully into consideration the Nietzschean distinction between the "master" and the "shepherd": only the former is a
"sovereign" type because while the shepherd is "a *means* of preserving
the herd," the master is "the *end* for which the herd exists" (note 903).
Whereas Smith still clings to the mentality of the shepherd—hence his
sympathy for and faith in the proles—O'Brien has already adopted the
mentality of the master, having complete contempt for them. Getting
emotionally involved in the herd mentality of the slave breeds guilt and
ressentiment, as well as envy and grudging admiration. These are precisely Smith's emotions toward the members of the inner Party, particularly O'Brien. The latter, on the other hand, maintains almost a "divine"
pathic distance regarding Smith and therefore is free of any rancor toward
him. He transforms Smith into a toy that he manipulates for his own
pleasure, just as a guiltless cat plays with a mouse purely for the sake of

the game, rejoicing in its feeling of power. Of course, O'Brien does not act in a purely disinterested, ludic fashion (any more than a cat does, who after all catches mice for food), insofar as Smith represents the median mentality of the outer Party and his elimination serves the purpose of increasing the distance between the inner Party and the proles, i.e., between the masters and the herd.

Although the world of *1984* may be described as postmodern (in my sense of the term), Orwell certainly does not share these postmodern values—hence the (median) reader's definite feeling that Orwell presents a dystopian, rather than a utopian, society in his novel. But it would be an error to assume, as many critics do, that he shares Smith's values instead. The latter belong as clearly to a mentality of power as those of O'Brien, and Smith appears to be little more than a mouse who fancies himself to be a cat for a while. For example, Smith is aware that his attraction for Julia has to do as much with sexual satisfaction as with the satisfaction of his Will to Power in the guise of rebellion; indeed, the two drives are inextricably intertwined. He becomes aroused only when he hears that Julia has had illicit affairs with other men before him: "That was above all what he wanted to hear. Not merely the love of one person, but the animal instinct, the simple undifferentiated desire: that was the force that would tear the Party to pieces."[48] After their embrace, Smith also reflects, "[Y]ou could not have pure love or pure lust nowadays. No emotion was pure, because everything was mixed up with fear and hatred. Their embrace had been a battle, the climax a victory. It was a blow struck against the Party. It was a political act" (105).

Julia herself shares Winston's mentality of power, being unable to imagine any alternatives to it. For her, "the Party was invincible. It would always exist, and it would always be the same. You could only rebel against it by secret disobedience or, at most, by isolated acts of violence such as killing somebody or blowing something up" (127). Moreover, when Winston and Julia enlist (or think they do) in the Brotherhood, Goldstein's alleged underground movement, they pledge before O'Brien to commit murder and acts of sabotage that "may cause the death of hundreds of innocent people," to betray their country to foreign powers, "to cheat, to forge, to blackmail, to corrupt the minds of children, to distribute habit-forming drugs, to encourage prostitution, to disseminate venereal disease," or to do anything else that would be "likely to cause demoralization and weaken the power of the Party" (142). When, in the cells of the thought police, Smith answers in the affirmative O'Brien's question whether he considers himself "morally superior to us, with our lies and our cruelty" (222), O'Brien simply plays back the tape on which he had recorded Smith's pledge to the Brotherhood.

It becomes obvious, then, that *1984* stages not only a conflict between an archaic and a median mentality but also a conflict between two forms of the Will to Power present within both these mentalities: collectivist and individualistic. Collective oligarchism is plainly unacceptable even to those who cannot imagine human life outside a world of power. In turn, Smith's anarchic-hedonistic individualism is not only ineffective but causes as much pain to himself as to others. In fact, it is his lack of responsive understanding toward the Other and otherness that precludes him from transcending the mentality of power that he abhors so much. The novel implicitly underlines this point in the scenes in which Smith guiltily reminisces about his childhood's selfish attitude toward his mother and little sister, or in the climactic scene in which Smith, reduced to an infant state, screams that Julia, and not himself, be given to the rats. His ratiphobia is an internalization typical of victims traumatized by aggression, and his way of dealing with it is no less typical of a victim's frame of mind. Instead of realizing that O'Brien's hold over him is nothing but his own fear, he falls back on the scapegoat mechanism that O'Brien had already employed against him and asks his torturer to deflect it in turn onto Julia.

If Smith comes to love Big Brother (as he already loves O'Brien, about whom he confesses with unconscious irony in his journal that it does not matter whether he turns out to be a friend or an enemy, since they obviously are kindred spirits), it is because he has been an all too willing victim, never imagining the possibility of an alternative world, be it a world that is completely alien from or incommensurable with the one he finds himself in. The novel emphasizes again and again that both Smith and Julia suffer from a failure in the imagination (and its liminal possibilities): for, if reality, as O'Brien argues, is indeed a manifestation of the inner being, then Smith is free to choose its intellectual, perceptual, and emotional content and does not have to accept the one imposed on him from outside.

Finally, if Orwell's novel is a warning at all, then, like Lowry's and

Nabokov's imaginative worlds, it is a warning against a mentality of power as a whole. The novel's dystopian and antiallegorical strategies, on the other hand, do not allow any explicit statement about its positive standard of evaluation. In this respect, *1984* remains deliberately ambivalent: its purpose is not to offer an ideal solution of the type one may find, say, in the rationalist utopias of the eighteenth and the nineteenth centuries but, rather, to stage the very real logical consequences of a kind of mentality that has, over the ages, been embraced by an ever larger number of human communities. Are readers to choose the lesser of two evils, between O'Brien's oligarchical collectivism and Smith's anarchic-hedonistic individualism? Or are they to turn away from both and move toward an irenic, alternative world? Orwell leaves it up to the individual reader to decide.

PART THREE

LUDIC-IRENIC APPROACHES TO CULTURAL CRITICISM

CHAPTER 7

CRITICISM AS IRENIC PLAY
The Case of the Victorian Sages

Throughout its long and complex history, Western criticism has often presented itself as a serious and dignified activity with lofty ethical and sociopolitical goals. Invoking high-minded standards, critics have often acted, at least since Socrates in Plato's *Republic*, as powerful arbiters of taste or culture brokers who have strictly regulated the artistic life of their communities. Given its claims of high seriousness, then, criticism has little to commend it as a ludic activity, unless by "ludic" one also understands the competitive spirit underlying any project undertaken by a mentality of power. In this latter agonistic sense, criticism is essentially playful, running neck in neck with other disciplines in an endless race for cultural authority within the community. But can criticism also be viewed as nonagonistic play—that is, from the perspective of an irenic world? Or, more specifically, can criticism also assume a ludic-liminal role? One could give a positive answer to these questions, if one were willing to emancipate criticism from its philosophical-scientific context and reaffirm its imaginative, artistic nature. Then, no less than literary discourse in general, criticism as play could also offer irenic alternatives to its community. By critical (and literary) "play" here, as in previous chapters, I primarily understand *staging*, or an as-if creative activity in which actual worlds and imaginary ones become interwoven, generating intermediary or liminal worlds separate from, yet contingent upon, the others. By reflecting on an actual or an imagined state of affairs and presenting it from multiple perspectives, critical discourse, no less than its literary counterpart, can articulate major existential choices open to the community at various historical junctures and can play a significant role in proposing models of historical change.

   The notion of criticism as ludic liminality is hardly new. One can find various elements of it in the aesthetic theories of Gorgias, Plato, Aristotle, Sidney, Baumgarten, Kant, Schiller, Goethe, and Shelley, among many others, and chapter 2 has highlighted some of these elements. The present chapter will take up and expand my liminal perspective on the history of literary criticism, examining the ludic spirit that animates the critical thought of Matthew Arnold, John Ruskin, and Oscar Wilde, who consistently seek to redefine the role of artistic discourse within their community. I also hope to show that the commonly accepted view of Victorian criticism as high seriousness is greatly misleading, at least in the case of these Victorians, and obscures the innovative nature of their thought. From a ludic-irenic standpoint, they continue the philosophical line of Schopenhauer, rather than that of Nietzsche, and as such they can serve as valuable models for those thinkers who are seeking genuine alternatives to a mentality of power.

1. Matthew Arnold and Criticism as A Ludic-Liminal Activity

Arnold is praised and damned, rejected and reclaimed by liberals and conservatives alike; his critical thought is deemed either confused, inconsistent, and reactionary, or complex, profound, and radical; either traditional and elitist, or progressive and democratic; either insufferably serious or irresponsibly playful. One reason for this wildly contradictory reception of Arnold's criticism in the Anglo-American world is the practical attitude toward the realm of ideas that Arnold himself, among many others, has identified as the main strength (and weakness) of the Anglo-Saxon mind and has in vain tried to counterbalance. This practical attitude has often led Anglo-American critics to enlist Arnold's critical concepts in the service of their own cultural politics. Consequently, they have often arrested that "free play of the mind" that for Arnold is the necessary condition of any intellectual activity. Here I shall mainly focus on "The Function of Criticism at the Present Time," attempting to see it "as in itself it really is," to borrow one of Arnold's most famous and controversial phrases. I shall suggest that this essay can best be read precisely as an attempt to redefine the function of Victorian criticism in ludic terms. Play, for Arnold, implies some of the basic elements that Western thinkers have always associated with the ludic phenomenon: creativity, freedom, curiosity, disinterestedness, and pleasure. But it also implies an irenic holistic view of the world, underlying all cultural, ethical, and critical values.

Arnold begins his essay by challenging the cultural cliché that criticism, because it is supposedly less creative, is inferior to literary production. Noting that both criticism and literary production are forms of creation, he argues that even though literature creates beauty, it "does not principally show itself in discovering new ideas"—that is philosophy's business. In this sense, literary creation is a "work of synthesis and exposition, not of analysis and discovery; its gift lies in the faculty of being happily inspired by a certain intellectual and spiritual atmosphere, by a certain order of ideas, when it finds itself in them."[1] By contrast, criticism is directly involved in discovering or creating new ideas, because it is a form of philosophical activity. It is the task of the "critical power" to "make an intellectual situation of which the creative power can profitably avail itself." The critical faculty "tends to establish an order of ideas, if not absolutely true, yet true by comparison with that which it displaces; to make the best ideas prevail." Soon these new ideas spread to the whole community and "there is a stir and growth everywhere; out of this stir and growth come the creative epochs of literature" (11).

At first sight, then, Arnold seems to substitute one cliché for another: echoing Socrates, he now implies that criticism as a form of philosophical activity is superior to literature, not vice versa. But he eventually disposes of this cultural cliché as well in the proposition that literature and criticism (read: literature and philosophy) do not necessarily engage in a Socratic agon, nor should one be regarded as superior to the other; rather, they are symbiotic cultural activities. Criticism is the crucial preparatory activity that creates the conditions of the possibility of great literary works. It selects and evaluates that very order of ideas which Arnold seems at first to attribute to philosophy, but then tacitly appropriates for literature. He draws a distinction between two kinds of literary periods: the "epochs of expansion," during which great literary works are created, and "epochs of concentration," during which the critical spirit prevails (17). Examples of the first kind are the epochs of Aeschylus and Shakespeare; examples of the second kind are the English romantic period and Arnold's own age. Arnold obviously implies that a period of expansion will be followed by a period of concentration and vice versa, so that the two are constantly engaged in a mutually enriching interplay.

Although Arnold ostensibly begins by replacing one critical cliché by another, by the end of his essay he transfigures both clichés into a fresh insight. He reestablishes the balance between what for him are two equally important literary functions: the aesthetic and the critical. These functions are interdependent; one cannot exist without the other. To drive his point home, Arnold employs a germinal metaphor. He compares the "epochs of Aeschylus and Shakespeare" with a "promised land, towards which criticism can only beckon." Although that promised land "will not be ours to enter, and we shall die in the wilderness . . . to have desired to enter it, to have saluted it from afar, is already, perhaps, the best distinction among contemporaries" (30). Making an obvious allusion to the biblical narrative of the Exodus, Arnold likens the periods of great literary production with the Promised Land toward which Moses leads his people after escaping from Egypt, and the periods of criticism with the wanderings in the wilderness of these people, whose leader can only glimpse their destination from afar, but can never reach it.

On the one hand, Arnold implies that literary production cannot exist without the criticism that prepares it any more than the Promised Land can exist apart from those who seek it. Furthermore, just as the Promised Land ultimately becomes one with its people, criticism at its best becomes literature, and literature at its best becomes criticism. On the other hand, Arnold's metaphor points to the liminal nature of literary discourse as a whole. Just as the Promised Land, at least from Moses' standpoint, can never be reached but only striven toward, the liminal worlds created by literature can never be actualized as such, but, rather, can serve as beacons for practical communal projects. For Arnold, then, literary discourse has a leading role in creating cultural values in at least two ways. Through its critical function, it selects and evaluates the ideas produced by philosophy and other nonliterary modes of discourse. Through its aesthetic function, it gives these ideas a beautiful, living body, but, most importantly, it can also transfigure and transvaluate them into an alternative, imaginary world that may in turn act as a general guide for the practical world.

But how can criticism, as part of literature as a whole, best fulfill its function? It is through its attitude toward culture, through its manner of approaching the world of ideas or, indeed, the world as such. For Arnold, this attitude can best be described as ludic. He develops his notion of playfulness by contrasting it to the purely practical notions of his countrymen: "The English-man has been called a political animal, and he values what is political and practical so much that ideas easily become objects of dislike in his eyes, and thinkers 'miscreants,' because ideas and thinkers have rashly meddled with politics and practice. . . . Practice is everything, a free play of the mind is nothing" (16).

The phrase "a free play of the mind" recurs frequently throughout the essay and is obviously central to Arnold's concept of criticism, but what does he mean by it? "Free play" sounds almost redundant because the ludic always already implies freedom.[2] It is, moreover, slightly inaccurate, if by it Arnold means cultural play, which is not absolute, but relative and self-restricted. The limits of play give it cultural content or structure: games must abide by rules. But here Arnold does not mean freedom from limits or rules; rather he means freedom from the blinkers of immediate political interest. He challenges the assumption that politics determines play rather than vice versa; it is precisely the politics of play practiced by a utilitarian, Philistine morality that he finds objectionable, and this is the basis of his critique of party-inspired cultural criticism: "Our organs of criticism are organs of men and parties having practical ends to serve, and with them those practical ends are the first thing and the play of the mind the second; so much play of mind as is compatible with the prosecution of those practical ends is all that is wanted."[3]

Arnold invokes the median dichotomy between play and utility only to dissolve it in the end. At first he argues that his contemporaries' utilitarian attitude toward existence can in and of itself become unsatisfactory, stultifying, and limiting, unless it is corrected by a ludic attitude that Arnold associates with spiritual development. The utilitarian and the playful should in fact go hand in hand: "[I]n spite of all that is said about the absorbing and brutalising influence of our passionate material progress, it seems to me indisputable that this progress is likely, though not certain, to lead in the end to the apparition of intellectual life; and that man, after he has made himself perfectly comfortable and has now to determine what to do with himself next, may begin to remember that he has a mind, and that the mind may be made the source of great pleasure" (17). Although Arnold grants that at present it is hard to discern a ludic tendency in "our railways, our business, and our fortune-making," he believes that "our ease, our travelling, and our unbounded liberty to hold just as hard and securely as we please to the practice to which our notions have given birth, all tend to beget an inclination to deal a little more freely with these notions themselves, to canvass them a little, to penetrate a little into their real nature" (17).

It is the inclination toward spiritual freedom, detachment, and adventure that ought to separate criticism from routine practical endeavors, and Arnold calls this inclination "curiosity." He points out that although curiosity is a word often used disparagingly in English, in other European languages it "is used in a good sense, to mean, as a high and fine quality of man's nature, just this disinterested love of a free play of the mind on all subjects for its own sake" (19). In his eyes, a free play of the mind fueled by curiosity, by the pure pleasure of finding things out, is what generates ever fresh human values. Pleasure is another key word here: criticism is fully satisfying only when it is animated by a joyful sense of creation, for "to have the sense of creative activity is the greatest happiness and the great proof of being alive" (35).

On the other hand, despite Arnold's optimistic prediction of the positive relationship between the practical and the ludic in English culture, it is obvious that he does not believe, as his contemporary Herbert Spencer does, that the ludic tendency will in due (evolutionary) course prevail over the utilitarian tendency. On the contrary, he is fully aware that as long as a utilitarian mentality prevails, it will subordinate the ludic tendency to its own practical aims and will therefore effectively block all genuine cultural change. So he points out that the critical postures assumed by the British press of his time are directly subordinated to their pragmatic, political interests: "We have the *Edinburgh Review*, existing as an organ of the old Whigs, and for as much play of the mind as may suit its being that; we have the *Quarterly Review*, existing as an organ of the Tories, and for as much play of the mind as may suit its being that; we have the *British Quarterly Review*, existing as an organ of the political Dissenters, and for as much play of mind as may suit its being that; we have the *Times*, existing as an organ of the common, satisfied, well-to-do Englishman, and for as much play of mind as may suit its being that" (18–19). By contrast, genuine criticism should go beyond political factions and parties, beyond pragmatic interests; it should be "not the minister of these interests, not their enemy, but absolutely and entirely independent of them" (19). Only as an autonomous, neutral entity can criticism best fulfill its role of both cultural mediator and agent of cultural change.

It is the twofold cultural role of criticism as mediator and catalyst that Arnold associates with the idea of disinterestedness (an idea that Arnoldian scholarship has variously traced back to Spinoza, Kant, Goethe, or Sainte-Beuve, but that actually recurs, as we have seen in chapter 2, throughout the Western poetic tradition, beginning with Gorgias). According to Arnold, criticism is to show disinterestedness by "following the law of its own nature, which is to be a free play of the mind on all subjects which it touches" and by "steadily refusing to lend itself to any . . . ulterior, political, practical considerations" (18). Arnold is fully aware, moreover, that one can transcend a utilitarian view of play only by restoring the original relationship between play and culture, in which the ludic both precedes and generates human activity. For him, genuine criticism is the creative act that rises above what is already given, returns to its original source in precultural play, and taps this source for a fresh stream of practical constructions. In other words, criticism as play adopts a liminal standpoint, placing itself in a no-man's land or "wilderness" from which it can point the way to fresh cultural alternatives.

But is Arnold's ludic notion of criticism anything more than a naive form of idealism condemned to political irrelevance? "It will be said," Arnold himself notes, "that it is a very subtle and indirect action which I am thus prescribing for criticism, and that by embracing in this manner the Indian virtue of detachment and abandoning the sphere of practical life, it condemns itself to a slow and obscure work" (25).[4] To this putative objection Arnold replies that such risks are worth taking precisely because ludic disinterestedness, far from rendering criticism politically irrelevant, allows it to ground politics itself in a supple and flexible practice, free of the blind constraints of immediate self-interest. Ludic detachment means, above all, that criticism "must not hurry to the goal because of its practical importance." On the contrary, it "must be patient, and know how to wait. It must be flexible and know how to attach itself to things and how to withdraw from them. It must know to praise spiritual perfection even in those agents which in the practical sphere seem maleficent. It must be apt to discern the spiritual shortcomings and illusions in those agents which in the practical sphere seem beneficent."[5]

Criticism must also show impartiality, "without any notion of favouring or injuring, in the practical sphere, one power or the other;

without any notion of playing off, in this sphere, one power against the other" (27). In short, criticism must not be tempted by party strife, but act as both an umpire and a corrective in relation to all political factions, in the interest of the community as a whole. Although criticism itself avoids any particular practice, it constantly generates new courses of action, new models of sociopolitical reality. Arnold's notion of disinterestedness then should not be understood as a flight from practical concerns or as a refuge into an ivory tower. Rather, as we have seen, it advocates a return to a precultural imaginative source—or a liminal time-space—from which new practical concerns can be drawn and implemented.

So far Arnold seems to have equated practice with politics, including church politics. But he himself is aware of having overstated the matter and observes that if he has "insisted so much on the course which criticism must take where politics and religion are concerned, it is because, where these burning matters are in question, it is most likely to go astray" (28). Of course, criticism should operate in relation to other fields as well, and Arnold adds: "I have wished, above all, to insist on the attitude which criticism should adopt towards things in general; on its right tone and temper of mind" (28). This is a crucial point that Arnold also echoes in his comments on Joubert's maxim, "[F]orce and right are the governors of this world; force till right is ready" (14). If force still prevails over right in practical matters, it is because we prefer it this way. This truth becomes especially evident in those cases in which we attempt to back up right by force. So Arnold emphasizes that right can never be achieved by applying external pressure; rather it must freely rise up from the groundless depths of the inner being in the Schopenhauerian sense: "[R]ight is something moral, and implies inward recognition, free assent of the will; we are not ready for right,—*right*, so far as we are concerned, *is not ready*,—until we have attained this sense of seeing it and willing it. The way in which for us it may change and transform force, the existing order of things, and become, in its turn, the legitimate ruler of the world, should depend on the way in which, when our time comes, we see it and will it" (14).

Arnold clearly associates the practical world, or "the existing order of things," with force, and right with his own irenic view of cultural play. It is from this irenic standpoint that criticism must remain neutral or politically ungrounded in relation to the practical world. It is a responsible play, involving an alternative mentality oriented toward right rather than force. It constantly beckons toward an irenic Promised Land without trying to compel anyone to follow. In this metaphorical sense, the chosen people will remain wandering in the desert until such time as they are ready to enter this Promised Land, the gates of which can never be forced open. Arnold notes that "for other people enamoured of their own newly discerned right, to attempt to impose it upon us as ours, and violently to substitute their right for our force, is an act of tyranny, and to be resisted. It sets at nought the second great half of our maxim, *force till right is ready*" (15). He believes that this was, for instance, "the grand error of the French revolution" because its "movement of ideas, by quitting the intellectual sphere and rushing furiously into the political sphere, ran indeed, a prodigious and memorable course, but produced no such intellectual fruit as the movement of ideas of the Renascence, and created, in opposition to itself, what I may call an *epoch of concentration*" (15).

When Arnold adds that "the great force of that epoch of concentration was England" and that its "great voice" was Burke (15), his notion of the interplay between the epochs of concentration and those of expansion receives full clarification. As long as our world is governed by force rather than right, it will ceaselessly oscillate between historical action and reaction in an attempt to regain its holistic balance, and one of the basic functions of criticism is to see to it that this balance is not tipped one way or another. Or, to change the metaphor somewhat, criticism, in Arnold's eyes, has the same function in relation to the body politic that homeopathy, as a holistic form of medicine, has in relation to the body physical. The aim of critical interventions, no less than that of homeopathic ones, is to adjust and maintain a healthful balance among various contending forces in the interest of the whole social and natural body.

From an irenic perspective, the free play of the mind equally implies a holistic quest for authenticity, which for Arnold can come only from within and which, in *Culture and Anarchy* for example, he constantly opposes to the mechanical routine of everyday practice. This inner quest for authenticity is also the basis for Arnold's devastating critique of dehumanizing technology in an industrial age, a critique that in many respects anticipates Heidegger's. But, unlike Heidegger, Arnold does not see the interplay between *Dasein* and Being as an agonistic one. On the contrary, he implies that this interplay can become authentic only in an irenic context. It is also for this reason that criticism as an irenic human activity must avoid "sterile conflict" (21) and "keep out of the region of immediate practice in the political, social, humanitarian sphere" (22). Only in this way can it hope eventually to "make its benefits felt even in this [practical] sphere, but in a natural and thence irresistible manner" (22).

Arnold's holistic or "homeopathic" notion of criticism as play gives rise to endless paradoxes in the pragmatic or political world, and this can explain the widely divergent ideological positions attributed to him. One may find a quotation from Arnold in support of practically any brand of politics. But this is because Arnold's political thought is profoundly unsystematic. He is well aware of the fact that systems, political and intellectual, are the wrong kind of totality. In this respect, his political notion of totality is certainly not totalitarian, but pluralistic. For example, in "The Function of Criticism" as well as in other works, notably in *Culture and Anarchy*, Arnold praises a political figure such as Burke for his ability "to return upon himself" and rise above narrow political partisanship, something that Arnold himself does frequently in his own writings. Although a liberal, he criticizes Bishop Colenso's mechanical view of the Bible; although he is for religious freedom, he criticizes the Nonconformists' sectarian efforts to disestablish the Irish Catholic Church; although he is a champion of the rational values of the French Revolution, he points out that its "mania for giving an immediate political and practical application for all these fine ideas of . . . reason was fatal" (16).

As we have seen, for Arnold the communal function of the critic is also to temper the political, intellectual, or cultural force that gains inordinate predominance at a given historical moment. In England one needs to counterbalance practicality by emphasizing speculative intellect; in France one needs to do the opposite. In hellenizing communities one needs to support the hebraizing forces; in hebraizing communities one needs to support the hellenizing forces. In predominantly rational and scientific communities one must stress faith and the imagination; in predominantly religious communities one must stress science and intellect to the ultimate benefit of what Arnold calls "imaginative reason."[6]

Arnold constantly contrasts polemics and controversy with an ideal of peace, suggesting that it is only the latter that can lead a human being "towards perfection, by making his mind dwell upon what is excellent in itself, and the absolute beauty and fitness of things."[7] It is with "a long peace" that the best "ideas of Europe steal gradually and amicably in, and mingle, though in infinitesimally small quantities at a time, with our own notions" (17). By learning and propagating "the best that is known and thought in the world," criticism reveals itself to be not only a pacific activity but also a cosmopolitan one, spontaneously transcending the ethnic and sociopolitical barriers of any one country. Criticism as ludic detachment should be able to rise above bigoted insularity and narrow-minded provincialism: "By the very nature of things, as England is not all the world, much of the best that is known and thought in the world cannot be of English growth, must be foreign; by the nature of things, again, it is just this that we are least likely to know, while English thought is streaming in upon us from all sides" (28).

By the "standard of the best that is known and thought in the world" (19), therefore, Arnold does not imply an exclusivist or elitist principle based on a sense of cultural superiority or even on "eternal truth"— after all, he does say that any order of ideas is not "absolutely true" but only "true by comparison with that which it displaces" (11); rather, he implies a cosmopolitan attitude of responsive understanding toward others and otherness. In this regard, Arnold urges the English critic to "try and possess one great literature, at least, besides his own; and the more unlike his own, the better" (29). At the same time, the English critic can be truly cosmopolitan only if he or she "regards Europe as being, for intellectual and spiritual purposes [*not* for political and economic ones, as in today's "European Community"], one great confederation, bound to a joint action and working to a common result" (29). Arnold also preempts charges of Eurocentrism when he adds that the members of his cosmopolitan critical community should have, "for their proper outfit, a knowledge of Greek, Roman, and Eastern antiquity, and of one another" (29). Here, then, Arnold advocates Goethe's principle of world literature based on a thorough knowledge of and mutual respect for all cultural traditions.

One could certainly argue that Arnold's desideratum for a holistic criticism oriented toward right (defined, irenically, as responsive understanding rather than force) founders on the historical or practical limitations of his own thought. In *Culture and Anarchy*, for example, Arnold advocates violent means in dealing with the so-called Hyde Park riots and so appeals to a mentality of power incommensurable with his principle of "sweetness and light": "Monster-processions in the streets and forcible irruptions into the parks, even in professed support of [a] good design, ought to be unflinchingly forbidden and repressed."[8] In typical rationalist fashion, Arnold fears "anarchy," which he interprets negatively as the war of all against all (rather than positively, as the absence of all war) and advocates social order at any cost, including violent repression. In the first edition of the book (1869), Arnold further justifies his rationalist position by citing his father's similar political views. After criticizing "the badness and foolishness of the government" as well as the "harm and dangerousness of our feudal and aristocratical constitution of society," Dr. Arnold, the Rugby school principal, adds: "As for rioting, the old Roman way of dealing with *that* is always the right one; flog the rank and file, and fling the ring leaders from the Tarpeian rock!"

Although this passage (excised from subsequent editions of *Culture and Anarchy*) could be construed as hidden irony, playfully invoking one of Dr. Arnold's classical admonitions to his Rugby students, it has drawn appropriate criticism from Arnold's contemporaries as well as from twentieth-century critics. For example, one Victorian critic, J. M. Robertson, notes: "The most odiously irrational advice ever given to a modern British Government in a time of perturbation comes from a professed cultivator of sweetness and light, echoing a dictum which, even in the darkened age when it was first pronounced, was stupidly and insanely cruel."[9] More recently, Lionel Trilling writes that, in *Culture and Anarchy* as a whole, Arnold "will have both 'force' and 'right'; confusion results— and Arnold's *criticism* retires before the brutal questions of power."[10] To turn Arnold upon himself, then, the function of criticism at the present time would also be to direct a free play of thought onto his rationalist views of force, responsibility, and social order—a complex task that exceeds the scope of the present discussion.

But one should not summarily dismiss Arnold's thought as an outgrowth of an elitist, bourgeois ideology, the way some contemporary Marxist critics tend to do in the wake of Lionel Trilling and Raymond Williams, who were, as a rule, less extreme and more sympathetic in their evaluations. It is unfair to apply to Arnold the kind of narrow, political interpretation that he himself attempts to steer away from in his critical work. Even though he is occasionally unable to rise above the practical limitations of his social and psychoemotional background, at least he makes a sincere attempt to formulate a mode of thinking, acting, and feeling that leaves this background behind. At any rate, one can perhaps further adjust Arnold's notion of cultural criticism as ludic-irenic play by comparing it with those of John Ruskin and Oscar Wilde.

2. Play and Irenic Mentality in Ruskin's "The Crown of Wild Olive"

Like Arnold, Ruskin is fully aware of the rejuvenating role that art and play can have in modern culture. No less than Arnold, Ruskin attempts to conceptualize his irenic holistic view of the world in ludic terms, but his interest also lies in the social aspects of play that in Arnold are somewhat muted. Ruskin's views on play, literature, and culture are scattered throughout his work. He, like Arnold, is an unsystematic thinker by choice. But for the present purpose we can focus on his collection of lectures entitled *The Crown of Wild Olive* (1866), particularly on the preface and the first three essays, "Work," "Traffic," and "War."

Ruskin's preface begins with a striking description of the deteriorating ecological condition of the lowland surrounding the springs of Wandel in South England, which to him is a symbol for the deteriorating condition of the modern soul in an industrial age. Like Arnold, he blames the practical, utilitarian mentality of his contemporaries, who are not only competitive, avaricious, and selfish, but also joyless, peaceless, and chronically unhealthy. He dispels the bourgeois myth of social and moral progress by arguing that, from the standpoint of the common man, the only difference between the feudal lord of yore and today's capitalist—or, as he puts it metaphorically, between the "modern acquisitive power of the capital" and "that of the lance and sword"—is that one "comes as an open robber, the other as a cheating peddler," for "the levy of black-mail in old times was by force, and is now by cozening."[11]

Ruskin challenges the utilitarian political economy of his day, contending that "the great question is, not so much what money you have in your pocket, as what you will buy with it, and do with it." So it matters less how much a man is paid for his work than what kind of work he is called upon to perform: "If his labor is so ordered as to produce food, and fresh air, and fresh water, no matter that his wages are low;—the food and fresh air and water will be at last there; and he will at last get them. But if he is paid to destroy food and fresh air or to produce iron bars instead of them, —the food and air will finally *not* be there, and he will *not* get them, to his great and final inconvenience" (14). Like Arnold, then, Ruskin believes that it is a certain mentality that produces certain favorable or unfavorable material conditions, rather than the other way around.

According to Ruskin, the adverse social effects of a utilitarian mentality are further aggravated by the modern loss of faith in a just, gentle, and forgiving God. By now an agnostic himself, Ruskin confesses that he does not know how to appeal to his audience in order to affect their mode of thought, feeling, and behavior. Nevertheless, he sets out to demonstrate that the ideals of peace and social justice, whether derived from Christian faith or not, ought to be as important to the nonbeliever as they presumably are to the believer, if indeed not more so. For this purpose, Ruskin employs an extended game metaphor, worth citing in full:

> If your life were but a fever fit,—the madness of a night, whose follies were all to be forgotten in the dawn, it might matter little how you fretted away the sickly hours,—what toys you snatched at, or let fall,—what visions you followed wistfully with the deceived eyes of sleepless phrenzy. Is the earth only an hospital? Play, if you care to play, on the floor of the hospital dens. Knit its straws into what crowns please you; gather the dust of it for treasure, and die rich in that, clutching at the black motes in the air with your dying hands;—and yet it may be well with you. But if this life be no dream, and the world no hospital, but your palace-inheritance;—if all the peace and power and joy you can ever win, must be won now; and all fruit of victory gathered here, or never;—will you still, throughout the puny totality of your life, weary yourselves in the fire for vanity? (24)

Here Ruskin's ludic metaphor reveals itself as both an ironic reversal of Pascal's bet and a Socratic reversal of the heroic contest. In a first move, Ruskin suggests that if the religious believer can afford to waste his earthly sojourn, wagering on God's existence and, consequently, on his infinite love and mercy, the nonbeliever has no such luxury because he must live a meaningful life here and now, having no hope for a future one.

In a second move, Ruskin attempts (much like Socrates in Plato's *Republic*) to transvaluate the agonistic values of his culture from a ludic-irenic perspective, pointing out that a joyful, peaceful, and healthy life is the most reasonable goal for the Christian and the non-Christian alike. It is in this context that he invokes the legend of the Olympic crown of wild olive through which, he implies, Zeus taught his worshippers the same lesson of peace and social harmony that Christ did. According to Ruskin, the ancient Greeks "knew that life brought its contest, but they expected from it also the crown of all contest: No proud one! no jewel-led circlet flaming through Heaven above the height of the unmerited throne; only some few leaves of wild olive, cool to the tired brow, through a few years of peace. It should have been of gold they thought; but Jupiter was poor; this was the best the god could give them. Seeking a greater than this, they had known it a mockery. Not in war, not in wealth, not in tyranny, was there any happiness to be found for them—only in kindly peace, fruitful and free" (25). On one level, by contrasting the Christian straw crown with the Hellenic wreath of wild olive, Ruskin actually contrasts bad play to good and, by extension, a misspent life to a well-spent one, regardless of religious belief. On another level, he transforms the wreath of wild olive, which Zeus originally presented to the victors in the Olympic games, into a symbol of the vanity of all contest, the goal of which, ironically, becomes peaceful joy.

As I pointed out in the introduction, Ruskin's irenic reading of Zeus's symbolic gesture finds further resonances in book 5 of *The Odyssey*, where a wild olive bush grows closely interwoven with a tame one on the Skherian shore, offering Odysseus an ideal hideout. The episode gains increased symbolical significance if one recalls that, throughout it, Pallas-Athena is hovering protectively over the prudent hero. In antiquity, the goddess herself was often associated with a victorious olive wreath, undoubtedly because of her prowess in battle—according to legend, she issued fully armed out of Zeus's head. Because of her cephalic origin, she was equally associated with rational wisdom. It was her twofold nature of physical and intellectual force that eventually turned her into a symbol of enlightened yet bellicose Reason.[12] Her wreath, then, can truly be said to be knit of wild and tame olive branches, of war and peace, even though the Western rationalist tradition (beginning with Socrates) has always subordinated peace to war, maintaining that right must always be backed up by might. We have seen, for instance, that Matthew Arnold reverted to this bellicose rationalist tradition when he adopted, in *Culture and Anarchy*, his father's violent solution in dealing with social unrest. Ruskin, on the other hand, attempts to transcend precisely this tradition by having the crown of wild and tame olive symbolize two incommensurable, alternative mentalities, rather than subordinating one to the other. One may further note that in *The Queen of the Air*, he examines in detail the figure of Athena, downplaying her traditional rationalist role in favor of a holistic view of the human faculties, for which reason and imagination are equal partners.[13] Thereby Ruskin implicitly both endorses and revises Arnold's notion of "imaginative reason" in *Culture and Anarchy*.

Ruskin's irenic interpretation of the Olympic crown of wild olive is obviously indebted to Christianity, and in this sense one might say that he idealizes the Greek notion of contest. Yet the point he wishes to make in his preface is not historical but ethical, in the tradition of the Victorian sage, to which Arnold equally belongs.[14] Only through a peaceful, playful approach to the world can one attain joy, happiness, and a sense of fulfillment here and now and, perhaps, also in the afterlife: "Free-heartedness, and graciousness, and undisturbed trust, and requited love, and the sight of the peace of others, and the ministry to their pain;— these, and the blue sky above you, and the sweet waters and flowers of the earth beneath; and mysteries and presences, innumerable, of living things,—these may yet be your riches; untormenting and divine: serviceable for the life that now is; nor, it may be, without promise of that which is to come."[15]

In his preface, Ruskin also uses the ambivalent Olympic crown in order to introduce the Platonic view of play as good and bad, or agonistic and peaceful, turning it into both a symbol of and a model for constructive or destructive human behavior. This double view of the ludic will run throughout the essays included in *The Crown of Wild Olive*. In "Work," the distinction between good and bad play is at the center of Ruskin's argument, although he will ultimately reverse and dissolve this distinction along with all the others he bases his lecture on.

Since Ruskin is addressing a Working Men's Institute, he begins his lecture by examining the dichotomy between the "idle" class and the "working" class, which is often used interchangeably with that between the rich and the poor. Ruskin points out, however, that there is "a working class—strong and happy—among both rich and poor" and that there is also "an idle class—weak, wicked and miserable—among both rich and poor" (33). He further observes that the idea of class struggle originates among the unjust elements of both classes, because "each class has a tendency to look for the faults of the other." So a "hard-working man of property is particularly offended by an idle beggar; and an orderly, but poor, workman is naturally intolerant of the licentious luxury of the rich." As a result, "what is severe judgment in the minds of the just men of either class, becomes fierce enmity in the unjust" (33). Ruskin suggests that class tensions, as well as social injustice, could be reduced considerably, if not eliminated, should each class castigate its own rather than the other's idle elements: "If the busy rich people watched and rebuked the idle rich people, all would be right; and if the busy poor people watched and rebuked the idle poor people, all would be right" (33).

Having established that there is an idle and an industrious class among both the upper and the lower classes, Ruskin proceeds to examine the dichotomy between work and play, which initially seems to be interchangeable both with the dichotomy between idle and industrious and with that between rich and poor, but which will ultimately prove to be cutting across all boundaries as well. To begin with, Ruskin attempts to dispel the common prejudices about play that arise among all social classes. He initially opposes play to work on the criterion of usefulness or disinterestedness, but immediately acknowledges that play "may be useful, in a secondary sense" (36). He then implies that this is a purely spontaneous side effect of play rather than its nature or goal. In other words, like Arnold, Ruskin implicitly acknowledges that play is trans-cultural in nature, even though it can be given cultural value when opposed to work, a central cultural activity. Precisely because of his awareness of the transcultural nature of the ludic, Ruskin will eventually dissolve the dichotomy between work and play, by constantly turning one into the other. For the time being, however, he concentrates on the sociocultural aspects of this dichotomy.

Play in its sociocultural guise can be given either positive or negative value—it can become either good or bad—so Ruskin provisionally divides English society into a playing class and a working class. The playing class engages only in bad forms of play, such as money-making for its own sake, gambling, hunting and shooting, the ladies' game of dressing, playing at literature and art, and playing at war, the deadliest game of all. Ruskin now employs his ludic metaphor as an instrument of social criticism, and his rhetoric is effective although not inflammatory:

> The first of all English games is making money. That is an all-absorbing game; and we knock each other down oftener in playing at that, than at football, or any other roughest sport: and it is absolutely without purpose; no one who engages heartily in that game ever knows why. . . . So all that great foul city of London there,—rattling, growling, smoking, stinking,—a ghastly heap of fermenting brickwork, pouring out poison at every pore,—you fancy it is a city of work?—not a street of it! It is a great city of play. It is only Lord's cricket-ground without the turf:—a huge billiard-table without the cloth, and with pockets as deep as the bottomless pit; but mainly a billiard-table, after all. (36–37)

Ruskin argues ironically that making money, the prime activity in a utilitarian society, is in reality completely gratuitous, since it is undertaken for its own sake, rather than for the sake of worthy communal and spiritual goals. In a utilitarian society, the very meaning of the word "play" is perverted, not only by the inauthentic games of the upper classes but also by the very nature of the "work" that this society imposes on its members. To illustrate the complete corruption of both concepts, Ruskin mentions the English coal miners and steelworkers "who have all the work and none of the play," and for whom play means "being laid up by sickness." Indeed, it is "a pretty example for philologists, of varying dialect, this change in the sense of the word as used in the black country of Birmingham, and the red and black country of Baden Baden. Yes, gentlemen and gentlewomen of England . . . this is what you have brought the word 'play' to mean, in the heart of merry England!" (41).

After examining several other interrelated binary oppositions, such as production versus consumption, intellectual work versus the physical kind, and profitable labor versus wasteful labor, and demonstrating that the meanings of all these words have been distorted into their opposites by a utilitarian mentality, Ruskin attempts to restore their true meanings, which in effect involves restoring the true meaning of "play" and "work." He urges his contemporaries to renounce their selfish, utilitarian ways and adopt childlike, innocent values, such as selfless love, gentleness, modesty, charity, spontaneous trust, and cheerfulness. Once they have adopted an alternative ethopathology, they will no longer perceive work and play as separate or conflictive experiences, and Ruskin conveys a sense of what this ethopathology would be like through his metaphor of the Sun as a cheerful worker: "For lovely human play is like the Sun. There's a worker for you. He, steady to his time, is set as a strong man to run his course, but also he *rejoiceth* as a strong man to run his course [see Ps. 19:5]. See how he plays in the morning, with the mists below, and the clouds above, with a ray here, and a flash there, and a shower of jewels everywhere; that's the Sun's play; and great human play is like his—all various—all full of light and life, and tender, as the dew of the morning" (75). Here, then, Ruskin concludes with the transcultural view of play that he presented in the preface and to which he alluded at the beginning of "Work." Like Arnold, he relates this view to an irenic holistic, but not necessarily religious, world outlook that grounds not only his critique of nineteenth-century capitalist mentality but also his aesthetic notions, developed in "Traffic."

Asked to speak before an audience of Yorkshire businessmen who were seeking his professional advice on building an Exchange, Ruskin chides them for their utilitarian frame of mind that separates act from thought, religion and morality from practical affairs, and art from its physical and spiritual environment. As to the latter, he takes issue with those of his opponents who argue that artistic "taste is one thing, morality is another," advancing the provocative proposition that taste "is not only a part and an index of morality—it is the ONLY morality" (83). Of course, what Ruskin means here is that art cannot be subordinated to morality any more than play can be subordinated to utility; rather, art becomes morality just as morality becomes art. The issue, for him, is not having people *do* the right thing, as traditional morality demands, but having them *enjoy* the right thing. The object of a truly liberal education would thus be to make people "not merely industrious, but to love industry—not merely learned, but to love knowledge—not merely pure, but to love purity—not merely just, but to hunger and thirst for justice" (85).

By making people "love" something, Ruskin obviously does not mean the kind of violent engineering of human pathos practiced by O'Brien in *1984*. On the contrary, just like Arnold, he believes that no form of ethics (or aesthetics) can ever be imposed upon an individual from outside, but has to arise from the inner being of that individual. This is why he tells his audience that he can never force upon them the right principles of architecture any more than he can force upon them the right kind of morality. It is precisely a mentality of force that has brought contemporary society into a state of disarray, and Ruskin takes up his game metaphor from "Work" to describe this mentality as a bad form of play: "[Y]ou liked pop-guns when you were schoolboys, and rifles and Armstrongs are only the same things better made: but then the worst of it is, that what was play to you when boys, was not play to the sparrows; and what is play to you now, is not play to the small birds of State neither" (91).

The ethopathology of a community—which in this essay Ruskin calls either "right states of temper and moral feeling" or "a state of pure national faith," to be distinguished from ecclesiastical religion—will find expression in its art forms. To illustrate his point, Ruskin distinguishes three kinds of ethopathology manifest in different forms of worship: "the Greek, which was the worship of the God of Wisdom and Power; the Mediaeval, which was the Worship of the God of Judgment and Consolation; the Renaissance, which was the worship of the God of Pride and Beauty" (99–100). All three kinds of worship resulted in "vast temple building" (103).

According to Ruskin, the architectural expression of the first kind is the Parthenon or the temple of Pallas-Athena. The goddess herself as portrayed in her statues is a symbolic epitome of the Hellenic ethopathology in its double guise of "imperfect" and "perfect" knowledge. Imperfect or rational knowledge is embodied in her aegis or "mantle with the serpent fringes" and the "Gorgon on her shield," which are "both representative mainly of the chilling horror and madness (turning men to stone as it were), of the outmost and superficial spheres of knowledge—that knowledge which separates, in bitterness, hardness, and sorrow, the heart of the full-grown man from the heart of the child" (100–101). This imperfect, outer or purely rational knowledge engenders "terror, dissension, and disdain." Perfect, inner, or intuitive knowledge, on the other hand, engenders "strength and peace, in sign of which [Pallas-Athena] is crowned with the olive spray and bears the resistless spear" (101). True to the modern classicist tradition from Winckelmann to Lessing to Goethe to Schiller to Arnold, Ruskin believes that when outer, rational knowledge lost its foundation in the inner being, it led to the destruction of the harmonious Hellenic mentality as a whole through the "Oppositions of science, falsely so called" (103; which is, incidentally, a buried quotation from Isaac Newton).

The second kind of ethopathology is manifest in the Christian faith, whose "great doctrine is the remission of sins" as well as moral and physical comfort. In art the practical consequence of this doctrine is "a continual contemplation of sin and disease, and of imaginary states of purification from them" (102). Christian architecture, for example, conveys "a mingled sentiment of melancholy and aspiration, partly severe, partly luxuriant, which will bend itself to every one of our needs, and every one of our fancies, and be strong and weak with us, as we are strong or weak ourselves." In this respect, Christian architecture "is, of all architecture, the basest, when base people build it—of all, the noblest, when built by the noble" (102). Not unlike Nietzsche, Ruskin points out that during certain phases of Christianity "sin and sickness themselves are partly glorified" (102), and this glorification results in "false comfort" and in "remission of sins given lyingly" (103). The Christian obsession with sin and sickness shows an imbalance of the various human faculties that ultimately led to the undoing of the Christian mentality as well. Finally, the third type of ethopathology has manifested itself since the Renaissance as a "religion of Pleasure." In this case, again, excess and imbalance led to destruction. Increasingly, "all Europe gave itself to luxury, ending in death. First, *bals masqués* in every saloon, and then guillotines in every square" (103).

After completing his historical survey, Ruskin proceeds to ask his audience how he should characterize their own ethopathology so that he can suggest a corresponding architectural form for it. He points out that their object of worship is neither the Hellenic goddess of wisdom, nor the medieval god of comfort, nor the Renaissance god of pleasure; rather, it is the "Goddess of Getting-on" or "Britannia of the Market" (104). He ironically proposes that they decorate their Exchange with "pendant purses" and make "its pillars broad at the base, for the sticking of bills" (108). In the innermost chamber of this Exchange they may erect a statue of the Britannia of the Market that may display, among other emblematic items connected with the money trade, "a partridge for her crest, typical at once of her courage in fighting for noble ideas; and of her interest in game; and round its neck the inscription in golden letters, 'Perdix fovit quae non peperit' [see Jer. 17, which compares the man who gets his riches in a crooked manner to the partridge who fosters what she has not brought forth and ends up a fool]" (108–9).

The serious point of Ruskin's mordant satirical portrait, however, is that the Goddess of Getting-on cannot serve its worshipers as well or as long as the other three divinities did. For example, "Pallas and the Madonna were supposed to be all the world's Pallas and all the world's Madonna. They could teach all men and comfort all men." But the Goddess of Getting-on is "not of everybody's getting on—but only of somebody's getting on" (112), because thousands of workers must live in poverty for a single family to live in comfort. Ruskin again urges his contemporaries to give up their disguised might-makes-right mentality, according to which "they should take who have the power, and they should keep who can" (114), and he attacks the utilitarian gospel according to which "To do the best for yourself is finally to do the best for others" (117). He reminds the Christians in his audience of Christ's obverse injunction that "to do the best for others, is finally to do the best for ourselves" (117), and the non-Christians, of Plato's unfinished account, in *Critias*, of the fall of Atlantis because of its worship of the idol of riches. Only if all of his audience—believers and nonbelievers alike—find it in their hearts to replace their grasping, competitive ways with a truly irenic mentality can they hope for a bright future for themselves and their children. And then they will also have no trouble in choosing the right kind of architectural design for their temples:

> But if you can fix some conception of a true human state of life to be striven for—life for all men as for yourselves—if you can determine some honest and simple order of existence; following those trodden ways of wisdom, which are pleasantness, and seeking her quiet and withdrawn paths, which are peace;—then, and so sanctifying wealth into "commonwealth," all your art, your literature, your daily labors, your domestic affection, and citizen's duty, will join and increase into one magnificent harmony. You will know then how to build, well enough; you will build with stone well, but with flesh better; temples

not made with hands, but riveted of hearts; and that kind of marble, crimson-veined, is indeed eternal. (120–21)

Note, here, as well as throughout his book, Ruskin's highly ornamented, exuberant language of the pulpit, full of biblical resonances, hyperbolic images, and elaborate wordplay. Even though this language may sound extravagant to the late-twentieth-century ear, Ruskin's rhetoric was effective in reaching the Victorian public, and his essays were carefully designed for specific live audiences rather than for an abstract, impersonal reader. This audience-oriented approach is equally evident in "War," in which Ruskin addresses the royal cadets at Woolwich.

In "Work" Ruskin focused on the dichotomy between play and work, and in "Traffic," on the ethics of art in order to guide his contemporaries toward an alternative mode of thought, feeling, and behavior. In "War" he returns, for the same purpose, to cultural play in its most violent manifestation. He begins with the startling proposition that contest, in the guise of war, produces all cultural phenomena, including art. This was, at the time, a fairly common notion on the Continent, advanced by such cultural historians as Ernst Curtius, Jacob Burckhardt, and Friedrich Nietzsche. But Ruskin partially modifies this notion when he draws upon an equally common distinction between good and bad contest, or good and bad war. Like Nietzsche, Ruskin divides humanity into two races, "one of workers, and the other of players—one tilling the ground, manufacturing, building and otherwise providing for the necessities of life;— the other part proudly idle, and continually therefore needing recreation, in which they use the productive and laborious orders partly as their cattle, and partly as their puppets or pieces in the game of death" (136).

Unlike Nietzsche, however, Ruskin does not approve of such unfair social practices: "If you, the gentlemen of this or any other kingdom, choose to make your pastime of contest, do so, and welcome; but set not up these unhappy peasant-pieces upon the green fielded board. If the wager is to be of death, lay it on your own heads, not theirs" (136). Ruskin decries as bad the kind of violent contest in which an aristocratic elite play at war not among themselves, but "with a multitude of small human pawns" (136). He thus moves away from Nietzsche's aristocratic view of war, adopting a median position toward it. He suggests that the good kind of war is the "creative or foundational" one, "in which the natural restlessness and love of contest among men are disciplined, by consent, into modes of beautiful—though it may be fatal—play: in which natural ambition and love of power of men are disciplined into the aggressive conquest of surrounding evil: and in which the natural instincts of self-defence are sanctified by the nobleness of the institutions, and purity of the households, which they are appointed to defend" (134). In other words, for Ruskin good war is the violent contest that is carried out not for one's own sake but for the sake of others.

Based on his median criteria of good and bad contest, Ruskin also divides war into three kinds: war for "exercise or play," war for "dominion," and war for "defence," seemingly endorsing only the third kind. The war for exercise or play is, to some extent, also acceptable when fought in single combat, for example among the Hellenic heroes or the medieval knights. But Ruskin employs all of these distinctions critically, expressing his disapproval of modern war, that is, "scientific war,—chemical and mechanic war, worse even than the savage's poisoned arrow" (145). His argument finally seems to be of the median kind that Socrates employs in the *Republic*: if one were to accept the common belief that humanity is violent by nature, then one must regulate this violence and turn it into something useful for the whole community.

Johan Huizinga points out in *Homo Ludens* that Ruskin's description of war as contest seems ambiguous. Huizinga goes on to say that there is a "taint of the Superman" and a "touch of cheap illusionism" in Ruskin's essay on "War."[16] But Huizinga does not read his Ruskin carefully enough. Unlike the Dutch cultural historian, Ruskin eventually condemns all war and violence from the standpoint of moral-religious principles. Huizinga takes into account neither the aristocratic audience Ruskin was addressing (the Royal Military Academy) nor the rhetorical strategy announced in his preface to *The Crown of Wild Olive*: "For I do not speak, nor have I ever spoken, since the time of first forward youth, in any proselytizing temper, as desiring to persuade any one to believe anything; but whomsoever I venture to address, I take for the time, his creed as I find it; and endeavor to push it into such vital fruit as it seems capable of."[17]

In "War," Ruskin clearly *stages* a conflict between the agonistic mentality of his aristocratic audience (the royal cadets) and their supposedly Christian upbringing, and it is Christian values such as kindness and justice that he elevates at the end of his lecture. The goal of all contest is the wreath of wild olive, or peace. So, he implies, would it not make more sense to dispense with violent contest altogether and put an end to all war? What needs to change, Ruskin suggests, is our "idea of power itself" (153), which should always be regarded as "wise and benevolent" (154). For, he goes on, "there is no true potency . . . but that of help; nor true ambition, but ambition to save" (155).

In fact, by the end of his lecture, Ruskin turns from the cadets to the women in his audience, "to you—wives and maidens, who are the souls of soldiers; to you,—mothers who have devoted your children to the great hierarchy of war" (172). Appealing to their Christian beliefs, he chides them for allowing war to go on when it is in their power to put a stop to it within the week. His playful argument is a Victorian, expurgated version of that of Aristophanes in *Lysistrata*: "Let but every Christian lady who has conscience toward God, vow that she will mourn, at least outwardly, for His killed creatures. . . . Let every lady in the upper classes of civilized Europe simply vow, that, while any cruel war proceeds, she will wear *black*;—a mute's black,—with no jewel, no ornament, no excuse for, or evasion into, prettiness.—I tell you again, no war would last a week" (176).

Ruskin becomes serious, however, when he observes that if upper-class ladies, instead of "shrieking in one voice" with the clergymen at their Bible being attacked, will simply obey the injunctions about "judgment and justice" therein, they "will never care who attacks" it (177), for their agonistic frame of mind will have changed. All they will have to do is to understand what the Christian god "means when he tells you to be just: and teach your sons, that their bravery is but a fool's boast, and their deeds but a firebrand's tossing, unless they are indeed Just men, and Perfect in the fear of God" (177). Should they find it in their heart to change their way of thinking and believing, the world "will soon have no more war, unless it be indeed such as is willed by Him, of whom, though Prince of Peace, it is also written, 'In Righteousness He doth judge, and make war'" (177).

Ruskin's concluding statement appears again to be ambiguous, seemingly endorsing at least one form of war—the righteous, divine kind. But here, again, one should keep in mind the audience he is addressing. Throughout his essay, Ruskin employs what his audience are most familiar with—the language of war—in order to guide them toward what they are most unfamiliar with: a world of peace. From Plato to the Christian mystics, thinkers have always turned to such rhetorical strategies, attempting to convey both the infinite proximity and the infinite distance between the two incommensurable worlds of war and peace. In his Letter to the Ephesians, for example, Paul employs an agonistic vocabulary familiar to his audience in order to express irenic values that are completely alien to it: "Stand therefore, having your loins girt about with truth, and having on the breastplate of righteousness; And your feet shod with the preparation of the gospel of peace; Above all, taking the shield of faith, wherewith ye shall be able to quench all the fiery darts of the wicked. And take the helmet of salvation, and the Sword of the Spirit, which is the word of God" (Eph. 6:14–17). It is exactly this kind of language that Ruskin employs in the conclusion of "War" in order to appeal to the Christian upbringing of his audience and steer them toward an irenic world. The "war" waged by the Christian God, he implies, is directed against a warlike mentality as such, and in this sense it is, indeed, a war to end all wars.

In reading Ruskin, therefore, the critic ought to keep in mind Arnold's words about Spinoza: "A philosopher's real power over mankind resides not in his metaphysical formulas, but in the spirit and tendencies which have led him to adopt these formulas."[18] In other words, what has a lasting impact on humankind is not a thinker's theoretical schemes, but his or her ethopathology as a whole—an observation found already in Plato's seventh letter. Ruskin's holistic mentality is animated by a ludic-irenic approach to the world that seeks to turn away from power and its accompanying hermeneutics of suspicion. To Ruskin, as to Arnold, a purely utilitarian mentality is unacceptable because it shackles the free play of the mind; it reduces the array of the possible to a contingency unrelated to the whole. Only through play can humanity ultimately address this whole.

But from his holistic perspective, Ruskin also fully realizes the ambivalent nature of play when considered purely from a practical standpoint, that is, from the standpoint of the competitive and violent values of Victorian culture. Unlike Arnold, he refrains from advocating social violence in any form and for any practical purposes, no matter how justified this violence may appear from a utilitarian point of view. In this respect, he seems more consistent than Arnold in employing an irenic, holistic notion of culture as play. Ruskin's "honest and simple order of existence" based on joyfulness and peace is no other than the childlike world of great human play that he envisions at the end of his lecture "Work" and that the wreath of wild olive symbolizes.

3. Oscar Wilde and the Ludic-Irenic Self

Although Wilde is perhaps the most playful of the three Victorian think-ers under consideration here, he seems all the more aware of both the advantages and the pitfalls of a holistic notion of the ludic as applied to specific cultural contexts. Despite the fact that he couches his critical views in a provocative vocabulary, his world outlook is similar to that of the other two Victorian sages. Like Arnold and Ruskin, Wilde turns away from the dehumanizing utilitarianism of the industrial age and regards art-play as both a critical standard and a valuable instrument in fashion-ing a gentle and humane mentality. But he goes even further than his predecessors in exploring the ways in which the free play of the mind can create new cultural realities and in insisting that these realities can arise only from within the individual. In what follows, I shall briefly consider "The Critic as Artist" and "The Soul of Man under Social-ism," in which Wilde attempts to develop his notion of a ludic-irenic self under the provocative banner of individualism.

"The Critic as Artist" (1890), written as a two-part dialogue, is a self-conscious continuation of Arnold's "The Function of Criticism." It largely adopts Arnold's holistic notion of criticism as play, even though it occasionally polemicizes with him.[19] More emphatically than his pre-decessor, Wilde asserts the close interdependence of the aesthetic and the critical functions. Whereas for Arnold periods of great literary pro-duction alternate with periods of criticism, for Wilde they go hand in hand at all times. Wilde also questions some of Arnold's formulations, which, having been so often cited out of context, had by now become critical shibboleths. Note, however, that both Arnold and Ruskin never attach more than heuristic and strategic value to a critical formulation or a critical term. They dispense with it or "deconstruct" it as soon as it outlives its usefulness, and this is consistent with their deliberate refusal

of any system. What Wilde's character Vivian playfully says about himself in "The Decay of Lying" applies not only to his creator but also to
Arnold and Ruskin: "Who wants to be consistent? The dullard and the
doctrinaire, the tedious people who carry out their principles to the bitter end of action, to the *reductio ad absurdum* of practice. Not I. Like
Emerson, I write over the door of my library the word 'Whim.'"[20]

In "The Critic as Artist," Gilbert, one of the characters in the dialogue, deplores the Victorian pragmatic mentality, echoing Arnold: "Anything approaching to the free play of the mind is practically unknown
amongst us."[21] Like Arnold, Gilbert calls "disinterestedness" the ability of the critic to engage in cultural play, that is, to rise above the narrow
political interests of various factions within the polis. In turn, Gilbert
associates ludic disinterestedness both with curiosity, which "is the real
root, as it is the real flower, of the intellectual life" (978), and with the
vita contemplativa, to which, following Plato, Aristotle, and the Stoics,
he ascribes a divine origin. According to Gilbert, the Hellenic gods live
either "brooding over their own perfection" or "watching with the calm
eyes of the spectator the tragi-comedy of the world that they have made"
(980–81). There is no reason why humans cannot live like them, training themselves "to witness with appropriate emotions the varied scenes
that nature and man afford." They can make themselves spiritual by
detaching themselves from action and "become perfect by the rejection of energy." To humans, at any rate, "the *bios theoretikos* is the true
ideal" (981). In other words, Gilbert, no less than Ruskin, proposes a
new kind of ethopathology for humans, one that would allow them to
experience an alternative state of being.

From the standpoint of a practical mentality, contemplative life appears immoral, "for every kind of action belongs to the sphere of ethics,"
and thus inaction transgresses this sphere. That is why "doing nothing"
or playing for the sake of play is condemned in the utilitarian world as
"laziness" and "irresponsibility." And that is also why the critic should
insist that the "sphere of Art and the sphere of Ethics [remain] absolutely distinct and separate" (987). But for Gilbert, as for Arnold, the
"doing nothing" of the *vita contemplativa* largely remains an ideal, and
criticism is never too far away from the *vita activa*, practical life, even as
it keeps clear of its borders. He is aware that criticism assumes its disinterested position only to ascertain what is beneficial and healthy for the

community as a whole. In "beholding for the mere joy of beholding, and contemplating for the sake of contemplation," the critic will no doubt be accused of selfishness or egotism. But it is only from a detached, liminal world that he can point to practical directions: "What we want are unpractical people who see beyond the moment, and think beyond the day. Those who try to lead people can only do so by following the mob. It is through the voice of one crying in the wilderness that the ways of the gods must be prepared" (982).

Here Gilbert obviously alludes to Arnold's notion of criticism as a prophesy, in the wilderness, of the Promised Land. Earlier he had developed and somewhat modified Arnold's formulation of the relation between criticism and this Promised Land in terms of the interrelation of criticism and the artwork. According to Ernest, the other character in the dialogue, Gilbert appears to suggest that "the primary aim of the critic is to see the object as in itself it really is not" (969). This, of course, is a reversal of Arnold's formulation, according to which the aim of criticism is "to see the object as in itself it really is," and is meant to advance Pater's theory of criticism as impressionistic experience. But perhaps one should not make too much of this Paterian revision of Arnold, because Gilbert seems to use Pater's notion of aesthetic impressionism largely in order to support Arnold's view of criticism as a creative act: "To the critic the work of art is simply a suggestion for a new work of his own, that need not necessarily bear any obvious resemblance to the thing it criticizes. The one characteristic of a beautiful form is that one can put into it whatever one wishes, and see in it whatever one chooses to see; and the Beauty, that gives to creation its universal and aesthetic element, makes the critic creator in his turn" (969).

What Gilbert develops in this passage is precisely the Arnoldian notion of art and criticism as eternally incomplete expressions of the Promised Land, which I have called the liminal Void and which Gilbert calls Beauty: "It is through its very incompleteness that Art becomes complete in beauty" (970). According to Gilbert, art appeals neither to the faculty of recognition nor to the faculty of reason, but to the aesthetic sense. Although this sense accepts both reason and recognition as stages of apprehension, it subordinates them to "a pure synthetic impression of the work of art as a whole." It takes "whatever alien emotional elements the work may possess [and] uses their very complexity as a means by which a richer unity may be added to the ultimate impression itself" (970). The creative process inherent in any genuine critical apprehension thus parallels the Arnoldian process by which criticism goes beyond practice (the aesthetic equivalent of what is explicit in an artwork) to the precultural, liminal world of the ludic in order to point to new practical directions.

Gilbert also radicalizes Arnold's notion of individuality understood not as utilitarian selfishness, but as an inner quest for authenticity. At first sight, he appears again to lend this notion the impressionistic overtones of Pater's aestheticism. According to Gilbert, art "springs from personality, so it is only to personality that it can be revealed" (973). Art would seem then to be purely subjective, and criticism "in its highest development, simply a mood" (973). In this light, the critic is never more true to himself than when he is inconsistent. But Gilbert immediately erases the opposition between subject and object when he says that "man is least himself when he talks in his own person" (984). He thereby brings two nonimpressionistic elements into play: his notions of mask and dialogue. According to Gilbert, masks enable the artist not to hide but to reveal the truth of the practical world, which is manifold and eternally changing. The practical world is a play of forces, in which subjectivity and otherness continually trade places. Consequently, Gilbert claims, to arrive at "what one really believes, one must speak through lips different from its own"; and to reach the truth "one must imagine myriads of falsehoods" (986). The artist will "realize himself in many forms, and by a thousand of different ways, and will ever be curious of new sensations and fresh points of view" (987). The artist is a multiplicity of persons and masks, a role-player par excellence, in whom mask and person are one, and for whom no role is more real or fictitious than another.

Literary dialogue, in turn, is the best mode of expression for an exuberant role-playing, or donning and doffing of masks, and Gilbert points out that, through it, the artist "can both reveal and conceal himself, and give form to every fancy, and reality to every mood." Through literary dialogue, he can "exhibit the object from each point of view, and show it to us in the round, as a sculptor shows us things" (985). Wilde expects the reader to relish the irony that "The Artist as Critic" itself is a dialogue. He playfully returns upon himself when he has Ernest say that through the dialogue the artist can also "invent an imaginary antagonist, and convert him when he chooses by some absurdly sophistical argument" (985). This is a delightful Platonic allusion that undercuts the present dialogue as well. Wilde indirectly warns his reader that what he writes is metacriticism: he "kicks around" various critical ideas borrowed from Arnold, Ruskin, and Pater, thereby detaching them from their original context and opening them to the free play of the reader's mind. Wilde's essay, then, becomes in turn a form of play through which he *stages* the critical views of his mentors in a dialogical manner. Such staging allows Wilde to subject the idea of the ludic itself to subtle critical play, both questioning and developing it. His dialogical perspective encompasses and at the same time transcends his fictional world, just as the holistic play of the cosmos both encompasses and transcends the practical experience that acts as its limited stage.

Wilde is fully aware, therefore, that while role-playing and dialogue belong to the world of games rather than to that of holistic play, it is holistic play that ultimately makes both of them possible. Once Gilbert returns to this holistic perspective, he leaves behind Pater's practical world of "high passions" and "quick pulsations" and goes back to the disinterested, contemplative play of criticism. Gilbert points out, for example, that only when criticism is inspired by such holistic play can it become truly cosmopolitan. Only by "insisting upon the unity of the human mind in the variety of its forms" (996) can it rise above all passions and pulsations, above all practical differences and prejudices. Yet one does not arrive at such unity by imposing a pragmatic program or system on others, but by moving away from all systems and practical schemes. Gilbert cites the failure of the Manchester school "to make men realise the brotherhood of humanity by pointing out the commercial advantages of peace" (995). According to him, this utilitarian school fell far short of its task because it "addressed itself to the lowest instincts," seeking to "degrade the wonderful world into a common market-place for the buyer and the seller." The consequence was that war "followed upon war, and the tradesman's creed did not prevent France and Germany from clashing together in bloodstained battle" (995).

Nor can one arrive at an irenic unity of the human mind by emotional appeals to "the shallow dogmas of some vague system of abstract ethics," such as are advanced by various peace societies with their pro-

posals for unarmed international arbitration, "so dear to the sentimen-
talists" and "so popular among those who have never read history" (995).
Echoing Ruskin in "War," Gilbert suggests that as long as one operates
within a mentality of power, one must obey its logic and maintain peace
by force: "There is only one thing worse than Injustice, and that is Justice without her sword in her hand. When Right is not Might, it is Evil"
(995). It is only by consistently developing the "habit of intellectual
criticism" that humankind will succeed in creating a cosmopolitan, alternative mentality based on the irenic principle of responsive understanding, the idea of which Gilbert, like Arnold, traces back to Goethe
(996). Then war, Gilbert points out, will also disappear in a natural and
spontaneous manner:

> If we are tempted to make war upon another nation, we shall remem-
> ber that we are seeking to destroy an element of our own culture, and
> possibly its most important element. As long as war is regarded as
> wicked, it will always have its fascination. When it is looked upon as
> vulgar, it will cease to be popular. The change will, of course, be slow,
> and people will not be conscious of it. They will not say "We will not
> war against France because her prose is perfect," but because the
> prose of France is perfect, they will not hate the land. Intellectual
> criticism will bind Europe together in bonds far closer than those that
> can be forged by shopman or sentimentalist. It will give us the peace
> that springs from understanding. (996)

By playfully arguing that people will not wage war against France
because French prose is perfect, Gilbert makes the serious Ruskinian
point that ethics and aesthetics can never be separated within an irenic
mentality. He further develops this point by comparing the relation between aesthetics and ethics with the relation between sexual and natural selection: "Ethics, like natural selection, make existence possible.
Aesthetics, like sexual selection, make life lovely and wonderful, fill it
with new forms, and give it progress, and variety and change" (997).
Most importantly, a consistent aesthetic approach to human life will
lead to a new form of morality, not based on compulsion, deprivation, or
suffering but on limitless, cosmopolitan free expression: "When we reach
the true culture that is our aim, we attain to that perfection of which the
saints have dreamed, the perfection of those to whom sin is impossible,

not because they make the renunciations of the ascetic, but because they can do everything they wish without hurt to the soul, and can wish for nothing that can do the soul harm" (997). It is precisely the composed, patient, and innocent quest for the inner soul, leading to responsive understanding and an awareness of the irenic unity of all being, that Wilde calls "individualism." This kind of individualism has little to do either with egotistic and voluntaristic individuality or with sociopolitical role-playing, for as Gilbert observes, "it is so easy to convert others," but it "is so difficult to convert oneself" (986), and Wilde explores its full implications in "The Soul of Man under Socialism" (1895).

The title of Wilde's essay might be misleading, especially for those readers who expect him to make the usual apology for socialism by opposing it to individualism. In fact, the reverse is true, for Wilde declares from the outset that "Socialism itself will be of value simply because it will lead to Individualism."[22] He also sounds a prophetic warning against socialist or communist totalitarianism: "If the Socialism is Authoritarian; if there are Governments armed with economic power as they are now with political power; if, in a word, we are to have Industrial Tyrannies, then the last state of man will be worse than the first" (1019). Whereas under the present capitalist system, "a very large number of people can lead lives of a certain amount of freedom and expression and happiness, under an industrial-barrack system, or a system of economic tyranny, nobody would be able to have any such freedom at all" (1021). According to Wilde, it is certainly regrettable that under capitalism "a portion of our community should be practically in slavery, but to propose to solve the problem by enslaving the entire community is childish" (1021). He points out, moreover, that "many of the socialistic views that I have come across seem to me to be tainted with ideas of authority, if not actual compulsion. Of course authority and compulsion are out of the question. All association must be quite voluntary. It is only in voluntary associations that man is fine" (1021).

For Wilde, as for many political thinkers today, the crucial question to be answered is how individualism, which seems always to have been "dependent on the existence of private property for its development, will benefit by the abolition of such private property" (1022), the latter being a main practical objective of any socialist program. Wilde believes, however, that the interdependence of individualism and private property is a utilitarian myth. In his eyes, the recognition of private property has had an adverse effect on the development of the individual "by confusing a man with what he possesses" and making gain, rather than growth, his main life goal. Humans have thus come to believe that the important thing is to have rather than to be. It is in this sense that private property "has crushed true Individualism, and set up an Individualism that is false" (1022).

According to Wilde, "the true perfection of man lies, not in what man has, but in what man is" (1022). This is also the meaning of the simple but profound message that Christ brought to the world: "Be thyself" (1024). Christ was not against wealth as such or even private property as such. He simply understood that obsession with outer material concerns inevitably hampered an individual's inner development. He believed that "It is within you, and not outside of you, that you will find what you really are, and what you really want" (1025). Christ taught his apostles to be true individualists, always to be themselves and not worry about accepted values or public opinion: "The things people say of a man, does not alter the man. He is what he is. Public opinion is of no value whatsoever" (1025). Although the world as presently constituted hates true individualists and invariably persecutes them, they should not allow themselves to be swayed from their course. If someone took their cloak, they should also give him their coat to show that material possessions are unimportant.

Individualism, therefore, means also doing away with selfishness and egotism, which are not unrelated to the idea of private property and equally hamper the inner development of the individual. Wilde argues that in a utilitarian society, selfishness "always aims at creating around it an absolute uniformity as a delightful thing, accepts it, acquiesces in it, enjoys it" (1040). On the other hand, thinking for oneself, as any true individualist will do, can be neither selfish nor egotistic: "For the egotist is he who makes claims upon others, and the Individualist will not desire to do that. It will not give him pleasure. When man has realised Individualism, he will also realise sympathy and exercise it freely and spontaneously" (1040).

Those who think for themselves will also realize that a mentality of power is intolerable and will not be afraid to dispense with any form of authority. So Wilde believes that socialism based on true individualism should renounce all idea of government. From an individualistic standpoint, all historical forms of government have failed: "Despotism is unjust to everybody, including the despot, who was probably made for better things. Oligarchies are unjust to the many, and ochlocracies are unjust to the few. High hopes were once formed of democracy; but democracy means simply the bludgeoning of the people by the people for the people. It has been found out. I must say that it was high time, for all authority is quite degrading. It degrades those who exercise it, and degrades those over whom it is exercised" (1026). What is degrading about authority is the inescapable logic of force on which it is based: "Wherever there is a man who exercises authority, there is a man who resists authority" (1023).

In Wilde's eyes, those who rebel are no better than those who rule, because they simply perpetuate the cycle of violence and injustice. He suggests that Christ was fully aware of this fact, for even though he questioned the root of all authority he did not rebel against it. For example, Christ "accepted the imperial authority of the Roman empire and paid tribute"; he also "endured the ecclesiastical authority of the Jewish Church, and would not repel its violence by any violence of his own" (1042). Therefore Christ was not only the first true individualist, but also the first true pacifist. He taught his disciples that even if someone resorts to physical violence against them, they should not be violent in turn. That would mean descending to the same low level: "After all, even in prison, a man can be quite free. His soul can be free. His personality can be untroubled. He can be at peace" (1025). For Christ, then, the "note of the perfect personality is not rebellion but peace" (1023).

According to Wilde, art is an avant-garde expression of the ludic-irenic mentality that socialism aspires toward and it can therefore serve as both a model and a goal for all human endeavor. Because art already represents the highest form of individualism available in our world, it appears to us as "a disturbing and disintegrating force," but precisely therein "lies its immense value"; for what art "seeks to disturb is monotony of type, slavery of custom, tyranny of habit, and the reduction of man to the level of a machine" (1030). A community's negative and inappropriate responses toward its aesthetic productions can be traced back to its "barbarous conception of authority," i.e., back to its mentality of power. Such responses derive "from the natural inability of a community corrupted by authority to understand or appreciate Individualism." They derive from "that monstrous and ignorant thing that is called Public Opinion, which, bad and well-meaning as it is when it tries to control action, is infamous and of evil meaning when it tries to control Thought or Art" (1033).

Wilde suggests that what art can teach the community is precisely a "temperament of receptivity" or responsive understanding, in other words, how to relate to the Other and otherness in an irenic manner: "If a man approaches a work of art with any desire to exercise authority over it and the artist, he approaches it in such a spirit that he cannot receive any artistic impression from it at all. The work of art is to dominate the spectator: the spectator is not to dominate the work of art. The spectator is to be receptive. He is to be the violin on which the master is to play. And the more completely he can suppress his own silly views, his own foolish prejudices, his own absurd ideas of what Art should be, or should not be, the more likely he is to understand and appreciate the work of art in question" (1035). By the same token, should the spectator seek to exercise authority over the artwork, "he becomes the avowed enemy of Art, and of himself." In that case, however, it is the spectator who suffers, not the aesthetic work, for "Art does not mind" (1036), always moving beyond the reach of those who do not know how to approach it.

What art can teach its community is not only an alternative ethos but also an alternative pathos. According to Wilde, within a world of power, human beings tend to sympathize only with suffering, illness, misery, and sacrifice. Art, on the other hand, teaches them how to sympathize "with the entirety of life, not with life's sores and maladies merely, but with life's joy and beauty and energy and health and freedom" (1040). Given the "modern stress of competition and struggle for place," one tends to sympathize with another's defeats rather than with another's victories. The latter kind of sympathy is "very much stifled by the immoral ideal of uniformity of type and conformity to rule which is so prevalent everywhere, and is perhaps most obnoxious in England" (1041). It would require an unselfish disposition, completely different from the present one, for an affirmative type of sympathy to take root in the community. As Wilde notes ironically, anyone can "sympathise with the sufferings of a friend, but it requires a very fine nature—it requires, in fact, that nature of a true Individualist—to sympathise with a friend's success" (1041).

Art can help create the kind of affirmative individualism that expresses itself through joy. It is a prime example of the fact that pain need not be "the ultimate mode of perception." Indeed, Wilde argues, pain "is merely provisional and a protest," being only a symptom of "wrong, unhealthy, unjust surroundings" (1042). On the other hand, pleasure, including the aesthetic kind, "is Nature's test, her sign of approval. When man is happy, he is in harmony with himself and his environment" (1043). Here Wilde's vision of the alternative irenic self that will replace its utilitarian counterpart comes very close to that of Ruskin, striking the same exhilarating, prophetic chord:

> It will be a marvelous thing—the true personality of man—when we see it. It will grow naturally and simply, flowerlike, or as a tree grows. It will not be at discord. It will never argue or dispute. It will not prove things. It will know everything. And yet it will not busy itself about knowledge. It will have wisdom. Its value will not be measured by material things. It will have nothing. And yet it will have everything, and whatever one takes from it, it will still have, so rich will it be. It will not be always meddling with others, or asking them to be like itself. It will love them because they will be different. And yet while it will not meddle with others, it will help all, as a beautiful thing helps us, by being what it is. The personality of a man will be very wonderful. It will be as wonderful as the personality of a child. (1023)

The question may be asked how Wilde proposes to carry out his socialist ideal in practice. A child of his age, he places his trust in technological progress. He believes that machines will carry out the manual labor that in the past was carried out by slaves, serfs, industrial workers, and so on. Although up to now "man has been, to some extent, the slave of machinery" (1028), individualistic socialism will create the proper conditions under which the relation between human beings and machines will be reversed. Consequently, "just as trees grow while the country gentleman is asleep, so while Humanity will be amusing itself, or enjoying cultivated leisure—which, and not labour, is the aim of man—

or making beautiful things, or reading beautiful things, or simply contemplating the world with admiration and delight, machinery will be doing all the necessary and unpleasant work" (1028).

Wilde believes, as Nietzsche does, that one cannot deny the fact that "civilization requires slaves," a fact that the ancient Greeks fully recognized: "Unless there are slaves to do the ugly, horrible, uninteresting work, culture and contemplation become almost impossible" (1028). Unlike Nietzsche, however, Wilde also believes that "human slavery is wrong, insecure, and demoralising" and that one should therefore resort to a different kind of slavery: "On mechanical slavery, on the slavery of the machine, the future of the world depends" (1028). Anticipating charges of utopianism, he adds: "A map of the world that does not include Utopia is not even worth glancing at, for it leaves out the one country at which Humanity is always landing. And when Humanity lands there, it looks out, and, seeing a better country, sets sail. Progress is the realisation of Utopias" (1028).

From a contemporary standpoint and from Wilde's own ludic-irenic critical perspective, one can hardly subscribe to his socialist practical vision. It seems obvious that Wilde was unable to rise entirely above the utilitarian mentality he abhorred so much. Although, a hundred years later, public opinion (in Wilde's sense) still shares his faith in industrial utopias or in technological progress as a cure of all social evils, there are also numerous visionary thinkers and artists who recognize that machines are simply extensions of ourselves and that, consequently, it will not do to treat them like slaves—for we would again only enslave part of ourselves. A consistently irenic-ludic frame of mind (which Wilde himself advances in this and other essays) would, on the contrary, approach machines with the same kind of responsive understanding that it approaches other human beings, or, indeed, the world as a whole. Nor can it accept the idea of utopia—whether political, economical, or spiritual—without first turning an Arnoldian fresh stream of thought on it, especially after the ghastly utopian experiments (mostly of the socialist kind) that have plagued our century. Rather than prescribing any specific practical course of action for humanity, whether socialist or otherwise, irenic-ludic criticism should simply endeavor to steer humans gently toward an alternative mentality. In turn, this mentality—as Arnold, Ruskin, and Wilde himself point out, will of itself create an infinite number of practical courses in a spontaneous manner. Then, indeed, many alternative worlds will come "naturally and inevitably out of man" (1039) rather than, in some utopian fashion, to him.

One can, however, wholeheartedly subscribe to Wilde's assumption regarding the infinite plasticity of human nature, without which no change would be conceivable at all. What I have predicated about a ludic-irenic mentality can find its support only in this assumption, and Wilde's argument is the best that anyone can employ in its favor: "It will, of course, be said that such a scheme as is set forth here [individualistic socialism in Wilde's case, a ludic-irenic mentality in the case of the present book] is quite unpractical, and goes against human nature. This is perfectly true. It is unpractical, and it goes against human nature. This is why it is worth carrying out, and that is why one proposes it. For what is a practical scheme? A practical scheme is either a scheme that is already in existence, or a scheme that could be carried out under existing conditions. But it is exactly the existing conditions that one objects to; and any scheme that could accept these conditions is wrong and foolish. The conditions will be done away with, and human nature will change. The only thing that one really knows about human nature is that it changes" (1039). As Wilde implies and as I have argued throughout this study, one cannot learn how to "fly beyond the atmosphere" (in Schopenhauer's words) unless one first completely accepts the possibility of such flying from an intellectual, imaginative, and emotional standpoint.

In conclusion, let us review briefly the common principles that inform Arnold, Ruskin, and Wilde's idea of cultural criticism. Their basic assumption is that a certain mentality (or a certain way of thinking, behaving, and feeling) determines the kinds of institutions and socioeconomic structures present in any community. To be sure, institutions and socioeconomic structures can in turn reinforce and perpetuate the mentality that produces them. But criticism begins by diagnosing the mentality of a certain community before it attempts to reform its institutions. This mentality, moreover, can never be changed by outside forces but only from within, for all genuine social transformation is self-transformation.

For the Victorian sages, criticism is a responsible activity, not in the sense of a moral imperative, but in the sense of a certain responsiveness or openness toward others and otherness. Thus, criticism is a creative activity grounded in the kind of responsive understanding that is characteristic of any irenic mentality. As such, it adopts an empathic rather than an agonistic or hostile attitude towards its object. Criticism becomes a form of holistic medicine in which the diagnosis takes into account the overall condition of the patient, both physical and spiritual, before any remedy can be prescribed.

Finally, for Arnold, Ruskin, and Wilde, criticism is a form of play, i.e., a liminal, *as if* mode of being that implies both involvement in and detachment from a practical state of affairs. In this latter sense, criticism becomes a playground suitable for the creation and imaginative enactment of human values that are often incommensurable with those embraced by the community out of which criticism arises and to which it is normally addressed. It is no longer called upon to establish literary canons and promote or demote literary reputations. It aims at healing and bringing together, rather than dividing, the polis it serves. Criticism as play avoids getting directly involved in partisan strife and places itself in a no-man's land, from which it can propose suitable courses of action. It moves continually between the contemplative life and the active, knowing, in Arnold's words, when to attach itself to things and when to disengage itself from them.

The playful critic, in turn, learns how to steer a delicate course between pragmatics and aesthetics, between history and the imagination. His or her critical stances are gentle and cosmopolitan, free in the interplay of mind and experience. Sociopolitically, the critic lacks prejudice and is open to dialogue. S/he respects plurality and otherness, fostering a sense of human justice, responsibility, and tolerance. Cultural play may be perceived as competitive and rough, but there are alternative perceptions and even alternative experiences. For all his extravagant metaphors, Ruskin gently reminds us that the reward for our creative pleasures lies in a wreath of wild olive rather than a crown—or even Mara's mountain—of gold.

Notes

Introduction

1. John Ruskin, *The Crown of Wild Olive* (New York, 1905), 25. I discuss Ruskin's collection at length in chapter 7, section 2, below.

2. Homer, *The Odyssey,* trans. R. Fitzgerald (New York, 1954), bk. 5, lines 498–503.

3. By "power" here, as well as throughout my study, I understand a self-generated, historical principle that organizes human existence and relations in terms of force, exerted by individuals and communities upon each other and upon their environment. Power can be either violent or nonviolent, coercive or persuasive, physical or psychological, and can assume both immediate and mediated symbolical forms. Whereas it can start out being concrete, specific, and obvious, especially in the early developmental stages of a particular community, it can end up being abstract, sublimated, and obscure, eluding all definition. In turn, by "mentality" I understand not only the predominant behavior and thought patterns of a certain community but also the psychophysiological and emotional makeup or the *pathos* that both underlies and upholds this community's body of values and beliefs. In this sense, for me, the mentality of a specific community produces certain kinds of socioeconomic and political structures or certain kinds of institutions (rather than the other way around), although these structures or institutions can in turn reinforce and perpetuate a certain mentality.

Finally, by an "irenic" mentality, I mean a mode of thought, behavior, and pathos grounded in the principle of peace (the adjective "irenic" comes from the Greek noun εἰρήνη, peace), understood not as antinomic to war, but as incommensurable with and therefore inaccessible to the power principle. For a full discussion of these basic assumptions, see chapters 1, 2, and 3 below.

*Chapter 1. Nietzsche or Schopenhauer: Can One
Construct an Alternative Mentality?*

1. See Mihai I. Spariosu, *Dionysus Reborn: Play and the Aesthetic Dimension in Modern Philosophical and Scientific Discourse* (Ithaca, N.Y., 1989), 68–99.

2. Friedrich Nietzsche, *The Genealogy of Morals: An Attack*, trans. Francis Golffing (New York, 1956), 151.

3. Although some of Nietzsche's etymologies may often sound fanciful to the modern philologist, in this particular case he seems to be on the right historical track. Many of his insights about the agonistic nature of archaic values, for example in ancient Greece, have been cast into acceptable scholarly form by such well-respected classicists as E. R. Dodds, Arthur W. Adkins, Eric A. Havelock, and Walter Burkert. One may also hope for a reversal in the current tendency of Anglo-American classicists to regard etymology as an unsound scientific method of investigation. This tendency may in part be an overreaction to the playful uses to which etymology has lately been put in literary and philosophical studies by certain Heideggerian poststructuralists. But even these playful etymologies, when used sparingly and tactfully, can be of help in illustrating certain theoretical points and need not be discarded out of hand.

4. Nietzsche, *Genealogy*, 167.

5. In *Dionysus Reborn*, 7–9, I offered a schematic list of the main features that give a predominantly archaic or median orientation to a certain community, ethnic-geographic area, or historical period. The terms I used there were "prerational" and "rational," but I have since then replaced them by "archaic" and "median" in order to eliminate the appearance of invoking an evolutionary model of cultural development based on rationalist criteria, which was definitely not my intention. I have substantially revised this list in other ways as well and, because I shall refer to elements of it throughout the present study, it may be useful to reproduce it here in its updated form:

(1) *Power.* An archaic mentality conceives of power as physical, naked, and immediate. Authority largely depends on physical strength and cunning intelligence. Competition takes precedence over cooperation, and violence or the threat thereof is commonly employed in resolving conflicts. An archaic mentality tends as a rule to create hierarchical and authoritarian forms of government.

By contrast, in a predominantly median community power becomes increasingly mediated and/or shared. Authority depends less on physical strength than on intellectual ability, superior knowledge, and public truthfulness. Cooperation and social consensus are increasingly emphasized, although they remain subordinated to competition. Violence is less commonly employed in resolving conflicts and is regulated by the social body at large. A median mentality can create a variety of forms of government, ranging from the more centralized and hierarchical kinds with a king or an autocrat representing the gods or the people, to more democratic kinds, in which power is shared by an elected, rotating body of citizens, delegated to represent the will of the majority.

(2) *Justice.* In an archaic world, customary law prevails according to the principle of might makes right. Justice is largely a private matter that concerns the community only indirectly. Right is restored by violent means, according to the principle of blood revenge or retribution *(lex talionis).* The interests of the strong take precedence over those of the weak. Shame rather than guilt is the most effective social censor.

By contrast, in a median world, written law often replaces or coexists with customary law, according to the principle of might *and* right. A median mentality effects a conscious separation between power and justice: right becomes separated from might, but also right is protected by might. Justice turns from a largely private matter into a public one. Moral responsibility toward the community takes precedence over individual merit. Although right is still restored by violent means, violence is strictly regulated by the community, and the principle of reciprocity generally prevails over the principle of retribution. The interests of the weak are, as a rule, emphasized over those of the strong, and guilt rather than shame becomes the most effective social censor.

(3) *Religion.* In an archaic world, religion is generally animistic and/or anthropomorphic with centralized, hierarchical, and violent societies of gods, conceived as extensions of human societies—the difference between men and gods resides in degree rather than kind of power. Gods communicate directly with humans, especially through voices, and they are amoral, violent, and arbitrary. Sacrificial rituals are the most effective mechanism of appeasing vengeful gods and purging human communities of violence.

By contrast, in a median world, gods become increasingly abstract and removed, and they can often be replaced by an impersonal, transcendental power, e.g., in monotheism. They generally hide from and no longer communicate directly with humans, appearing only to a privileged few, indirectly, in portents and visions or in oracular states of possession-madness. Religious cults remain sacrificial, although scapegoat rituals become increasingly abstract and symbolic. Human sacrifice comes to be perceived as "unnatural," and real scapegoats are replaced by surrogates. Religious ritual becomes less and less violent and the gods become increasingly moral and rational.

(4) *Consciousness.* An archaic mentality is often also a preconscious one, with the auditory taking precedence over the visual. In many cases, an archaic mentality is a predominantly oral one as well. The voice is an important source of authority: to hear is to obey. Speech is "thought" whose seat is not the brain, but the lungs or the diaphragm. An archaic mentality does not distinguish between speech and action, cognition and emotion. Language is concrete and practical, having poetical or performative power and being structured according to mnemonic rather than visual, rational principles.

By contrast, a median mentality is largely a conscious one, with the preconscious mind becoming gradually incorporated into it as its "unconscious" or "subconscious" component. The visual replaces the auditory as the main seat of perception. Whereas emotions remain located in the diaphragm or the lungs, understanding moves to the brain, and consciousness is born as a result of this split. Language becomes increasingly abstract and logical, whereas thought becomes dialectical or based on binary oppositions. Writing emerges and spreads to an ever broader section of the community, and a median mentality is often also a literate one.

(5.) *Education and Knowledge.* In an archaic community, education consists mainly of physical and occupational training as well as of what archaic Greece calls μουσική, that is, an amalgam of poetry-reciting, music-making, and dancing. Although archaic communities practice a division of labor, their idea of knowledge (as distinguished from that of individual skills) is holistic. Μουσική is "wisdom" (σοφία in its archaic sense), that is, a mechanism of preservation and transmission of dominant cultural values as well as a mechanism of ethnic and social cohesion. Poetic performance is carried out by the singer of tales, who is the mouthpiece of tradition rather than an individual "author." There is a complete identification between rhapsode and audience through mimesis-play.

By contrast, in median, literate communities there occurs a division of knowledge, with philosophy, history, rhetoric, natural science, jurisprudence, and so on, replacing μουσική as main cultural authority. Μουσική itself breaks up into individual "arts" (poetry, music, dancing, and the like) while poetry is written down and becomes literature. The science of interpretation (hermeneutics) develops from the old art of divination and becomes the most important critical instrument of producing texts. History as written documentation replaces oral tradition as μῦθος (which a literate mind treats as fiction) in its function of preserving and transmitting dominant cultural values. The singer of tales becomes separated from the audience and turns into a "poet" (a maker of literary texts) or an individual author-authority.

For a full examination of these archaic and median features in ancient Greece, see Mihai Spariosu, *God of Many Names: Play, Poetry, and Power in Hellenic Thought, from Homer to Aristotle* (Durham, N.C., 1991). In the present chapter, as well as in subsequent ones, I have also chosen many of my historical examples from ancient Greece: Hellenic culture was obviously what Nietzsche knew and loved best, drawing most of his philosophical and historical insights from it.

6. For the Mycenaean notion of king-priest or "steward of the gods," see, among others, L. R. Palmer, *Mycenaeans and Minoans* (London, 1960), esp. 90–99. For example, citing Nausicaa's conversation with Odysseus in the *Odyssey*, Palmer notes: "We learn that Alcinous, Wanax of Scheria and father of Nausicaa, had his τέμενος [land allocated to the Mycenean king and warriors] closely conjoined with the precincts of Athena. The link of the royal τέμενος with his religious functions appears clearly even in post-Homeric times. Herodotus records that when the constitution of Cyrene was reformed on the advice of Delphi, King Battus was allowed to keep his '*temenea* and his priesthoods'" (95). The notion of priest-king would seem to indicate that early archaic Greece was strongly influenced by its Near Eastern neighbors and did not exhibit proto-Indo-European ideological features, if we were to

believe Georges Dumézil's thesis that archaic Indo-European cultures draw a clear distinction between a priestly and a warrior caste (a thesis that Dumézil might have partly derived from Nietzsche; see, for example, Georges Dumézil, *L'idéologie tripartite des Indo-Européens* [Brussels, 1958]). It may well be, however, that the separation between a religious and a martial function is a historical rather than a generic factor, and can take place in any archaic community that is, or becomes, open to a redistribution of power among its members; this was presumably the case with some archaic communities on the Greek mainland in the aftermath of the collapse of the Mycenaean palace-culture. One therefore discerns the first signs of a "slave ethics" or a median morality both in the Greek shaman-priests or the Delphi oracle and in some of the traditional, aristocratic sages (such as Pittacus and Solon, who were legislative, political, and religious leaders in their communities, all in one). The same median mentality is equally present in Homer and Hesiod, alongside with its heroic, aristocratic counterpart.

7. Nietzsche, *Genealogy*, 165.

8. Nietzsche himself mentions the Jesuit order as promoters of a "healthy," archaic mentality. See, for example, *The Will to Power*, ed. Walter Kaufmann, trans. W. Kaufmann and R. J. Hollingdale (New York, 1967), note 783.

9. Nietzsche, *Genealogy*, 281–82.

10. For a full historical demonstration of this thesis, see Spariosu, *God of Many Names*, esp. chaps. 4 and 5.

11. Nietzsche, *Genealogy*, 217–18.

12. For a detailed examination of the relationship between Freud and Nietzsche, see, for example, Paul-Laurent Assoun, *Freud et Nietzsche* (Paris, 1980). Within the psychoanalytical movement itself, there are those who, like Otto Rank, Otto Gross, Alfred Adler, Carl Jung, and Wilhelm Reich, openly acknowledge the relevance of Nietzsche's psychological theses (particularly as developed in the *Genealogy of Morals*) to psychoanalysis, and those who, like D. W. Winnicott, Erik Erikson, and most American analysts, downplay this relevance. Since psychoanalytical theory in general attempts to deal with the modern mentality of guilt *without* envisioning, as a rule, a return to its "innocent," archaic counterpart, Nietzsche's psychological theses can also be used against psychoanalysis. A good example of a contemporary attack on psychoanalysis from a Nietzschean, "archaic" position is Gilles Deleuze and Félix Guattari's *L'anti-Oedipe: capitalisme et schizophrénie* (Paris, 1972).

13. Nietzsche, *Genealogy*, 151.

14. Nietzsche, *Will to Power*, note 814.

15. Ibid., note 815. For numerous other examples of Nietzsche's view of artistic asceticism as a positive manifestation of the will to mastery, see especially *Will to Power*, bk. 3, pt. 4: "The Will to Power as Art."

16. Nietzsche, *Genealogy*, 262.

17. Arthur Schopenhauer, *The World as Will and Representation*, trans. E. F. Payne (New York, 1958), 2:615.

18. In reference to Being, Heidegger says in *Der Satz vom Grund*: "Es spielet weil es spielet" (it plays while [or because] it plays). Of course, *Der Satz vom Grund*

itself testifies to the fact that Heidegger is vitally interested in the imaginary debate between Nietzsche and Schopenhauer regarding "mystical" and philosophical knowledge. But, as I imply in *Dionysus Reborn*, 117–24, Heidegger ultimately remains divided between the two thinkers and the two kinds of knowledge. See also my discussion of Heidegger's agonistic notion of difference in chapter 3, section 1, below.

19. Nietzsche, *Will to Power*, note 692.

20. Schopenhauer, *World as Will*, 2:613.

21. Paul Feyerabend, *Against Method: Outline of an Anarchistic Theory of Knowledge* (London, 1975), 257.

22. Feyerabend, *Against Method*, 257.

23. See Friedrich Nietzsche, *The Birth of Tragedy*, trans. F. Golffing (New York, 1956), 10.

24. Nietzsche, *Genealogy*, 290.

25. Compare Oscar Wilde's similar argument in his essay, "The Decay of Lying," where he opposes art to modern ethics in a Nietzschean fashion. For a detailed discussion of Wilde's notion of art, see chapter 7, section 3, below.

26. Nietzsche, *Genealogy*, 290.

Chapter 2. Liminality, Literary Discourse, and Alternative Worlds

1. For a detailed historical examination of the origins of the "quarrel" between poetry and philosophy in Western culture, see Spariosu, *God of Many Names*, esp. 141–235.

2. For a discussion of some of these studies in terms of a philosophy of difference, see chapter 3 below.

3. See Itamar Even-Zohar, *Polysystem Studies*, special issue of *Poetics Today* 11, nos. 1–2 (1990): 91. For further discussion of polysystem theory, see section 3 of this chapter. For Yuri Lotman's dynamic cultural functionalism, see especially *Analysis of the Poetic Text*, ed. and trans. D. Barton Johnson (Ann Arbor, Mich., 1976) and *Universe of the Mind: A Semiotic Theory of Culture*, trans. Ann Shukman (Bloomington, Ind., 1990).

4. Victor Turner, "Liminal to Liminoid, in Play, Flow, and Ritual: An Essay in Comparative Symbology," in *From Ritual to Theatre: The Human Seriousness of Play* (New York, 1982), 26.

5. In this sense, both Brian Sutton-Smith and Victor Turner can be seen as precursors of the "chaos" theory that has recently gained significant support not only in physics and the natural sciences but also in literary studies.

6. Turner, "Liminal," 28.

7. Victor Turner, *Dramas, Fields, and Metaphors: Symbolic Action in Human Society* (Ithaca, N.Y., 1974), 14.

8. Victor Turner, *The Ritual Process: Structure and Anti-Structure* (Ithaca, N.Y., 1969), 166–67.

9. Turner, "Liminal," 44.

10. See especially Giuseppe Mazzotta, *Dante, Poet of the Desert: History and Allegory in the "Divine Comedy"* (Princeton, 1979) and *The World of Play in Boccaccio's "Decameron"* (Princeton, 1986), which I shall discuss shortly; as well as the critical essays collected in *Victor Turner and the Construction of Cultural Criticism: Between Literature and Anthropology*, ed. Kathleen M. Ashley (Bloomington, Ind., 1990).

11. For Turner's exploratory, indeed ludic, temperament see Frederick Turner's fine essay entitled "'Hyperion to a Satyr': Criticism and Anti-Structure in the Work of Victor Turner," in Ashley, *Victor Turner and the Construction of Cultural Criticism*, 147–63.

12. Turner, "Liminal," 55.

13. Chögyam Trungpa, Rinpoche, commentary to *The Tibetan Book of the Dead: The Great Liberation through Hearing in the Bardo* (Boston, 1987), 10–11.

14. Turner, "Liminal," 44.

15. For Turner's attempt to distinguish between marginality and liminality, see, for example, his *Dramas, Fields, and Metaphors*, esp. 233f.

16. Compare my discussion of alternative and liminal worlds in this chapter, section 3 below.

17. Turner, "Liminal," 40.

18. For a detailed argument, see Spariosu, *God of Many Names*, 141–94.

19. See Gorgias, Fr. B 23, in H. Diels and W. Kranz, *Die Fragmente der Vorsokratiker*, 6th ed., 3 vols. (Berlin, 1952). The English translations of Gorgias are mine.

20. For a full discussion of the Platonic and Aristotelian notions of *mimesis* and their ludic implications, see Spariosu, *God of Many Names*, esp. 149–60, 197–210.

21. Aristotle, *Poetics* 1460b9–11.

22. Sir Philip Sidney, *The Defense of Poesie*, in *Literary Criticism. Plato to Dryden*, ed. Allan H. Gilbert (Detroit, 1962), 420. Sidney's essay was probably written between 1580 and 1583 and published, after Sidney's death, in two versions in 1595: *An Apologie for Poetry* (the Henry Olney edition) and *The Defense of Poesie* (the William Ponsonby edition). Most critics prefer the Ponsonby edition, which seems to have incorporated Sidney's last revisions. Allan Gilbert adopts this version as prepared by Albert Feuillerat in his edition of Sidney's *Works* (Cambridge, 1922–26).

23. For a full discussion of Schiller's theory of art as play see Spariosu, *Dionysus Reborn*, 53–65.

24. Friedrich Schiller, "Letter 23," in *On the Aesthetic Education of Man, in a Series of Letters*, ed. and trans. Elizabeth M. Wilkinson and L. A. Willoughby (Oxford, 1967), 161.

25. See Percy Bysshe Shelley, "A Defence of Poetry," in *Peacock's Four Ages of Poetry, Shelley's Defence of Poetry, and Browning's Essay on Shelley*, ed. H. F. B. Brett-Smith (Boston and New York, 1921), 23.

26. For both a history and a development of the Western concept of imagination, see Murray Wright Bundy, *The Theory of Imagination in Classical and Mediaeval Thought* (Urbana, Ill., 1927); and more recently, Cornelius Castoriadis, *L'institution imaginaire de la société* (Paris, 1975); James Engell, *The Creative Imagination: Enlightenment to*

Romanticism (Cambridge, Mass., 1981); Richard Kearney, *The Wake of Imagination: Toward a Postmodern Culture* (Minneapolis, Minn., 1984); Eva T. H. Brann, *The World of the Imagination: Sum and Substance* (Savage, Md., 1991); and Wolfgang Iser, *The Fictive and the Imaginary: Charting Literary Anthropology* (Baltimore, 1993), esp. 171–246.

27. Jean-Paul Sartre, *The Psychology of Imagination* (London, 1972), 218.

28. Giuseppe Mazzotta, *"Communitas* and its Typological Structure," in *Dante, Poet of the Desert,* 109.

29. Mazzotta, *World at Play in Boccaccio's "Decameron,"* 56.

30. Virgil Nemoianu, *A Theory of the Secondary: Literature, Progress and Reaction* (Baltimore, 1989), 202.

31. Iser, *Fictive and the Imaginary,* 4.

32. Here Iser employs D. W. Winnicott's term in *Playing and Reality* (London and New York, 1971). For Winnicott a "transitional object" is a material object such as a corner of blanket or napkin, a bundle of wool, etc., which has a special value for the infant between the ages of four and twelve months. The transitional object occupies the neutral space between the inner and the outer world of the infant, before the final split between the two occurs with the development of a self. It has lasting effects on individuals even after their infant stage is over, however, being retained throughout life "in the intense experiencing that belongs to the arts and to religion and to creative scientific work" (14). Thus Iser uses Winnicott's notion of transitional object in both a ludic and a liminal sense. For various applications of Turner's notion of liminality in psychotherapy, see Nathan Schwartz-Salant and Murray Stein, eds., *Liminality and Transitional Phenomena* (Wilmette, Ill., 1991). See also my mention of Jane Flax's application of the term in developing a feminist theory of justice in chapter 3, section 2, below.

33. See Gustavo Pérez-Firmat, *Literature and Liminality. Festive Readings in the Hispanic Tradition* (Durham, N.C., 1986), xviii.

34. See Alvin Plantinga, *The Nature of Necessity* (Oxford, 1974); Raymond Bradley and Norman Swartz, *Possible Worlds* (Oxford, 1979); Paul Davies, *Other Worlds* (London, 1980); and Saul Kripke, *Naming and Necessity* (Oxford, 1980).

35. See J. L. Austin, *How to Do Things with Words* (Cambridge, Mass., 1962); and John Searle, *Speech Acts* (Cambridge, 1969) and, especially, idem, "The Logical Status of Fictional Discourse," *New Literary History* 6 (1975): 315–30. Of course, as we have seen, the relevance of a "sincerity rule" in the case of literary discourse has already been dismissed effectively by literary theorists from Gorgias to Sidney.

36. See Nelson Goodman, *Ways of Worldmaking* (Indianapolis, Ind., 1978), 4.

37. See Floyd Merrell, *Pararealities: The Nature of Our Fictions and How We Know Them* (Amsterdam and Philadelphia, 1983), x.

38. See Thomas G. Pavel, *Fictional Worlds* (Cambridge, Mass., 1986), 26. One may also consult Pavel's short essay, "Narratives of Ritual and Desire," in Ashley, *Victor Turner and the Construction of Cultural Criticism,* where he refers directly to Turner's anthropological theory.

39. For an extensive discussion of this topic, see, for example, Terence Parsons, *Nonexistent Objects* (New Haven, 1980).

40. See Doreen Maitre, *Literature and Possible Worlds* (London, 1983), 117.

41. Merrell, *Pararealities*, x.

42. Goodman, *Ways of Worldmaking*, 7–17.

43. Itamar Even-Zohar's "polysystem theory" provides an excellent description of worlds that are organized on power-oriented or dynamic principles. For instance, defending his concept of dynamic functionalism, Even-Zohar states:

> Heterogeneity is reconcilable with functionality if we assume that rather than correlating with each other as individual items (elements or functions), the seemingly non-reconcilable items (elements or functions) constitute partly alternative systems of concurrent options. These systems are not equal, but hierarchized within the polysystem. It is the permanent struggle between the various strata, Tynjanov has suggested, which constitutes the (dynamic) synchronic state of the system. It is the victory of one stratum over another which constitutes the change on the diachronic axis. In this centrifugal vs. centripetal motion, phenomena are driven from the center to the periphery while, conversely, phenomena may push their way into the center and occupy it. However, with a polysystem one must not think of *one* center and *one* periphery, since several such positions are hypothesized. A move may take place, for instance, whereby a certain item (element, function) is transferred from the periphery of one system to the periphery of an adjacent system within the same polysystem, and then may or may not move on to the center of the latter. (*Polysystem Studies*, 13–14)

Polysystem theory, however, does not consider the possibility of worlds with radically different reference frames that are incommensurable with dynamic principles. See my argument and diagrams in this section, below.

44. See Max Jammer, *Concepts of Force: A Study in the Foundations of Dynamics* (Cambridge, Mass., 1957), 5. For introductions to Jainism, the reader may consult Jagmanderlal Jaini, *Outlines of Jainism* (1940; reprint, Westport, Conn., 1982); Bimal Krishna Matilal, *The Central Philosophy of Jainism (Anekanta-Vada)* (Ahmedabad, 1981); and Paul Dundas, *The Jains* (London and New York, 1992).

45. Early versions of these diagrams were drawn and commented upon by my former student, Cal Clements, with whom I had many delightful debates about postmodernism, alternative worlds, and higher dimensions.

46. For an extensive discussion of the incommensurability between worlds in *The Bacchae*, see Spariosu, *God of Many Names*, 103–39. I shall return to this topic in chapters 4, 5, and 6 of the present study.

47. See *The Mara Suttas*, chap. 4 in *The Book of the Kindred Sayings (Samyutta-Nikaya) or Grouped Suttas*, trans. Mrs. Rhys Davids (London, 1950), 1:145–46. I am grateful to Wyatt Benner for pointing out this passage to me.

48. See Johan Huizinga, *Homo Ludens: A Study of the Play Element in Culture* (Boston, 1950), 13.

49. Turner, "Liminality," 50.
50. Nietzsche, *Birth of Tragedy*, 24.

Chapter 3. Difference, Identity, and Otherness: A Ludic-Irenic Perspective

1. The next few paragraphs are a summation of my argument in *God of Many Names*, 58–75.
2. See Heraclitus, DK B 52, translated in Kathleen Freeman, *Ancilla to the Pre-Socratic Philosophers: A Complete Translation of the Fragments in Diels* (Oxford, 1956).
3. A primary task of an irenic mentality would therefore be to separate the notion of being from that of power and allow each to go its own way. See my argument below, in section 3 of this chapter.
4. See Martin Heidegger, *Identity and Difference*, trans. J. Stambaugh, bilingual ed. (New York, 1969), 50–51.
5. The next few pages sum up my discussion of the "artist-metaphysicians" in *Dionysus Reborn*, 99–124, shifting its focus from the question of play to that of difference. My remarks on de Man and Bataille, however, are entirely new.
6. See Georges Bataille, *Théorie de la religion*, in *Œuvres complètes* (Paris, 1974), 328; my translation.
7. Gilles Deleuze, "Renverser le Platonisme," in *Logique du sens* (Paris, 1969), 303.
8. Deleuze, *Logique du sens* (Paris, 1969), 10. All English translations are mine.
9. Jacques Derrida, "Différance," in *Margins of Philosophy*, trans. Alan Bass (Chicago, 1982), 11.
10. Derridian *différance*, as well as Derridian deconstruction, can be read in ways that do not necessarily link it to an agonistic philosophy of difference. For instance, there have been attempts to compare both *différance* and deconstruction to certain Eastern modes of thinking. See, among others, Robert Magliola, *Derrida on the Mend* (West Lafayette, Ind., 1984), Harold Coward, *Derrida and Indian Philosophy* (Albany, N.Y., 1990) and David Loy, *Nonduality: A Study in Comparative Philosophy* (New Haven, 1988). Moreover, Derrida himself speaks of deconstructions rather than deconstruction, and the more his critics attempt to pin him down as to a definition of the term, the more he resists such definitions, somewhat in the fashion of a Zen master. For instance, in "Letter to A Japanese Friend" he notes: "Deconstruction takes place, it is an event that does not await the deliberation, consciousness or organization of a subject, or even of modernity. *It can be deconstructed. It deconstructs itself* [Ça se déconstruit]"—see Derrida, "A Letter to A Japanese Friend," trans. Andrew Benjamin, in *Derrida and Différance*, ed. David Wood and Robert Bernasconi (Evanston, Ill., 1988), 4. In "Some Statements and Truisms about Neologisms, Newisms, Positisms, Parasitisms, and Other Small Seismisms," Derrida further distinguishes between deconstruction as open-ended process and "deconstructionism" as dogma and states: "Deconstruction is neither a theory nor a philosophy. It is

neither a school nor a method. It is not even a discourse, nor an act, nor a practice. It is what happens, what is happening today in what they call society, politics, diplomacy, economics, historical reality, and so on and so forth. Deconstruction is the case" (*The States of "Theory": History, Art, and Critical Discourse*, trans. Anne Tomiche, ed. David Carroll [New York, 1990], 85). Of course, this view of deconstruction as a way of life or a dynamic process rather than a philosophical method recalls certain Taoist and Buddhist claims. But here the analogy between an Eastern master and the French philosopher stops, because Derrida remains, both intellectually and professionally, well within the Western philosophical tradition and Western cultural institutions. As such, Derrida claims both too much and too little: on the one hand, deconstruction appears to be only a local, not a generalized event, perhaps only a storm in an academic teapot; on the other hand, as an event or that which is the case, it can trigger a long chain of reactions that escape the will or intention of the person who occasioned this event. Socratically speaking, moreover, the "midwife" of deconstruction cannot very well disclaim responsibility—in Derrida's own sense of the term—for its unwanted or unpredictable effects, including "deconstructionism" (which was only too predictable, however). Judging from its intellectual and institutional effects so far, I cannot regard deconstruction, barring a few argumentative and rhetorical strategies, as a Western equivalent of, say, Zen Buddhism. Nor has deconstruction turned away from a mentality of power, although it has substantially contributed to a better understanding of this mentality. In all fairness to Derrida, however, deconstruction is still "playing itself out" (even as it has temporarily gone out of fashion), so it is perhaps too early to assess its full intellectual and emotional impact in contemporary Western thought. For further consideration of Derrida in the context of (nonlogocentric) Eastern thought, see below, section 3 of this chapter.

11.   Paul de Man, "Criticism and Crisis," in *Blindness and Insight: Essays in the Rhetoric of Contemporary Criticism* (New York, 1971), 17–19.

12.   Georges Bataille, "The College of Sociology," in *The College of Sociology (1937–39)*, ed. Denis Hollier (Minneapolis, Minn., 1988), 339.

13.   See especially Georges Bataille, *La part maudite* (Paris, 1949). Interestingly enough, though, the principle of heterogeneity ultimately remains tied to what Bataille calls a "lost totality" (a version of the Nietzschean primordial, Dionysian unity or violent play of the world). As Bataille notes in "The Sorcerer's Apprentice," an essay included in the *College of Sociology* papers, he seeks to revive the power of archaic myth, which depends in turn on a "total existence." Violent play is a mode of manifestation of this "total existence" or "Being," and practicing it would rejuvenate decadent, bourgeois culture. According to Bataille, archaic myth is (re)born "in ritual acts concealed from the static vulgarity of a disintegrated society, but the violent dynamic belonging to it has no other object than the return to a lost totality" (22). Violent play as a reaffirmation of archaic myth in contemporary culture seems also to have been the purpose of Bataille's secret society, Acéphale. The members of this society were reportedly looking for a volunteer to be sacrificed in a scapegoat ritual. A willing human victim seems to have been found, but no willing

executioner, and the members ended up sacrificing a ram instead. Thus Bataille's secret society clearly operated on the same ludic principles as Artaud's theater of cruelty or Breton's random, "surrealist" violence.

14. *Republic* 4.431a, trans. Paul Shorey, in *The Collected Dialogues of Plato*, ed. E. Hamilton and H. Cairns (Princeton, 1961).

15. Nietzsche, *Will to Power*, note 636.

16. See G. W. F. Hegel, *Early Theological Writings*, trans. T. M. Knox (Philadelphia, 1948), 309.

17. Ibid., 186. Hegel's opposition between the Judaic and the Christian spirit could be fruitfully compared with Nietzsche's opposition between Roman and Jew. Ironically and probably polemically, Nietzsche attributes to the Roman precisely what Hegel attributes to the Jew: a competitive frame of mind that ceaselessly seeks mastery. One can also point out that Hegel's view of the Jew as an eternally unhappy and shiftless character, as a potentially unsettling element in a well-integrated community, is similar to Socrates' view of the foreigner who threatens the unity of the polis. This view, no less than Nietzsche's, was also popularized with horrifying consequences by Nazi propaganda during the Third Reich. It is obvious, then, that ethnicity and race equally become part of a conflictive dialectic of master and slave, or identity and alterity, in which the Other must be either victimized or exalted, either demonized or beatified. For a discussion of the foreign Other as both idealized and vilified, see chapter 5, section 3, below.

18. See Jean-Paul Sartre, *Being and Nothingness*, trans. Hazel E. Barnes (Secaucus, N.J., 1956), 340.

19. See Jacques Lacan, *Ecrits* (Paris, 1966), 1:95.

20. See also Lacan's remarks in "Fonction et champ de la parole et du langage": "Cet *ego*, dont nos théoriciens définissent maintenant la force par la capacité de soutenir une frustration, est frustration dans son essence. Il est frustration non d'un désir du sujet, mais d'un objet ou son désir est aliéné et qui, tant plus il s'élabore, tant plus s'approfondit pour le sujet l'aliénation de sa jouissance. Frustration au second degré donc, et telle que le sujet en ramenerait-il la forme en son discours jusqu'à l'image passivante par où le sujet se fait objet dans la parade du miroir, il ne saurait s'en satisfaire puisque à atteindre même en cette image sa plus parfaite ressemblance, ce serait encore la jouissance de l'autre qu'il y ferait reconnaître. . . . L'aggressivité que le sujet éprouvera ici n'a rien à faire avec l'aggressivité animal du désir frustré. Cette référence dont on se contente, en masque une autre moins agréable pour tous et pour chacun: l'aggressivité de l'esclave qui repond à la frustration de son travail par un désir de mort" (*Ecrits*, 1:125–26).

21. In much poststructuralist criticism, the subject is no longer called a "subject" but an "agent" in order to conform with the poststructuralist claim of transcending the Cartesian and Hegelian dualism of subject and object. For a detailed justification of this practice, see, most recently, Paul Smith, *Discerning the Subject* (Minneapolis, Minn., 1988).

22. Michel Foucault, "The Subject and Power," afterword to *Michel Foucault:*

Beyond Structuralism and Hermeneutics, by Hubert L. Dreyfus and Paul Rabinow, 2d ed. (Chicago, 1983), 219.

23. I have found particularly useful: Luce Irigaray, *Ethique de la différence sexuelle* (Paris, 1984); Barbara Johnson, *A World of Difference* (Baltimore, 1987); Diana Fuss, *Essentially Speaking* (New York, 1989); Jane Flax, *Thinking Fragments: Psychoanalysis, Feminism, and Postmodernism in the Contemporary West* (Berkeley and Los Angeles, 1990) and idem, *Disputed Subjects: Essays on Psychoanalysis, Politics, and Philosophy* (New York, 1993); Linda Nicholson, ed., *Feminism/Postmodernism* (New York, 1990); Diane Elam, *Feminism and Deconstruction: Ms. en abyme* (London and New York, 1994); and Linda Nicholson and Steven Seidman, eds., *Social Postmodernism: Beyond Identity Politics* (Cambridge, 1995). My own ludic-irenic approach is especially sympathetic to those postmodern feminist approaches (Flax, Elam, etc.) that stress a need for an alternative human ethics over any rigid ideology or party line.

24. See Judith Butler, *Gender Trouble: Feminism and the Subversion of Identity* (London and New York, 1990), 3–4.

25. Michael Warner, "From Queer to Eternity: An Army of Theorists Cannot Fail," in *Voice Literary Supplement*, June 1992, 19.

26. See Monique Wittig, *The Straight Mind and Other Essays* (Boston, 1992), 5. By contrast, Jane Flax is fully aware of the pitfalls of such a position. For example, she notes:

> Indeed, the notion of a feminist standpoint that is truer than previous (male) ones seems to rest upon many problematic and unexamined assumptions. These include an optimistic belief that people act rationally in their own interests and that reality has a structure that perfect reason (once perfected) can discover. . . . This position assumes that the oppressed have a privileged (and not just different) relation and ability to comprehend a reality that is out there waiting for our representation. It also presupposes gendered social relations in which there is a category of beings who are fundamentally like each other by virtue of their sex—that is, it assumes the otherness men assign to women. Such a standpoint also assumes that women, unlike men, can be free of determination from their own participation in relations of domination such as those rooted in the social relations of race, class, or homophobia. ("Postmodernism and Gender Relations in Feminist Theory," in Nicholson, *Feminism/Postmodernism*, 56)

In *Disputed Subjects*, moreover, Flax develops a ludic theory of justice—based on Winnicott's idea of transitional, or what I would call liminal, objects—and a notion of "responsibility without grounds" (cf. Elam's "groundless solidarity" [*Feminism and Deconstruction*, 68ff.]) that come close to my own ideas of ludic liminality and responsive understanding. See below, section 3 of this chapter.

Among the postcolonial studies that are aware of the need to go beyond a dialectic of victim and victimizer and that question the Western notion of otherness, see, for example, Frantz Fanon, *The Wretched of the Earth* (Harmondsworth, U.K., 1969) and, more recently, Henry Louis Gates Jr., *The Signifying Monkey: A Theory of Afro-American Literary Criticism* (New York, 1988), Djelal Kadir, *The Other Writing: Postcolonial Essays in Latin America's Writing Culture* (West Lafayette, Ind., 1993), and Homi Bhabha, *The Location of Culture* (London and New York, 1994).

27. For a full discussion of Oscar Wilde's concept of human individuality, see below, chapter 7, section 3.

28. M. M. Bakhtin, *The Dialogic Imagination: Four Essays*, ed. Michael Holquist, trans. Caryl Emerson and Michael Holquist (Austin, Tex., 1981), 272.

29. See Michael Holquist, introduction to ibid., xviii.

30. Bakhtin, *Dialogic Imagination*, 280.

31. See Tzvetan Todorov, *Mikhail Bakhtin: The Dialogical Principle*, trans. Wlad Godzich (Minneapolis, Minn., 1984), 106. Todorov's book is not only a useful account of Bakhtin's life and work but also an excellent collection of citations from Bakhtin's works not readily available in this country.

32. See Paul de Man's interesting essay, "Dialogue and Dialogism" (in *The Resistance to Theory* [Minneapolis, Minn., 1986], 106–14) devoted to Bakhtin. De Man's insight into Bakhtin's dialogical impulse, however, is blinded by his own will to power, which denies the irenic aspects of that impulse by formulating the issue in deconstructive terms as an aporia between poetics and hermeneutics: "The relationship between poetics and hermeneutics, like that between R the author and N the reader [in Rousseau's *Dialogue on the Novel*], is dialogical to the precise extent that the one cannot be substituted for the other, despite the fact that the non-dialogical discourse of question and answer fully justifies the substitution. What one has to admire Bakhtin for (that is, want to be in his place in having written what he wrote), as all his present readers, including myself, do, is his hope that by starting out, as he does, in a poetics of novelistic discourse one may gain access to the power of a hermeneutics" (113). It is precisely the power-oriented nature of any traditional or contemporary hermeneutics (as well as antihermeneutics) that de Man is not interested in exploring. For a detailed discussion of hermeneutics as a median, allegorical form of power and its postmodern deconstruction, see chapter 6 below. For the disturbing ethical implications of de Man's own will to power, see Stanley Corngold's fine essay, "Remembering Paul de Man: An Epoch in the History of Comparative Literature," in *Building a Profession: Perspectives on the Beginnings of Comparative Literature in the United States,* ed. Lionel Gossman and Mihai I. Spariosu (Albany, N.Y., 1994), 177–92.

33. Todorov, *Mikhail Bakhtin*, 110f.

34. See Emmanuel Levinas, *Totalité et infini: Essai sur l'exteriorité* (The Hague, 1965), 266f.

35. See especially ibid., xviii; and idem, *Autrement qu'être; ou Au-delà de l'essence* (The Hague, 1974), 6–9, 195–207.

36. Witness, in this respect, the sharp criticism of several feminist deconstruc–tionists, who attempt to separate Derrida from Levinas, whose ethics they consider

"blatantly patriarchal" (Elam, *Feminism and Deconstruction*, 147). Cf. also the remarks on Levinas's "sentimentalization" of women by Drucilla Cornell, in *The Philosophy of the Limit* (New York, 1992), 85–90. Derrida himself attempts to remove what he perceives to be patriarchal and sexist overtones in Levinas's thinking, most recently in *Psyche: inventions de l'autre* (Paris, 1987). For an extended comparison between Derrida and Levinas, see Simon Critchley, *The Ethics of Deconstruction: Derrida and Levinas* (Oxford, 1992). Whether the feminist negative perception of Levinas's ethics is justified or not, it certainly dramatizes the risks of attempting to "retrieve" the Western ontotheological tradition from an incommensurable standpoint. Nor do I harbor any illusions that my own irenic discourse will not be seen as sharing all the rhetorical ambiguities and unwanted practical consequences that I have pointed out in the case of Levinas, Derrida, Butler, and others. In a sense, such misunderstandings (including my own) are inevitable, but can ultimately have positive dialogical effects as well.

37. See *The Zen Teaching of Huang Po: On the Transmission of Mind*, trans. John Blofeld (New York, 1958), 115. For a general introduction to Zen Buddhism, see Heinrich Dumoulin, S.J., *A History of Zen Buddhism*, trans. Paul Preachy (New York, 1963). For specific studies of Zen Buddhism in relation to Western thought, see, among many others: Alan Watts, *The Way of Zen* (New York, 1957); Roshi Philip Kapleau, *The Three Pillars of Zen* (New York, 1965); and Masao Abe, *Zen and Western Thought* (Honolulu, Hawaii, 1985).

38. *Zen Teaching of Huang Po*, 122–23. Of course, for the Western reader, "One Mind" sounds suspiciously like a Neoplatonic or Hegelian type of idealism and, therefore, the question of translating *hsin* by a different English term might be raised. The point, however, is that no translation (and any translation!) will do, because not only the concept of *hsin* but the practice of conceptualization as such are deconstructed by Huang Po in the course of his teaching.

39. Robert Magliola, for example, points out that Derrida's wholesale charge that "the East offers no more than variations of logocentrism" is "egregiously misinformed" (*Derrida on the Mend*, 88). Magliola draws a distinction between "centric" and "differential" Buddhism, showing that such "differential" Buddhists as Nagarjuna deconstruct logocentric thought as thoroughly as Derrida does, by employing a similar notion of *différance*, which Nagarjuna calls *sunyata* (translated by Magliola as "devoidness" [89]). Magliola, however, has a tendency to see Zen Buddhism as centric, but this is again a wholesale judgment, as the case of Huang Po conclusively demonstrates.

40. For a fine study of the Western misunderstanding of (Indian) Buddhist thought as nihilism, see Dorothy M. Figueira, "The Poetics of Despair: Irrational Responses to Exoticism," in *The Exotic: A Decadent Quest* (Albany, N.Y., 1994), 92–161.

41. Deleuze, *Difference and Repetition*, trans. Paul Patton (New York, 1994), 29.

42. Levinas, *Totalité et infini*, xii.

43. Magliola makes a similar distinction (based on pathos) between Nagarjunist differential thinking and Derridian deconstruction:

1) while the Derridean alternately celebrates and anguishes, hopes and waxes nostalgic, the Nagarjunist is aware and serene, and has the security that comes with liberation; 2) while the Derridean performs the logocentric and differential self-consciously and piecemeal, the Nagarjunist performs them by means of a grace which is spontaneous but "at will," a kind of off/ self that moves freely between the objectivism of ego and pure devoidness. The Nagarjunist freely, fully, and gracefully "moves" because he has *prajna*-knowing, or realization; and because he has that enabling power which smoothly exercises the shift to and fro between the logocentric and the differential—that is, he has *tathata* ("thusness/suchness"). (Magliola, *Derrida on the Mend*, 126)

44.   For the first rudiments of a science of peratology, albeit from a Heideggerian perspective, see Gabriel Liiceanu, *Despre limita* (About limit) (Bucharest, 1994).

45.   Thus, what is generally perceived as an incommensurable gap between Eastern and Western ways of thinking does not have much to do with "thinking" at all, but mostly with psychological limits. For instance, Harold Coward notes in the conclusion of his comparative study of Derrida and Bhartrhari:

At this point the disagreement between Derrida and Bhartrhari repeats the views of other Western scholars such as Kant and Jung that a pure perception of the real transcends the limitations of human experience and is therefore simply not possible. Eastern views like those offered by Bhartrhari, Sankara, Aurobindo, Nagarjuna, and others are incorrect because they are imagining a human experience that does not exist. As Jung put it, Eastern intuition is simply overreaching itself. At its base this disagreement between East and West is a disagreement as to the definition of human nature, its epistemological and psychological (ego) limitations. (*Derrida and Indian Philosophy*, 149–50)

46.   See Michel Foucault, "Language to Infinity," in *Language, Counter-Memory, Practice*, ed. D. F. Bouchard, trans. D. F. Bouchard and S. Simon (Ithaca, N.Y., 1977), 53.

47.   What is so striking for a Westerner upon reading *The Tibetan Book of the Dead* for the first time is the great number of choices that the soul is presented with in the bardo state, before *it* finally chooses (and not someone else for it) either to reincarnate or to enter Nirvana. The Christian ethopathology of death, when compared with the Buddhist one, is not only positive but also uplifting and, therefore, it tends to be co-opted by the Will in the guise of an all-forgiving divine Power. Of course, during the later stages of Christianity, this all-forgiving divine Power is further (mis)interpreted by the Will as a judgmental and retributive one as well. For a fine literary description of the Christian ethopathology of death see, for example, Leo Tolstoy's story, "The Death of Ivan Ilyich." See also, below, my discussion of

Dostoevsky in chapter 4, section 1, and my discussion of Rebreanu, Eliade, and Devi in chapter 5.

48. If I were to articulate the nonagonistic difference between these two irenic models in ludic terms, Levinas's model is perhaps slightly overinvested with tragic (but *not* negative) pathos—an overinvestment that is fully understandable and justifiable in the light of the tragic historical fate of Levinas and the Jewish people; whereas the Zen Buddhist model presupposes an emotionally neutral detachment that allows for a certain degree of playfulness and freedom (assuming that these latter values are properly assessed and revaluated along the irenic lines envisioned by Levinas himself). So the Zen Buddhist model I have described here can be called "ludic-irenic" in order to distinguish it from Levinas's irenic model. I cannot stress enough, however, that all the distinctions I have drawn in this study, including those between a mentality of power and an irenic mentality, are nonagonistic in spirit, even though a power-oriented criticism will inevitably regard them as either oppositional and subversive or naive, defeatest, and impractical. For me, however, theoretical distinctions are simply a way of clarifying my ethical preferences and choices as well as the mental and emotional paths that have led me to these choices and preferences. Thus my study will hopefully be read not as authoritative exhortation, but as edifying personal testimony.

49. Levinas, *Totalité et infini*, 283.

Chapter 4. Homicide as Play: Dostoevsky, Gide, Aiken

1. For a full argument, see Spariosu, *Dionysus Reborn*, 33–52.
2. Nietzsche, *Birth of Tragedy*, 9.
3. An attempt to understand murder as an aesthetic phenomenon in terms of a romantic interplay of art and life, extending into American popular culture, can be found in Joel Black, *The Aesthetics of Murder: A Study in Romantic Literature and Contemporary Culture* (Baltimore, 1991).
4. For a perceptive discussion of this kind of detective fiction, see Dennis Porter, *The Pursuit of Crime: Art and Ideology in Detective Fiction* (New Haven, 1981).
5. See Fyodor Dostoevsky, *Crime and Punishment*, trans. Jessie Coulson, ed. George Gibian (New York, 1964), 250. It would be impossible to acknowledge the hundreds of studies on Dostoevsky in general and on *Crime and Punishment* in particular that have, over the years, shaped my view of this novel. Here I shall content myself with listing the ones I have found most useful: André Gide, *Dostoievski* (Paris, 1921); M. M. Bakhtin, *Problemy poetiki Dostoevskogo* (Problems of Dostoevsky's poetics) (Moscow, 1963); K. Mochulsky, *Dostoevsky: zhisn' i tvorchestvo* (Dostoevsky's life and work) (Paris 1947); Philip Rahv, "Dostoevsky in *Crime and Punishment*," *Partisan Review* 27, no. 3 (summer 1960): 393–425; René Girard, *Dostoievski: Du double à l'unité* (Paris, 1963); Edward Wasiolek, *Dostoevsky: The Major Fiction* (Cambridge, Mass., 1964), as well as idem, ed., *Crime and Punishment and the Critics* (San Francisco,

1961); Roger B. Anderson, *Dostoevsky: Myths of Duality* (Gainesville, Fla., 1986); and Joseph Frank, *Dostoevsky: The Seeds of Revolt, 1821–1849* (Princeton, 1976); idem, *Dostoevsky: The Years of Ordeal, 1850–1859* (Princeton, 1983); and idem, *Dostoevsky: The Stir of Liberation, 1860–1865* (Princeton, 1986).

    6. Dostoevsky, *Crime and Punishment*, 251.

    7. Nietzsche, *Will to Power*, 18.

    8. Dostoevsky, *Crime and Punishment*, 264.

    9. André Gide, *Lafcadio's Adventures*, trans. Dorothy Bussy (1953; reprint, Cambridge, Mass., 1980), 7. The critical studies on Gide and *Les caves du Vatican* that I have found particularly useful include: W. Wolfgang Holdheim, *Theory and Practice of the Novel: A Study on André Gide* (Geneva, 1968); George D. Painter, *André Gide. A Critical Biography* (New York, 1968); D. A. Steel, "'Lafcadio Ludens': Ideas of Play and Levity in *Les caves du Vatican*," *Modern Language Review* 66 (1971): 554–64; Claude Martin, *Gide* (Paris, 1974); G. W. Ireland, *André Gide. A Study of His Creative Writings* (Oxford, 1970); John McClelland, "The Lexicon of *Les caves du Vatican*," *PMLA* 89 (1974): 256–67; Bertrand Fillaudeau, *L'univers ludique d'André Gide: Les soties* (Paris, 1985); and Doris Y. Kadish, "Games of De(con)struction in Gide's *Les Caves du Vatican*," *French Review* 59, no. 4 (March 1986): 571–80.

    10. Gide, *Lafcadio's Adventures*, 7.

    11. Clarence Darrow and Benjamin Bacharach, introduction to Maureen McKernan, *The Amazing Crime and Trial of Leopold and Loeb* (1924; reprint, Chicago, 1986), vii.

    12. See Vincent McHugh, *Primer of the Novel* (New York, 1950), 34. Likewise, Frederick J. Hoffman writes: "If I seem to be overlong in describing Aiken's failures, it is only with the aim of setting the stage for a discussion of his major failure—in fiction, that is. All of the contrivances, half-starts, hollowness and thinness of characterization culminate in the novel *King Coffin*. Its hero, Jasper Ammen, descends from Dostoevski, Poe and Nietzsche; and in each case he loses much of the inheritance. . . . On the edge of Harvard Yard, Ammen plots the 'perfect crime'. . . . He is the Emersonian soul gone sour, an Ahab turned Raskolnikov, with the motive of neither for planning his acts" (*Conrad Aiken* [New York, 1962], 53–54). Hoffman in effect blames *King Coffin* for not being the kind of Fosterian novel of manners it was never meant to be. He seems to take the narrative at its face value, ignoring the fact that it is presented from Ammen's point of view, and consequently failing to perceive the ironical standpoint of the narrator. Hoffman also fails to inform his reader that Ammen never kills anyone, but rather attempts suicide. Hoffman thus misses the final ironic twist in the narrative. Hoffman is equally cavalier in treating Aiken's short story, "Smith and Jones"—a sort of prototype for *King Coffin*. He states that Jones kills Smith, again missing the final twist, in which Smith, the supposed victim, kills Jones.

    13. Conrad Aiken, *King Coffin*, in *The Collected Novels of Conrad Aiken* (New York, 1967), 328.

    14. The violent, archaic kind of play that Ammen envisages is equally shared by the surrealists. Witness, for example, André Breton's desideratum of shooting

real pistol bullets, at random, into a live audience; or Antonin Artaud's project of stabbing a fellow actor on stage in order to implicate the audience in ritual murder, thereby recovering the "sacred" origin of drama in sacrificial victimage. Georges Bataille's secret society, Acéphale (which I have already mentioned in chapter 3), belongs to the same ludic category. Ammen would undoubtedly have been embraced by the surrealists as a kindred spirit. For surrealism as archaic play (and as an aesthetic foundation of French poststructuralism), see Mihai I. Spariosu, "Surrealism and Play: Notes Toward a Cultural Historical Evaluation," *Boletin de Literatura Comparada* 16–18 (1991–93): 97–110.

Chapter 5. Race, Ethnicity, and Irenic Mentality: Rebreanu, Eliade, Devi

1. Liviu Rebreanu, *The Forest of the Hanged*, trans. A. V. Wise (London, 1967), 16.

2. George Schöpflin, "The Political Traditions of Eastern Europe," *Daedalus* 119, no. 1 (winter 1990): 55–89 at 79.

3. Before his self-exile in 1945, Eliade published several novels among which these stand out: *Isabel si apele diavolului* (Isabel and the devil's waters), *Maitreyi*, *Întoarcerea din rai* (Return from Eden), *Nopti la Serampore* (Nights at Serampore), *Lumina ce se stinge* (Fading light), *Secretul doctorului Honigberger* (Dr. Honigberger's secret), and *Huliganii* (The hooligans). He also published a number of remarkable short stories such as "La Tiganci" (With the Gypsies), "La curtea lui Dionis" (At Dionysius's court), and "Ivan." In Paris, his home until 1957 when he came to America, Eliade also wrote what many, including its author, consider his masterpiece: *Noaptea de sînziene* (French title: *Forêt interdite*, 1955; English title: *The Forbidden Forest*, 1978).

4. Mircea Eliade, *No Souvenirs: Journal 1957–1969* (New York, 1977), ix.

5. Mircea Eliade, *The Forbidden Forest*, trans. Mac Linscott Ricketts and Mary Park Stevenson (Notre Dame, Ind., 1978), vi.

6. Eliade, *No Souvenirs*, ix.

7. See, for example, Dumitru Micu in his preface to the first postwar Romanian edition of *Maitreyi* and *Nunta în cer* (Bucharest, 1969).

8. See, for example, Anita Desai's recent review of both Eliade's and Devi's novels: "Oh Calcutta!" *New Republic*, 15 August 1994, 43–45.

9. Mircea Eliade, *Maitreyi* (Bucharest, 1969), 15. All the English translations from the Romanian text are mine. *Maitreyi* has recently been published in English under the title of *Bengal Nights* (Chicago, 1994). I have not used this English edition here because it is a rather unreliable translation of the French version of the novel, *Les nuits bengali* (Paris, 1958).

10. Maitreyi Devi, *It Does Not Die* (Chicago, 1994), 226.

11. For a definition of the term *bardo*, see chapter 2, section 1 above.

12. See Frank Kermode, *The Sense of an Ending* (New York, 1967).

13. Devi, *It Does Not Die*, 257.

Chapter 6. Allegory, Power, and the Postmodern
Game of Interpretation: Lowry, Nabokov, Orwell

1.   For extensive discussions of modernism and postmodernism as period concepts, see, among many others: Ihab Hassan, *The Dismemberment of Orpheus: Toward
a Postmodern Literature* (New York, 1971) and *The Postmodern Turn: Essays in Postmodern
Theory and Culture* (Columbus, Ohio, 1987); Ihab Hassan and Sally Hassan, eds., *Inno-
vation/Renovation: New Perspectives on the Humanities* (Madison, Wisc., 1983); Alan Wilde,
Horizons of Assent: Modernism, Postmodernism and the Ironic Imagination (Baltimore,
1981); Andreas Huyssen, *After the Great Divide: Modernism, Mass Culture, Postmodernism*
(Bloomington, Ind., 1986); Matei Calinescu, *Five Faces of Modernity* (Durham, N.C.,
1987); Jean-François Lyotard, *The Postmodern Condition: A Report on Knowledge* (Minneapolis, Minn., 1984); Linda Hutcheon, *A Poetics of Postmodernism* (New York, 1988);
Brian McHale, *Postmodernist Fiction* (New York, 1987) and *Constructing Postmodernism*
(London and New York, 1992); John McGowan, *Postmodernism and Its Critics* (Ithaca,
N.Y., 1991); Marcel Cornis-Pope, *Hermeneutic Desire and Critical Rewriting* (New York,
1992); and Patricia Waugh, *Practising Postmodernism, Reading Modernism* (London
and New York, 1992). I may add that many contemporary critics will in all likelihood
see the present study, with its emphasis on constructivist perspectives and alternative
worlds, as a postmodern one. This again depends on how one defines postmodernism
and on how much one is willing to place under a "postmodern" umbrella. For a discussion of my earlier work in a postmodern context, see, for instance, Marcel Cornis-
Pope, "Contest vs. Mediation: Innovative Discursive Modes in Postmodern Fiction,"
in *Violence and Mediation in Contemporary Culture,* ed. R. Bogue and M. Cornis-Pope
(Albany, N.Y., 1996), 181–200. As to works of art in general, my consistently constructivist position has been, and still is, that although many of them can be approached
from classical, romantic, realist, modernist, postmodern, and other perspectives (including a ludic-irenic one), they will always exceed any and all of these perspectives, as well as all critical labels. Cf., especially, my analysis of *Pale Fire* in this chapter
and Oscar Wilde's own views on the subject, which I discuss in chapter 7, below.
      2.   Cf. my description of the main features of the archaic and the median men-
tality in chapter 1, note 5, above.
      3.   For the early allegorical readings of Homer, see among others, William B.
Stanford, *The Ulysses Theme: A Study in the Adaptability of a Traditional Hero* (Oxford,
1954) and F. Buffière, *Les mythes d'Homer et la pensée grecque* (Paris, 1956).
      4.   For an examination of the historical origins of the opposition between alle-
gory and symbol in romanticism, see Hans-Georg Gadamer, *Truth and Method,* trans.
G. Garden and J. Cumming (New York, 1975), 65–73.
      5.   The contemporary rehabilitation of allegory finds its clearest expression in
Paul de Man's work, including *Allegories of Reading: Figural Language in Rousseau,
Nietzsche, Rilke, and Proust* (New Haven, 1979).
      6.   One of the most influential critical statements indicative of the antiherme-
neutical orientation of postmodernism is Susan Sontag's "Against Interpretation,"
in *Against Interpretation and Other Essays* (New York, 1966).

7. See Spariosu, *God of Many Names*, 155–59.

8. Vladimir Nabokov, *Pale Fire* (New York, 1962), 86. My present reading of the novel has taken into consideration many of the over one thousand critical pieces written on Nabokov and his work to date, including *Pale Fire*. Here I can mention only the ones that I have found most useful: Mary McCarthy, "A Bolt from the Blue," *New Republic*, June 1962, 21–27 and "Vladimir Nabokov's *Pale Fire*," *Encounter* 19, no. 4 (October 1962), 71–84; Carol T. Williams, "'Web of Sense': *Pale Fire* in the Nabokov Canon," *Critique* 6, no. 3 (winter 1963–64), 29–45; R. H. W. Dillard, "Not Text but Texture: The Novels of Vladimir Nabokov," *Hollins Critic* 3, no. 3 (June 1966): 1–12; Page Stegner, *Escape into Aesthetics: The Art of Vladimir Nabokov* (New York, 1966); Andrew Field, *Nabokov: His Life in Art, A Critical Narrative* (London, 1967); A. Appel and Ch. Newman, eds., *Nabokov: Criticism, Reminiscences, Translations, and Tributes* (London, 1971); Julia Bader, *Crystal Land: Artifice in Nabokov's English Novels* (Berkeley, Calif., 1972); Douglas Fowler, *Reading Nabokov* (Ithaca, N.Y., 1974); Carl R. Proffer, ed., *A Book of Things about Vladimir Nabokov* (Ann Arbor, Mich., 1974); Robert Alter, *Partial Magic: The Novel as Self-Conscious Genre* (Berkeley, Calif., 1975), 180–217; William Woodin Rowe, *Nabokov's Spectral Dimension: The Other World in His Works* (Ann Arbor, Mich., 1981); Phyllis A. Roth, ed., *Critical Essays on Vladimir Nabokov* (Boston, 1984); Margaret Peller Feely, "'Warp and Weft': Patterns of Artistry in Nabokov's *Pale Fire*," in *The Scope of the Fantastic—Theory, Technique, Major Authors*, ed. R. A. Collins and H. D. Pearce (Westport, Conn., 1985), 239–45; Michael Seidel, *Exile and the Narrative Imagination* (New Haven, 1986), 164–96; Priscilla Meyer, *Find What the Sailor has Hidden: Vladimir Nabokov's "Pale Fire"* (Middletown, Conn., 1988); Leona Toker, *Nabokov: The Mystery of Literary Structures* (Ithaca, N.Y., 1989); Vladimir Alexandrov, *Nabokov's Otherworld* (Princeton, 1991); and David Rampton, *Vladimir Nabokov* (New York, 1993).

9. Nabokov, *Pale Fire*, 25.

10. Nietzsche, *Birth of Tragedy*, 42.

11. Nabokov, *Pale Fire*, 226.

12. "God's playing will become world." See Martin Heidegger, *Der Satz vom Grund* (Pfullingen, 1958), 170.

13. Nabokov, *Pale Fire*, 63.

14. William Carroll, "Nabokov's Signs and Symbols," in Proffer, *A Book of Things about Vladimir Nabokov*, 203.

15. Nabokov, *Pale Fire*, 299.

16. For an extensive list of the literary games that Nabokov plays with his reader, see Meyer, *Find What the Sailor has Hidden*.

17. See Alfred Appel Jr., "An Interview with Vladimir Nabokov," in *Nabokov, the Man and his Work*, ed. L. S. Dembo (Madison, Wisc., 1967), 29. In the same interview, Nabokov's facetious advice to "a budding literary critic" is to "ask yourself if the symbol you have detected is not your own footprint" and to "[i]gnore allegories" (23)—an excellent postmodern injunction, to be sure.

18. Nabokov, *Pale Fire*, 265.

19. These questions have first been raised and variously answered by Mary

McCarthy, Carol T. Williams, Page Stegner, and Julia Bader. I tend, however, to agree with Margaret Peller Feeley's observation that the problem with these critics' readings is that "they clash with the spirit of pluralism in the book and Vladimir Nabokov's world generally" ("'Warp and Weft,'" 239). But Feely ignores her own caveat when she says that Kinbote is an "obvious impostor," being "no king but an eccentric Russian refugee" (244).
    20. Nabokov, *Pale Fire*, 306.
    21. See Appel, "An Interview with Vladimir Nabokov," 43.
    22. Nabokov, *Pale Fire*, 301.
    23. See Kenneth Burke, *"Coriolanus*, or the Delights of Faction," in *Language as Symbolic Action* (Berkeley, Calif., 1966).
    24. Malcolm Lowry, *Under the Volcano* (London and New York, 1971), 79. The critical material that I have found most useful in updating and substantially revising the present essay on Lowry (first published in 1982) includes: Chris Ackerley and Lawrence J. Clipper, *A Companion to "Under the Volcano"* (Vancouver, B.C., 1984); Gordon Bowker and Paul Tiessen, eds., *Proceedings of the London Conference on Malcolm Lowry 1984* (London, 1985); Gordon Bowker, ed., *Malcolm Lowry: Under the Volcano: A Casebook* (London, 1987); Sue Vice, ed., *Malcolm Lowry Eighty Years On* (New York, 1989); and Sherrill Grace, ed., *Swinging the Maelstrom: New Perspectives on Malcolm Lowry* (Montreal, 1992).
    25. Lowry, *Under the Volcano*, 210.
    26. For an extensive examination of cabalistic symbolism in *Under the Volcano*, see Perle Epstein's *The Private Labyrinth of Malcolm Lowry: "Under the Volcano" and the Cabbala* (New York, 1969). Her cabalistic interpretation of Lowry's text is so extravagantly detailed, however, that it caused Dale Edmonds to call it "the *Pale Fire* of Lowry criticism."
    27. See Malcolm Lowry, "Letter to Jonathan Cape," in *The Selected Letters of Malcolm Lowry*, ed. H. Breit and M. Bonner Lowry (New York, 1965), 65. For the Consul as artist, see also Patrick McCarthy, "Wrider/Espider: The Consul as Artist in *Under the Volcano*," *Studies in Canadian Literature* 17, no. 1 (1992): 30–51.
    28. For a full discussion of the modern cultural implications of the archaic scapegoat ritual, see René Girard, *La violence et le sacré* (Paris, 1972) and *Le bouc émissaire* (Paris, 1985), as well as Philippe Lacoue-Labarthes's critique of Girard's theory of the scapegoat as mimetic desire in "Typographie," *Mimésis/des articulations*, ed. J. Derrida et al. (Paris, 1975). For a general critique of Girard's thought, see Mihai Spariosu, "Mimesis and French Contemporary Theory," in *Mimesis in Contemporary Theory*, vol. 1: *The Literary and Philosophical Debate*, ed. M. Spariosu (Philadelphia and Amsterdam, 1984).
    29. Lowry, *Under the Volcano*, 234–35.
    30. Lowry, *Selected Letters*, 71.
    31. For a detailed discussion of *Under the Volcano* and film, see Paul G. Tiessen, "Malcolm Lowry and the Cinema," *Canadian Literature* 44 (spring 1970): 38–49.
    32. Of course, here I am mainly concerned with rereading as an improper or

vicious form of the hermeneutical circle. For proper or benign forms of rereading, see Matei Calinescu's excellent study, *Rereading* (New Haven, 1993).

33. As Lowry wrote to Harold Matson in November 1951, *The Voyage that Never Ends* was supposed to comprise: *The Ordeal of Sighjørn Wilderness I*, an untitled sea novel, *Lunar Caustic*, *Under the Volcano* (the center of the entire cycle), a trilogy including *Dark as the Grave Wherein my Friend is Laid*, *Eridanus*, and *La Mordida*, as well as *The Ordeal of Sighjørn Wilderness II*. See Douglas Day, *Malcolm Lowry* (New York, 1973), 426. Lowry scholars, on the other hand, see this project as a modern-day *Divine Comedy*, with *Under the Volcano* as the *Inferno*, *Lunar Caustic* as the *Purgatorio*, and "The Forest Path to the Spring" as the *Paradiso*—see, for example, David Benham, "Lowry's Purgatory: Versions of *Lunar Caustic*," in *Malcolm Lowry: The Man and his Work*, ed. George Woodcock (Vancouver, B.C., 1971). A comparison of Lowry's *The Voyage that Never Ends* with Dante's trilogy, however, is precisely the kind of hermeneutic allegorizing that Nabokov ridicules.

34. Critics have often seen *Dark as the Grave* as thinly disguised autobiography because the novel is based on the diary of a Mexican trip undertaken by Malcolm and Margerie Bonner Lowry—see, for example, George Woodcock, "Art as the Writer's Mirror: Literary Solipsism in *Dark as the Grave*," in Woodcock, *Malcolm Lowry*. But Lowry himself pointed to the fictional nature of this diary when, upon rereading it, he exclaimed, "By God, we have a novel here," and thus started the process of separating himself from it. A perceived critical difficulty in discussing *Dark as the Grave* stems from the fact that the published version has been edited by Margerie Lowry and Douglas Day, who have drastically revised Lowry's chaotic, original typescript of over seven hundred pages. Consequently, critics have raised questions about the "authenticity" of this work. But in Lowry's case these questions are rather ironical, because much of his fiction, including *Under the Volcano*, seems to have been the result of symbiotic teamwork with his wife, Margerie. The whole scholarly controversy around the issue of authenticity smacks of Kinbote's misguided editorial "labor of love."

35. Lowry, *Selected Letters*, 180.

36. Malcolm Lowry, *Dark as the Grave Wherein My Friend is Laid*, ed. Margerie Bonner Lowry and Douglas Day (New York, 1968), 3.

37. Lowry, *Selected Letters*, 331.

38. José Ortega y Gasset, *Toward a Philosophy of History* (New York, 1941), 108.

39. Lowry, *Dark as the Grave*, 70.

40. *Macbeth* 3.3.

41. Lowry, *Dark as the Grave*, 217.

42. Miguel de Unamuno, *Mist*, in *Selected Works*, vol. 4: *Novela/Nivola*, trans. Anthony Kerrigan (Princeton, 1976), 226.

43. Nietzsche, *Will to Power*, note 504.

44. See George Orwell, *1984* (1949; reprint, New York, 1984), 205. Among the great number of recent studies devoted to Orwell's novel I have found these most useful: Irving Howe, ed., *1984 Revisited: Totalitarianism in our Century* (New

York, 1983); J. M. Richardson, ed., *Orwell x 8: A Symposium* (Winnipeg, Man., 1986); C. T. Wemyss and A. Ugrinsky, eds., *George Orwell* (Westport, Conn., 1987); William Casement, "*Nineteen Eighty-Four* and Philosophical Realism," *Midwest Quarterly* 30, no. 2 (winter 1989): 215–28; William Lutz, ed., *Beyond Nineteen Eighty-Four: Double-speak in a Post-Orwellian Age* (Urbana, Ill., 1989); Earl Ingersoll, "The Decentering of Tragic Narrative in George Orwell's *Nineteen Eighty-Four,*" *Studies in the Humanities* 16, no. 2 (December 1989): 69–83; Kenneth Matthews, "'Guardian of the Human Spirit': The Moral Foundation of *Nineteen Eighty-Four,*" *Christianity and Literature* 40, no. 2 (winter 1991): 157–67; and Erika Gottlieb, *The Orwell Conundrum: A Cry of Despair or Faith in the Spirit of Man?* (Ottawa, 1992).

45. Nietzsche, *Will to Power,* note 267.
46. Orwell, *1984,* 177.
47. Nietzsche, *Will to Power,* note 891.
48. Orwell, *1984,* 105.

Chapter 7. Criticism as Irenic Play: The Case of the Victorian Sages

1. Matthew Arnold, "The Function of Criticism at the Present Time," in *Matthew Arnold's Essays in Criticism,* ed. Sister Thomas Marion Hoctor, S.S.J. (Chicago, 1968), 10.

2. The phrase "free play" is also used in deconstructive criticism, designating the loose relationship between signifier and signified. In a certain sense, this deconstructive use parallels Arnold's: for the deconstructionist, the playful signifier can break loose from the signified, just as for Arnold the playful mind can detach itself from the practical world. But this is where the analogy ends, because, as we shall presently see, Arnold effects this ludic detachment for cultural reasons that are radically different from those of the deconstructive critic.

3. Arnold, "Function of Criticism," 21.

4. Here it becomes obvious that Arnold is not unaware of the relation between his idea of criticism as ludic disinterestedness and the Buddhist notion of liminal detachment. Sister Hoctor notes his interest in the *Bhagavad Gita* and cites a passage from his *Letters to Clough* in which he praises Indian meditative practices; she adds that "Arnold's notion of disinterestedness in criticism no doubt derives something from the 'Indian virtue [of detachment].'" See *Matthew Arnold's Essays in Criticism,* explanatory notes, 277.

5. Arnold, "Function of Criticism," 26.

6. For a full explanation of this terminology see, especially, "Hebraism and Hellenism," chapter 4 of *Culture and Anarchy: An Essay in Political and Social Criticism,* ed. Ian Gregor (Indianapolis and New York, 1971), where Arnold associates "Hebraism" with practical and rational tendencies and "Hellenism" with a free or imaginative play of thought and argues that these two primary cultural forces should always be kept in balance—hence his ideal of imaginative reason.

7. Arnold, "Function of Criticism," 19.

8. Arnold, *Culture and Anarchy*, 170.

9. J. M. Roberts, *Modern Humanists* (London, 1891), 166.

10. Lionel Trilling, *Matthew Arnold* (New York, 1939), 217–18.

11. John Ruskin, *The Crown of Wild Olive* (New York, 1905), 12.

12. For a brief discussion of Athena as a rationalist symbol, particularly in Schiller's *Letters on the Aesthetic Education of Man*, see Spariosu, *Dionysus Reborn*, 63.

13. Ruskin speculates on the cultural symbolism of Pallas-Athena along the same lines in "Traffic," which I shall examine shortly.

14. For an examination of the figure of the Victorian secular prophet, see John Holloway, *The Victorian Sage: Studies in Argument* (London, 1953); and, more recently, George P. Landow, "Ruskin as Victorian Sage," in *New Approaches to Ruskin*, ed. R. Hewison (London, 1981).

15. Ruskin, *Crown of Wild Olive*, 26.

16. Huizinga, *Homo Ludens*, 103.

17. Ruskin, *Crown of Wild Olive*, 18.

18. Matthew Arnold, "Spinoza and the Bible," in *Matthew Arnold's Essays in Criticism*, 209. Of course, this observation equally applies to Arnold.

19. The original title of Wilde's piece intentionally echoed Arnold's: "The True Value and Function of Criticism: With Some Remarks on the Importance of Doing Nothing." As Richard Ellmann says, throughout the essay Wilde "tweaks Arnold's nose." See Ellmann, "The Artist as Critic as Wilde," in *Oscar Wilde*, ed. Harold Bloom (New York, 1985). For contemporary perspectives on Wilde's work in general, see all of the contributions in that volume. Ellmann remains, however, the most consistently perceptive and thought-provoking critic of Oscar Wilde to date.

20. See Oscar Wilde, "The Decay of Lying," in *The Works of Oscar Wilde*, ed. G. F. Maine (New York, 1954), 910.

21. Oscar Wilde, "The Critic as Artist," in *Works of Oscar Wilde*, 996.

22. Oscar Wilde, "The Soul of Man under Socialism," in *Works of Oscar Wilde*, 1019.

Selected Bibliography

Abe, Masao. *Zen and Western Thought.* Honolulu, Hawaii, 1985.

Ackerley, Chris, and Lawrence J. Clipper. *A Companion to "Under the Volcano."* Vancouver, B.C., 1984.

Aiken, Conrad. *The Collected Novels of Conrad Aiken.* New York, 1967.

Alexandrov, Vladimir. *Nabokov's Otherworld.* Princeton, 1991.

Alter, Robert. *Partial Magic: The Novel as Self-Conscious Genre.* Berkeley, Calif., 1975.

Anderson, Roger B. *Dostoevsky: Myths of Duality.* Gainesville, Fla., 1986.

Appel, A., and Ch. Newman, eds. *Nabokov: Criticism, Reminiscences, Translations, and Tributes.* London, 1971.

Aristotle. *Poetics.* Translated by S. H. Butcher. In *Aristotle's Theory of Poetry and Fine Art,* by Samuel H. Butcher. 1894. Reprint, 4th ed., New York, 1951.

Arnold, Matthew. *Culture and Anarchy: An Essay in Political and Social Criticism.* Edited by Ian Gregor. Indianapolis and New York, 1971.

———. *Matthew Arnold's Essays in Criticism: First Series.* Edited by Sister Thomas Marion Hoctor, S.S.J. Chicago, 1968.

Ashley, Kathleen M., ed. *Victor Turner and the Construction of Cultural Criticism: Between Literature and Anthropology.* Bloomington, Ind., 1990.

Assoun, Paul-Laurent. *Freud et Nietzsche.* Paris, 1980.

Austin, J. L. *How to Do Things with Words.* Cambridge, Mass., 1962.

Bader, Julia. *Crystal Land: Artifice in Nabokov's English Novels.* Berkeley, Calif.,1972.

Bakhtin, M. M. *The Dialogic Imagination: Four Essays.* Edited by Michael Holquist. Translated by Caryl Emerson and Michael Holquist. Austin, Tex., 1981.

329

Bataille, Georges. *Œuvres complètes.* Paris, 1974.

Bhabha, Homi. *The Location of Culture.* London and New York, 1994.

Bloom, Harold, ed. *Oscar Wilde.* New York, 1985.

Bogue, Ronald, and Marcel Cornis-Pope, eds. *Violence and Mediation in Contemporary Culture.* Albany, N.Y., 1996.

Bradley, Raymond, and Norman Swartz. *Possible Worlds.* Oxford, 1979.

Brann, Eva T. H. *The World of the Imagination: Sum and Substance.* Savage, Md., 1991.

Brett-Smith, H. F. B., ed. *Peacock's Four Ages of Poetry, Shelley's Defence of Poetry, and Browning's Essay on Shelley.* Boston and New York, 1921.

Bruner, Jerome. *Actual Minds, Possible Worlds.* Cambridge, Mass., 1986.

Buffière, F. *Les mythes d'Homer and la pensée grecque.* Paris, 1956.

Bundy, Murray Wright. *The Theory of Imagination in Classical and Mediaeval Thought.* Urbana, Ill., 1927.

Burke, Kenneth. *Language as Symbolic Action.* Berkeley, Calif., 1966.

Butler, Judith. *Gender Trouble: Feminism and the Subversion of Identity.* London and New York, 1990.

Calinescu, Matei. *Five Faces of Modernity.* Durham, N.C., 1987.

———. *Rereading.* New Haven, 1993.

Carroll, David, ed. *The States of "Theory": History, Art, and Critical Discourse.* New York, 1990.

Casement, William. *"Nineteen Eighty-Four and Philosophical Realism." Midwest Quarterly* 30, no. 2 (winter 1989): 215–28.

Castoriadis, Cornelius. *L'institution imaginaire de la société.* Paris, 1975.

Collins, R. A., and H. D. Pearce, eds. *The Scope of the Fantastic—Theory, Technique, Major Authors.* Westport, Conn., 1985.

Cornell, Drucilla. *The Philosophy of the Limit.* New York, 1992.

Corngold, Stanley. *The Fate of the Self: German Writers and French Theory.* New York, 1986.

Cornis-Pope, Marcel. *Hermeneutic Desire and Critical Rewriting.* New York, 1992.

Coward, Harold. *Derrida and Indian Philosophy.* Albany, N.Y., 1990.

Critchley, Simon. *The Ethics of Deconstruction: Derrida and Levinas.* Oxford, 1992.

Davies, Paul. *Other Worlds.* London, 1980.

Day, Douglas. *Malcolm Lowry.* New York, 1973.

Deleuze, Gilles. *Différence et répétition.* Paris, 1968. Translated by Paul Patton under the title *Difference and Repetition* (New York, 1994).

————. *Logique du sens.* Paris, 1969.

Deleuze, Gilles, and Félix Guattari. *L'anti-Œdipe: capitalisme et schizophrénie.* Paris, 1972.

de Man, Paul. *Allegories of Reading: Figural Language in Rousseau, Nietzsche, Rilke, and Proust.* New Haven, 1979.

————. *Blindness and Insight: Essays in the Rhetoric of Contemporary Criticism.* New York, 1971.

————. *The Resistance to Theory.* Minneapolis, Minn., 1986.

Dembo, L. S., ed. *Nabokov, the Man and his Work.* Madison, Wisc., 1967.

Derrida, Jacques. *Margins of Philosophy.* Translated by Alan Bass. Chicago, 1982.

————. *Psyche: inventions de l'autre.* Paris, 1987.

Derrida, Jacques, et al. *Mimésis/des articulations.* Paris, 1975.

Devi, Maitreyi. *It Does Not Die.* Chicago, 1994.

Diels, H., and W. Kranz, eds. *Die Fragmente der Vorsokratiker.* 6th ed. 3 vols. Berlin, 1952.

Dostoevsky, Fyodor. *Crime and Punishment.* Translated by Jessie Coulson. Edited by George Gibian. New York, 1964.

Dreyfus, Hubert L., and Paul Rabinow, eds. *Michel Foucault: Beyond Structuralism and Hermeneutics.* 2d ed. Chicago, 1983.

Dumézil, Georges. *L'idéologie tripartite des Indo-Européens.* Brussels, 1958.

Dumoulin, Heinrich, S.J. *A History of Zen Buddhism.* Translated by Paul Preachy. New York, 1963.

Dundas, Paul. *The Jains.* London and New York, 1992.

Elam, Diane. *Feminism and Deconstruction: Ms. en abyme.* London and New York, 1994.

Eliade, Mircea. *The Forbidden Forest.* Translated by Mac Linscott Ricketts and Mary Park Stevenson. Notre Dame, Ind., 1978.

————. *Maitreyi.* 1933. Reprint, Bucharest, 1969. French version: *Les nuits bengali* (Paris, 1958). English version: *Bengal Nights* (Chicago, 1994).

————. *No Souvenirs: Journal, 1957–1969.* New York, 1977.

Ellmann, Richard. *Oscar Wilde.* New York, 1988.

Engell, James. *The Creative Imagination: Enlightenment to Romanticism.* Cambridge, Mass., 1981.

Epstein, Perle. *The Private Labyrinth of Malcolm Lowry: "Under the Volcano" and the Cabbala.* New York, 1969.

Even-Zohar, Itamar. *Polysystem Studies.* Special issue of *Poetics Today* 11, nos. 1–2 (1990).

Fanon, Frantz. *The Wretched of the Earth.* Harmondsworth, U.K., 1969.

Feyerabend, Paul. *Against Method: Outline of an Anarchistic Theory of Knowledge.* London, 1975.

Field, Andrew. *Nabokov: His Life in Art, A Critical Narrative.* London, 1967.

Figueira, Dorothy. *The Exotic: A Decadent Quest.* Albany, N.Y., 1994.

Fillaudeau, Bertrand. *L'univers ludique d'André Gide: Les soties.* Paris, 1985.

Flax, Jane. *Disputed Subjects: Essays on Psychoanalysis, Politics, and Philosophy.* New York, 1993.

————. *Thinking Fragments: Psychoanalysis, Feminism, and Postmodernism in the Contemporary West.* Berkeley and Los Angeles, 1990.

Foucault, Michel. *Language, Counter-Memory, Practice.* Edited by D. F. Bouchard. Translated by D. F. Bouchard and S. Simon. Ithaca, N.Y., 1977.

Fowler, Douglas. *Reading Nabokov.* Ithaca, N.Y., 1974.

Frank, Joseph. *Dostoevsky: The Seeds of Revolt, 1821–1849.* Princeton, 1976.

————. *Dostoevsky: The Stir of Liberation, 1860–1865.* Princeton, 1986.

————. *Dostoevsky: The Years of Ordeal, 1850–1859.* Princeton, 1983.

Freeman, Kathleen. *Ancilla to the Pre-Socratic Philosophers: A Complete Translation of the Fragments in Diels.* Oxford, 1956.

Fuss, Diana. *Essentially Speaking.* New York, 1989.

Gadamer, Hans-Georg. *Truth and Method.* Translated by G. Garden and J. Cumming. New York, 1975.

Gates, Henry Louis, Jr. *The Signifying Monkey: A Theory of Afro-American Criticism.* New York, 1988.

Gennep, Arnold van. *Rites de passage.* Paris, 1909.

Gide, André. *Les caves du Vatican: sotie.* Paris, 1922. Translated by Dorothy Bussy under the title *Lafcadio's Adventures* (1953; reprint, Cambridge, Mass., 1980).

Gilbert, Alla H., ed. *Literary Criticism: Plato to Dryden.* Detroit, 1962.

Girard, René. *Dostoievski: Du double à l'unité.* Paris, 1963.

————. *La violence et le sacré.* Paris, 1972.

————. *Le bouc émissaire.* Paris, 1985.

Goodman, Nelson. *Ways of Worldmaking.* Indianapolis, Ind., 1978.

Gossman, Lionel, and Mihai I. Spariosu, eds. *Building a Profession: Autobiographical Perspectives on the Beginnings of Comparative Literature in the United States.* Albany, N.Y., 1994.

Gottlieb, Erika. *The Orwell Conundrum: A Cry of Despair or Faith in the Spirit of Man?* Ottawa, 1992.

Grace, Sherrill, ed. *Swinging the Maelstrom: New Perspectives on Malcolm Lowry*. Montreal, 1992.

Gurwitsch, Aron. *Marginal Consciousness*. Edited by Lester Embree. Athens, Ohio, 1985.

Hassan, Ihab. *The Dismemberment of Orpheus: Toward a Postmodern Literature*. New York, 1971.

—. *The Postmodern Turn: Essays in Postmodern Theory and Culture*. Columbus, Ohio, 1987.

Hegel, G. W. F. *Early Theological Writings*. Translated by T. M. Knox. Philadelphia, 1948.

—. *Phenomenology of Mind*. Translated, with introduction and notes, by J. B. Baillie. New York, 1931.

Heidegger, Martin. *Der Satz vom Grund*. Pfullingen, 1958.

—. *Identity and Difference*. Translated by J. Stambaugh. Bilingual ed. New York, 1969.

Hewison, R., ed. *New Approaches to Ruskin*. London, 1981.

Holdheim, Wolfgang W. *Theory and Practice of the Novel: A Study on André Gide*. Geneva, 1968.

Hollier, Denis, ed. *The College of Sociology (1937–39)*. Minneapolis, Minn., 1988.

Holloway, John. *The Victorian Sage: Studies in Argument*. London, 1953.

Homer. *The Odyssey*. Translated by R. Fitzgerald. New York, 1954.

Howe, Irving, ed. *"1984" Revisited: Totalitarianism in our Century*. New York, 1983.

Huang Po. *The Zen Teaching of Huang Po: On the Transmission of Mind*. Translated by John Blofeld. New York, 1958.

Huizinga, Johan. *Homo Ludens: A Study of the Play Element in Culture*. Boston, 1950.

Hutcheon, Linda. *A Poetics of Postmodernism*. New York, 1988.

Huyssen, Andreas. *After the Great Divide: Modernism, Mass Culture, Postmodernism*. Bloomington, Ind., 1986.

Ireland, G. W. *André Gide: A Study of His Creative Writings*. Oxford, 1970.

Irigaray, Luce. *Ethique de la différence sexuelle*. Paris, 1984.

Iser, Wolfgang. *The Fictive and the Imaginary: Charting Literary Anthropology*. Baltimore, 1993.

—. *Prospecting: From Reader Response to Literary Anthropology*. Baltimore, 1989.

Jaini, Jagmanderlal. *Outlines of Jainism*. 1940. Reprint, Westport, Conn., 1982.

Jammer, Max. *Concepts of Force: A Study in the Foundations of Dynamics*. Cambridge, Mass., 1957.

Johnson, Barbara. *A World of Difference*. Baltimore, 1987.

Kadir, Djelal. *The Other Writing: Postcolonial Essays in Latin America's Writing Culture*. West Lafayette, Ind., 1993.

Kapleau, Roshi Philip. *The Three Pillars of Zen*. New York, 1965.

Kearney, Richard. *The Wake of Imagination: Toward a Postmodern Culture*. Minneapolis, Minn., 1984.

Kermode, Frank. *The Sense of an Ending*. New York, 1967.

Kripke, Saul. *Naming and Necessity*. Oxford, 1980.

Lacan, Jacques. *Ecrits*. 2 vols. Paris, 1966.

Levinas, Emmanuel. *Autrement qu'être; ou Au-delà de l'essence*. The Hague, 1974.

———. *Totalité et infini: Essai sur l'extériorité*. The Hague, 1965.

Liiceanu, Gabriel. *Despre limita*. Bucharest, 1994.

Lotman, Yuri. *Analysis of the Poetic Text*. Edited and translated by D. Barton Johnson. Ann Arbor, Mich., 1976.

———. *Universe of the Mind: A Semiotic Theory of Culture*. Translated by Ann Shukman. Bloomington, Ind., 1990.

Lowry, Malcolm. *Dark as the Grave Wherein My Friend is Laid*. Edited by Margerie Bonner Lowry and Douglas Day. New York, 1968.

———. *The Selected Letters of Malcolm Lowry*. Edited by H. Breit and M. Bonner Lowry. New York, 1965.

———. *Under the Volcano*. London and New York, 1971.

Loy, David. *Nonduality: A Study in Comparative Philosophy*. New Haven, 1988.

Lutz, William, ed. *Beyond Nineteen Eighty-Four: Doublespeak in a Post-Orwellian Age*. Urbana, Ill., 1989.

Lyotard, Jean-François. *The Postmodern Condition: A Report on Knowledge*. Minneapolis, Minn., 1984.

Magliola, Robert. *Derrida on the Mend*. West Lafayette, Ind., 1984.

Maitre, Doreen. *Literature and Possible Worlds*. London, 1983.

Martin, Claude. *Gide*. Paris, 1974.

Matilal, Bimal Krishna. *The Central Philosophy of Jainism (Anekanta-Vada)*. Ahmedabad, 1981.

Mazzotta, Giuseppe. *Dante, Poet of the Desert: History and Allegory in the "Divine Comedy."* Princeton, 1979.

———. *Dante's Vision and the Circle of Knowledge.* Princeton, 1993.

———. *The World at Play in Boccaccio's "Decameron."* Princeton, 1986.

———. *The Worlds of Petrarch.* Durham, N.C., 1993.

McCarthy, Mary. "Vladimir Nabokov's *Pale Fire.*" *Encounter* 19, no. 4 (October 1962): 71–84.

McGowan, John. *Postmodernism and Its Critics.* Ithaca, N.Y., 1991.

McHale, Brian. *Constructing Postmodernism.* London and New York, 1992.

———. *Postmodernist Fiction.* New York, 1987.

McKernan, Maureen. *The Amazing Crime and Trial of Leopold and Loeb.* 1924. Reprint, Chicago, 1986.

Merrell, Floyd. *Pararealities: The Nature of Our Fictions and How We Know Them.* Amsterdam and Philadelphia, 1983.

Meyer, Priscilla. *Find What the Sailor has Hidden: Vladimir Nabokov's "Pale Fire."* Middletown, Conn., 1988.

Morson, Gary Saul, and Caryl Emerson, eds. *Rethinking Bakhtin: Extensions and Challenges.* Evanston, Ill., 1989.

Nemoianu, Virgil. *A Theory of the Secondary: Literature, Progress, and Reaction.* Baltimore, 1989.

Nicholson, Linda, ed. *Feminism/Postmodernism.* New York, 1990.

Nicholson, Linda, and Steven Seidman. *Social Postmodernism: Beyond Identity Politics.* Cambridge, 1996.

Nietzsche, Friedrich. *The Birth of Tragedy* and *The Genealogy of Morals: An Attack.* Translated by Francis Golffing. New York, 1956.

———. *The Will to Power.* Edited by Walter Kaufmann. Translated by W. Kaufmann and R. J. Hollingdale. New York, 1967.

Ortega y Gasset, José. *Toward a Philosophy of History.* New York, 1941.

Orwell, George. *1984.* 1949. Reprint, New York, 1984.

Painter, George D. *André Gide: A Critical Biography.* New York, 1968.

Palmer, L. R. *Mycenaeans and Minoans.* London, 1960.

Parsons, Terence. *Nonexistent Objects.* New Haven, 1980.

Pavel, Thomas G. *Fictional Worlds.* Cambridge, Mass., 1986.

Pérez-Firmat, Gustavo. *Literature and Liminality: Festive Readings in the Hispanic Tradition.* Durham, N.C., 1986.

Plantinga, Alvin. *The Nature of Necessity.* Oxford, 1974.

Plato. *The Collected Dialogues of Plato.* Edited by E. Hamilton and H. Cairns. Princeton, 1961.

Porter, Dennis. *The Pursuit of Crime: Art and Ideology in Detective Fiction.* New Haven, 1981.

Proffer, Carl R., ed. *A Book of Things about Vladimir Nabokov.* Ann Arbor, Mich., 1974.

Rahv, Philip. "Dostoevsky in *Crime and Punishment.*" *Partisan Review* 27, no. 3 (summer 1960): 393–425.

Rampton, David. *Vladimir Nabokov.* New York, 1993.

Rebreanu, Liviu. *The Forest of the Hanged.* Translated by A. V. Wise. London, 1967.

Rhys Davids, Mrs. [Caroline], trans. *The Book of Kindred Sayings (Samyutta-Nikaya) or Grouped Suttas.* London, 1950.

Richardson, J. M., ed. *Orwell x 8: A Symposium.* Winnipeg, Man., 1986.

Roberts, J. M. *Modern Humanists.* London, 1891.

Roth, Phyllis A., ed. *Critical Essays on Vladimir Nabokov.* Boston, 1984.

Ruskin, John. *The Crown of Wild Olive.* New York, 1905.

———. *The Queen of the Air: Being a Study of the Greek Myths of Cloud and Storm.* New York, 1869.

Sartre, Jean-Paul. *Being and Nothingness.* Translated by Hazel E. Barnes. Secaucus, N.J., 1956.

———. *The Psychology of Imagination.* Translator unknown. London, 1972.

Schiller, Friedrich. *On the Aesthetic Education of Man, in a Series of Letters.* Edited and translated by E. M. Wilkinson and L. A. Willoughby. Oxford, 1967.

Schopenhauer, Arthur. *The World as Will and Representation.* Translated by E. F. Payne. 2 vols. New York, 1958.

Schwartz-Salant, Nathan, and Murray Stein, eds. *Liminality and Transitional Phenomena.* Wilmette, Ill., 1991.

Searle, John. "The Logical Status of Fictional Discourse." *New Literary History* 6 (1975): 315–30.

———. *Speech Acts.* Cambridge, 1969.

Sidney, Sir Philip. *Works.* Edited by A. Feuillerat. Cambridge, 1922–26.

Smith, Paul. *Discerning the Subject.* Minneapolis, Minn., 1988.

Sontag, Susan. *Against Interpretation and Other Essays.* New York, 1966.

Spariosu, Mihai I. *Dionysus Reborn: Play and the Aesthetic Dimension in Modern Philosophical and Scientific Discourse.* Ithaca, N.Y., 1989.

———. *God of Many Names: Play, Poetry, and Power in Hellenic Thought from Homer to Aristotle.* Durham, N.C., 1991.

———. *Literature, Mimesis, and Play: Essays in Literary Theory.* Tübingen, 1982.

————, ed. *Mimesis in Contemporary Theory*, vol. 1: *The Literary and Philosophical Debate*. Philadelphia and Amsterdam, 1984.

Stanford, William B. *The Ulysses Theme: A Study in the Adaptability of a Traditional Hero*. Oxford, 1954.

Stegner, Page. *Escape into Aesthetics: The Art of Vladimir Nabokov*. New York, 1966.

Taylor, Charles. *Sources of the Self: The Making of the Modern Identity*. Cambridge, Mass., 1989.

Taylor, Mark. *Altarity*. Chicago, 1987.

Todorov, Tzvetan. *Mikhail Bakhtin: The Dialogical Principle*. Translated by Wlad Godzich. Minneapolis, Minn., 1984.

Toker, Leona. *Nabokov: The Mystery of Literary Structures*. Ithaca, N.Y., 1989.

Trilling, Lionel. *Matthew Arnold*. New York, 1939.

Trungpa, Chögyam, Rinpoche. Commentary to *The Tibetan Book of the Dead: The Great Liberation through Hearing in the Bardo*. Boston, 1987.

Turner, Victor. *Dramas, Fields, and Metaphors: Symbolic Action in Human Society*. Ithaca, N.Y., 1974.

————. *From Ritual to Theater: The Human Seriousness of Play*. New York, 1982.

————. *The Ritual Process: Structure and Anti-Structure*. Ithaca, N.Y., 1969.

Unamuno, Miguel de. *Selected Works*, vol. 4: *Novela/Nivola*. Translated by Anthony Kerrigan. Princeton, 1976.

Vice, Sue, ed. *Malcolm Lowry Eighty Years On*. New York, 1989.

Watts, Alan. *The Way of Zen*. New York, 1957.

Waugh, Patricia. *Practising Postmodernism, Reading Modernism*. London and New York, 1992.

Wemyss, C. T., and A. Ugrinsky, eds. *George Orwell*. Westport, Conn., 1987.

Wilde, Alan. *Horizons of Assent: Modernism, Postmodernism, and the Ironic Imagination*. Baltimore, 1981.

Wilde, Oscar. *The Works of Oscar Wilde*. Edited by G. F. Maine. New York, 1954.

Winnicott, D. W. *Playing and Reality*. London and New York, 1971.

Wittig, Monique. *The Straight Mind and Other Essays*. Boston, 1992.

Wood, David, and Robert Bernasconi, eds. *Derrida and Différance*. Evanston, Ill., 1988.

Woodcock, George, ed. *Malcolm Lowry: The Man and his Work*. Vancouver, B.C., 1971.

Woodin Rowe, William. *Nabokov's Spectral Dimension: The Other World in His Works*. Ann Arbor, Mich., 1981.

Index

Abe, Masao, 317
Ackerley, Chris, 324
Adam, Villiers de L'Isle, 123
Adkins, Arthur W., 304
Adler, Alfred, 307
Aeschylus, 265–66
Aestheticism, xiv, 124–25, 147–48,
  157, 217, 220, 291–92
Aesthetics, xii, xiii, xiv, 28, 281–85,
  297–99, 302, 308. *See also* Agon
Against Method (Feyerabend), 27, 308
Agon, xv, 5, 10, 31, 74, 76–77, 79, 81,
  84–85, 88–89, 98–100, 119, 126,
  169, 171, 199–200, 202–3, 211,
  214, 221, 242–43, 259, 263, 270,
  276, 285–57, 298, 302; between
  ethics and aesthetics, xii, 28, 40,
  46, 123–25, 146–48, 157–58, 281–
  82, 294–95, 308; between poetry
  and philosophy, xii, 13–16, 31, 40,
  45, 46, 263, 265, 308; between
  science and religion, 17, 143–45.
  See also Play
Aiken, Conrad, xiv, 123, 155–57, 165,
  167, 320

Alcman, 9
Alexandrov, Vladimir, 323
Alice in Wonderland (Carroll), 61
Allegory, xv, 211–60. *See also*
  Hermeneutics
Alter, Robert, 323
Alterity. *See* Otherness
Anaximander, 76, 81
Anderson, Roger B., 320
Appel, Alfred, 323, 324
Aristarchus, 54
Aristophanes, 287
Aristotle, 24, 41–42, 206, 220, 263,
  290, 309
Arnold, Matthew, xvi, 264–75, 278,
  279, 281, 283, 288, 289–92, 293,
  294, 301–2, 326, 327
Artaud, Antonin, 321
"Artist as Critic as Wilde, The"
  (Ellmann), 327
Artist-Metaphysician, 47, 312. *See
  also* Deleuze, Gilles; Derrida,
  Jacques; Fink, Eugen; Gadamer,
  Hans-Georg; Nietzsche,
  Friedrich